# European
# Christian
# Democracy

*Critical Problems in History*

The University of Notre Dame Press gratefully acknowledges the generous support of the Dilenschneider family in the publication of titles in this series.

# European Christian Democracy

## Historical Legacies and Comparative Perspectives

*edited by*

## Thomas Kselman and Joseph A. Buttigieg

University of Notre Dame Press
*Notre Dame, Indiana*

*The editors wish to acknowledge the support of the Nanovic Institute for European Studies, and in particular J. Robert Wegs, its founding director, for his support of this project, which began as an international conference on Christian democracy held at the University of Notre Dame in April 1999.*

Manufactured in the United States of America

*Library of Congress Cataloging-in-Publication Data*
European Christian democracy : historical legacies and comparative perspectives / Thomas Kselman and Joseph A. Buttigieg, editors.
p.   cm. — (Critical problems in history)
Includes bibliographical references and index.
ISBN 0-268-02275-5 (alk. paper)
ISBN 0-268-02276-3 (pbk. : alk. paper)
1. Christian Democratic parties—Europe, Western—History.
2. Christian democracy—Europe, Western—History.   I. Kselman, Thomas A. (Thomas Albert), 1948–   II. Buttigieg, Joseph A.
III. Series.
JN94.A979 E8469    2003
324.2'182'094—dc21

2002013120

∞ *This book is printed on acid-free paper.*

As the history of the Christian Democratic parties in Europe reveals, religion and politics have never stopped jousting with each other, even in modern times. This collection of essays analyzes that engagement in a variety of ways. The authors explore the sometimes contentious relationship between the Catholic Church and the Christian Democratic parties, primarily in the postwar period, and probe the rise and fall of those parties in Germany, Italy, France, and elsewhere. They also provide a number of shrewd insights. Those perceptions could not come at a better time. In addition to providing a fresh analysis of Christian Democracy in recent European history, they shed light on broader questions: When do religiously inspired political parties flourish? How do religious institutions adapt to politics on the ground? What is the relationship between religious parties and religious hierarchies? And what parallels can we see in the world today?

The rise of Christian evangelicalism as a potent political force in the United States certainly provides one parallel. The growing influence of Islamic fundamentalism around the world offers another ripe area for comparison. And there are more.

The authors provide a great service to the reader who seeks to understand the forces that shape history. By studying the successes and failures of Christian Democratic parties we deepen our understanding about the intersection of religion and politics. That knowledge is desperately needed, now more than ever.

Putting these developments into context is a daunting task. The articles that make up this book provide useful tools in that endeavor. I applaud the publication of this book and am proud to be associated with it.

—Robert L. Dilenschneider

# Contents

# European
# Christian
# Democracy

# Introduction

## The History and Legacy
## of European Christian Democracy

THOMAS KSELMAN

In the 1990s historians and political scientists began to take notice of
Christian Democracy. Virtually all of the studies that have appeared
over the past few years acknowledge the crucial role Christian Democratic parties have played in the history of Europe since the end of World
War II and express surprise at the paucity of previous work on the topic.
The British scholar David Hanley may have overstated the case when he
wrote that until recently the scholarship on Christian Democracy was
nonexistent, but his assertion suggests the degree to which this major
political movement has been understudied.[1]

Academics take up new topics for a number of reasons, not excluding a taste for what is fashionable, but the emerging interest in Christian Democracy can clearly be linked to a number of recent political
and intellectual developments. In the early 1990s the collapse of the
Soviet Union and the end of the Cold War created a new context for
international relations and contributed to a reorientation of domestic
politics as well. This development was most clearly evident in Italy,
where the absence of a Soviet threat to western Europe contributed to
the meltdown in 1994 of a Christian Democratic party that had relied
on fear of Communism as a trump card in domestic politics. Of course,
the breakup of Christian Democracy in Italy had a number of other
causes as well, which no doubt will preoccupy scholars for the next generation or so. The inability of the government to respond to catastro-
phes, such as the 1980 earthquake in Naples, a fluctuating economy that
suggested an inability to sustain the postwar prosperity, a weakening

1

attachment to the Roman Catholic Church, and the public revelation of massive political corruption in the judical investigations known as *mani pulite* were among the factors that led to a decline in public confidence in Christian Democracy.[2] However one analyzes it, the Italian Christian Democratic party's loss of its central role in government in 1994, after being the major governing force since the end of World War II, marked the end of a stage in Italian politics. This signal event focused attention not only on the Italian case, however, but also on the general significance of Christian Democracy in the construction of postwar Europe.

In Germany, the historical significance of Christian Democracy was also thrown into sharp relief as the Cold War ended and the Berlin Wall collapsed. For it was the Christian Democratic chancellor, Helmut Kohl, heading the most durable government of the past half century, who oversaw the reunification of Germany. Nothing could point up more dramatically the importance of Christian Democracy (the Christian Democratic Union and its Bavarian partner, the Christian Social Union) as the dominant force in German domestic politics and a crucial player in international relations. The financial scandal involving Kohl's acceptance of illegal campaign contributions that broke after he left office in 1998 has led to problems for the party not unlike those that preceded the demise of Italian Christian Democracy. German Christian Democracy seems more likely to survive this crisis intact, but the departure of Kohl following his remarkable run as chancellor nonetheless seems to suggest a turn in the history of German Christian Democracy, the close of a period that began with the dominance of Adenauer in the 1950s.

At the same time that political events were focusing attention on Christian Democracy, scholars were pursuing with new energy the more general problem of the relationship between religion and politics. The wave of fundamentalist movements around the world has drawn attention since the 1970s, a trend that reached a kind of climax with the publication of five massive volumes coming out of the Fundamentalist project sponsored by the American Academy of Arts and Sciences.[3] The growth of interest in religion as a force in the contemporary world runs counter to a deep-rooted belief among scholars that secularization is an ineluctable process. The success of Islamic movements in the Middle East and evangelical Protestantism in the United States has confounded this view and created a climate within which Christian Democracy is more likely to receive serious scholarly attention.

The scholarship on European Christian Democracy promises in turn to contribute important evidence to the more general discussion about religion and politics as both an empirical problem and a conceptual issue.

The essays in this volume are intended to contribute to the growing interest in Christian Democracy in a number of ways. It is first of all an interdisciplinary collection, with contributions from historians and political scientists. It also brings together the perspectives of both Anglo-American and European scholars, many of whom have been prominent in the recent burst of scholarship on Christian Democracy. Several of the essays are self-consciously comparative in their methdology and in some cases stretch beyond Europe in making the case for the broader significance of Christian Democracy. Although the essays do not follow a particular formula, they can be understood as raising four major themes for readers who wish to place Christian Democracy in a historical and scholarly context: the historical roots of Christian Democracy; Christian Democracy and the relationship between religion and politics, church and state; methodological approaches to Christian Democracy, both case studies and comparative analyses; and the legacy of Christian Democracy.

## THE HISTORICAL ROOTS OF CHRISTIAN DEMOCRACY

Most of the essays deal in some way with the question of historical continuity between Catholic political movements from the nineteenth and early twentieth centuries and the Christian Democratic parties that emerged at the close of World War II.[4] Raymond Grew sees nineteenth-century Catholic political and social movements as bridges to Christian Democracy, a metaphor that suggests a direct relationship between the two even while it maintains a sense of their distinctiveness. In Grew's view, postwar Christian Democracy takes up themes from Catholic liberalism and social Catholicism but looks back as well to an integralism that put its faith in traditional hierarchies and corporations rather than parliamentary institutions.[5] Paul Misner focuses on Catholic social thinking during the interwar period and distinguishes between the Fascist "third way," which emphasized state domination as an alternative to the capitalist/socialist debate, and the ideas of the Jesuits Heinrich Pesch and Oswald von Nell-Breuning, which helped to shape Pius XI's 1931 encyclical, *Quadragesimo Anno.* Their call for the cooperation

of employers and employees in the administration of social programs reso-
nates, according to Misner, with the kind of welfare systems introduced
in Europe after World War II. Steven F. White also takes a nuanced position in favor of continuity, seeing Alcide De Gasperi's parliamentary pluralism of the post–World War II era as derived from Luigi Sturzo's People's
Party (1919–26), while Pius XII was the spokesman for an integralist defense
of Catholic institutions that also had roots in the interwar period. Maria
Mitchell's essay shows how prewar tensions between Catholics and Protestants continued in the late 1940s. Her close reading of the speeches and correspondence of Christian Democratic politicians shows them struggling
to find a vocabulary that could bring together Christians without evoking
historical memories in which political identity was based on confessional
attachment.

Martin Conway offers a revisionist critique of a view according to which
the postwar movements grew naturally from political parties such as the
Center in Germany but broke free from the narrow confessionalism of the
earlier movement. Conway is also skeptical about the influence of social
Catholicism derived from thinkers such as Félicité de Lamennais and from
Leo XIII's 1891 encyclical, *Rerum Novarum*. Instead, he sees Christian Democracy after World War II as moving rapidly to the Right, with only attenuated
links to an earlier commitment to the social question. Carolyn M. Warner
interprets the different relationships between church and party in Italy,
France, and Germany as dependent in part on the distance between the
Church and the prewar authoritarian regimes. Winfried Becker also acknowledges a break between the Catholic politics of the Center Party and postwar
Christian Democracy, stressing in particular the effort to reach across confessional lines. But he sees at the same time in both movements a suspicion
of the state and a concern for spiritual values. Finally, Michael Gehler and
Wolfram Kaiser trace the history of transnational contacts between Christian Democrats from the interwar period through the 1960s. Here the experience of the war seems to have been a major impetus in pushing Christian
Democrats to pursue a more intensive and institutionalized relationship
across national boundaries. Kaiser and Gehler's archival research illuminates
the importance of Christian Democratic gatherings under the rubric of the
Nouvelles Equipes Internationales and the more informal gatherings of the
Geneva Circle as a basis for the establishment of the European Economic
Community.[6]

## RELIGION AND POLITICS, CHURCH AND STATE

A second theme that emerges in a number of essays is the relationship between Christian Democracy and the Catholic Church. This complex question involves both ideological and institutional ties that have varied across time and place. The political experiments of the French Revolution, which included an anticlerical assault on Roman Catholicism, contributed to Vatican skepticism about democratic institutions, a position that was reinforced when Pius IX was forced to flee Rome during a Republican revolution in 1848.[7] Papal suspicion of democratic political institutions was clearly expressed by Leo XIII in his 1901 encyclical, *Graves de Communi*, where he insisted the label "Christian Democracy" "must be employed without any political significance, so as to mean nothing else than . . . beneficent Christian action in behalf of the people."[8] Subsequently, the Catholic hierarchy was more comfortable dealing with authoritarian regimes, signing concordats with Mussolini in 1929 and Hitler in 1933, even while it undermined Christian Democratic movements led by Marc Sangnier and Luigi Sturzo.[9] As Emiel Lamberts points out in his survey of Christian Democracy in the postwar period, it was only at the end of World War II that the Vatican finally accepted parliamentary democracy. Even then, many on the Left remained suspicious about the political orientation of Christian Democracy; Martin Conway recalls that the French Christian Democratic party known as the MRP (Mouvement Républicain Populaire) was cast as the "Mouvement des Révérends Pères." Without accepting this hyperbole, Conway links the success of Christian Democracy to the organizational efforts of the Church, which was in some places the only institution to survive the collapse of 1945. And he emphasizes as well the influence of Pius XII's anticommunism as setting the ideological tone for Christian Democracy in the postwar era. White's study, however, illuminates the tension between the reverend fathers, including Pius XII himself, and the lay leaders of Christian Democracy, particularly De Gasperi, as they faced the Roman municipal elections in 1952. Warner also emphasizes the tensions between Church and party by employing a model in which clerical authorities negotiate contracts with Christian Democratic politicians to deliver policy benefits. Rather than see the party as an extension of the Church, her approach underlines the distinct goals of buyer and seller.[10]

Several of the essays, however, take a less institutional view of the relationship between the Catholic Church and Christian Democracy and stress instead the influence of social doctrines. In different ways the essays of Misner, Becker, and Mitchell suggest how a commitment to the poor, a concern for the integrity of the family, and a critique of the materialist assumptions undergirding socialist ideology provided common ground for Christian Democrats. Antonio A. Santucci focuses his essay on the Communist leader Enrico Berlinguer's 1981 critique of Christian Democracy, in which he placed "the moral question" at the center of Italy's political problems. In Santucci's view, Berlinguer is an heir of the moral tradition of Sturzo and De Gasperi, Christian Democratic leaders who put the general interests of Italy over the narrow concerns of party. Although their political perspectives are very different, Santucci and Becker both suggest that contemporary European politics would benefit from an injection of the moral fervor that Christian Democracy drew on to create parliamentary governments and generous social welfare programs in the 1940s and 1950s.

## CHRISTIAN DEMOCRACY IN
## COMPARATIVE PERSPECTIVE

The advantages of different methodological approaches constitute a third issue raised in this volume. Half of the essays are explicitly comparative in their methodology (Grew, Conway, Warner, Lamberts, Strikwerda, Kalyvas), though this means different things to different scholars. The political scientists (Warner and Kalyvas) develop their ideas through the use of general models, whereas the historians are more inclined to read their cases against each other with little reliance on a theoretical vocabulary. But all of the comparative essays point up the value of such study in illuminating common characteristics that allow us to see Christian Democracy as something more than a set of national parties that share a label but little else.

Two of the authors reach beyond European Christian Democracy to suggest fascinating parallels with religious movements elsewhere. Carl Strikwerda proposes that Christian Democracy understood as a social movement that organized its members through myriad youth, labor, charitable, and devotional groups bears comparison with the organizational efforts of evangelical Protestants in the United States. For Strikwerda, this comparison suggests an alternative and potentially more effective route for influencing and ameliorating social conditions than the traditional political party.[11] Stathis N. Kalyvas sees contemporary Islamic and Hindu movements as exercises in religious mobilization comparable to the Catholic mobilization of Europe through Christian Democracy, a point that leads him to criticize what he terms the "indiscriminate alarmism" that sometimes accompanies analyses of religious politics in the Middle East and India. It is worth noting that the comparative essays included here rely extensively on the kind of detailed case studies that make up the balance of the volume, suggesting the sustained value of such analyses.

## THE LEGACY OF CHRISTIAN DEMOCRACY

Fourth, and finally, this volume raises the question of the legacy of Christian Democracy. Of course, such a question might be considered premature, as Christian Democratic parties continue to be active in much of Europe. Conway insists nonetheless that "the age of Christian Democracy in Europe has ended," and Grew believes that the parties "may have fulfilled their historical function." If this is the case, what have been the major contributions of Christian Democracy? Lamberts summarizes a number of achievements that are discussed in other essays as well: Christian Democracy was instrumental in the writing of new constitutions, the establishment of parliamentary government, the acknowledgment of human rights, acceptance of the role of communities that mediate between the individual and the state, and European integration. This positive assessment comes from a European scholar who writes with sympathy about the history of the movement, an example of what Conway calls a tendency for Christian Democracy "to write its own history." Becker writes from a similar perspective, emphasizing in his case the ability of Christian Democracy to define an agenda that broke from the materialist assumptions of National Socialism. Santucci faults the Christian Democrats of the last two decades for abandoning the mission of their founding fathers. In effect he identifies two legacies of the movement, an older tradition dating to Sturzo and De Gasperi in which the party genuinely worked to advance general social welfare based on broad political participation and a more recent version in which Christian Democracy represents a corrupt political system serving only party bureaucrats and their clients.

The current troubles of Christian Democratic parties in Italy and Germany suggest that they may well play a diminished role over the next few decades, especially when compared to the power they have wielded over the past fifty years. Even if this is the case, however, this volume suggests that European political and social institutions will continue to bear for a long time the imprint of Christian Democracy. We hope these essays will provide students and scholars with a helpful guide to the genealogy, achievements, and legacy of this movement.

## NOTES

1. David Hanley, "Introduction: Christian Democracy as a Political Phenomenon," in *Christian Democracy in Europe: A Comparative Perspective* (New York: Pinter, 1994), 1. Stathis Kalyvas described the literature as "underdeveloped" in *The Rise of Christian Democracy in Europe* (Ithaca: Cornell University Press, 1996), 6. Kees von Kersbergen noted that "Christian democracy has attracted surprisingly little scholarly attention" in *Social Capitalism: A Study of Christian Democracy and the Welfare State* (New York: Routledge, 1995). Emiel Lamberts, in his introduction to *Christian Democracy in the European Union, 1945–1995*, ed. Emiel Lamberts (Leuven: Leuven University Press, 1997), 9, recalls that in 1992 an international symposium concluded that the literature on Christian Democracy was "virtually non-existent" but notes as well growing interest in the 1990s. Carolyn Warner refers to the "lack of scholarly attention" to Christian Democracy in her recent study, *Confessions of an Interest Group: The Catholic Church and Political Parties in Europe* (Princeton: Princeton University Press, 2000), 14. Some of the older studies that recur in the bibliographies are Mario Einaudi and François Goguel, *Christian Democracy in Italy and France* (Notre Dame: University of Notre Dame Press, 1952); Michael Fogarty, *Christian Democracy in Western Europe, 1820–1953* (Notre Dame: University of Notre Dame Press, 1957); R.E.M. Irving, *The Christian Democratic Parties of Western Europe* (London: Royal Institute of International Affairs, 1979).

2. Patrick McCarthy, *The Crisis of the Italian State* (New York: Macmillan, 1995).

3. Scott Appleby and Martin Marty, eds., *The Fundamentalism Project*. 5 vols. (Chicago: University of Chicago Press, 1991–95). General studies concerned with the revival of religion as a political and social force in the modern world include Gilles Kepel, *The Revenge of God: The Resurgence of Islam, Christianity, and Judaism in the Modern World* (University Park: Pennsylvania State University Press, 1994); and

Scott Appleby and Martin Marty, *The Glory and the Power: The Fundamentalist Challenge to the Modern World* (Boston: Beacon Press, 1992).

4. For a recent overview that stresses the nineteenth-century heritage of Christian Democracy, see Jean-Dominique Durand, *L'Europe de la Démocratie Chrétienne* (Paris: Complex, 1995). Other recent works that emphasize this theme are Pierre Letamendia, *La Démocratie Chrétienne*, 2d ed. (Paris: Presses Universitaires de France, 1993); Noel Cary, *The Path to Christian Democracy: German Catholics and the Party System from Windthorst to Adenauer* (Cambridge, Mass.: Harvard University Press, 1996); Stathis Kalyvas, *The Rise of Christian Democracy in Europe* (Ithaca: Cornell University Press, 1996); Ellen Lovell Evans, *The Cross and the Ballot: Catholic Political Parties in Germany, Switzerland, Austria, Belgium, and the Netherlands, 1785–1985* (Boston: Humanities Press, 1999). Martin Conway's elegant survey, *Catholic Politics in Europe, 1918–1945* (New York: Routledge, 1997), recalls the ties of Catholics to the right-wing politics of that era as well as their democratic inclinations.

5. Grew pursues some of these themes in an important essay, "Liberty and the Catholic Church in Nineteenth-Century Europe," in *Freedom and Religion in the Nineteenth Century*, ed. Richard Helmstadter (Stanford: Stanford University Press, 1997), 196–232.

6. The importance of Christian Democracy for European integration is developed in the work of Roberto Papini, *L'Internationale Démocrate-Chrétienne: La coopération internationale entre les partis Démocrates-Chrétiens de 1925 à 1986* (Paris, Editions du Cerf, 1988), and *Il coraggio della democrazia: Sturzo e l'Internazionale popolare tra le due guerre* (Rome: Studium, 1995). See also Philippe Chenaux, *Une Europe Vaticane? Entre le Plan Marshall et les Traités de Rome* (Paris: Ciaco, 1990). Christian Democratic parties now cooperate in the European Parliament, under the name of the European People's Party. See Thomas Jansen, *The European People's Party: Origins and Development*, trans. Barbara Steen (New York: St. Martin's, 1998).

7. Owen Chadwick, *A History of the Popes, 1830–1914* (New York: Oxford University Press, 1998); Roger Aubert, *Le pontificat de Pie IX (1846–1878)* (Paris: Bloud et Gay, 1952).

8. Etienne Gilson, ed., *The Church Speaks to the Modern World: The Social Teachings of Leo XIII* (Garden City, N.Y.: Image Books, 1954), 318.

9. Frank Coppa, ed., *Controversial Concordats: The Vatican's Relations with Napoleon, Mussolini, and Hitler* (Washington, D.C.: Catholic University Press of America, 1999); Jean Caron, *Le Sillon et la Démocratie Chrétienne* (Paris: Plon, 1967); John Molony, *The Emergence of Political Catholicism in Italy: Partito Popolare, 1919–1926* (Totowa, N.J.: Rowman and Littlefield, 1977). Kalyvas emphasizes the reticence of the institutional church when faced with Christian Democratic movements in the late nineteenth century and argues that "the extension of religion into the

(democratic) political realm through the creation of confessional parties was inevitably opposed by the church." *The Rise of Christian Democracy*, 49.

    10. Warner develops this model more fully in *Confessions of an Interest Group: The Catholic Church and Political Parties in Europe* (Princeton: Princeton University Press, 2000).

    11. Strikwerda's point here resembles the view of José Casanova, *Public Religions in the Modern World* (Chicago: University of Chicago Press, 1994).

# 1 Suspended Bridges to Democracy

## The Uncertain Origins of Christian Democracy in France and Italy

RAYMOND GREW

Studies of Christian Democratic parties in western Europe make at least two points: these parties have been at the center of continental politics since World War II, and they combine diverse currents within Catholicism, each of which is more than a century old.[1] That long history exposes persistent obstacles to political success, including opposition from the hierarchy and the Vatican, disagreements among Catholics about political and social policies, and antagonistic governments. Having had to swim upstream against strong currents in both church and state, Catholic political movements might be expected to founder. Similar difficulties obtained in most of Europe, yet effective Catholic parties were established much earlier in some countries than in others.

There is some disagreement about where in western Europe Christian Democratic parties have mattered most,[2] but France and Italy stand out in any such ranking. They are Catholic countries, as Switzerland and Germany are not, and have been of unsurpassed importance to the Church throughout the history of Catholicism. Both countries have a record of vigorous parliamentary politics. Yet France and Italy were among the last to have powerful Catholic parties, and that surprising outcome suggests that reflection on the history of Christian Democracy in these nations that would seem to have been its natural home may reveal something of its strengths and weaknesses more generally.[3] Christian Democracy means much more than winning elections, of course;

and to concentrate on political parties, as I propose to do, is to underplay the role of ideas, of Catholic social action, and of local notables and popular religion. But it highlights the extent to which any political party with Catholic ties was instantly seen as a threat by many influential Catholic laymen, most of the Catholic hierarchy, nearly all state officials, and all other political parties. Christian Democrats have suffered ostracism, denunciation, condemnation, and the Church's full range of formal punishments. Often fatal to Christian Democratic movements, these reactions caused terrible anguish for leaders who acted from vibrant faith, moved by visions of Catholic community. Despite its hierarchical structure and emphasis on obedience, the Catholic Church is not a monolith. The decision as to whether to ignore, discourage, disband, or work with a Catholic political party may or may not (more often not) be taken in the Vatican or by the national hierarchy—and not necessarily on strictly political grounds, for the attitudes of priests and laity, the nature and interests of Catholic organizations, relations with the national state, regional differences, and traditions and specific interests are likely to weigh as heavily as political calculation.

As the historical literature on Christian Democracy rightly emphasizes, to advocate democracy from within a hierarchical church was in itself disquieting. In such overwhelmingly Catholic nations as France and Italy, the very idea of a Christian Democratic party contained an antecedent oxymoron, acceptance of being one party among many. By definition, parties distinguish their members from nonmembers; they are not catholic.[4] In addition, for many nineteenth-century liberals as well as Catholics, "party" had pejorative connotations of faction, sect, or cabal. Anticlericals denounced the Church as a semisecret party; and the hierarchy consistently fought against that charge, even while employing its long experience in how to apply pressure to governments. In the nineteenth century Catholicism became the clearest marker of political cleavage in both Italy and France; yet leaders of the Church battled throughout the century to maintain Catholicism as an inextricable part of all social and public, as well as spiritual, life. Prefects and bishops corresponded constantly about accusations of clerical involvement in politics; and, whatever the reality, to one side combating the danger and to the other denying the accusation was a matter of high principle. Thus, bishops who anticipated a change of regime, bishops determined to fight secularization and efforts to isolate the Church, bishops who looked to concordats as the safest model for church-state relations, and bishops who found occasions to cooperate with state officials (as a remarkable number did) all had reasons to watch with unease the formation of a Catholic political party.

In thinking about Christian Democratic parties, however, too much can be made of these obvious conflicts. Admittedly, especially in modern France, voting behavior correlates more strongly with Church attendance than with any other single social measure. In both France and Italy, Catholicism did much to shape the confrontation with communist parties and to contribute to their political isolation (although not necessarily to their subsequent decline). Indicators of cleavage should not, however, obscure the diversity among Catholics and the complexity of their participation in social life. Religious behavior and political behavior do not always predict each other, even when they tend to overlap. Even Catholics eager to join in defending the Church were not always willing to follow clerical dictates in casting their ballots. There have been Catholic anticlericals and pious socialists and ongoing, shifting debates in all camps about which issues fall within the religious sphere and which are secular.

The ideas to which a Christian Democratic party should adhere, the social ties it should claim, and the positions it should hold are not automatically determined. French and Italian Catholics had long lived with the dissonances that rang from conflicts between church and state, lord and peasant, and employer and worker, between Sunday sermons and the pleasures of dance and drink and between neighbor and neighbor. That created special problems for Catholic parties. Intellectual tradition required that any specific position be justified on the basis of lasting principles; yet rigid policies usually could not be sustained. Worse, any stand on controversial questions was likely to lose the party some potential support. Many currents of Catholic concern had to be woven together to form an effective Christian Democratic party. In trying to disentangle distinctive strands, I have rather artificially separated elements that of course were never experienced in isolation. These categories are meant rather as analytic devices for identifying the problems that had to be overcome for a Christian Democratic party to be successful.

## THE INTEGRALIST URGE

Early in the nineteenth century, the potential power and limitations of a Catholic party were demonstrated by men of faith determined to reconquer society for religion. They wanted religion to permeate all of society.

The integralism that resulted was more of an attitude than a movement or any single program, and that attitude was influential in Catholic circles throughout the century. Integralists wanted to reconquer the state, by putting it back in reliably Catholic hands; they embraced the need for firm discipline within a Church militant reaching from the pope through the clerical hierarchy to the laity; and they organized pious associations intended to spread their influence into families, parishes, public behavior, and all of society. Politically, such efforts were usually closely associated with conservatives and reactionaries, the most fervent supporters of the restoration of legitimist, monarchical regimes. Within the Church, integralists tended to embrace authority and doctrinal rigidity while denouncing the sins of modern society, including love of money and liberal "indifferentism."

It can thus seem odd to begin a discussion of Christian Democracy with integralism, which in France especially emphasized the need to combat the ideas and undo the evil effects of the French Revolution. That, however, required converting a population considered to have been de-Christianized. The first steps were to restrict the press and to disseminate Catholic publications. Admirably organized campaigns involved members of the laity (primarily legitimist nobles). Missions conducted by eloquent preachers traveled from city to city, leading crowds in prayer and song and planting crosses in central squares. The songs praised king as well as God, and the crosses carried Bourbon along with Christian symbols. Although these campaigns bore many of the marks of a right-wing political party, they provided training in the techniques of popular appeal. Similar, less urgent campaigns were conducted in Italy, where the Amicizie Cattoliche circulated pamphlets on the lives of saints and tales of moral uplift that echoed the efforts in France.[5]

This missionary urge was fired by an enthusiastic vision of a society made whole through piety, and a similar, indeed related, vision inspired many Christian Democrats, of whom Félicité de Lamennais was the most influential. In his own career he carried the emphasis on applying Christian principles to society, on social action, on the importance of politics, and on the need to reach and mobilize the masses from one end of the political spectrum to the other. Like the most intransigent integralists, Christian Democrats would frequently be judged inconvenient by the officials of the Church; and hence the fate of integralism, which had the sympathy of most of the hierarchy, is instructive for understanding the evolution of Christian Democracy, which never enjoyed such strong clerical support.

As the integralist urge inevitably led into political activities, resistance and opposition rose. In France, local notables complained of agitation that threatened to stir up the public and weaken their hold on local affairs. Even the government of Louis XVIII found reasons for concern, pressured bishops for constraint, and moved to restrict the activities of diocesan seminaries, seen as potential centers of political agitation. To the July Monarchy, the Second Empire, and the Third Republic alike, integralists were Legitimists, that is to say, a subversive party. Although the social program of the Society of St. Vincent de Paul could be understood as an effort to heal the breach between social classes and to train the poor in the hard work and thrift that industrialization required, the Society was disbanded by the Second Empire, fearful that in fact a Legitimist network was being created. By tying their conception of a Catholic society so closely to the Bourbon restoration, integralists were vulnerable to its political failures and risked undermining their own social programs.

In Italy the alliance of throne and altar was generally more old-fashioned. Sanfedisti were reactionary without much integralist zeal, and closed political systems offered little incentive to rouse popular support (indeed, the successes during the bloody riots against the French in 1796 and 1799 had frightened even their clerical sponsors). The integralist aspiration grew stronger in Italy after unification stripped the papacy of its territory and put church and state at loggerheads. Then, Catholic social action in the north included a strong integralist current, one particularly prominent in the Opera dei Congressi, a loose federation of thousands of lay activists, both devotional and social. Although it proclaimed defense of the pope as its principal goal, the Opera's disparate activities and lay leadership troubled the Vatican. In 1904, as the Opera edged toward increased political engagement, the pope dissolved it. What appeared to the government an instrument for challenging national unity was seen by the Vatican as a threat to clerical control.

The nineteenth-century trend toward increased centralization within the Church, which strengthened the authority of bishops over priests and of clergy over laity, added a further obstacle to Catholic political engagement, making it easier for the hierarchy to circumscribe partisan activity by Catholics and increasing the risk that the public activities of Catholics would be taken to represent the official policy of the Church. In fact, French integralists tended to be ultramontane and eager to accept papal authority, but that made them especially vulnerable to signs of official disapproval. The very energy that made them seem a party soon drew disciplinary attention from a hierarchy that did not welcome risky intermediaries in its unending negotiations with the state. Sermons in support of the Holy Father or such demonstrations as the campaigns for Peter's Pence were welcome but only as adjuncts to a defense of the Church left safely in the hands of its authorities.

Not surprisingly, the integralist impulse retreated into devotional associations, then periodically burst forth in grander public efforts. It did not produce a successful political party. After all, sustaining an organized commitment to approach all issues in terms of the community of faith is difficult in itself, even within a religious order. Within the Church, an integralist dream of a harmonious Christian society never died, and it would crop up in new movements in every generation. If there were lessons to be learned, the hierarchy learned them more readily than did the founders of parties. Integralist efforts failed to lead to an effective political party because the integralists were too much like a party while lacking a party's flexibility. They divided Catholics, who disagreed on too many matters of policy, and they stimulated anticlerical reactions. Above all, they ran counter to the Church's institutional interests. Accommodation to the French state was a central and sometimes rewarding necessity throughout the nineteenth century, as it was to the Italian state from the turn of the century on. Being able to insist that priests were not engaged in politics strengthened bishops in demanding as a quid pro quo that the state not interfere in matters they considered purely religious. The secularization that the Church so loudly denounced permitted a useful, institutional modus vivendi. That modus vivendi could be endangered by a Catholic party, for the existence of such a party implied that Catholics were only one interest group among many. Nevertheless, integralist ideas and instincts continued to influence Catholic movements, including many associated with the democratic Left,[6] which would have to overcome similar obstacles.


## THE DEMOCRATIC DREAM

Integralism, as historians use the term, left little room for democracy (aside from an interest in reaching and mobilizing the public), but many of those remembered as the founding fathers of Christian Democracy held a quite integralist concept of what their success would bring. Lamennais and Vincenzo Gioberti became democrats (at a time when such views were rare among educated Europeans) in large part because they believed that the demos was Catholic.[7] Sensitive to popular opinion, they rejected sharp distinctions between politics and religion. Political liberty, a Church revitalized, and the end in Italy of foreign rule and in France of conflict between church and state would all be achieved through democracy. The Church itself, these two priests and many of their followers believed, would prosper once it was trusted by a more contented flock. The culmination of this first phase of Christian Democracy occurred during the revolutions of 1848, as priests blessed liberty trees; bishops recalled the biblical basis of liberty, fraternity, and equality; and priests and bishops sat in constituent assemblies.[8] The failure of the revolutionary regimes left Christian Democrats marginalized within the Church and underscored their reliance on political conditions outside of it.

At the very least, anything like a Christian Democratic party required the tolerance of the government in power and a fair prospect that democracy might come to pass. The intermittent rise and decline of Christian Democratic movements in France and Italy had a lot to do with the government in power. Inhibited, when not absolutely forbidden, by the policies of the restoration regimes and then by those of the Second Empire, programs for Christian Democracy were discouraged by limited suffrage in united Italy and by constraints on Catholic political activity, which was considered inherently antirepublican in France and antinational in Italy.

Christian Democracy also required Vatican acceptance, and that was slow to come. The policies and encyclicals of Gregory XVI and Pius IX made opposition to Christian Democracy seem a principle of the Church. The language of democratic enthusiasm incorporated a possibility that the Church itself might democratize, and to many in the Vatican any such hint evoked the ghosts of the French Revolution's juring priests and of Italian Jansenists. Priests on the hustings triggered inquiries about correct doctrine and clerical discipline, and lay leaders with a Catholic following could threaten clerical authority. To churchmen engaged at the end of the nineteenth century in a further round of intense conflict with the state, much of what Christian Democrats did seemed at best inopportune. For a Vatican beginning its repressive campaign against the vaguely defined dangers of modernism, Christian Democrats often sounded similarly indifferent to authority.[9]

Indeed, the meaning of Christian Democracy had never been very precise. Associated with Lamennais in France, it had come to Italy through Carlo Maria Curci, a Neapolitan priest exiled for political activities who left Paris for Rome in 1850. There, he was one of the principal figures in the founding of *Civiltà Cattolica*, a publication not otherwise associated with democracy. The multiple Christian Democratic movements in France and Italy toward the end of the nineteenth century were quite different from those a half century earlier. They centered on more organized and delimited groups and concentrated on more concrete issues. In France Christian Democrats sought to combine the lasting structures of a party with the enthusiasms of a movement. That proved difficult. Many Catholic parties preferred to call themselves popular rather than democratic, suggesting a populist groundswell rather than an ordinary political party and implying perhaps that elections or even constitutional procedures were not their primary interest.

By the end of the century, the connotations of the term were still not clear. Christian Democracy had implied attitudes not automatically associated with Catholics: a certain vague optimism about the possibilities of progress and reform, willing engagement in the electoral process, and acceptance of a united Italy or a republican France. Until after World War II, Christian Democracy remained more successful as a movement than as a political party. The activities of the Fascio Democratico of Milan or the 1899 Festa della Democrazia Cristiana (first celebrated in Turin on May 15 as a counter to the socialists' May 1st demonstrations) gained as much attention as any electoral efforts. Despite important variations in style, tone, leadership, and program, none of these efforts can be counted a great political success,[10] with the exception of the Partito Popolare Italiano (PPI), founded in 1919. In Italy, Romolo Murri's Lega Democratica Nazionale, though it denied being a party, had been squelched by the Vatican.[11] Marc Sangnier fared better with the Vatican than his predecessors, but his movement did not. Neither did the PPI: forbidden to deal with socialists and abandoned by the Vatican, Don Luigi Sturzo had to leave Italy to the Fascists.

Democracy in itself was only part of the problem, for democratic movements tended to form all sorts of alliances and address all sorts of issues. The archbishop of Lyon refused to support the movement for La Démocracie Chrétienne in 1896 not because it was democratic but because of the participation of the stridently anti-Semitic local paper, *La France Libre*. Christian Democratic movements always risked getting out of hand and offending both state and church, and they had great difficulty following a steady course. When, in order to broaden their appeal, they loosened their ties to the Church and carefully declined to give their party a Catholic name, they risked reduced support and increased criticism from part of their core constituency. When Catholics willing to embrace a Christian Democratic party announced allegiance to the Republic and then, like Léon Harmel, gave voice to fears of a "Masonic, Jewish, and Protestant coalition," they were hurt on several fronts. The rhetoric they inherited and their positions on disparate issues tended to be both too divisive and too *intégriste* to win a large following in or out of the Church. On the other hand, electoral battles fought on Catholic issues, while not guaranteeing massive Catholic support, risked isolating Christian Democrats from the party alliances and compromises on which parliamentary influence depended—as in the French elections of 1924 and 1928 and the Italian referendum on divorce in 1974. Christian Democratic parties did better when they could pick their issues, but too often opponents and even other Catholics made sure that they could not. As a party like all the others, they risked the indifference or contempt that greeted most parties; as an expression of Catholic idealism, they risked consignment to a Catholic subculture.

For a long time Christian Democrats were more effective as a movement than a party and as one focused especially on youth. That offered a number of advantages. It was a way to define coherent social groups without acknowledging class divisions (although in reality only the middle and upper classes could construct youth as a distinctive way of life between elementary school and employment). Concentration on youth also fit contemporary culture's concern with education and civic training, implied acceptance of much of the modern world, and quietly distanced Christian Democrats from French legitimists and Italian intransigents. It also allowed them to build on the wide-ranging social action of religious orders and Catholic laity. Scores of young Christians' groups, such as the Association des Jeunes Catholiques Françaises, the Unione Giovani, and the Federazione Universitaria Cattolica Italia, brought an energy and idealism to Christian Democracy reminiscent of Mazzini's Young Italy.[12] Here, too, there were dangers. Sangnier's Sillon,[13] with its uniformed Jeunes Gardes, theaters, exercises, lectures, and study groups, struck many as too exclusive, more like a subculture than a party; and its endorsements of democracy were oddly balanced by aggressive references to "sterile parliamentarianism." (Today, Communione e Liberazione has similarly been torn between political engagement and a more sectarian purity.) The successes of Christian Democracy after World War II in a new political context would permit a legislative program and organizational structure never achieved before.

A successful Christian Democratic party in France or Italy had to overcome a distrust woven into the structure and memory of the Church. From Lamennais through Murri and Sangnier, the pattern was one of failure and condemnation, which extended to worker-priests even after Christian Democratic parties were successfully established. More remarkable than these recurrent failures, however, has been the persistent reemergence of Christian Democratic movements, evidence that they tapped values nourished within the faith itself, despite the distrust that greeted them.[14] Eventually, effective Christian Democratic parties would find a way to embrace a range of activist Catholic traditions and establish their essential independence from the Church while remaining cautious on matters of substance and tactically flexible. In these two Catholic nations at least, so delicate a balance apparently required a particular set of political circumstances.

## THE LIBERAL COMPROMISE

During most of the nineteenth century, neither France nor Italy had much experience of democracy, but liberalism was strong in both countries. In neither nation, however, did liberal Catholicism achieve the kind of political organization and continuity that might have been expected or that it achieved in Belgium. Political liberalism required a confidence in the electorate that Catholic experience in France from the 1820s on rarely seemed to justify. The tragic emblem of liberal Catholicism's political promise and dramatic failure was Pellegrino Rossi. An Italian political exile, then liberal economist at the Collège de France and Louis-Philippe's ambassador to the Holy See, he became prime minister of Pius IX's liberal government—which died with Rossi when he was assassinated in 1849. Throughout the century Catholics who favored representative government tended to be driven to cautious retreat by attacks from the Catholic press, disapproval from the hierarchy, and their own fears of revolution. Although influential Catholic economists and businessmen were drawn to economic liberalism, denunciations of avarice and social alienation got much more attention.[15] The repeated warnings from Rome about the dangers of untrammeled speech and the continuing thunder from pulpits against liberal individualism made the political battles surrounding the anticlericalism of France's liberal regimes and the Vatican's opposition to Italy's liberal monarchy seem the expression of an inevitable and fundamental opposition.

For the political historian, that impression can be reinforced by liberal Catholicism's limited political success in France and Italy. Even in the calmest times, Catholics on the Right were too numerous and those on the Left too loud and inventive to allow the contradictions of liberal accommodation to go unexposed. The practical attractions of liberal compromise were simply not great enough to win electoral support from a majority of Catholics, and in Italy for more than a generation the temptation to accommodate to liberal practice and win elections was mitigated by the Church's prohibition against participation in national politics. Isolated within the Church and distrusted outside it, liberal Catholicism had the aura of a losing and dubious cause.

Despite all this, liberal Catholics were in fact influential throughout the century and played important roles in the development of the parliamentary system and the awkward compromises that supported political moderation. Most political liberals in Italy and France thought of themselves as Catholics, and liberal regimes were not so consistently opposed to the Church as the bitter conflicts during and after the Risorgimento, the July Monarchy, and the Third Republic made them seem. Liberal Catholics were central figures in Italian public and intellectual life from the Risorgimento to De Gasperi.[16] Their number included admired theologians such as Rosmini Serbati and other notable members of the clergy as well as many political figures close to Pius IX in his liberal phase, many who held political power during the Risorgimento, and many prominent legal experts and intellectuals around the turn of the century.[17] In France every Chamber of Deputies and Senate included influential liberal Catholics, from Charles de Montalembert and generations of Cochins to Henri Wallon, whose narrowly passed amendment acknowledged the establishment of the Third Republic. Suspected of Gallicanism and often out of favor with both the ultramontane Catholic press and the Vatican, they remained loyal to the Church while increasingly tempted by the practical benefits of parliamentary engagement. Leo XIII's call to French Catholics to rally to the Republic was in a sense their triumph.[18]

In both countries liberal Catholics sensed the possibilities of electoral participation. By the end of the century, figures like the abbé Lemire had learned to work effectively even in an often hostile parliament, and the abbé Garnier could think about a nonconfessional party.[19] Without quite accepting in principle the merits of pluralistic freedoms, figures like Albert de Mun were in fact pursuing essentially liberal tactics. His Action Libérale and then the Parti Démocrate Populaire were in many respects liberal ventures.[20] In Milan and Turin liberal Catholics participated in local elections and city councils even while the *non expedit* remained in effect. That training in how to win elections, work with other parties, and develop attractive programs made it possible for Filippo Meda to form the Unione Elettorale Cattolica Milanese in 1890. It led to the Opera dei Congressi's electoral committees, which survived the Opera's dissolution to become the Unione Elettorale under Giuseppe Toniolo within Azione Cattolica. By the end of the century Don Romolo Murri spoke openly of a national Catholic party. In some respects, the pope's agreement in 1905 that Catholics might vote in national elections (in dioceses that received papal permission to do so because of a socialist threat) and his subsequent acquiescence in Catholic electoral cooperation with Giolitti was a victory for Catholic liberals. Its ironic effect was to discourage formation of an independent Catholic party.

Catholic liberals never won more than grudging support, more private than public, from the Church, nor did they gain a mass following. Their contribution was rather in their demonstration of how to work with parliamentary democracy and how to use the arguments of liberalism in the Church's defense.[21] Balanced between a wholehearted embrace of liberty and a concern to antagonize as few Catholics as possible, Catholic liberals appeared more pragmatic than principled, their positions uncomfortable, their contributions overshadowed by difficulties with bishops and secular liberals and by the more activist stands other Catholics took on social issues. After World War II the great Christian Democratic parties of Italy and France cited their roots in early programs for Christian Democracy and social Catholicism with greater pride than they did the greater debt owed to a century of Catholic liberalism. Yet it is not hard to imagine a Montalembert working with Georges Bidault, a Pierre-Antoine Berryer assisting Robert Schuman, and a Terenzio Mamiani or a Stefano Jacini sitting in De Gasperi's cabinet.

## THE ORGANIZATIONAL EFFORT

Potentially the greatest asset of any Christian Democratic party was the vast array of Catholic organizations, one of the wonders of modern Church history. They took many forms.[22] There were hundreds of new religious orders, most of them devoted to such social services as teaching, nursing, and welfare and many of them local or regional. There were new diocesan groups, devotional, social, and recreational. There were lay associations dedicated to good works and others organized among particular groups: mutual aid societies, apprentices, young people, and so forth. These latter were the ones with the greatest political potential, but they have been much criticized for their paternalism.

Ongoing connections between notables and peasants or employers and artisans could be politically very valuable, however, especially in Catholic areas like the Veneto or Brittany. Sometimes these organizations competed against each other; more often they simply overlapped. Until the 1880s more extensive in France than in Italy, they tended in both countries to establish national ties—except where their culture was highly regional (which tended to be the case where they were strongest and largest).[23] The Vatican often encouraged the proliferation of Catholic organizations, as it did in France after the failure of De Mun's Action Libérale Populaire; and they in turn helped to counter the impression that Catholic connections led to right-wing activities.

Still, for all their social engagement, such organizations had difficulty shedding their association with movements on the Right, which continued into the 1920s, although by the time of the MRP they could be cited as evidence of "progressive" Catholic engagement.[24] When at its first meeting, the Opera dei Congressi declared itself to be Catholic and nothing else, neither liberal nor tyrannical, that was understood to be a statement by Catholics who refused to accept Italy's liberal constitution. It would take a generation before such a statement could be read as a claim to political neutrality. Indeed, the dynamic organizations known collectively as Catholic Action, especially strong among young adults, never sustained a common political stance. Agreement that religion should transform society did not mean agreement as to what a truly Catholic society might be like.

In Italy Catholic Action moved from intransigent opposition to the new state to social action in the time of Leo XIII and became more ambiguous in its relation to secular society and political life under Pius X. In fact, the institutional advantages of claiming political neutrality proved to be great, and many lay Catholics were reluctant to give it up. The thousands of Catholic mutual aid societies and cooperatives and organizations of social groups (of veterans, agricultural workers, fishermen, and so forth) were invaluable to the early electoral success of the PPI. By 1921, however, many of these groups, dominated by a rural middle class, had begun to pull away from the PPI and its social programs were denounced as "white Bolshevism." Catholic Action's traditional claim to political neutrality led it away from the PPI and in practice to considerable sympathy for Fascism, until years later Fascist attacks made Catholic Action a center of quiet opposition to the regime. After the fall of Fascism, the strong desire within Italian Catholic Action (now including labor unions) to claim political neutrality was, under Vatican pressure, subordinated to cooperation in an anti-Marxist front.[25] After playing an essential part in the great mobilization of Italian Catholics from 1946 to 1948, these organizations similarly tended in a few years to become more critical of and even somewhat distant from the Christian Democrats.[26] Thus, although Catholic organizations were potentially invaluable to Christian Democratic parties, their political loyalty was far from assured, and making effective use of them remained problematic.

The denial that Catholic organizations were political had at first been primarily a self-protective effort to forfend against pressure from a frightened Church or an angry state. But this isolation from politics was also built into the ideology of much Catholic social action, which emphasized harmony and showed a certain disdain for mundane controversies. Such caution had the further advantage of giving an organization led by laymen a better chance of escaping heavy-handed clerical control, and these associations were pioneers in establishing the legitimacy and effectiveness of independent Catholic lay organizations. In terms of concrete, continuing active support, Catholic organizations gave Christian Democratic parties only limited help.

In terms of the broad appeal Christian Democratic parties needed to make, Catholic organizations could even be a hindrance. Catholic youth groups, savings banks, and recreational clubs competed with similar organizations that had no religious affiliation, often with some name calling. Although this divisiveness probably did not cost Catholic candidates many votes if they had a realistic chance of winning, it may well have kept some who sang in the secular choral society or belonged to the secular hiking club from voting for a Catholic party; and the very existence of such alternatives reinforced local divisions that Christian Democratic parties sought to overcome. In addition to this Catholic separatism, the tendency of parish priests to discourage membership in organizations that were not Catholic and the hierarchy's concern to maintain clerical control inflamed anticlerical visions of conspiracy. This was not wholly imaginary. Inside the meetings of Catholic organizations, denunciations of the French Republic or of the new Italian state were likely to be accepted as indications of religious fervor; and the paternalism that was often part of their local and regional social fabric left them likely to be considerably more conservative than the Christian Democratic party.

Disassociating themselves from such attitudes was a constant challenge for Christian Democratic parties,[27] made more difficult by the virulence of the Catholic press. Newspapers like Louis Veuillot's *L'Univers* and Davide Albertario's *L'Osservatorio Cattolico* not only denounced the secular governments of their day but also rarely missed a chance to lambaste any Catholics, including bishops, thought guilty of compromise. The Assumptionists, with their newspaper, *La Croix,* may well have been politically more effective, as well as noisier, than any Christian Democratic movement. In any case, Catholic social concerns, however expressed, often had a political valence; and the lay leaders of Catholic Action were often known to be opponents of the current form of government. Thus, no matter what their policies, Catholic social organizations seemed political.

Nevertheless, parish groups and local clergy (more than Catholic Action) were crucial to the early success of Catholic candidates in local Italian elections, and they continued to be important in the early years of the Partito Popolare.[28] That was somewhat less true of Christian Democratic efforts in France. In both countries the fact that support for Catholic parties was strongest in certain regions heightened clerical influence there. It was widely believed that priests could swing elections in some electoral colleges, and they learned to be less demanding with regard to the party platform than they were with regard to social action. Christian Democratic parties thus had to seek a balance between enjoying the benefits of clerical support and demonstrating the independence of the clergy that their programs required. That tactical paradox, which reinforced the tendency of Christian Democratic parties to send mixed messages and to seem opportunist, was accompanied by a structural one. Catholic parties were not the most effective means of mobilizing Catholic opinion. That was more effectively done in parishes, by Catholic newspapers, and through Catholic Action directing, and sometimes inflaming, Catholic opinion by concentrating on divisive issues like education or policy on the papacy. Christian Democratic parties, in contrast, wanted not merely to represent Catholic interests but rather through politics to extend to the nation their genial vision of a Christian society. They could neither fully use the network of Catholic associations nor rely on having the support of Catholic militants. Democracy divided Catholics without healing the divisions between them and the rest of secular society.

## THE SOCIAL PROGRAM

Social Catholicism was the most important single element in the formation of Christian Democratic parties, although its contribution came intermittently.[29] In practice differences in attitudes and values divided Catholic social activity into two types. Some groups of men and women in religious orders and of laypeople sought to establish an integrated religious life, preferring to build from formal Christian communities and through devotional societies to social action. Other groups of religious orders and also of lay men and women concentrated on performing specific social services in the name of Christian charity, supplementing and sometimes competing with secular and state-run organizations. Organizations of the first type tended to turn their backs on political activity; those of the second type were more readily drawn to party politics while believing, often correctly, that their interests were best served by protestations of political neutrality. Social Catholicism could thus point in many different directions, politically as well as ideologically. Leo XIII sought to separate social action from questions of democracy, and the French priests who campaigned for a Christian Democratic movement met more resistance for their political program than their economic one.[30] In both countries social engagement contributed fresh energy to all forms of Catholic activity (in Italy, the economic-social section of the Opera dei Congressi was by far its most active).[31] For many Catholics, the deeper knowledge of society acquired through the activities of social Catholics argued for a political program different from the traditional Catholic one, and the network of connections social Catholics built was more amenable to Christian Democracy than much of Catholic Action was. Ultimately, then, the development of effective, modern Christian Democratic parties in both Italy and France owed a great deal to social Catholicism, but that was not always the direction in which social Catholicism seemed headed.

The best-known social Catholic projects were not directed by democrats. In France the sponsors of mutual aid societies, visits to workers' homes, day care centers, societies for the protection of apprentices, and mixed unions of Christian employers and respectful workers were led by figures like René de la Tour du Pin, De Mun, Léon Harmel, and the conservative notables who ran the committees of the St. Vincent de Paul Society—all people associated with legitimism. In Italy most of the Catholic agricultural societies, peasant cooperatives, and savings banks for workers and peasants were led by local notables, aristocrats who were political conservatives and who considered the guidance of peasants their historic obligation. Even the French social Catholics who early in the century conducted the remarkable investigations of social conditions that are at the origin of modern sociology were legitimists or liberals rather than democrats. Whatever their inspiration, however, the concerns of social Catholics addressed modern society, even when their solutions were cautious, paternalistic, or vaguely utopian. Social Catholics helped to inform the middle class of the conditions faced by the poor and spoke more about some issues, such as migration and housing, than most liberals or socialists. The effect of this increased awareness led Christian Democrats to propose specific social measures and then campaign for them. That gave them a distinctive voice and facilitated their turning attention away from the symbolic issues that traditionally preoccupied Catholic politics. Christian Democrats were simply inclined to let others worry about dancing and immodest dress, restrictions on religious processions, and the loss of the papal states.

*Rerum Novarum,* which lent papal authority to social Catholicism, was also important in the formation of Christian Democratic parties. It legitimated attacks on economic liberalism, which, like De Mun's, had been criticized by many French Catholics as having gone too far;[32] it outlined reassuring limits, between campaigns for social justice and the protection of private property, within which to operate. In their avoidance of classic conflicts and their insistence on acceptance of established governments, Christian Democrats sounded like the more accommodating bishops who sought to depoliticize old controversies. In reality, they accepted many traditional Catholic strictures against contemporary society but argued that democratic politics could be a corrective. That very acceptance of politics, of course, implied some ultimate acceptance of awkward alliances and compromise, but that was not something many early Christian Democrats had to face.

Social engagement as well as their political principles led Christian Democrats into controversy and into conflicts with many conservative Catholics, state officials, and established interests. When they shed association with French legitimists or Italian intransigents, Christian Democratic leaders soon experienced the dangers of being radical. From Buchez's campaigns for workers in the 1840s through some of the activities of the Sillon at the turn of the century and the support of peasant strikes in Sicily that got Don Sturzo and his companions in trouble, Christian Democratic movements paid a price for acknowledging that there were class interests.[33] Indeed, any involvement in public disturbances cost them much Catholic support as well as an official reprimand from the hierarchy. However progressive and democratic Christian Democratic parties started out to be, experience from the first pushed them toward being parties of the center.

Social Catholics tended to see themselves as part of an international movement. They observed social activities and conditions in a variety of countries, and they met each other at international congresses. These international ties, valuable in practical terms as well as for lifting morale, also helped lay leadership to assert its independence of clerical control. Having a social program enabled Christian Democratic parties to position themselves to gain support outside Catholic circles and, with the rise of socialist competitors, to win wider support among Catholics as the best defense against socialism. In Italy that seemed to enjoy Vatican approval. Then after 1904 Pius X began to put heavy pressure on Catholics in France and Italy to form parties more narrowly dedicated to defending papal positions. Although weakened by such pressures, Christian Democrats were able to assert their autonomy, which may have been enough to assure their survival and pushed them toward a reassertion of their social commitment. In its early stages the Partito Popolare, like the Mouvement Républicain Populaire (MRP) a generation later, sounded quite anticapitalist. But even when social programs won votes, they also frightened many Catholics, including important members of the hierarchy. It would take something more, a greater sense among Catholics of social outrage or political urgency, to win Christian Democrats a share of power in France or to protect them from a papal veto in Italy.

## CHRISTIAN DEMOCRATIC PARTIES AFTER WORLD WAR II

The emergence of strong Christian Democratic parties in Italy and France at the end of World War II can be seen as the culmination of a century-long evolution toward a democratic Catholic party.[34] Alternatively, the strands in this evolution can be viewed as historically separate and even antagonistic; only after each had failed to achieve its goals did they finally come together in the stress of war and defeat.[35] That might help to explain the failure of progressive Catholic parties in the 1840s, the 1890s to 1910, and the 1920s. Or maybe the historical lesson lies in the more recent decline even of the MRP[36] in the 1960s and Democrazia Cristiana (DC) in the 1990s, suggesting that the victories of Christian Democracy in Italy, the home of the papacy, and in France, the eldest daughter of the Church, were momentary achievements possible only in special circumstances.[37]

In both countries the end of the war necessitated a fresh start politically at a time when the parties of the Left had gained unprecedented strength and those of the center—the Giolittian liberals in Italy and the conservative republicans and Radical Socialists in France—had been greatly weakened. Newly established modern democracies required parties capable of rapid, national organization and of using the techniques of mass appeal. That gave Catholic parties an important advantage, much as had the introduction of universal suffrage in Italy just before World War I.[38] After World War II women voted in France and Italy for the first time, which benefited Christian Democratic parties in particular (although less overwhelmingly so than anticlericals had feared). Modern parties also needed professional politicians, and the Catholic parties, having shaken off the dominance of aristocrats and notables in Catholic affairs, could now provide them. Involvement with the Vichy regime and Italian Fascism had largely silenced Catholics dubious about democracy, and fear of the Marxist tide gave French and Italian Catholics new political cohesion. Suddenly politics divided Catholics less than ever before, and the Church muted its earlier insistence on the clerical direction of lay activities. Opposition to the separation of church and state and to the loss of the papal states was no longer the litmus test of Catholic loyalty. Many Catholics had taken part in the Resistance; and Christian Democrats, sharing the values it proclaimed, could also share in the prestige it bestowed and the optimism it encouraged.[39]

Christian Democratic parties were at last truly nonconfessional, genuinely political parties.[40] They were more socially engaged than most parties of order, more committed to liberal procedures and closer to the national bureaucracy than most parties with progressive social programs. Ironically, they quickly became parties of government, defenders of the state they had battled for a century. Advocates of progressive programs and protectors of private property, they were positioned to be the negotiators of coalitions, interlocutors with other parties that were willing to share power. This political indifferentism extended to the far Right and the Left; for, in contrast to every other party, the Christian Democrats included some members willing to negotiate with neo-fascists and some prepared to engage publicly and deal privately with communists.[41] A major political strength, this broad reach could also become a vulnerability. A charismatic De Gaulle could neutralize the Christian Democrats' advantage in terms of political networks and steal their votes by appealing to a large part of their constituency (Catholics who, unlike the leaders of the MRP, were more concerned with order and protecting the Church's interests than with the rest of the party's program).[42] In Italy Christian Democrats held power for nearly fifty years, their various factions making the party itself a broad coalition; but without a strong Communist opponent to hold them together and make that a sufficient goal in itself, their talent for complicated and semisecret political deals became a liability. As the Christian Democratic party began to break up, Silvio Berlusconi, a far less charismatic figure than General De Gaulle, was able with a skillful media campaign and a network of advertising agencies to drive them from power. Out of power, the postwar Christian Democratic parties of France and Italy dissipated.[43]

## CHALLENGES TO CHRISTIAN DEMOCRACY IN FRANCE AND ITALY

Christian Democratic parties in France and Italy had so many assets, so much to build on, that their relatively late development into effective political instruments suggests the presence of some formidable barriers beyond those faced by similar parties in other countries. I will mention four of them. France and Italy after 1860 had highly centralized administrative systems. Issues of church-state relations therefore almost always became the subject of national, political controversy. That tended to make these conflicts more ideological and longer lasting than they might otherwise have been, and it largely disallowed flexible local or regional resolutions, at least officially. This mattered all the more in France and Italy because of the regional concentration of Catholic political strength in each country—in Brittany and Alsace-Lorraine (where its absence between 1870 and 1918, a particularly important period for party formation, seriously weakened French Christian Democracy), in the Veneto but not in southern Italy (where the political use of patronage networks helped to stifle democratic political movements).[44]

Nationalism (a Catholic political asset in Belgium, Ireland, and Poland) was another distinctive barrier in France and Italy. In both countries the political strength of nationalism until late in the century lay primarily on the Left, for nationalism was associated with the principles of the French Revolution and the Risorgimento and included a strong dose of anticlericalism. At a time when nationalism was particularly powerful, Catholics struggled to establish their claim to participate in national sentiment.[45] A major element of the Dreyfus affair was the assertion of nationalism on the Right, and Catholics in both countries used their support of imperialism to demonstrate their importance to the nation. French Catholics also boasted of how well Catholic schools prepared their graduates for military careers. Such claims came more easily, however, to conservative Catholics than to Christian Democrats. Constructing a Catholic nationalism was particularly difficult in Italy. Reconciliation, which had still seemed possible in the 1860s when liberal Catholics were prominent in the new government, was nearly impossible once Rome became the capital. The cardinal who opened the first Italian Catholic congress in 1874 regretted those youth who had "abandoned the banner of Christ to drape themselves in the flag of the devil." Everyone understood what flag he had in mind. Twenty years later *Civiltà Cattolica* still referred to the Italian *tricolore* as the antipapal flag.[46] The alternative patriotism intransigents offered, which stressed Italy's special mission as the seat of the papacy and the glory of medieval communes, was not very useful in electoral campaigns. It took the experience of war, in Ethiopia and Libya and most notably World War I that Italian Catholics had wanted not to enter, to enable Catholics to establish their nationalist credentials.[47]

Potentially, however, nationalism and especially the universalistic nationalisms of France and Italy could have a deeply Catholic appeal, associating land and religion, mores and morality, secular rituals and religious liturgy, community and church. Those affinities functioned in Catholic regions; the difficulty lay in extending them to the French Republic and Italy's liberal monarchy. Still, Catholics often accomplished that, as, in effect, did priests and bishops when they celebrated victories with a Te Deum, sat on platforms at civic ceremonies, and hailed national achievements at the opening of railroads. Christian Democrats made this loyalty explicit. In 1899 the Catholic paper *Il Popolo Italiano* took as its subtitle, *Risorgimento Sociale Cattolico*, a brave assimilation of the national, democratic, and social to Catholicism. Although a toast to Italian unity offered at a meeting of Christian Democrats in Lombardy scandalized many Catholics in 1901, Don Sturzo dared a few years later to speak of Italian unity as a good thing and, moved by sympathy for Italy's Libyan venture, to refer to a *nazionalismo cattolico*. If few French Catholics could equal the eloquence of Charles Péguy, more and more of them shared some of his affection for the Republic as well as the *patrie*. On the other hand, Catholics drawn to conservative nationalisms were slow to discover that their values were ancillary at best to the Action Française, the Vichy regime, and Italian Fascism. The importance of Catholic participation in the Resistance lay in part in its demonstration that national, democratic, and religious values could reinforce each other. No one found it surprising that national pride was a prominent theme at Christian Democratic and MRP congresses. At a more theoretical level, however, the relationship between Catholicism and nationalism remained unresolved. Yet that made it all the easier for Christian Democrats to embrace international cooperation and to work more consistently than any other political party for the formation of the European Community.

Social class was another important barrier to the formation of Christian Democratic parties in France and Italy.[48] Here, too, theory was a factor. Catholic social thought rejected ideas of class conflict at a time when national politics seemed increasingly to divide along class lines. Social Catholics played an important and easily overlooked role in the evolution of social policies in both countries, and their organizations sometimes exercised significant influence locally. Instances of industrial conflict, and they were numerous, were likely to divide Catholics, however, and to cost Catholic parties politically. Christian Democratic parties never gained strong working-class support at the national level.[49] There was a better chance for establishing a political base among the peasantry, but that, too, proved limited. The tendency of small landowners in France to give their votes to republicans was one of the enduring legacies of the French Revolution. The politicization of rural society increased markedly in France from the 1860s on, and the intensely local issues often involved conflicts with the village priest or a religious order over rights to a well, an orchard, or a roadway. In the parts of rural France where Catholic political influence was great, the mixture of local loyalties, interests, social hierarchy, and ideology left limited room for a Catholic Democratic party. Later, when at its height, the MRP would declare that half of its leadership should be workers or peasants but then found it necessary to count civil servants and managers as workers. When the MRP was one of France's four largest parties, five others received more votes from peasants.

In Italy limited suffrage excluded peasants until the beginning of the twentieth century. Then the landowning peasants of Piedmont voted, rather like their French neighbors, for progressive liberals. A more radical Left found significant support among day laborers in the Romagna and the rice fields of Lombardy. In Tuscany and Umbria sharecropping turned out not to have cemented the social, let alone political, ties its advocates had claimed. In the short time they had, Catholic parties impressively mobilized peasants only in the Veneto and Sicily, and those efforts antagonized conservative Catholics. Although in the Veneto economic demands troubled landlords, the Catholic peasant movement there was too much under the thumb of local notables to be the basis for a national Christian Democratic party. In Sicily the PPI's involvement in strikes by landless peasants contributed to the suspicion with which Catholic leaders outside Sicily viewed the party. In both nations, then, social structure and ideology inhibited development of the kind of Catholic peasant party so important in much of Europe.

Historically, much of the middle and lower middle class in France and Italy disliked clerical involvement in politics more than they feared the Left, and in both nations the political influence of the aristocracy was circumscribed by the 1880s, when Christian Democratic parties began to show promise. Unable to establish a strong class base, although class mattered politically, Christian Democratic parties needed to develop an appeal across class. That the PPI began to do in the early 1920s,[50] and the Christian Democrats and MRP did after World War II, helped by the weakness of the Right and the threatening presence of two strong communist parties.

The fourth barrier to the establishment of strong Christian Democratic parties in France and Italy, although the least tangible, may have been the most important. Catholics held on to the view that theirs were Catholic nations, or at least were meant to be. Defensive, angry, or alienated as many Catholics were, French and Italian Catholicism did not accept minority status. Even as they constructed the practices and institutions that allowed Catholics to live their social life within distinctly Catholic groups, they did not accept being relegated to a subculture. The diverse, multiform, fissiparous qualities that gave French and Italian Catholicism great vitality, creativity, and adaptability cost Catholic politics the cohesion and Catholic parties the reliable political support available in other European countries.

## A FEW CONCLUDING GENERALIZATIONS

Their history in France and Italy suggests some points about Christian Democratic parties more generally. They benefit from, indeed may require, a clearly identified, politically powerful opponent. The chances of forming a lasting coalition among Catholics and of compressing them into a coherent party are greatly enhanced by the presence of a strong competitor. Without Protestants to play that role, communists were invaluable. Ireland pioneered a Catholic, nationalist party when under English rule; there was no need for one after independence.

An effective Christian Democratic party must intertwine strands of liberal Catholicism, integral Catholicism, and social Catholicism without invoking opposition from the hierarchy. Needing to appeal at the parish level, a national Catholic party must also honor local loyalties. This complex balancing of traditions, interests, and ideologies is especially challenging in a country where nearly everyone is said to be Catholic and in which Catholics are accustomed to public disagreement with each other on political and social questions.

Christian Democratic parties are stronger at a time when there is a distinctive political advantage in having a network of extra-party ties: unions, lay associations, social and charitable activities, and parish organizations. They thus are more likely to flourish when mass parties are new and democracy has been recently established or restored, and that is especially true when only Marxist opponents enjoy comparable networks.[51]

In Catholic countries Christian Democratic parties enlarge their support by being nonconfessional and quite secular parties. At the height of church-state conflict, a Catholic politician was someone concerned to protect the Church; since World War II, he or she has preferred to be defined in terms of a social program and opposition to communism. Christian Democrats thus tend to distance themselves from clerical structures (and to claim more autonomy than they have). This broadens their electoral support and facilitates an often remarkable tactical flexibility. This independence of the Church's institutional concerns becomes especially appropriate when the Church is not under attack and faith itself is understood as inward-looking and personal, in little need of a specifically Catholic party for its public expression. The sorts of issues called wedge issues in American political jargon, such as aid to Catholic schools, can at times effectively mobilize the support of Catholic voters. Often, however, outspoken clerical campaigns instead strengthen opposition to clerical influence even among Catholics, encouraging Christian Democratic parties to become still more secular.

To avoid association with Catholic traditions of intolerance and distrust of freedom, Christian Democratic parties have an interest in staying away from old issues of church-state conflict.[52] For its 1949 congress, where Marc Sangnier was one of the honorary presidents, the MRP published a pamphlet describing its program. Its enumeration of such general goals as equality and justice was mixed with allusions to a proud past and boasts of the party's ties to youth and workers, but its Catholicism surfaced almost inadvertently—in a passing reference to the scandalous behavior of other parties. The scandalous, the MRP explained (presumably for the benefit of its secular supporters), is defined as that which provides an occasion for sin.[53]

These tendencies can sap a Christian Democratic party's electoral strength, risking the loss of its idealism as connections to the Church are loosened and integralist aspirations disappear. Catholics in France and Italy not only remain divided on political issues, they seem increasingly comfortable with such disagreements.[54] More than anything else their attentuated and often neglected social programs distinguished the Christian Democrats from other parties of the center-Left, and political reality tended to make those programs ever more cautious.

Large Christian Democratic parties tend to be coalitions (much like parties in the United States) held together by a common opponent and the magnetism of political power. On many issues that divide Left and Right, they are freer to choose their positions than are parties that rest on explicit political traditions and specific interests. This helped leaders like De Gasperi and Bidault to establish a pattern of acting as arbiters among other parties. Christian Democratic parties are thus parties of the center, and they tended to replace more old-fashioned parties of the center because they proved more skillful at making mass appeals than did liberals or progressive intellectuals. Embarrassingly comfortable with the compromises that follow from being a party of government, Christian Democratic parties risk becoming parties of stasis while sustaining an air of intellectual seriousness by insisting that their positions (like those of communists) stem from a coherent philosophy of society and history—a claim subverted by the compromises on which they thrive.

For reasons historical and philosophical as well as tactical, Christian Democrats have performed a healing function in France and Italy. On the whole, they have been readier than other parties to forgive those who fought on the wrong side before 1945. They have helped to soften class and regional divisions and been quick to rise above domestic dissension by stressing the merits of international cooperation. When Christian Democrats from Belgium, France, Germany, Italy, and the Netherlands attend each other's party conferences and campaign for the European Union, it is as if they believe in progress after all.

Having assisted Catholics to reconcile with contemporary society, having helped divided nations wounded by repression and war to make the transition to modern democracy, having joined in making social welfare one of the responsibilities of the European state, and having led in the creation of the European Union, Christian Democratic parties may have fulfilled their historic function. Religious faith will continue to stimulate battles for social justice, and Catholic social thinkers will continue to be powerful social critics and to stimulate social action; but will giant Christian Democratic parties remain the most effective agents of such programs? The political skills that Christian Democratic parties precociously mastered are now familiar to all. When Christian Democratic parties in Catholic countries find themselves out of power and without the threat of Marxist enemies, their coalitions readily dissipate, allowing smaller groups to lobby for more consistent and demanding programs. In such circumstances, visions of a truly Christian democracy might even gain new power, but will Catholics or society at large have a need in the future for centrist, compromising, mass parties that are vaguely Christian, uncomfortably Catholic, and no more democratic than any other?

## NOTES

1. R. E. M. Irving, *The Christian Democratic Parties of Western Europe* (London: Royal Institute of International Affairs, 1979): "Christian Democratic parties have dominated the politics of Western Europe for more than a century. . . ." Stathis N. Kalyvas, *The Rise of Christian Democracy in Europe* (Ithaca: Cornell University Press, 1996), 1–2, declares that Christian Democratic parties "are frequently in power in five major European countries" and adds that the federation of these parties, along with the socialists, "dominates the European parliament." He cites the *Economist* as stating that "Christian Democracy is rightly considered the most successful western European political movement since 1945."

2. John H. Whyte, *Catholics in Western Democracies: A Study in Political Behavior* (Dublin: Gill and Macmillan, 1981), 12, finds thirteen countries that are economically advanced (a criterion that allows him to eliminate Latin America), have long democratic traditions (which excludes Spain and Portugal), and in which Catholics constitute a significant part of the population. Of these, nine are European. Ireland and the United Kingdom, however, do not have strong Catholic parties; and Catholics are not a clear majority in two others. That leaves Austria, Belgium, Italy, and France as Europe's Catholic and democratic countries with a history of Catholic parties.

3. For an excellent brief assessment of the history of political Catholicism in France and Italy, see James F. McMillan, "France," and John Pollard, "Italy," in *Political Catholicism in Europe, 1918–1965* (Oxford: Clarendon Press, 1996), 34–96.

4. In Italy after World War I the idea that a Catholic party might be just one among many parties troubled many Catholics. Agostino Giovagnoli, *La cultura democristiana: Tra chiesa cattolica e identità italiana, 1918–1948* (Bari: Laterza, 1991), 23–55.

5. Emile Sévrin, *Les missions réligieuses en France sous la Restauration (1815–1830)*, 2 vols. (Paris: J. Vrin, 1948–59); Robert L. Locke, *French Legitimists and the Politics of*

*Moral Order in the Early Third Republic* (Princeton: Princeton University Press, 1974); Hans Maier, *Revolution and the Church: The Early History of Christian Democracy, 1789–1907* (Notre Dame: University of Notre Dame Press, 1969); Adolfo Omodeo, *Le Amicizie Cattoliche* (Turin, 1954).

   6.  Yvon Tranvouez, *Catholics d'abord: Approches du mouvement catholique en France (xix<sup>e</sup>–xx<sup>e</sup> siècle)* (Paris: Editions Ouvrières, 1988), 107–92.

   7.  Alec R. Vidler, *Prophecy and Papacy: A Study of Lamennais, the Church, and the Revolution* (New York: Charles Scribner's Sons, 1954); Mario Sancipriano, *Vincenzo Gioberti: Progetti etico-politici nel Risorgimento* (Rome: Studium, 1997).

   8.  At a more popular level, too, there were many groups in this period for whom religious feeling and democratic values naturally went together. Edward Berenson, *Populist Religion and Left-Wing Politics in France, 1830–1852* (Princeton: Princeton University Press, 1984).

   9.  Alec Vidler, *A Century of Social Catholicism* (London: SPCK, 1964), 70–76, 112–23; Emile Poulat, *Catholicisme, démocratie et socialisme: Le mouvement catholique e Mgr. Benigni de la naissance du socialisme à la victoire du fascisme* (Paris: Casterman, 1977).

   10.  Robert F. Byrnes, "The French Christian Democrats in the 1890's: Their Appearance and Failure," *Catholic Historical Review* 36 (October 1950): 286–306.

   11.  Pietro Scoppola, "La Lega democratica nazionale," in *Il Cattolicesimo politico e sociale in Italia e Germania dal 1870 al 1914*, ed. Ettore Passerin d'Entrèves and Konrad Repgen (Bologna: Il Mulino, 1977), 103–21.

   12.  Giorgio Vecchio, *Alla ricerca del partito* (Brescia: Morcelliana, 1987), 81–113.

   13.  Jeanne Caron, *Le Sillon et la démocratie chrétienne en France, 1891–1902* (Paris: Plon, 1965).

   14.  Maurice Montuclard, *Conscience religieuse et démocratie chrétienne en France, 1891–1902* (Paris: Editions du Seuil, 1965).

   15.  Bernard Reardon, *Liberalism and Tradition: Aspects of Catholic Thought in Nineteenth-Century France* (New York: Cambridge University Press, 1975).

   16.  Marcella Pincherle, *Moderatismo politico e riforma religiosa in Terenzio Mamiani* (Milan: Giuffrè Editore, 1975); Ornella Confessore, *Conservatorismo politico e reformismo religioso: La "Rassegna Nazionale," dal 1898 al 1908* (Bologna: Il Mulino, 1971).

   17.  Among them, Alessandro Manzoni, Gino Capponi, Rafaello Lambruschini, Cesare Cantù, Niccolò Tommaseo, Marco Minghetti, and Giovanni Pasolini. For the later period, see Alessandro Pellegrini, ed., *Tre Cattolici liberali: Alessandro Casati, Tommaso Gallarati Scotti, Stefano Jacini* (Milan: Adelphi, 1972). In his essay on Jacini, Arturo Carlo Jemolo, himself a prominent liberal Catholic and historian in the twentieth century, says many of them were Catholic integralists, even if they built on a "platform of liberal Catholicism." Ibid., 41.

18. The old Gallicans had, of course, been routed earlier. See Austin Gough, *Paris and Rome: The Gallican Church and the Ultramontane Campaign, 1848–1853* (Oxford: Clarendon Press, 1986); on the Raillement, Alexander Sedgwick, *The Ralliement in Franch Politics, 1890–1898* (Cambridge, Mass.: Harvard University Press, 1965).

19. Jean-Marie Mayeur, *Un prêtre démocrate, l'abbé Lemire, 1853–1928* (Paris: Casterman, 1968).

20. Benjamin F. Martin Jr., *Count Albert de Mun: Paladin of the Third Republic* (Chapel Hill: University of North Carolina Press, 1978).

21. Note the interesting discussion between De Gasperi and Benedetto Croce on the Church and liberty in Giovagnoli, *Cultura democristiana*, 49–57.

22. William Bosworth, *Catholicism in Modern France: French Catholic Groups at the Threshold of the Fifth Republic* (Princeton: Princeton University Press, 1962); Gabriele De Rosa, *Storia del movimento cattolico in Italia: Dalla Restaurazione all'età giolittiana* (Bari: Laterza, 1972).

23. Bosworth, *Catholicism in Modern France*, 96–261, discusses these organizations in France and their importance for the MRP. On the party in Italy, see Gabriele De Rosa, *Storia del movimento cattolico in Italia: Il Partito Popolare Italiano* (Bari: Laterza, 1966).

24. Adrien Dansette, *Destin du catholicisme française, 1926–1956* (Paris: Flammarion, 1957).

25. Gianfranco Poggi, *Catholic Action in Italy: The Sociology of a Sponsored Organization* (Stanford: Stanford University Press, 1967), passim; Maria Casella, *L'Azione Cattolica alla caduta del fascismo* (Rome: Edizioni Studium, 1984), 44–59, 239 ff.; Maria Casella, *L'Azione cattolica nell'Italia contemporanea (1919–1969)* (Rome: Editrice AVE, 1992), 31–66, 189–203; Paolo Pombeni, *Le Cronache Sociale di Dossetti, 1947–1951: Geografia di un movimento di opinione* (Florence: Valechhi, 1976).

26. Alfred Canavero, *I Cattolici nella società italiana* (Brescia: Editrice La Scuola, 1991), 152, 248–64.

27. Even though Catholic campaigns against the state's restrictions can be seen as a contribution to liberty: Raymond Grew, "Liberty and the Catholic Church in Nineteenth-Century Europe Italy," in *Freedom and Religion in the Nineteenth Century*, ed. Richard Helmstadter (Stanford: Stanford University Press, 1997), 196–232.

28. De Rosa, *Partito Popolare*; John N. Molony, *The Emergence of Political Catholicism in Italy: Partito Popolare, 1919–1926* (London: Croom Helm, 1977).

29. The literature is immense: Jean-Baptiste Duroselle, *Les débuts du catholicisme social en France, 1822–1870* (Paris: Presses Universitaires de France, 1951), is fundamental. Among others, see also Emmanuel Barbier, *Histoire du catholicisme libéral et du catholicisme social en France, 1870–1914* (Bordeaux: Imprimerie Caadoret,

1923), 5 vols.; Charles Maignen, *Maurice Maignen directeur du Cercle Montparnasse et les origins du mouvement sociale catholique en France (1822–1890)* (Luöcon: S. Pacteau, 1927); Henri Rollet, *L'Action sociale des catholiques en France* (Paris: Boivin, 1947) and *Etapes du catholicisme sociale* (Paris: La Colombe, 1949); Sanor Agocs, *The Troubled Origins of the Italian Catholic Labor Movement, 1878–1914* (Detroit: Wayne State University Press, 1988); Carlo Falconi, *Luigi Gedda e l'Azione Cattolica* (Florence: Parenti, 1958); Paul Misner, *Social Catholicism in Europe: From the Onset of Industrialization to the First World War* (New York: Crossroad, 1991).

30. Paul Droulers, *Politique sociale et christianisme: Le Père Desbuquois et l'Action Populaire* (Paris: Editions Ouvrières, 1968), 60–73.

31. On the importance of the social question in prying Italian Catholics from the intransigent position, see Canavero, *I Cattolici nella società italiana*, 45–103.

32. Tranvouez, *Catholics d'abord*, 61–67.

33. Marxists as well as Catholics were surprised and confused by a social Catholicism seriously engaged in workers' issues. Robert S. Stuart, "'A "De Profundis" for Christian Socialism': French Marxists and the Critique of Political Catholicism, 1882–1905," *French Historical Studies* 22:2 (Spring 1999): 241–61.

34. And as part of a larger long-term development toward modern ideas of justice and equality in the Church: Jean-Dominique Durand, *L'Europe de la Démocratie Chrétienne* (Brussels: Editions Complexe, 1995); Thomas Bokenkotter, *Church and Revolution: Catholics in the Struggle for Democracy and Social Justice* (New York: Doubleday, 1998).

35. A delegate to the constitutional convention of the MRP in November 1944 could proudly point to a heritage that included Lamennais, Lacordaire, Montalembert, De Mun, and the social Catholics, in addition to Marc Sagnier and the Sillon, cited in Mario Einaudi and François Goguel, *Christian Democracy in Italy and France* (New York: Archon Books, 1969), 109. The impression that so diverse a group represented a single "venerable ideal" was, of course, one of the achievements of the MRP.

36. Pierre Letamendia, *Le Mouvement Républicain Populaire* (Paris: Beauchesne, 1995); R. E. M. Irving, *Christian Democracy in France* (London: George Allen & Unwin, 1973).

37. On the particular culture that nurtured Italy's Christian Democratic party, see Giovagnoli, *Cultura democristiana*.

38. The wartime experience also proved Catholics to be patriots. On the experience in France, see Nadine-Joselle Chaline, ed., *Chrétiens dans la première guerre mondiale* (Paris: Editions du Cerf, 1993); Jacques Fontana, *Les Catholiques français pendant la grande guerre* (Paris: Editions du Cerf, 1990).

39. Hugues Petit, *L'Eglise, le Sillon et l'Action Française* (Paris: Nouvelles Editions Latines, 1998), 301–20, sees important continuity between the Sillon and the MRP,

yet stresses the importance for the MRP of the Resistance and the profound changes in the Church after 1945.

40. Qualities that did not automatically appeal to all Catholic voters. A contemporary French observer believed that the Right got more Catholic votes than the MRP, the Left fewer but still a large proportion, and considered the MRP's appeal strongest among younger Catholics: Georges Suffert, *Les Catholiques et la gauche* (Paris: François Maspero, 1960), 36–46.

41. Ibid.; Francis J. Murphy, *Communists and Catholics in France, 1936–1939* (Gainesville: University of Florida Press, 1989); Rosanna Mulazzi Giammanco, *The Catholic-Communist Dialogue in Italy, 1944 to the Present* (New York: Praeger, 1989).

42. Jean-Dominique Durand, *L'Europe de la démocratie chrétienne* (Brussels: Editions Complexe, 1995), 273–85.

43. Enzo Pace, *L'Unità dei cattolici in Italia: Origini e decadenza di un mito collettivo* (Verona: Guerini e Associati, 1995).

44. Caroline C. Ford, *Creating the Nation in Provincial France: Religion and Identity in Brittany* (Princeton: Princeton University Press, 1993); Suzanne Berger, *Peasants against Politics: Rural Organization in Brittany, 1911–1967* (Cambridge, Mass.: Harvard University Press, 1972); Nadine-Josette Chaline, *Des Catholiques normands sous la Troisième République: Crises, combats, renouveaux* (Roanne/Le Coteau: Editions Horvath, 1995); Angelo Gambasin, *Parroci e contadini nel Veneto* (Rome: Edizioni Studium, 1974).

45. Note the comment of René Rémond, "Il nous manque une théologie de la nation," in *Entretien avec René Rémond* (Paris: Politiques et Chrétien, 1992), 44.

46. Guido Formigoni, *L'Italia dei cattolici: Fede e nazione dal Risorgimento alla Repubblica* (Bologna: Il Mulino, 1998).

47. John A. Thayer, *Italy and the Great War: Politics and Culture, 1870–1915* (Madison: University of Wisconsin Press, 1964).

48. Ralph Gibson, *A Social History of French Catholicism, 1789–1914* (London: Routledge, 1989).

49. Which is not to say that workers did not have varied and important relations with the Church: Pierre Pierrard, *L'Eglise et les ouvriers en France (1840–1940)* (Paris: Hachette, 1984).

50. Vecchio, *Ricerchio del partito*, 211–68.

51. This is in a sense the other side of the argument of Kalyvas, *Rise of Christian Democracy*, 114–66, that the absence of an effective Christian democratic party in France before World War II resulted from electoral failures due to the failure to organize (and this essay attempts to suggest some of the reasons for that). For an interesting example of the importance of using such networks at the beginning of a new political regime, see Sudhir Hazareesingh, "The Société Républicaine and the

Propagation of Civic Republicanism in Provincial and Rural France, 1870–1877," *Journal of Modern History* 71:2 (June 1999): 271–307.

52.  Kalyvas, *Rise of Christian Democracy,* 1, makes this point in somewhat different terms.

53.  *En Marche vers l'avenir: Travaux du Vᵉ Congrès National MRP,* Strasbourg, May 26–29, 1949.

54.  See Jean-Marie Donegani, *La liberté de choisir: Pluralisme religieux et pluralisme politique dans le catholicisme français contemporain* (Paris: Press de la Fondaton Nationale des Sciences Politiques, 1993).

# 2

# The Age of Christian Democracy

## The Frontiers of Success and Failure

MARTIN CONWAY

The age of Christian Democracy in Europe has ended. The political parties that use its name and owe loyalty to its past for the most part have not disappeared and show few signs of doing so in the foreseeable future. The current social democratic quasi-hegemony in European politics will prove transient, and new opportunities will present themselves for Christian Democratic parties to regain the political initiative, both in the European Union and in the new (or restored) democracies farther east. None of this, however, negates the fact that Christian Democracy is now the object of historical study rather than a contemporary reality. As historical rather than political science perspectives of the development of postwar Europe have come to the fore in recent years, so it has become increasingly evident that the thirty years after World War II constituted the heyday of Christian Democracy as a political force in much of western and central Europe. The temporal and geographic frontiers of this phenomenon can be delineated without much difficulty. It began during Europe's transition from war to peace between 1943 and 1948 and ended in the economic difficulties and concomitant political realignments of the late 1970s. During that era, Christian Democracy was the dominant form of center-Right politics in a region that stretched roughly from the mouth of the Rhine in the north to the Veneto and Lombardy in the south and from northeastern France in the west to the artificially abrupt frontier of the Iron Curtain in the east.[1]

The remarkable success of Christian Democracy during these *trente glo-rieuses* as well as its rather precise geographic contours present a double-headed agenda for those who seek to examine it as a historical phenomenon. The twin tasks that will preoccupy historians as they probe the history of Christian Democracy in its myriad political, economic, cultural, and ideological dimensions over the coming decades will be to explain its rapid growth after 1945 and why this success was confined, with some French and Iberian exceptions, to particular areas of western and central Europe. The purpose of this chapter is not to prejudge this research; this is a historical field where the serious work is only just beginning. I seek instead merely to analyze some of the principal lines of current historical work on Christian Democracy and to suggest some tentative conclusions.

Given the dominance Christian Democracy achieved in center-Right politics after World War II, it is not surprising that accounts of that success have tended to be written primarily by those sympathetic to the movement. In this way Christian Democracy, it might be said, has come to write its own history of its origins and postwar development. Stated briefly, these accounts stress the organic growth of a democratic Christian politics from its origins in the 1890s through Catholic opposition to the antidemocratic forces of the Left and Right during the interwar years and, more especially, resistance against Nazism and its affiliated evils during World War II. The intellectual heritage and political experience derived from this long gestation then burst forth decisively in the new Catholic and interconfessional political movements founded after the war that, by offering a "third way" between Communist and Fascist totalitarianism and an outmoded liberal individualism, rallied a cross-class coalition of support for their democratic politics, social-market corporatism, and personalist humanism.[2]

Summarized in this way, this interpretation of Christian Democratic success inevitably seems somewhat simplistic. It rests, however, on two central assumptions: first, the Christian Democracy that emerged after World War II was the product of a half century of gradual maturation; and second, it was initially as much an ideology as a political movement. Both of these theses have considerable plausibility. Nobody would deny that the Christian Democrats of the 1940s drew on the ideas developed by their predecessors of the interwar years and, perhaps more especially, of the 1890s. As Jean-Marie Mayeur has perceptively remarked, there was much in the initial programs of the Christian Democratic parties of the 1940s that marked a return to the language and preoccupations of the social Catholicism of the pre-1914 era.[3] Moreover, the ideological dynamism of Christian Democracy in the years after World War II was one of its outstanding characteristics. Far from limiting themselves to narrowly confessional concerns, the parties drew up wide-ranging and ambitious programs that mobilized their supporters by presenting a radical alternative to capitalism and communism.[4] Though the pragmatic dictates of government subsequently blunted this ideological energy, Christian Democrats retained a strong sense of their distinctiveness through their commitment to a social-market economy, limited state power, and a society of intermediate bodies.[5]

Nevertheless, both elements of this interpretation can, indeed should, be questioned. As historians have not been slow to point out, accounts of the long-term origins of Christian Democracy rest on a rather tendentious account of the nature of Christian-democratic politics of the 1890s that, far from embracing democratic values, predominantly defined itself against such modern heresies in favor of an essentially antimodern social Catholicism.[6] Moreover, by bracketing out the collaboration of many Catholic individuals and groups with the antidemocratic Right in the 1920s and 1930s, such an interpretation risks presenting a distinctly sanitized account of Catholic politics during the first half of the twentieth century.[7] The more profound problem raised by such an approach is, however, not so much the validity, or otherwise, of elements of its interpretation of the prehistory of Christian Democracy but how far this emphasis on its long-term origins can adequately explain the success of Christian Democratic politics after 1945. Perhaps the most influential recent political science study, by Stathis N. Kalyvas, for example, is significantly entitled *The Rise of Christian Democracy* and presents the decades prior to World War I as the decisive era when the essential components of twentieth-century Christian Democracy were forged.[8] The logic of such an approach is questionable. In its most extreme form, it relegates the post-1945 history of Christian Democracy to little more than the proof of prior events and deflects attention from the political context and material circumstances within which Christian Democratic parties emerged and continued to change after World War II.

The emphasis on the initial programmatic energy of Christian Democracy raises similar problems. Once again, it privileges its origins over its subsequent development and more especially presents World War II as a decisive moment when resistance to foreign oppression and totalitarian rule forged a new Catholic ideology of democratic engagement in a pluralist society.[9] This, however, is based on a selective reading of the events of the war years and risks making the undoubted impact of the war on certain intellectual elites (notably in France and, during the latter war years, in Italy) stand as representative of the experiences of millions of European Catholics. In reality, Catholic Resistance possessed neither the scope nor always the progressive character that is often attributed to it, and, as with other Resistance ideologies, its impact on the postwar world proved highly ephemeral.[10] Thus, whatever the initial debt owed by Christian Democratic parties to Resistance ideas, it was rapidly overlaid not merely by the return of more durable and conservative mentalities but also by the pervasive materialism of much postwar politics.[11]

There would, thus, seem to be scope for a new approach to the history of Christian Democracy that, while not neglecting its long-term origins and initial ideological character, resituates it in the immediate context of postwar Europe. Perhaps the most appropriate analogy for this change in historical perspective is the historiography of the development of Socialist movements in pre-1914 Europe. There are obvious similarities with Christian Democracy after 1945. In both cases a new political movement emerged that, within the space of a generation, acquired a powerful position in many western and central European states. Not surprisingly, historians initially tended to write wide-ranging histories of nineteenth-century socialism that presented its "rise" in somewhat Whiggish terms as the organic growth of a unitary movement with a clearly defined ideology.[12] Times change, however, and so do historical perspectives. In recent decades there has been a new wave of historical writing that has analyzed much more critically the nineteenth-century development of socialist and labor movements, examining both ruptures and continuities, instances of failure alongside successes, and the external as well as the internal influences on the development of socialism. The consequence has been a historiography of pre-1914 socialism that is much less concerned with origins and ideological manifestos and much more attentive to the particular factors that molded the development and character of individual Socialist movements.[13]

A similar process of change, it would seem fair to assume, is likely to occur in studies of post-1945 Christian Democracy. Broad accounts and teleological narratives are likely to be replaced by a more specific and contextual approach in which the influence of national political systems and mentalities, of internal tensions and of external developments will all come to the fore. Above all, there needs to be a recognition that Christian Democracy was not a uniform movement that arrived "ready-made" in the history of post-1945 Europe but a dynamic and evolving phenomenon that was molded more by circumstance than by intent. In the remainder of this chapter, I therefore wish to sketch out a number of the factors, both internal and external to Christian Democracy, that seem to have played a role in explaining both its success in some areas and its failure or absence in others.

Religion might seem the obvious place to begin. Nothing would appear less controversial than to suggest that the history of Christian Democracy might have been related to trends within Catholicism as a religious faith in twentieth-century Europe. Yet one of the remarkable features of much of the writing about Christian Democracy is the limited attention it has paid to religious history. Somewhat ironically, those who have studied it have tended to accept secular notions of a divorce between politics and religion that would certainly have been alien to the founders of Christian Democratic parties.[14] One of their reasons for doing so may have been that, at least superficially, the character of postwar European Catholicism seems at odds with the pluralist and progressive tone of many of the founding charters of Christian Democratic parties. While the parties presented themselves as Christian rather than Catholic, open to men and women of all faiths and of none, Catholicism in the 1940s and 1950s was intransigent, hierarchical, and dismissive of the values of other denominations and political traditions. Indeed, in many respects the era of Pius XII (1939–58) marked the high point of a Catholic faith that defined itself as the fortress of truth in a corrupt and decadent world. The collective excommunication of Communists by the pope in 1949, his defiant declaration of the Assumption of the Virgin Mary in 1950, and the self-conscious majesty adopted by Pius XII in his dealings with the faithful all betokened a confrontational approach to the contemporary world that was much more profound than the pope's often-quoted but circumstantial and conditional espousal of democracy in his Christmas Message of 1944.[15] Nor were such attitudes limited to the papacy. Throughout Europe the postwar years witnessed a resurgence of a traditionalist and self-confident Catholicism that made few concessions to the modern world. The world of postwar Catholicism was one of banners, parades, and youth movements in which, for example, the five hundred thousand Catholics who paraded through Budapest in August 1945 behind the uncorrupted hand of Saint Stephen or the Marian imagery that suffused so much of popular piety were more characteristic of the dominant mentality than the philo-Communism displayed by certain Catholic intellectuals or the pastoral experiments of the worker priests.[16]

How are we to square this Catholicism with postwar Christian Democracy? Primarily, no doubt, by recognizing that, however sincere the protests of their founders, the Christian Democratic parties were for the most part emphatically Catholic parties. In Germany, of course, the rupture provoked by the demise of the Third Reich enabled the foundation of a party that was nominally interconfessional but largely Catholic in terms of its electorate and overwhelmingly so in terms of its membership and inspiration.[17] Elsewhere, hopes of a deconfessionalization of politics proved short-lived. The designation of the Mouvement Républicain Populaire (MRP) by the satirical newspaper *Le Canard Enchaîné* as the "Mouvement des Révérends Pères" might have been a cruel jibe leveled at a party that genuinely wished to transcend France's entrenched clerical-anticlerical frontier, but as a rough approximation of the reality of its electoral base (once it had separated from Gaullism) it was not inaccurate.[18] A reconfessionalization of politics occurred rapidly in much of Catholic Europe after the disruptions of the war years, and religious practice became once again a more reliable determinant for electoral sociologists than any other variable, including social class, of an individual's political loyalty.[19]

This ineluctable psephological reality served as a sheet anchor for postwar Christian Democratic politics. However far leaderships and intellectuals might have wished to lead their parties from a narrow confessionalism, electoral needs and grassroots pressure obliged the parties to act as the guarantors of Catholic interests and as spokesmen for distinctly Catholic values. In Belgium, for example, the Christian Social Party (CVP-PSC) was a loyal defender of the interests of the Catholic educational system, while in Germany the Christian Democratic Union (CDU) advocated (and enacted) an uncompromisingly Catholic approach to family structures and social morality.[20] There was, therefore, no secret to the postwar electoral success of Christian Democracy: it relied primarily on the successful yoking of political choice to religious commitment. Catholicism in the 1940s and 1950s was certainly more pluralist than the self-deluding cult of Pius XII might suggest. Beneath the surface, there were many who quietly rejected the Church's guidance on moral and social issues, as well as intellectuals, priests, and even bishops who refused the ghetto or fortress mentality evident in papal rhetoric.[21] But for the most part these trends remained submerged and did not contradict the underlying reality that for millions of European Catholics of all social classes the link between their religious faith and their political loyalty seemed natural.

This interconnection between religion and electoral behavior owed much to the weight of an inherited tradition that stretched back, in many regions of Europe, to the foundation of Catholic political parties in the late nineteenth century. It was, however, a connection that had been reinforced by the events of World War II. In most areas of Europe the war was a far from "de-Christianizing" experience. Though the social changes brought about by the war may have accelerated long-term processes of secularization, its more immediate impact was the enhanced importance it gave religion and, more especially, the Church in the lives of many Catholics.[22] Statistical trends are all but impossible to trace, but there seems little doubt that participation in religious practice (especially attendance at the principal feast days) increased as a consequence of the war. In some cases, the reasons were very immediate: fear and unpredictability often provoked what Jean-Louis Clément has aptly described as a *piété panique*.[23] But the war also had a more durable impact by drawing back into the patterns of the faith many of those who had formerly been only on the penumbra of Catholicism. This recourse to religion often had a crudely intercessionary character. The war narrowed horizons, provoking an overriding concern with personal security and that of loved ones. Soldiers visited neighborhood shrines before departing to the army; the threat of aerial bombardment led the faithful into churches for reasons more profound than the relative solidity of the buildings; and the impact of prolonged separation on the close nuclear family structures of western Europe provoked many earnest nocturnal prayers. Marianism featured prominently in this wartime Catholicism. The remarkable success of the procession through France during the German occupation of the statue of Notre Dame de Boulogne and the mass pilgrimage by Catholic scouts to Notre Dame du Puy in August 1942 reflected the consolatory and protective appeal of the Virgin Mary.[24] In the Belgian province of Luxembourg, which, as the Ardennes offensive was to demonstrate a few days later, remained uncomfortably close to the military front line, the Feast of the Immaculate Conception of December 1944 was the occasion of a remarkable ceremony at which the bishop of

Namur and the provincial governor jointly dedicated the entire province to the Virgin Mary.[25]

Christian Democracy was the inheritor and beneficiary of these wartime trends. By consolidating the loyalty of the faithful to the Church, the war provided reserves of confessional solidarity that enabled Christian Democratic parties to burst so dramatically onto the stage of postwar politics. Much of the surge in wartime religiosity may have been too circumstantial to have survived the transition to peace. The intense materialism of the immediate postwar years, as Europeans sought almost frantically to compensate for wartime privations, seems inevitably to have taken its toll on levels of religious practice. Even in Germany, the upsurge in religious practice evident in summer 1945 proved short-lived, prompting the pope's personal representative, Father Zieger, to declare the country at the initial postwar Katholikentag in Mainz in 1948 to be a "Missionsland."[26] It would be wrong, however, to accept clerical denunciations of postwar decadence at face value. Not all Europeans abandoned Catholicism to worship the idols of postwar consumerism, and the very slow erosion of religious practice that seems to have been the norm in Catholic Europe during the twenty years after World War II would appear to have been related more to rural-urban migration and the changing age structure of the population than to any conscious rejection of the Church.[27] Indeed, in some regions that remained relatively immune to these broader social changes, the more structured and energetic forms of pastoral work developed by the clergy during the 1930s reaped a belated reward in terms of a modest but emphatic rise in postwar levels of religious practice.[28]

The war also reinforced the authority of the Church. By suspending the rituals of public life in almost all of Europe, the war demobilized the political and social leaders who in more normal times had acted as the lay leaders of the Catholic community. In their place, it was the ecclesiastical hierarchy—the clergy and the bishops—who became the sole spokesmen not merely for Catholicism but also, in some regions, for the local population.[29] This enhanced importance of the Church continued into the postwar world. The Catholic Church was one of the few social institutions in much of Europe to have survived the war with its reputation and structures largely intact. Indeed, in many areas of western and southern Germany in 1945, it was almost the only institution of importance, and Catholic social and welfare organizations acquired a remarkable prominence as the providers of food, shelter, and charity.[30] Not surprisingly, therefore, the role of the Church in the initial rallying of support for Christian Democratic parties was fundamental. At the top, it was the bishops and hierarchy who, by giving their clear approval to the re-creation of Catholic parties, ensured their success and the failure of their interconfessional rivals;[31] while at the base, in the improvised circumstances of the immediate postwar elections, the clergy acted as the essential mobilizers of the Catholic vote.[32]

Above all, the war injected a sense of purpose and even of urgency into Catholic politics. The profound cultural crisis that the war seemed to express provoked among many Catholics a conviction that the only salvation for the world lay in a categorical return to the teachings of the Catholic faith.[33] A new mentality of "mission" was evident in postwar Catholicism, prompted in part by the findings of surveys that revealed the extent of popular de-Christianization in implacable statistical terms. The *christianisme de choc* of postwar pastoral methods such as the worker-priest experiment was one expression of this mood,[34] but so too was the rhetorical radicalism of much early Christian Democracy. This tone was especially evident in Germany where, in the aftermath of the catastrophic collapse of Nazism, the Catholic clergy and intellectuals called with remarkable uniformity for a "re-Christianization" of German society. Nazism, so they argued, had not been a peculiar German phenomenon but the product of the perverted ideals of the Enlightenment. Only by returning to their lost Catholic heritage, a spiritual *Abendland,* could the Germans recover from this crisis. As Heinrich Krone, a former Catholic youth leader in the Weimar Republic and one of the founders of the CDU, declared:

> Failed are the gods the European man himself created. Now we stand naked and bare before the true God. . . . Failed is the hope in progress and paradise on earth. Failed is the belief in man as the law and rule himself.[35]

Such extravagant rhetoric was highly characteristic of a moment when everything had been destroyed but also when much seemed possible. The demise of the centralized German state and the subsequent partition of Germany created an unprecedented context in which the Catholic populations of southern and western Germany could finally achieve, in the form of the Bundesrepublik, the first Catholic national state on German soil. After almost a century of Protestant Prussianism, German Catholics felt the moment had come when, at the national and local levels, they could create their "politische Heimat."[36]

In launching themselves on this task, the German Christian Democrats, like their colleagues elsewhere in Europe, accepted representative democracy as the only political system that respected human rights and guaranteed political freedoms. The significance of this change has understandably come to be seen in retrospect as having something of the character of a "historic compromise" whereby the Catholics of western Europe belatedly but decisively espoused pluralist politics. Elements of such a sea change in Catholic mentalities were indeed present in the founding of Christian Democratic parties. The war had decisively destroyed the infatuation with authoritarian models of government that had influenced so much of Catholic politics of the 1930s[37] and had established parliamentary democracy as the compulsory language of postwar politics. This espousal of democracy was not, however, a surrender of Catholic ideals. Democracy, as the pope was at pains to stress, must not mean the tyranny of the (secular) majority.[38] Moreover, as the manifestos of the new parties frequently declared, their ambition was not to restore the liberal democracy of the past but to create a new form of democracy, in which the natural communities of family, workplace, and region would play as important a role as national parliaments.[39] In this sense, the social and political vision contained within Christian Democratic politics remained, more than ever, the antithesis of liberal individualism. Their goal was the achievement of the new social, economic, and political order that had been expounded for almost a century in papal encyclicals and reiterated, developed, and popularized by innumerable Catholic intellectuals, priests, and politicians.

The radical rhetoric of early postwar Christian Democracy therefore always had a double-edged character. While it signified a break with the defensive preoccupations of much previous Catholic politics, it also reflected a new determination to place Catholic ideals at the center of modern society. An essential stimulus for this ambition was the pervasive and often intense fear of Communism in Catholic ranks. The destructive and imposing advance of the Red Army through eastern and central Europe in 1944–45, as well as the presence of Communists in the postliberation governments of several western European countries, created almost a mood of panic in the Vatican. Communism, as Pius XII never tired of declaring, was an unambivalent evil, and he was suspicious of those progressive Catholic politicians, such as De Gasperi in Italy, whom he suspected of wishing to grasp the *main tendue* offered by the Communists.[40]

The pope's warnings on the whole found a ready audience. Anticommunism had become firmly embedded in Catholic mentalities since at least the Spanish Civil War and had scarcely been diminished by the plethora of wartime anti-Bolshevik propaganda in German-occupied Europe. Thus anticommunism remained firmly embedded in the progressive language of early Christian Democratic manifestos. As Pierre Letamendia rightly stressed, the MRP's famous *révolution par la loi* was always intended as the antithesis to the totalitarian revolution of Communism, and hostility to Communism was the great mobilizing force behind the rapid development of the DC in Italy after 1943.[41] Such anticommunism was complemented by more long-established fears of an anticlerical alliance. The broad Popular Fronts of progressive forces that emerged in many areas of liberated Europe were a source of apprehension to the Church, as well as to many lay Catholics, because they seemed to presage a return to the offensive secularizing policies on issues such as education that had haunted the Catholic political imagination since the late nineteenth century. Anticlericalism was in many areas of Europe a more immediate and familiar danger than communism after 1945, encouraging the nervous and defiant mood expressed in the Swiss Catholic Party's slogan in the elections of 1947: "Wir lassen uns nicht ausmanövrieren."[42]

These anti-Communist and antisecularizing dynamics in postwar Christian Democracy make it easier to understand the "conservative turn" that took place in the parties at the end of the 1940s. Historians predominantly sympathetic to the progressive rhetoric of the early postwar years often have been tempted to present this evolution as a deviation from or even betrayal of the parties' initial character. This, however, seems somewhat misleading. It is certainly true that the circumstances of the Cold War gave confidence to the conservative elements within Christian Democratic ranks and contributed to the marginalization of more radical voices such as Dirks in Germany or Dossetti in Italy.[43] But the reality was more complex than that the Cold War caused a rightward shift in Christian Democracy. The opposite was also true, in the sense that the Cold War was not entirely of the superpowers' making and that much of the initial momentum behind opposition to the Soviet Union and international Communism was generated by

European political elites, among whom Christian Democrats played a prominent role.[44] In Switzerland, for example, it was Catholic opinion, notably the principal Catholic daily newspaper *Vaterland*, that led the way in adopting the rhetoric of the Cold War, warning as early as 1945 of the urgent need to counter Soviet-inspired communism.[45] The bipolar logic of the Cold War, with its emphasis on anti-Communist political alliances and Western diplomatic and military cooperation against the menace from the east, was not a transplantation into the culture of Christian Democracy but a natural extension of existing and deeply held Catholic fears.

Moreover, anticommunism was not the only factor that drew the Christian Democratic parties toward the Right. Social interest also played a powerful role. The point has frequently been made that the Christian Democratic parties were cross-class in nature: compared with their principal Socialist and Liberal rivals, they drew their support from all strata of society, including the industrial working class.[46] They should not, however, be regarded as class-neutral parties. Within Christian Democratic ranks, there was a continual struggle for influence between professional and sectional lobby groups, each of which sought to ensure that their interests prevailed in the making of party and, more important, governmental policy. In this internal party contest, it was on the whole the interests of the middle classes and of the rural populations that prevailed. In many respects, this outcome reflected a broader marginalization of the industrial working class from power in post-1945 Europe. Though it is customary to refer to the leftward shift in European politics provoked by the war, one of its more striking consequences was to fragment the working class and to isolate many of its most representative leaders in a Communist ghetto that was rigorously excluded from political and social power. Within Catholic ranks, trade unionism continued to flourish, but the new parties created after 1945 proved less susceptible than their predecessors to their lobbying. In Belgium, for example, the more centralized and professional party structure introduced after 1945 in effect shifted power away from the class-specific *standen* organizations to a party bureaucracy in which working-class influence was diminished though certainly not excluded.[47] Perhaps the most striking case was Germany. The Zentrumspartei (Center Party) of the Weimar Republic contained a considerable and vocal trade union lobby. After 1945, however, its influence within Adenauer's CDU was often secondary to that of farmers' groups and of predominantly middle-class party elites.[48]

This farmer-bourgeois alliance proved the durable reality on which the politics of the center-Right in postwar Europe was built. Compared to the volatile class conflicts that had characterized interwar Europe, it provided a social anchor for democratic parliamentary politics and marginalized the appeal of the extreme Right among those groups—the middle classes and disgruntled farmers—who had provided many of its most active supporters during the interwar years.[49] Conversely, this class basis gave Christian Democratic politics a social identity that reinforced and, to some extent, transcended their confessional identity. Thus all of the successful Christian Democratic parties pursued to a greater or lesser extent a twin-track electoral policy—rallying the faithful by appealing to their Christian values while also posing as the guarantors of the material interests of their core electors.[50] This was most obvious in the case of the rural population. The devolved welfare systems established after World War II reinforced the role of Catholic social organizations such as the Boerenbond in Belgian Flanders or the Coldiretti in northern Italy as the quasi-monopoly providers of a range of social and economic services to the rural population and enabled Christian Democratic parties to emerge as the vehicle for the articulation of rural interests in the political sphere.[51]

This rural–middle class alliance brought considerable electoral rewards for the Christian Democrats but at the same time acted as a brake on their reformist ambitions. It was the voices of farmers' pressure groups, industrialists, and middle-class professional organizations that enjoyed the greatest influence within Christian Democratic ranks and that to a considerable degree determined the policies adopted by the parties. This underlying reality helps to explain the remarkable transition that took place in Christian Democratic economic policy at the end of the 1940s from social corporatism to a largely free-market system. Catholic hostility to the abuses of the capitalist economic system could be traced back to the founding text *Rerum Novarum* in the 1890s, and all of the party programs of the immediate postwar era made much of their commitment to wide-ranging reforms intended to sweep away the anarchy and exploitation of the capitalist system and replace it with a new economic order and a social community within the factory.[52] Opposition to a Communist state-directed economy soon began to moderate this initial radicalism; it was, however, only at the end of the 1940s that Christian Democratic policies moved markedly to embrace market capitalism. In part, the reasons for this change were pragmatic. It was the free-market principles enshrined in the Marshall Plan that seemed to be delivering the high growth rates necessary for European reconstruction. But this change also reflected the pervasive influence within the parties of economic producers, both industrial and agricultural, for whom the overriding ambition was removal of wartime price and production controls and restoration of a free market, albeit supplemented when convenient by protectionist tariffs and guaranteed minimum price levels.[53]

The farmer-bourgeois alliance was also a major driving force behind the Catholic espousal of European integration. The role of Christian Democracy in this process is one of the most sacred myths of the parties' self-perception. Alas, like many such myths, it is gradually succumbing to historical revisionism. Their espousal of a limited pooling of nation-state sovereignty in the 1950s and 1960s was always more pragmatic, less idealist, and less comprehensive than some simple accounts might suggest.[54] Christian Democratic politicians supported the European Coal and Steel Community (ECSC), the European Defense Community (EDC), and, subsequently, the European Economic Community (EEC) because these organizations were a means of achieving their priorities of economic growth and anti-Communism and because they were encouraged to do so by sectional pressure groups within their own ranks. Certainly, in the case of Belgium it is almost impossible to discover any interest in European integration among Catholic political leaders until they began to realize in the late 1940s that the illusory panacea of export-led growth needed to be supplemented by agricultural protectionism and pan-European policies of restructuring in the coal, iron, and steel sectors.[55]

Another important element of the Christian Democratic social coalition, albeit a much less influential one within the counsels of the parties, was women. Women did of course constitute the majority of the electorate in all those European countries that had suffered demographically from the ravages of war: in Germany, for example, women outnumbered men by seven million in 1946.[56] Moreover, it seems clear that women voted disproportionately for Catholic parties: the electorate of the MRP in the elections of 1951 was estimated to have been 61 percent female.[57] In some respects, this female predominance was no more than one might expect, given the female bias in levels of religious practice that had been evident in Catholic Europe since at least the nineteenth century. There was no automatic link between these two statistical realities, however, and the women voters of postwar Europe, the majority of whom had never previously voted in multi-party elections,[58] had to be appealed to not merely in terms of their confessional loyalties but also in terms of their material interests. The nuclear family structures of much of western and central Europe had been considerably damaged by the traumas of war. Not surprisingly, much emphasis was therefore placed in state policy during the postwar years on the need to rebuild the family as the principal social unit. No party captured this theme more successfully than did the Christian Democrats, who not merely preached the virtues of the family with a confidence rooted in long-standing Catholic rhetoric but also constructed effective and largely pillarized structures of social welfare that materially favored the interests of women, children, and families.[59]

The electoral basis of Christian Democracy was thus both material and confessional. Indeed, it was the parallel existence of both of these elements that surely explains the rapid growth of the parties after 1945 and, with the significant exception of France, their durability. The one could not work without the other: confessional solidarity required material rewards, but its enduring power supplied the essential glue that bound the diverse social components of the Christian Democratic coalition. The process of "reconfessionalization" that took place in much of western Europe during the decade after World War II provided the Catholic milieu within which the parties could recruit their members and leaders, raise the funds they required, and disseminate their propaganda. The electoral consequences were often impressive. In Germany, 64.8 percent of registered Catholics voted for the CDU-CSU in the 1953 elections, a figure that, despite all the upheavals during the intervening years, matched almost identically the proportion of German Catholics who had voted for the Zentrumspartei and the Bavarian People's Party (BVP) during the Weimar Republic.[60] It was, however, the Netherlands that indisputably provided the most extreme example of "pillarization": in the 1956 elections, it is estimated that as many as 95 percent of churchgoing Catholics voted for the party.[61]

The connections between the Christian Democratic parties and the wider Catholic community were not always uncomplicated. Though the bishops and clergy frequently advised the faithful in scarcely coded terms to vote only for parties loyal to Catholic values, the hierarchy of the Church (and more especially the pope) often regarded Christian Democratic parties as insufficiently attentive to clerical interests and direction.[62] The most serious tension, however, was between the parties and the organizations of the Catholic working class. Catholic workers had been one of the strongest components of the Catholic electoral coalition since the nineteenth century; while the Catholic trade unions, strengthened by a half century of competition with their Socialist and then Communist rivals, had been among the most loyal adherents to a distinctive confessional politics. After some hesitation, the Catholic trade union federations in France, Italy, and the Low Countries opted to remain faithful to their confessional heritage after 1945. But their loyalty brought them scant material rewards. The absence of wideranging social reform, especially in the workplace, combined with the close links that developed between the Christian Democrats and farmers' and employers' groups, gradually but remorselessly wore away at the bonds of Catholic unity and culminated in the declarations of "political independence" made by many Catholic trade unions during the 1960s.[63]

The slow (and often incomplete) divorce of Christian Democratic parties from much of the Catholic working class demonstrated both the strength of confessional solidarity and its ultimate limits. From the perspective of the social changes that overwhelmed Catholicism from the 1960s onward, it is obviously tempting to see the concept of Catholic unity as an anachronism in Europe after 1945. What Margaret Anderson, borrowing from a namesake, has termed the "imagined community" of Catholicism appears destined to be dissolved by the rapid economic growth, urbanization, and educational changes that characterized postwar Europe.[64] In many respects, this was indeed true. As Patrick Pasture's comparative study of Catholic labor movements well demonstrates, the viability of a Catholic socioeconomic pillar was being steadily undermined by processes of social change, some internal to Catholicism but many others external to it, which reached their conclusion in the fragmentation of the Catholic community that occurred during the 1960s and 1970s.[65]

Yet, as always, hindsight can be a dubious privilege. Though what one might term the classic pillarized model of a self-contained Catholic world of trade unions, welfare organizations, educational systems, and social movements was coming under increasing strain in Europe after 1945, the eventual demise of these institutions did not signify the end of a Catholic milieu. The frontiers and mentality of the Catholic *Lagerkultur* remained firmly etched in the social texture of much of western and central Europe long after 1945[66] and gave a defining framework to Christian Democratic politics. Perhaps one of the most striking demonstrations of its strength is provided ironically by the ultimate failure of the MRP in France. There were many circumstantial reasons for its decline from 28 percent of the vote in the elections of 1946 to a mere 8 percent in 1962. The rival appeal of Gaullism and its involvement in colonial disasters and lack of attention to the interests of farmers, as well as the more general unpopularity that enveloped the Fourth Republic were all factors that hastened its demise. Nevertheless, especially in a comparative perspective, the underlying weakness of the MRP appears to be its lack of integration into a clearly defined Catholic milieu. In part, this reflected the party's Resistance origins: the young and predominantly intellectual leaders of the MRP were a Paris-based elite devoid of links with the enduring political cultures of provincial France.[67] It also reflected, however, the historic factionalization of Catholicism in France that had hindered the development of a unitary Catholic milieu equivalent to those that existed slightly farther east or south in Europe. Significantly, it was in those regions of eastern and northern France where confessionalization was more firmly rooted in the textures of local society that the MRP (and its successors) proved to have a more durable electoral appeal.[68]

In conclusion, then, the success of Christian Democracy appears to have been a complex but not incomprehensible phenomenon. It rested on a series of factors, some of which were of the parties' own making but many of which were related to the broader nature of European society and politics in the decades after World War II. In that sense, they were parties that went with the grain of the postwar world. Certainly, the more long-term heritage of Catholic political ideas since the end of the nineteenth century and the ideological innovations prompted by the war years were important elements in their success. But their significance should not be exaggerated. As perhaps with all such successful political movements, Christian Democratic success ultimately derived from a particular conjuncture. The resilience of the structures and mentality of confessional loyalty, the emergence of influential middle-class and rural interest groups, and the electoral space provided by the demise of many existing political parties of the center and the Right created an unprecedented opportunity that on the whole they proved able to seize with both hands. In doing so, it was not so much their ideological program as their flexibility that was important. Indeed, it was precisely because the Christian Democrats of Germany, Italy, Austria, and the Low Countries recognized the power of confessional identities and proved capable of adapting to the rapidly changing political and social landscape after World War II that their success proved more durable than that of the more programmatic MRP.[69]

What one might term this "circumstantial" interpretation of Christian Democratic success also suggests conversely why that success remained confined to certain regions of western and central Europe. The explanation for the absence of significant equivalent movements in Ireland, Britain (despite the steady growth in the Catholic component of its population), the Iberian Peninsula, or, after the 1950s, France clearly defies reduction to a glib checklist of factors. Nevertheless, common to all the "missing lands" of Christian Democracy was the absence of a profound political rupture provided by World War II and the structures of confessional pillarization akin to those that characterized its regions of success. This is perhaps especially evident in the case of Ireland. While political circumstance in Britain and the repressive dictatorships in Spain and Portugal more obviously militated against the success of Christian Democratic parties, its absence in Ireland is at first sight more puzzling. However, the status of Catholicism in Ireland, with the peculiar (and in many respects artificial) symbiosis that existed between national and religious identity, created a political culture in which the interpenetration of church and society left little space for confessional boundaries. Consequently, both of the major political parties, Fine Gael and Fianna Fáil, adopted much of the rhetoric and goals of Catholicism without thereby becoming Christian Democratic parties.[70]

If, as I have sought to suggest, historians can now begin to venture some explanations for Christian Democracy's initial success and geographic borders, what is much less evident from our present perspective is why the age of Christian Democracy ever ended. The Second Vatican Council, the social changes of the 1960s, and the economic difficulties of the subsequent decade constitute a cat's cradle of factors, the importance of which seems self-evident but within which it would be dangerous to trace crude lines of cause and effect. Only the conclusion seems inescapable: by the end of the 1970s there was a perceptible crisis within Christian Democracy that subsequent events have only reinforced.[71] None of this was of course apparent to those who witnessed with some astonishment the initial rapid surge in Christian Democratic politics after World War II. On June 5, 1946, the Belgian foreign minister, Paul-Henri Spaak, and the British ambassador to Belgium, Sir Hughe Knatchbull-Hugessen, met for one of their frequent private conversations in Spaak's office in the Foreign Ministry in Brussels. The results of the French parliamentary elections had just been announced in which to their (and many other people's) great surprise the MRP had emerged as the largest single party. The two men, one a Socialist politician of marked anticlerical opinions, the other an Anglican and in every respect a conservative diplomat, welcomed what the success of the MRP seemed to suggest in terms of a popular reaction against Communism. But to both of them the appeal of the Catholic political party was inexplicable. Perhaps, Knatchbull-Hugessen jokingly suggested, it meant they were destined to be burned at the stake as heretics. Spaak, the diplomat's diary records, "answered that it really was a question whether we were to be burnt by the Catholics or hung by the Communists, but we agreed that we might succeed in dodging both these fates for a few more years."[72] In retrospect, the half-sanguine, half-nervous humor of the two men seems to have been fully justified. Some fifty years later, Communism has all but disappeared from the European political stage while Christian Democracy, if distinctly more visible, has become something very different from the initial inspiration of its Catholic founders. Quite why that should have proved to be the case is, however, much less clear. But endings are perhaps always destined to be more mysterious than beginnings.

## NOTES

This contribution, and the conference paper from which it emerged, owes much to illuminating and stimulating discussions with Laura Gellott, Wolfgang Kaiser, Paul Misner, and Maria Mitchell.

1. This geographic delineation omits southern Italy, an area of considerable electoral strength for the Christian Democrats but which can, I think, legitimately be regarded as a special case. For an excellent study of Christian Democratic politics in the Italian south, see P. Allum, *Politics and Society in Post-War Naples* (Cambridge, 1973).

2. Such an interpretation unites, for example, both the first major account of Christian Democratic politics and one of the most recent collective volumes on the subject: M. Fogarty, *Christian Democracy in Europe, 1820–1953* (London, 1957); E. Lamberts, ed., *Christian Democracy in the European Union* (Leuven, 1997), especially J.-D. Durand, "La mémoire de la Démocratie Chrétienne en 1945: Antécédents, expériences et combats."

3. J.-M., Mayeur "Catholicisme intransigeant, catholicisme social, Démocratie Chrétienne," *Annales Economies, Sociétés, Civilisations* 27 (1972): 494. See also P. Misner, *Social Catholicism in Europe: From the Onset of Industrialization until the First World War* (London and New York, 1991).

4. E.g., M. Van den Wijngaert, *Ontstaan en stichting van de CVP-PSC: De lange weg naar het kerstprogramma* (Brussels, 1976); H. Bakvis, *Catholic Power in the Netherlands* (Kingston and Montreal, 1981), 67.

5. A.J. Nicholls, *Freedom with Responsibility* (Oxford, 1994); K. Van Kersbergen "The Distinctiveness of Christian Democracy" in D. Hanley, ed., *Christian Democracy in Europe: A Comparative Perspective* (London and New York, 1994), 31–47.

6. P. Nord, "Three Views of Christian Democracy in Fin-de-Siècle France," *Journal of Contemporary History* 19 (1984): 713–27; E. Poulat, "Pour une nouvelle compréhension de la Démocratie Chrétienne," *Revue d'Histoire Ecclésiastique* 60 (1975): 5–38.

7. M. Conway, *Catholic Politics in Europe, 1918–1945* (London and New York, 1997).

8. S. Kalyvas, *The Rise of Christian Democracy in Europe* (Ithaca and London, 1996). Elements of this interpretation are also evident in N. Cary, *The Path to Christian Democracy: German Catholics and the Party System from Windthorst to Adenauer* (Cambridge, Mass., and London, 1996).

9. B. Béthouart, "L'apport socio-économique de la Démocratie Chrétienne en France," in Lamberts, *Christian Democracy in the European Union*, 337–38; M. Kelly, "Catholics and Communism in Liberation France, 1944–47," in F. Tallett and N. Atkin, eds., *Religion, Society and Politics in France since 1789* (London and Rio Grande, Ohio, 1991), 187–202.

10. E. Fouilloux, "La Résistance spirituelle: Approche comparée," M. Bergère, "Tensions et rivalités entre les pouvoirs issus de la Résistance en Maine-et-Loire," and J. Papp, "Construction des mémoires collectives dans l'Eure: Enjeux et protagonistes," in J. Sainclivier and C. Bougeard, eds., *La Résistance et les français* (Rennes, 1995), 75–83, 295–305, 325–35; P. Lagrou, *The Legacy of Nazi Occupation: Patriotic Memory and National Recovery in Western Europe, 1945–1965* (Cambridge, 2000).

11. The history of the Mouvement Républicain Populaire (MRP) exemplifies this evolution. See the excellent study by Pierre Letamendia: *Le Mouvement Républicain Populaire: Histoire d'un grand parti français* (Paris, 1995).

12. E.g., G. Lichtheim, *A Short History of Socialism* (London, 1970).

13. G. Eley, "Joining Two Histories: The SPD and the German Working Class, 1860–1914," in G. Eley, *From Unification to Nazism: Reinterpreting the German Past* (Boston, 1986), 171–99; T. Judt, *Socialism in Provence, 1871–1914: A Study in the Origins of the Modern French Left* (Cambridge, 1979); M. Nolan, *Social Democracy and Society: Working-Class Radicalism in Düsseldorf, 1890–1920* (Cambridge, 1981);

P. Heywood, *Marxism and the Failure of Organised Socialism in Spain 1879–1936* (Cambridge, 1990).

14. Lamberts, *Christian Democracy in the European Union*, and Hanley, *Christian Democracy in Europe*, are both good examples of this approach.

15. O. Logan, "Pius XII: *Romanità*, Prophecy and Charisma," *Modern Italy* 3 (1998): 237–47; M. Walsh, "Pius XII," in A. Hastings, ed., *Modern Catholicism: Vatican II and After* (London and New York, 1991), 20–26; P. Hebblethwaite, *John XXIII: Pope of the Council* (London, 1984), 225–30; *Selected Letters and Addresses of Pius XII* (London, 1949), 299–318.

16. J. Mindszenty, *Memoirs* (London, 1974), 31; J. Pirotte, *Images des vivants et des morts: La vision du monde propagée par l'imagerie de dévotion dans le Namurois, 1840–1965* (Louvain-la-Neuve and Brussels, 1987).

17. K.-D. Rohe, *Wahlen und Wählertraditionen in Deutschland* (Frankfurt am Main, 1992), 171; M. Mitchell, "Materialism and Secularism: CDU Politicians and National Socialism, 1945–1949," *Journal of Modern History* 67 (1995): 281. See also Maria Mitchell's contribution to this volume. The appeal of the Bavarian CSU to confessional Catholic values was always even more explicit. See the text of its *Grundsatzprogramm* of December 1946, which is overwhelmingly Catholic in inspiration and content: O. K. Flechtheim, ed., *Dokumente zur parteipolitischen Entwicklung in Deutschland seit 1945*, vol. 2 (Berlin, 1963), 213–19.

18. Letamendia, *Mouvement Républicain Populaire*, 281.

19. J. Whyte, *Catholics in Western Democracies: A Study in Political Behaviour* (Dublin, 1981), 86–95; K. Schmitt, *Konfession und Wahlerverhalten in der Bundesrepublik Deutschland* (Berlin, 1989); W. Müller, F. Plasser, and P. Ulram, "Wähler und Mitglieder der ÖVP 1945–1994," in R. Kreichbaumer and F. Schausberger, eds., *Volkspartei—Anspruch und Realität* (Vienna, 1995), 167; J. Billiet, "Les électeurs du PSC et du CVP," in *Un parti dans l'histoire: 50 ans d'action du Parti Social Chrétien* (Louvain-la-Neuve, 1996), 297–325.

20. M. Conway, "Belgium," in T. Buchanan and M. Conway, eds., *Political Catholicism in Europe* (Oxford, 1996), 211–12; E. Heineman, "Complete Families, Half Families, No Families at All: Female-headed Households and the Reconstruction of the Family in the Early Federal Republic," *Central European History* 29 (1996): 26.

21. U. Altermatt, *Katholizismus und Moderne: Zur Sozial- und Mentalitätsgeschichte der Schweizer Katholiken im 19. und 20. Jahrhundert* (Zurich, 1989), 161–64; J. Coleman, *The Evolution of Dutch Catholicism, 1958–1974* (Berkeley, 1978); A. Hastings, "Catholic History from Vatican I to John Paul II," in Hastings, *Modern Catholicism*, 3–4.

22. See the important if occasionally somewhat polemical study of V. Drapac, *War and Religion: Catholics in the Churches of Occupied Paris* (Washington, D.C., 1998).

23. J. L. Clément, *Monseigneur Saliège, archevêque de Toulouse, 1929–1956* (Paris, 1994), 275; J. Chélini, *L'Eglise sous Pie XII: La tourmente (1939–1945)* (Paris, 1983), 290; F. Maerten, "La vie religieuse dans le Brabant wallon sous l'occupation allemande," *Revue d'Histoire Religieuse du Brabant Wallon* 5 (1991): 3–24.

24. S. Laury, "Le culte marial dans le Pas-de-Calais (1938–1948)," *Revue d'Histoire de la Deuxième Guerre Mondiale* 128 (1982): 23–47; D. Avon, "Le pèlerinage du Puy 12–15 août 1942," *Revue d'Histoire de l'Eglise de France* 83 (1997): 395–434.

25. *L'Avenir du Luxembourg,* December 9–10, 1944, 1, "Le Luxembourg à Marie."

26. K. Repgen, "Die Erfahrung des Dritten Reiches und das Selbstverständnis der deutscher Katholiken nach 1945," in V. Conzemius, M. Greschat, and H. Kocher, eds., *Die Zeit nach 1945 als Thema kirchlicher Zeitgeschichte* (Göttingen, 1988), 140–41; C. J. Barry, *American Nuncio: Cardinal Aloisius Muench* (Collegeville, Minn., 1969), 105–8.

27. K. Repgen, "Kardinal Frings im Rückblick: Zeitgeschichtliche Kontroverspunkte einer künftigen Biographie," *Historisches Jahrbuch* 100 (1980): 294; K. Dobbelaere, "La dominante catholique," *Recherches Sociologiques* 16, no. 3 (1985): 193–220.

28. V. Adoumié, "Le réveil religieux landais au XXᵉ siècle," *Annales du Midi* 108 (1996): 377–94.

29. J.-D. Durand, "L'épiscopat italien," in Sainclivier and Bougeard, *La Résistance et les français,* 95–108; F. Marten, "Le monde catholique dans la guerre: La Wallonie et Bruxelles," in F. Marten, F. Selleslagh, and M. Van den Wijngaert, eds., *Entre la peste et le choléra: Vie et attitudes des catholiques sous l'occupation* (Gerpinnes, 1999), 25.

30. E. Frei, "Brot und Sinn: Katholizismus und Caritasarbeit in der Zusammenbruchgesellschaft 1945," *Historisches Jahrbuch* 117 (1997): 129–46; W. Blessing, " 'Deutschland in Not, wir im Glauben . . .': Kirche und Kirchenvolk in einer katholischen Region, 1933–1949," in M. Broszat, K.-D. Henke, and H. Woller, eds., *Von Stalingrad zur Währungsreform: Zur Sozialgeschichte des Umbruchs in Deutschland* (Munich, 1988), 3–111.

31. Bakvis, *Catholic Power in the Netherlands,* 33; W. Beerten, *Le rêve travailliste en Belgique: Histoire de l'UDB, 1944–1947* (Brussels, 1990), 117–24.

32. E.g., Clément, *Monseigneur Saliège,* 323; J. Sagnes, "Les élections à l'Assemblée Constituante du 21 octobre 1945 en Languedoc-Roussillon," *Annales du Midi* 108 (1996): 326.

33. Hebblethwaite, *John XXIII,* 184, 191; J.-D. Durand, *L'église catholique dans la crise de l'Italie (1943–1948)* (Rome, 1991), 250–259.

34. L. Beinaert, *Pour un christianisme de choc* (Brussels, 1943); Y. Daniel and H. Godin, *La France, pays de mission?* (Paris, 1943); O. Arnal, *Priests in Working-Class Blue: The History of the Worker Priests (1943–1954)* (New York and Mahwah, N. J., 1986).

35. Mitchell, "Materialism and Secularism," 287; Repgen, "Die Erfahrung des Dritten Reiches," 127–79.

36. W. Löhr, "Rechristianierungsvorstellungen im deutschen Katholizismus 1945–1948," in J.-C. Kaiser and A. Doering-Manteuffel, eds., *Christentum und politische Verantwortung: Kirchen im Nachkriegsdeutschland* (Stuttgart, 1990), 25–41; M. Phayer, "The German Catholic Church after the Holocaust," *Holocaust and Genocide Studies* 10 (1996): 151–67; A. Doering-Manteuffel, *Katholizismus und Wiederbewaffnung: Die Haltung der deutschen Katholiken gegenüber der Wehrfrage 1948–1955* (Mainz, 1981), 56. R. Boehling, *A Question of Priorities: Democratic Reform and Recovery in Postwar Germany* (New York and Oxford, 1996), illustrates this process at the local level.

37. R.J. Wolff and J.K. Hoensch, eds., *Catholics, the State and the European Radical Right, 1919–1945* (Boulder, Colo., 1987).

38. *Selected Letters and Addresses of Pius XII*, 307.

39. E.g., *Principes et tendances du Parti Social Chrétien* (Brussels, [1946]).

40. E. Carrillo, "The Italian Catholic Church and Communism 1943–1963," *Catholic Historical Review* 77 (1991): 645–47; L. Papeleux, "Le Vatican et l'expansion du communisme (1944–1945)," *Revue d'Histoire de la Deuxième Guerre Mondiale et des Conflits Contemporains* 127 (1985): 63–84.

41. Letamendia, *Mouvement Rèpublicain Populaire*, 75–86; Durand, *L'église catholique dans la crise de l'Italie*.

42. U. Altermatt, "Die Stimmungslage im politischen Katholizismus der Schweiz von 1945," in Conzemius, Greschat, and Kocher, *Die Zeit nach 1945*, 72–96; H. Kleger, "Die nationale Bürgergesellschaft im Krieg und Nachkrieg: 1943–1955" in K. Imhof, H. Kleger, and G. Romano, eds., *Konkordanz und Kalter Krieg* (Zurich, 1996), 116–18, 127–28; R. Aubert, "L'Eglise catholique et la vie politique en Belgique depuis la seconde guerre mondiale," *Res Publica* 15 (1973): 187–88.

43. J. Pollard, "Italy," and K.-E. Lönne, "Germany," in Buchanan and Conway, *Political Catholicism in Europe*, 88–91, 181–83.

44. D. Reynolds, ed., *The Origins of the Cold War in Europe: International Perspectives* (New Haven and London, 1994).

45. K. Imhof, "Wiedergeburt der Geistigen Landesverteidigung: Kalter Krieg in der Schweiz," in Imhof, Kleger, and Romano, *Konkordanz und Kalter Krieg*, 184–207.

46. E.g., R. Koole, "The Societal Position of Christian Democracy in the Netherlands," in Lamberts, *Christian Democracy in the European Union*, 140–41; R.E.M. Irving, *Christian Democracy in France* (London, 1973), 88.

47. J. Smits, "De afbouw van de autonome politieke actie van het ACW en de oprichting van de CVP," in E. Gerard and J. Mampuys, eds., *Voor Kerk en Werk* (Leuven, 1986), 313–53.

48. G. Pridham, *Christian Democracy in Western Germany* (London, 1977), 292, 297–98.

49. G. Luebbert, *Liberalism, Fascism or Social Democracy: Social Classes and the Political Origins of Regimes in Inter-War Europe* (New York and Oxford, 1991). Poujadism was in this respect very much the exception that proved the rule.

50. Rohe, *Wahlen und Wählertraditionen*, 175.

51. P. Pasture, "Entre église et citoyen," in *Un parti dans l'histoire*, 270; A. Parisella, "La base sociale della Democrazia Cristiana italiana: Elettorato, iscritti e organizzazione" in Lamberts, *Christian Democracy in the European Union*, 197; Müller, Plasser, and Ulrani, "Wähler und Mitglieder der ÖVP," 171–72.

52. E.g., the Ahlen Programme of the CDU of 1947: Flechtheim, *Dokumente*, vol. 2, 53–58. See also Béthouart, "L'apport socio-économique," 338.

53. Lönne, "Germany," 182–83; G. Noël, *France, Allemagne et "Europe verte"* (Berne, 1995).

54. See notably A. Milward, *The European Rescue of the Nation-State*, rev. ed. (London, 1994); and P. Chenaux, *Une Europe vaticane?* (Brussels, 1990).

55. L. Van Molle, *Chacun pour tous: Le Boerenbond belge 1890–1990* (Leuven, 1990), esp. 347–48; A. Mommen, *The Belgian Economy in the Twentieth Century* (London and New York, 1994), 75–98.

56. Heineman, "Complete Families, Half Families, No Families at All," 21.

57. Letamendia, *Mouvement Républicain Populaire*, 188–91. See also Parisella, "La base sociale," 200.

58. Women were of course only enfranchised in France and Belgium after the war, while in Italy and Germany there had been no free elections for almost a generation.

59. H. Wilensky, "Leftism, Catholicism and Democratic Corporatism: The Role of Political Parties in Recent Welfare State Development," in P. Flora and A.J. Heidenheimer, eds., *The Development of Welfare States in Europe and America* (New Brunswick and London, 1981), 345–82; E.R. Dickinson, *The Politics of German Child Welfare from the Empire to the Federal Republic* (Cambridge, Mass., 1996), 247–51; Béthouart, "L'apport socio-économique," 349.

60. Schmitt, *Konfession und Wählerverhalten*, 123, 129.

61. Koole, "Societal Positum of Christian Democracy," 139. See also P. Luykx, "The Netherlands," in Buchanan and Conway, *Political Catholicism in Europe*, 219–47.

62. W. Plavsic, 'L'Eglise et la politique en Belgique," *Res Publica* 10 (1968): 234–37; Bakvis, *Catholic Power in the Netherlands*, 24, 33–34; J.-D. Durand, *L'Europe de la Démocratie Chrétienne* (Brussels, 1995), 248.

63. P. Pasture, "Diverging Paths: The Development of Catholic Labour Organisations in France, the Netherlands and Belgium since 1944," *Revue d'Histoire Ecclésiastique* 89 (1994): 54–90; P. Pasture, "Herstel en expansie (1945–1960)" in E. Gerard, ed., *De christelijke arbeidersbeweging in België* (Leuven, 1991), 245–97;

P. Vignaux, *De la CFTC à la CFDT: Syndicalisme et socialisme. "Reconstruction" (1946–1972)* (Paris, 1980).

64. M. Anderson, "The Limits of Secularization: On the Problem of the Catholic Revival in Nineteenth-Century Germany," *Historical Journal* 38 (1995): 670.

65. Pasture, "Diverging Paths"; Whyte, *Catholics in Western Democracies*, 100–111E

66. Müller, Plasser, and Ulram, "Wähler und Mitglieder der ÖVP," 163–71.

67. J. Sainclivier and C. Bougeard, eds., *Les pouvoirs locaux dans l'Ouest 1935–1953*, special issue, *Annales de Bretagne et des pays de l'ouest* 103 (1996); C. Warner, "Getting out the Vote with Patronage and Threat: The French and Italian Christian Democratic Parties, 1944–1958," *Journal of Interdisciplinary History* 28 (1998): 570–72.

68. Letamendia, *Mouvement Républicain Populaire;* R. Vinen, *Bourgeois Politics in France, 1945–1951* (Cambridge, 1995), 137–72.

69. This is the perhaps rather too emphatic but certainly not unjustified conclusion of Carolyn Warner: "Getting out the Vote," 553–82.

70. D. Keogh, *The Vatican, the Bishops and Irish Politics* (Cambridge, 1986); R. Dunphy, *The Making of Fianna Fáil Power in Ireland, 1923–1948* (Oxford, 1995); D. Keogh and F. O'Driscoll, "Ireland," in Buchanan and Conway, *Political Catholicism in Europe*, 275–300.

71. See the trenchant comments of Jean-Dominique Durand in *L'Europe de la Démocratie Chrétienne*, 331–39.

72. Diary of Sir Hughe Knatchbull-Hugessen, June 5, 1946 (Churchill Archives Centre, Churchill College Cambridge, KNAT 1/15). I am indebted to the archivist of Churchill College for permission to use these papers.

# 3 Christian Democratic Social Policy

## Precedents for Third-Way Thinking

PAUL MISNER

When speaking of a "third way" in today's politics, one is most likely referring to Tony Blair[1] or Bill Clinton or Gerhard Schröder, all politicians who have nudged their parties from the left toward the center of the political spectrum. There have been other notable "third ways," however, and some of them have played significant roles in the history of the Christian Democratic movement.

The most pertinent context in which to place the notion of a third way for present purposes is that of the period between the world wars in Europe, 1920–40. The continental liberalism of the late nineteenth century was shaken in its self-confidence by the Great War and assaulted on the Left by its socialist adversaries. The industrial revolution had generated sharp class-based alignments that were organized in two camps. The bourgeois, or "liberal," camp placed a premium on property rights and hence on capitalist control of the economy with minimum government interference. Liberals, most of whom were anticlerical, had dominated parliaments until World War I. The socialist camp aimed to end liberal hegemony and establish a regime in which the interests of the working class would prevail. Whether such a transition would take place through democratic means or by revolution, it would curtail capitalist exploitation of the economy. Given these two behemoths locked in strife, it was natural that those who were repulsed or disappointed by both options would seek a third way. Definitely in this category were Catholic supporters of the cause of social justice through political means—"Christian Democrats."

This chapter sets out to cast some light on a paradox. Given that third-way thinking was so closely associated with authoritarian and Fascist regimes in the 1930s, how and why did this paradigm survive in the Christian Democracy of Europe after World War II? One cannot but be impressed by how persistent the awareness of a third way different from liberalism and collectivism has been in social and political Catholicism, even after political democracy was embraced. In the 1930s and 1940s, for example, one could expect that any third-way notions would be framed as an alternative to Fascism and Nazism, on the one hand, and Soviet Communism, on the other. Yet this does not seem to have been the dominant note; instead, one still sought an alternative to liberalism qua individualistic and capitalistic, on the one hand, and an alternative to Communist collectivism, on the other.

Why, after the Nazi-Fascist threat had been defeated and the triumph of Western democracy was welcomed, did the previous pattern retain its hold in Christian Democratic parties? The continued opposition to Communism was no surprise in the Cold War era. The continued resistance to social democracy and especially democratic capitalism is more intriguing. Its residue can be traced in the generic differences that distinguish western European (continental) welfare states and economies as a group from the "Anglo-Saxon" variety of Britain and North America. Each nation has or had its variant, of course, but the "European" or "continental" varieties have a recognizable cast that derives from the historical sparring of "liberal" (i.e., conservative), socialist, and Christian Democratic forces.

A major complication in the story stems from the fact that nondemocratic ideologies also presented themselves as a third way. Various Fascist or fascistoid movements exalting national unity regarded themselves as bringing an authoritarian alternative to liberalism and socialism. "Corporatism" is the term that Catholic social thinkers and activists used to name their third way. It was also the term used by Mussolini for his way of gaining control over the labor movement and the economy in general. Indeed, after *Quadragesimo Anno*, the social encyclical of Pope Pius XI of 1931, Catholic social thinkers and activists often proposed a corporatist socioeconomic order as the Third Way par excellence, the necessary cure for the ills of both liberal capitalism and socialism. In this utopia, "networks of socio-economic corporations would bring together employers and employees to resolve conflicts of interest as well as assuring the ascendancy of social justice."[2]

Is not corporatism necessarily an antidemocratic project? Here a terminological clarification is required. In German, for example, there is a clear distinction between the phrase used in the interwar period, *berufsständische Ordnung* (awkwardly translated as "vocational order"), and another phrase, "social partnership," used in the 1950s. In English, however, "corporatism" may serve for either expression, and one has to gauge its bearing from the context. Thus 1930s Catholic corporatist notions in the wake of *Quadragesimo Anno* have to do with "vocational order," whereas 1950s *soziale Partnerschaft* in western Europe refers to institutionalized labor-management-government consultation and balancing of interests. With the aid of a distinction formulated only in 1974 but helpful for sorting out the crucial differences in 1930s corporatisms, we may call the type espoused even then by Christian Democrats "societal corporatism," as opposed to the "state corporatism" imposed by Mussolini and his emulators.[3] The crucial difference between the two types of "corporatist" third ways may be framed as follows: did the proposed system replace political democracy (with its elected, policy-setting parliaments), or did it presuppose and support such democracy?

The question arises: was there a *distinctive* third way that Christian *Democrats* pursued? To what extent was it consonant with genuinely democratic and pluralist political practice? This third way was distinctive by virtue of grounding itself in a Christian understanding of human persons, persons destined to share a common life as children of God. Because of this Catholic Christian character, it remained detachable from other right-wing third ways. This third way renounced authoritarian means but claimed its democratic right to toleration and participation in the larger society. Hence it was capable of contributing to the formation of postwar democratic political economies.

In the three sections that follow, I present a background sketch, through the major phases of its career, of the notion of a third-way political economy differing from both capitalism and socialism; explore the more prominent role it played in the 1930s, with *Quadragesimo Anno* stimulating attention to concrete corporatist projects; and finally, address the issue of the persistence of the third-way theme in postwar Christian Democracy.

## BEFORE AND AFTER WORLD WAR I

From whence did the distinct features of the Christian Democratic third way come? From what is called "social Catholicism." Jean-Dominique Durand, for instance, repeatedly emphasizes the significance of characteristically "social Catholic" thinking during the formative phases of the history of Christian Democracy.[4] With the postwar ascendancy of democracy in western Europe, Christian Democrats revived the memory of Félicité de Lamennais who, at the time of the 1830 revolution, called on the papacy to ally itself with the democratic aspirations of the people. Although Lamennais provided powerful stimuli, his condemnation by Pope Gregory XVI and the anticlerical attitude of most liberals left his "liberal Catholicism" a very much diminished and even marginal element in nineteenth-century ultramontane Catholicism. Much more germane to the further development of social Catholicism was the antirevolutionary thinking that took form in reaction to the political and social revolution of 1848.

In 1851 Juan Donoso Cortés published a book with a striking title that would have considerable impact: *Essay on Catholicism, Liberalism and Socialism.* In "Catholicism" Donoso Cortés saw a theory and practice devoted to social "solidarity." By contrast, "liberalism cultivated only individuality, even isolation. Socialism, for its part, having caught the infection of materialism from the liberals, reacted against the prospect of savage competition with anarchism or with regimentation and collectivism."[5] There were of course many other polarities between which to seek a middle way or a third way, but this pair of rival ideologies was the one to which Catholics kept recurring. The rivals in question were economic as well as political ideologies. Indeed, before socialism loomed so large (Donoso Cortés, alarmed by 1848, was a bit prescient in this regard), Enlightenment liberalism, seen as the progenitor of the French Revolution, was the foe in a battle for civilization, a Kulturkampf. There were some "liberal Catholics" who made serious efforts to assimilate Enlightenment advances into the Catholic spirit. But the tendency opposed to "liberal Catholicism" gained the upper hand in the Church. It was ultramontane or "intransigent" Catholicism that would form the seedbed of social Catholicism in the nineteenth century.[6] It is important to note, though, that this social Catholicism, sensitive to the injustices inflicted on the working class, was only one strand among the Catholic opponents of modernity.

It is true that intransigent Catholicism did not value the democratic elements that would be so important to Christian Democracy, but then democratic aspirations were not dominant in the liberal camp either. The worldviews of both nineteenth-century Catholicism and nineteenth-century continental liberalism took for granted that the vast majority of people were incapable of conducting or even meaningfully participating in the running of societal affairs. The educated elite had to take charge, bourgeois property owners in the liberal view or clergy in the Catholic one. The masses, after all, could not be expected to know where their own or the nation's best interests lay. As the radicals and socialists started to make a dent in this commonsense assumption among liberals, so the Christian democrats of the pre–World War I era challenged paternalist assumptions among intransigent Catholics. A pioneer social Catholic like Bishop Wilhelm Emmanuel von Ketteler (1811–77) recognized already that justice would not come for the workers in an industrializing society without autonomous labor unions capable of representing the interests of the working class. Hence workers could not remain permanently under the tutelage of their "betters." He advocated the interest and participation of the clergy in such associations, not so as to keep the workers docile, but for the sake of the common good and social peace—and because the clergy were not employers. As outsiders to the industrial establishment, priests could take a disinterested or sympathetic view of the "worker question." He even thought it worthwhile to float the idea of a collaboration between Catholic forces and the early social democracy of Ferdinand Lassalle (1825–64). Early in 1864 Ketteler offered to collect some start-up capital and put it at the disposition of Lassalle if the latter would use it to set up productive associations[7]—a third way of sorts.

However, even apart from the circumstances that pitted socialist labor against Catholicism and the new German Reich against both after 1870, the stimuli from Ketteler's engagement and writings led to developments in social Catholicism that can best be called reactionary and corporatist. The Prussian convert in Vienna, Baron Karl von Vogelsang (1818–90), and the French nobleman, René de La Tour du Pin (1834–1924), spearheaded the development of corporatist theory that would henceforth be the most conspicuous variant of third-way thinking among social Catholics.[8] In 1891, when Pope Leo XIII decided to issue an encyclical, *Rerum Novarum,* on economics and the social question, such ideas still seemed at least a bit risky and perhaps unrealistic; the distinctively corporatist elements in the social Catholic thought of the time were not incorporated into the encyclical.[9] Which is not to say that the third-way placement of this first papal foray into economic ethics was not perfectly clear. The opening words declared that the lust for revolutionary change (*rerum novarum cupido*) had invaded relations between employers and workers. The pope placed blame primarily on the exclusive sway of the liberal law of the market in labor relations and only secondarily on socialist ideas. All persons, workers as well as employers, have the same basic worth ("human dignity," nos. 20 and 40), which means that workers or the unemployed cannot be treated merely as factors of production. Private property is defended as essential to human dignity.

Corporatist thinking remained alive in Catholicism, fed by the medieval Christendom ideal, but it was not so prominent for the next quarter century in vital sectors of social Catholicism such as the Christian labor union movement. *Abbés démocrates* and other "Christian Democrats" emerged after *Rerum Novarum*. They were not generally so keen to bring labor and a recalcitrant capitalist class together into a premature harmony as they were to create an effective autonomous movement that could press labor's claims to fairer treatment. In terms of the distinction introduced earlier (after Schmitter), they foreshadowed, not the thoroughgoing authoritarian corporatist themes that would become prominent in the interwar period, but the democratic and autonomous labor movements that could hold their own with owners and managers of industry in a manner characteristic of the "societal corporatism" of post–World War II Europe.

For the interwar period no up-to-date comprehensive scholarly synthesis of social and political Catholicism in Europe exists.[10] It is safe to say, however, that the third-way theme will loom large when it is written. World War I led to the formation of economic councils and a degree of interventionism or economic controls in affected countries, with workers' welfare also taken into account. In Germany after the defeat, this practice was institutionalized in the so-called Zentralarbeitsgemeinschaft (ZAG). The measure of cooperation and sharing of the burdens of war provided by such mandatory joint deliberations commended them to some observers as a vast improvement in labor relations over what existed before the war.[11] There was some readiness to engage in such common efforts even among socialist labor leaders and more so among Catholic ones, provided they were also given a place at the table.

After a period of interclass hanging together during tough postwar times, the bourgeoisie managed, as Charles Maier has put it, to "recast Europe" in a form more to its liking. In Germany the ZAG was hollowed out by 1923. Still, industrialists could not "ignore working-class aspirations; for until 1930 at least, the powerful Christian Trade Union representation in the Center Party precluded a reactionary policy. The Catholic trade-union leader Brauns [the Reverend Heinrich Brauns, 1868–1939] held the pivotal Ministry of Labor with its power of compulsory arbitration from 1924 until 1928 and bargained consistently for restoring the eight-hour legislation that had been suspended in 1923."[12] This was a sort of middle course or third way between liberal (read: employers') and socialist ideas of how labor relations should be handled. In the solidarist economic theory of Heinrich Pesch, such practice was viewed as an initial example of where a third way beyond economic liberalism and communism might lead. From 1927 on, however, even the Christian unions would no longer cooperate, as they saw workers consistently getting the short end of the stick.

To get a closer look at how the third-way theme in social Catholicism was developed in the 1920s and to form a baseline against which to view the conspicuous corporatist developments of the 1930s, it will help to examine both Catholic theorists (mostly Catholic priest-scholars) and practitioners in the Christian labor movement. The theorist most influential on *Quadragesimo Anno* was Heinrich Pesch, S.J. (1854–1926), who thus deserves special attention. In general, he was in perfect agreement with other Catholic authorities on economic ethics such as Giuseppe Toniolo (1845–1918), the Belgian Jesuits Arthur Vermeersch and Albert Muller, and Charles Antoine in France and Johannes Messner (1891–1984) in Austria. They all situated themselves explicitly in a third school of social thought that rejected liberalism and socialism as ruinous of the dignity of the human person. The prevailing diagnosis was that Enlightenment individualism was at the root of the deviations. "No man is an island," said the poet, and the Catholic writers opposed the view that all one's relationships with other persons could or should be thought of as the result of contracts entered into for the sake of the advantages they might offer. Instead, their view stressed community, the web of relationships that exists before a given individual comes on the scene. In the 1920s the rediscovery of "community," as contrasted by Ferdinand Tönnies (in his 1887 book) with "society," gave a timely cachet to this critique of liberalism.[13] On this view, socialism, too, although a reaction against liberalism, accepted its basically materialistic conception of the individual from the same Enlightenment root when it advocated the collectivization of the means of production through coercive majoritarian politics, or worse, revolution. This subjection of the person-in-community to society at large—as of a means to an end—was no cure for the disease of individualism but rather another kind of devastation of community.

Pesch's principal interest was to relate the realm of economic activity to the ultimate end of human beings. Aristotelian and neo-Thomistic, he always had final causes and the nature-grace constitution of human life and destiny in mind. The latter gave him leave to explore the factors of production and exchange in their own "natural" frame of reference, without prematurely bringing in religious norms. It enabled him as well to belong to those students of economics who do not really regard it as a "dismal science" focusing on the disposition of scarce commodities. For him, it was a matter of understanding how human activity, at the level of material goods and services rendered for compensation, was intrinsically oriented and adapted to the satisfaction of human needs in community.

His teachers belonged to the "historical school" of economics; this alone set him apart from the earlier Catholic corporatists, whose economics was of a more doctrinaire and less well-informed character. In the history of economic analysis, Pesch followed in the wake of the so-called *Kathedersozialisten,* or academic socialists. In particular, he saw one of his teachers in Berlin, Adolph Wagner (1835–1917), as a pivotal figure, because he was not merely interested in ameliorating steps on the part of government, but aimed for a sane theoretical alternative to individualism and socialism. Wagner missed the mark, as Pesch saw it, for want of an adequate (i.e., Thomistic) political philosophy and a consistent systematic perspective, and strayed into "state socialism."[14] Pesch could relate well to the leading economists of his generation, who were already convinced of the shortcomings of classic liberal economic theory, yet were not willing to jump on the Marxist bandwagon. To Pesch, therefore, his teachers practiced a discipline in search of an explicit theoretical basis. He was anxious to provide this with his teleological (purpose-oriented) approach.

Hence Pesch stressed the common economic enterprise in which all human beings are variously engaged, according to their abilities. To meet the needs of all is the ultimate purpose of work and trade. This implies a third way, for the economic agent is neither the atomistic individual of liberal economics nor the mere member of a collectivity of the socialist alternative. No, the persons driving the economic process as producers and consumers are realizing their joint social-individual nature as unique human persons tending toward a common destiny. Working and enjoying the fruits of one's labor with one's family are the humanizing and socializing factors that loom the largest in most persons' lives. When they are subjected to relentless modern commodification, persons lose their dignity and their solidarity. Pesch defined his third way at the level of social philosophy, dubbed "solidarism," as the "system that validates the solidary connection of human beings as such" (i.e., one for all and all for one). It legitimated and advocated, he went on to say, a development "of cooperative, representative and corporative associations" limited only by practical considerations. Their aim was to promote human interaction that instrumentalized commodities rather than the other way around.[15] "Catholic solidarism," in the words of Matthew Lamb, "aimed at transposing pre-modern understandings of natural law, of human beings as essentially social, and of society itself as organic and cooperative, into the modern contexts of industrialized societies with complex exchange economies."[16]

In this comprehensive view of human nature and society, Pesch went on to develop an economic system, which he called the "social labor system" or "solidarist labor system," as distinct from the "liberal" (i.e., actually existing capitalist) and socialist labor theories.[17] Socialization was definitely needed, but its most crucial type was "socialization of persons," not of things.[18] Shops, firms, trade associations, labor unions, chambers of commerce, and the ZAG were already examples, if still scattered, of what such socialization of persons would entail. It was Pesch's conviction that a defective organic development in the socioeconomic sector, imbalanced to the detriment of labor (working people), meant that issues of equity proper to the economy were left to the government to deal with, bureaucratically, with the crude tools of coercive intervention. What was needed was a set of organs enhancing the marketplace that would permit the economic actors themselves to face and deal with economic issues of import to society; in other words (to translate a bit crudely and rapidly into more familiar terms), a comprehensive set of economic associations in the several sectors that would include representation of all the stakeholders and would have the ability to take corrective action.

The interaction between these national organizations at the summit would eventually have to be organized. Pesch did not shrink from speaking of an "Economic Parliament"[19] as the logical central clearinghouse of this decentralized organic development, but he left its structure to the future. In general, Pesch did not venture into the political aspects of political economy if he could avoid them. Only once, in the run-up to the elections just after World War I, did he enter the political fray with a pamphlet advocating "Christian socialism" (a phrase he did not use again). He also stayed aloof from the Center Party, whether through scholarly asceticism, an unwillingness to expose the Jesuits again to public criticism, or the recognition that his disciples would be more capable than he of furthering solidarism in the political arena. Because he banked on a slow process of organic socialization from below and on reforms carried out piecemeal rather than abruptly, by decree, we can number him among the intellectual authors of "societal corporatism" according to the typology I have borrowed from Schmitter.

In terms of political economy, the mainstream social Catholic authors I have named, including also the 1927 *Code social*[20] of Malines that summed up the thinking of French-speaking social Catholics, breathed a different spirit than the other antiliberal prophets of the time. True, principled pro-democracy arguments are missing from the social Catholic corpus apart from Sturzo's and Maritain's pioneering works—and this was a grievous lack, conditioned by papal pronouncements such as *Graves de Communi* of 1901. But these authors assumed parliamentary democracy as a practical matter at least. Where this was not the case, as in some of the so-called *Wiener Richtungen*, the influence of broader antiliberal tendencies in postwar Europe at large may be seen, as well as that of the first generation of corporatist thought, that of Vogelsang and La Tour du Pin. Albert de Mun, who died in 1918, for example, was well known as a "paladin" of papal social thought, but also of revanchism or nationalistic militarism. He once called for a "counterrevolution." La Tour du Pin was more than sympathetic with the proto-Fascist Action Française because of its support of the monarchical principle. It is a fact that he and some of the Viennese felt that *Rerum Novarum* was much too timid in its analysis of the ills of modern capitalism and the need for far-reaching corporatist reform. There were, therefore, respected social Catholics of an earlier generation who struck tones congenial to some Fascist or proto-Fascist ideologists. Such dark thoughts, however, were foreign to the moral philosophy of Antoine, Pesch, and other *auctores probati*, because of their championing of the dignity of the human person.

Turning to the activists of the Catholic labor movements between the world wars, particularly their programmatic documents, one sees the same

basic rejection of the worldviews of liberal capitalism and Marxist socialism. Christian labor activists were sensitive to the charge that they played
into the hands of employers by creating divisions. They were determined
to be no less militant in defending workers' rights than socialist unions.
However, they could not make common cause, except on a tactical basis,
with the anticlericalism (more exactly, the deriding of religious faith and
practice) and class struggle ideology of the socialist labor movement. In 1922
the fledgling International Federation of Christian Trade Unions (IFCTU)
met in Innsbruck and adopted a platform. The first part, laying out the
philosophical foundations of the Christian labor movement, adopted the
basic thrust of social Catholicism in steering a course between the individualistic extreme of "the liberal economic school" and the collectivist
tendencies of socialist or Marxist doctrine. The explicitly stated presup-
position is the unsurpassable human dignity of each person, realizable
only with the orientation of all to the common good. Private ownership
is a good thing, but "the forms of property can vary according to cultural
differences, whereas the acquisition and the use made of property are
subject to moral obligations incumbent on all."[21] The second part, on the
social economy, identified the most pressing problem as the sharp tensions existing between the providers of capital and the providers of
labor, with management for the most part representing capital. Labor,
too, should have a role in management and a part in the profits of the
common enterprise. Here occurs a widely shared idea with a future, *Mitbestimmung* (codetermination or coresponsibility).[22] This characteristic
program point of the Catholic labor movement was forged in ideological
struggle with capitalist control on the side of the employers and the alternative of state ownership and control commonly advocated in the socialist labor movement.

All of this may strike us, as it struck some even then, as something less
than the essentially different economic system suggested by the rhetoric of
"a third way." Even if the social philosophy from which the Catholics started
insisted that society was an organic whole, not a mere collection of atom-
ized individuals (*homo homini lupus*), the practical application seemed a
modification of capitalism, not its replacement; or as Goetz Briefs put it, an
adjustment of economic capitalism from its "liberal phase" to a more
socially responsible form, such as the social market economy of the 1950s.[23]
However, with the advent of Fascism in Italy, the depression, and the 1931

encyclical of Pope Pius XI, *Quadragesimo Anno*, third-way proposals got concrete frames of reference and entered a new phase.

## CORPORATIST THIRD WAYS OF THE DEPRESSION

The first effect of *Quadragesimo Anno* (henceforth *QA*) was to lift *Rerum Novarum* out of the run of encyclicals and endow it with special force as the Magna Carta of papal social teaching. To be sure, Catholic labor associations had given special attention to *Rerum Novarum*, but now its special and highly authoritative status for all Catholics was emphatically restated by Pius XI. *QA* roundly condemned socialism; it criticized the unjust workings of capitalist economies as well and its individualistic spirit but not its basic mechanisms as such. The particular stimulus it gave to third-way thinking was contained in paragraphs 91 through 96, commenting on Mussolini's corporatist "reforms" of the Italian labor-management scene. The principal drafter of the encyclical, Oswald von Nell-Breuning, S.J., disclosed forty years later that these paragraphs came from the pope himself and seemed to Nell-Breuning to be perfectly apposite and in keeping with the Peschian solidarist lines in which the rest of the encyclical was framed.[24]

Apart from these paragraphs and preceding them in the final text of the encyclical, there were some idealistic formulations that reflected the solidarism of Nell-Breuning's friends in the Königswinter Kreis. (This was a sort of Catholic study group of social scientists affiliated with the Volksverein, the training ground for Catholic labor leadership in Mönchengladbach. Quite independently, the *Code social* of Malines contained very similar ideas.) Particularly influential for Nell-Breuning was the thought of Gustav Gundlach, a fellow Jesuit and disciple of Pesch who advised Eugenio Pacelli when the latter was nuncio in Germany in the 1920s. (He later provided the same service for him in Rome when he became Pope Pius XII.) The Jesuit General who oversaw the writing of the draft encyclical wondered at including in the document far-reaching thoughts about overcoming class conflict. Nell-Breuning writes: "I recall . . . his doubting question: 'How long do you think it will take to achieve this?' and my disarming reply, 'It will never be achieved; it is much too sensible for people ever to do it.'"[25]

Let us briefly recall what *QA* contained that seemed to suggest a corporatism with a marked distance between it and prevailing capitalist assumptions.

There is first the ringing call for a reconstruction of the social(-economic) order according to the principle of subsidiarity (76–80).[26] The sound elements of communitarian solidarity that were once incarnated in the concrete structures of society have given way to state centralization and economic monopolization. What many liberals might have seen as progress appears in the encyclical's perspective as the inevitable and ruinous results of individualism without a counterbalancing sense of the common good. The remedy to this structural weakness, most evident in the endemic class struggle of modern nations, is set forth in an emphatic formulation in paragraph 81 that could be interpreted as an appeal for strong authoritarian measures.

> The State and every good citizen ought to look to and strive toward this end: that the conflict between the hostile classes be abolished and harmonious cooperation of the Industries and Professions be encouraged and promoted.

In the Latin, "industries and professions" is simply "*ordines*," as opposed to "*classes*"; both were put in quotation marks as an indication that they stand for modern terms. In Nell-Breuning's or Gundlach's German, the terms were *Stände* (economic "estates") and *Klassen*. This key sloganlike formulation was lifted from an address that Gundlach wrote and nuncio Pacelli delivered at the 1929 Katholikentag in Freiburg: "Aus der Auseinandersetzung der Klassen zur einträchtigen Zusammenarbeit der Stände."

The encyclical concretizes this cooperation of the professions first as a remedy for the dog-eat-dog workings of the labor market that lead to social strife (83–84). The common good would be better served by self-governing trade associations that would have the authority to set standards for contentious issues such as wages, working conditions, management prerogatives, and profits according to economic conditions. It is recognized that employers and workers will have divergent interests in some respects and that each should be able to take counsel separately on the way to an agreement acceptable to both sides and in conformity with the common good of society (85). Clearly, the idea is that the state's responsibility is not to command the economy or even to regulate it in detail; nor is the market capable of self-regulation by an invisible hand; therefore the requirements of good economic order point to cooperative trade associations or "professions"

(*Stände*) to take responsibility for justice in the economic arena, for the good of all—the common good. This would have to start from small beginnings to allow a full-blown solidarist (or corporatist) economic system to develop organically (87).

Although much Catholic social thinking of the time suffered from anti-modern shortcomings and hence minimized the positive significance of capital investment and competition, the encyclical reflected the moderate stance of Peschian economic ethics in acknowledging the benefits of competition for the common good (88). Also in paragraph 88 there is an implicit criticism of state takeovers of the economy, because state control throttles all kinds of voluntary initiatives and cooperative undertakings. There follow, however, paragraphs 91–96, which Nell-Breuning received from the pope at a late stage of the drafting process. They refer unmistakably to the Italian situation and the corporatist associations set up by the Fascist regime shortly before. After a neutral description of the system, the pope notes in paragraph 95 its "obvious advantages" in terms of social peace. The same paragraph, however, states an objection in principle: this system is imposed by the state; it unfortunately results in the kind of detailed governmental intervention and control that the solidarist project was meant to render unnecessary. The criticism is muted in that the pope attributes this objection to unnamed others. All the same, the pope in his own name states that "the reconstruction and improvement of a better social order" will not succeed without the contribution of good Catholics schooled in the ranks of Catholic Action (96). (This was a reminder to Mussolini to leave Catholic Action alone, as agreed in the Lateran Pacts.)

Only after this nod to and critique of the most conspicuous corporatist experiment of the time, taking place in the pope's own country, does the encyclical return to a more general train of thought. It develops at great length the overall history of the modern "capitalist economic regime" (103), pointing out its fatal flaws, such as monopolistic control of markets, as well as those of the socialist alternative (98). The impetus all this lent in the following decade to the search for a further alternative, a third way, was great in some circles, including Christian Democratic ones. The papal comments on the Fascist corporatist state were taken as an endorsement. After all, the criticism uttered in these paragraphs was milder than the encyclical's critique of the two older systems. In Italy itself, the Catholic response to home-grown Fascism may be summed up as "characterised by compromises, by moments of optimism and conviction and by much confusion."[27] Christian Democratic impulses were able to be nurtured under cover of some Catholic Action groups, particularly that of the academics (Movimento Laureati) and the Federation of Italian Catholic University Students (FUCI).[28]

In what is surely a unique occurrence in the annals of encyclical commentaries, Nell-Breuning has avowed:

> It is clear to me today [1971] that the insertion of Pius XI's comments on fascism bears the chief blame for the total misunderstanding of . . . the outline of a social order developed in *QA*, which in the German translation [his own!] goes by the unhappy word "occupational" and in French by "corporatist."[29]

In other words, Pope Pius XI read everything that Nell-Breuning had written about moving from a class-riven to a corporatist social order through his own authoritarian lenses, whereas Nell-Breuning had borrowed them from his fellow Peschian, Gustav Gundlach, and from the democratically minded Catholic labor leaders with whom he had contact and meant them in a basically democratic sense. None of these circles was prepared to give up Weimar constitutionalism voluntarily.

In Austria, a *Ständestaat* tried to master the difficult situation of 1934 to 1938. This was a "corporatist state" under Catholic dictatorial auspices that suppressed socialist organizations and liked to see itself as a "*QA* state." Pius XI blessed the undertaking and thus gave to this authoritarian third way the highest Catholic stamp of approval. "As Pius XI's enthusiasm for the dictatorial regimes of Salazar in Portugal and Dollfuss in Austria during the 1930s illustrated," he regarded "a strong central power . . . as essential to maintain social and political order but it was to be accompanied by the application of the principle of subsidiarity, by which responsibility for many socio-economic issues should be devolved from the central state to the 'natural' communities of region, profession, and family."[30] For Nell-Breuning's part, he did not see *QA* as in any way favoring antidemocratic state corporatism; in his mind, precisely the cases of Austria and Portugal completely discredited the expressions "corporatism" and "vocational order" but not the reformist approach of solidarism.

In France, too, social Catholics—Christian Democrats, Young Christian Workers (JOC), activists of the Catholic Youth Association (ACJF), trade unionists, and intellectuals who presented their ideas in lively periodicals and at the Semaines Sociales—were looking for a Catholic third way. A distinctive variant, however, began to stir in the form of Emmanuel Mounier's influence and that of his periodical, *Esprit*. Mounier wished to avoid both the political Left and the Right and indeed the whole "established disorder" of parliamentary electoral practices. The few Christian Democrats in the French parliament in 1932, when Mounier and friends first called for a "third force" relative to capitalism and communism, were in *Esprit*'s view part of the problem, not the solution.[31] On the other hand, it is interesting to note that the French Christian labor federation, the CFTC, eschewed the terms "corporatism" and "corporatist" and the like when it presented its own reform plan in 1936. A Jesuit commentator avowed, in terms anticipating Schmitter's, that a "corporatisme d'association" is what social Catholics had in mind, not the "corporatisme d'Etat" of the dictators.[32]

Jacques Maritain provided Mounier with much of his starting intellectual and human capital, notably his move beyond individualism and collectivism to personalism, though Maritain had to object to his younger friend's tolerance for fascistoid third-way elements.[33] Maritain's native liberalism allowed him to see more clearly than most Catholics what we might call "the third threat," namely, from Fascism as well as capitalism and collectivism. Maritain elevated the third-way approach to the level of a full-blown philosophy of human dignity and justice, one that required the exercise of democracy and the defense of human rights for the common good. This was a departure from the standard conservative third way of more representative but less original thinkers of the period. His ideal of a New Christendom still steers a clear course between the Scylla of individualism and the Charybdis of collectivism.[34] Before Maritain's personalism could be assimilated, however, a different "New Order" had its hour on the European scene.

## DESIGNS FOR RECONSTRUCTION

When Hitler invaded there were Catholic public figures in Belgium, the Netherlands, and Vichy France who supposed that the time for a corporatist new order had arrived. Others, more pragmatic, simply sought to make what use they could of the inevitable Nazi ascendancy. Several examples of Catholic social thought and approaches will make clear, however, that the third-way reflections of the interwar period had its effect not only among collaborators or passive victims of Nazi power but also among the most decided Resistance circles. This, too, then, will help to explain the persistence of third-way thinking after the war, when Nazi or Fascist associations left a very black mark.

Mounier himself, for a while, lent his name and his periodical to the Vichy attempt at limited self-government under German oversight. In fact, "social Catholics were particularly attracted to the new order," with its promise of a labor charter free of liberal or collectivist taint. "Many social Catholics readily identified with Vichy and for the first year of its existence, at least, chose to regard it as the embodiment of their own aspirations for a Christian state."[35] In occupied Belgium, similar efforts to adjust to the new order, seemingly in place for the duration, manifested themselves. In the Netherlands as elsewhere, there had already been much discussion of social reorganization along the lines suggested by *QA;* in 1938 a concerted "Action for a New Community" was started with the support of the strong Catholic labor movement. However, Dutch Catholics and Protestants demonstrated less readiness to collaborate with the new Nazi order than was evident in France and Belgium. The Dutch episcopate simply did not allow Catholic organizations, including the unions and the party, to continue to exist as tools of a Nazi occupation.[36]

Throughout occupied Europe and in Germany itself, clandestine groups laid plans as best they could for the reconstruction after the defeat of Fascism and Nazism. Perhaps the best known of the non-Communist resistance groups in Germany was the Kreisauer Kreis led by two Prussian gentlemen, Helmuth James von Moltke and Peter Yorck von Wartenburg. Both were upper-class Protestants from Silesia, but with an eye to action after the demise of Nazism, von Moltke in particular was determined to find socialist and Catholic (Jesuit) dialogue partners for this subversive activity, all with a background in their respective youth movements.[37] In this group, too, opposed as it was to any "new order" leanings of the authoritarian kind so common between the world wars, one finds a third way between individualism and collectivism.

Von Moltke was much impressed by the anticentralist political teaching of the early-nineteenth-century liberal Karl vom Stein (1757–1831), with its recognition of the importance of local communities for the exercise of personal responsibility. As it happened, one of the Jesuits initiated into the underground group, Alfred Delp (1907–45), had not only picked up Pesch's solidarism and studied *QA* but, in 1938, also had been intrigued by vom Stein's emphasis on the self-governance of communes, institutions, and associations. Delp saw subsidiarity at work there without the word.[38] He called his third way "personal socialism"; the basic approach was its simultaneous emphasis on the individual and the collective. What Delp brought to the infrequent and secretive conferences in 1942 and 1943 undergirded Count von Moltke's previous convictions. On the whole, the surviving documentation from the Kreisau group's deliberations attest an explicit third way along personalist and solidarist lines, overcoming the shortcomings of capitalism and Marxism. Given the arrests and executions of the principal members of the Kreisauer Kreis shortly after the famous attempt of July 20, 1944, to assassinate Hitler, it is not easy to say how far Delp's ideas carried weight with the socialist dialogue partners. In one case, however, the social democratic labor leader Wilhelm Leuschner (1888–1944), who was in contact with the Kreisauers, put it this way: "After individualism yielded to the epoch of collectivism, . . . 'there still remained a third reality, beyond individuality and collectivity, something that is no compromise, but different and higher: the person.'" As Hans Mommsen has commented, "That was precisely the Kreisau formula."[39]

When the war ended the hour of social or Left Catholicism seemed to have struck, with the emergence of worker-priests in France and Belgium and of left-wing Christian Democratic groups. Moreover, politically interested Catholics, taking to heart some themes of Sturzo and Maritain, felt that the time had come to create parties that would promote the welfare of all citizens and groups and that would no longer be identified as dedicated primarily to defending Catholic sectoral interests. The waning of anticlerical sentiment over the years and especially during the war meant that Church interests were not under concerted attack. In combination, such considerations led Catholic and socialist labor elements to contemplate the formation of broad labor parties in several countries, or at least a unitary labor movement. A single labor union confederation did come about in Germany and Austria, whereas Belgium and the Netherlands were too pillarized for such attempts to succeed.[40] In Italy, a unified labor confederation was formed, only to experience a Catholic secession in 1948. On balance, then, one might say that third-way hopes led some Catholics to throw in their lot with other labor democrats to shape a "laborist" political economy equidistant from capitalism and communism, while other social Catholics feared their third-way paradigm would succumb to socialist outlooks redolent of class struggle. These latter, allied with other classes in Catholicism, favored the creation of centrist, anti-Communist Christian Democratic parties. In any case, their point of departure was the familiar third-way paradigm.[41]

What drove the bulk of Catholic voters to support the Christian Democrats in the immediate postwar years, then, was not so much the intrinsic appeal of the far-reaching social justice platforms of those parties as the lack of a respectable right-wing democratic party to vote for. Where such more conservative parties emerged, as in France, the Christian Democratic party's Catholic constituency was split electorally. In Germany, all the same, the success of the new Christian Democratic Union in breaking through the confessional barrier and attracting Protestant members of a communitarian bent kept the conservative "liberal" Free Democratic Party in a distinctly minoritarian position. The electoral placement of the Christian Democratic parties to the Right of the social democratic parties, together with the weight of the middle-class and rural vote, as well as the necessities of postwar reconstruction under largely American auspices, had the effect of settling the Christian Democratic parties into a moderate conservative position on the political spectrum. These processes entailed a substantial "dilution of the ideological patrimony"[42] of the social Catholic tradition, to be sure. The combination of the experience of Nazi excesses, a relatively magnanimous occupation on the part of the Anglo-Saxon victors, and the fear of Soviet Communism tempered the critique of capitalism, especially once the postwar boom started to show its effects in the general standard of living. The search for a third way soon lost much of its appeal or was seen as substantially fulfilled in a mitigated democratic capitalist regime.

Yet beneath this picture of the Americanization of western European political economies observers have noticed some enduring characteristics that show roots in communitarian third-way thinking. For one thing, Christian Democratic parties did not simply lose their labor wing. As interclass parties, part of their raison d'être was to foster partnership between labor and capital, between city and country, between sectoral interests of all kinds. The shape of the welfare state reflected third-way thinking where the state delegated its authority to the social partners, for example, for the administration of medical and old-age insurance coverage.[43] The principle of subsidiarity is a feature of the social Catholic third way that has emerged again in post-1945 Europe, as has the "societal corporatism" described by Schmitter. The "intransigent" goal of re-Christianizing society as a whole gradually gave way to the conviction that pluralism, dialogue, and coopera- tion with those of other worldviews were more conducive to the common good under actual conditions, also as seen from a faith perspective. The postwar experience of Catholics and their bishops with Christian Demo- cratic politics certainly contributed to the new stance taken by the Second Vatican Council vis-à-vis contemporary pluralistic culture and politics. The route actually taken by Christian Democrats differed considerably from pre- vious third-way expectations.

The economic miracle of the 1950s made possible the joint develop- ment of democracy and capitalism that was not the intention of those social and political activists who threw themselves into the creation of a new Christendom but which they nevertheless helped to create with their per- sonalist orientation and dedication.[44] In the process institutions such as codetermination (*Mitbestimmung*) took root, a development, as noted, that Christian trade unionists had called for since the 1920s. In the Netherlands, the prewar proposals of Catholic labor to devolve substantial regulative powers over industry on corporatist industrial councils were taken up again after the war, with, again, unintended but not unwelcome consequences. In 1950, with support from the Labor Party as well as the Dutch Catholic Party, a law on Public Industrial Organization was passed, marking the official adoption of such proposals, reminiscent of *QA*. However, implementation lagged. The goal of economic growth was more pressing, and the coalition of Christian parties set about to encourage export industry in parts of the country that needed the jobs. Then prosperity set in. The enduring upshot was not active and determinative industrial councils in every enterprise but "a substantial network of governmental institutions and advisory councils in which employers, employees, and the government consulted with each other and discussed matters of common concern."[45]

It is of interest to note the declarations of recent popes that the magis- terium has no economic system, properly speaking, to propose as the ideal. The recent papal disclaimers of a specifically Catholic economic system that would constitute a third way apply to the authoritarian corporatist regimes that received Pius XI's blessings in the 1930s but also to any other project of describing *the* Catholic economic system. Nevertheless, a pronounced dis- satisfaction with the liberal and collectivist models remains characteristic of even the most recent papal social teaching.[46] The recent clarifications were called for precisely because the quest for a third model besides capitalist or socialist economic systems has loomed large in historical manifestations of social Catholicism.

Having disowned that pipe dream, proponents of the social Catholic heritage may nevertheless claim that much of the third-way paradigm has been accepted in Europe as a common possession of all parties. Unexpected developments turned out to convey the concerns of person-oriented social thinking. Instead of third-way talk, the United Nations Declaration of Human Rights (1948) and the European Human Rights Convention (1950) framed the language in which one can defend the dignity of the human person in society most widely today. The human person as individual-in-community commands respect in principle before public authorities and powers. The period of globalization that set in with the collapse of the Soviet socialist regime has not resulted in a wholesale neoliberalism, despite the painful adjustments that have to be made.

In conclusion: the kind of third-way projects and realizations that prevailed after World War II in many western European nations drew from the social Catholic tradition. In the Christian Democratic movements, with their political aspirations, the importance of subsidiarity, intermediate bodies, and social justice for a humane democratic regime was stressed. The system of "social partnership" represents a legacy of the third-way thinking that had such a notable career in European social and political Catholicism. Facing the challenges of globalization, the parties of Christian Democratic heritage retain a critique of capitalism that sets them apart from their American cousins in ways it will be increasingly important to note at the beginning of the third millennium.

## NOTES

1. See Anthony Giddens, *The Third Way: The Renewal of Social Democracy* (London: Polity Press, 1998).

2. Martin Conway, Introduction to *Political Catholicism in Europe, 1918–1965,* ed. Tom Buchanan and Martin Conway (Oxford: Clarendon, 1996), 15 and index, s.v. "corporatism" and "third way."

3. Philippe C. Schmitter, "Still the Century of Corporatism?" *Review of Politics* 36 (1974): 85–131 (reprinted in *The New Corporatism: Social-Political Structures in the Iberian World* [Notre Dame: University of Notre Dame Press, 1974], 102–5), sets up the typology of two varieties of "corporatism"; the authoritarian or Fascist "corporations" of the 1930s represent "state corporatism," whereas the latter-day arrangements in a democratic environment constitute "societal corporatism." Schmitter sees all such institutionalized systems of interest representation as the alternative to Anglo-Saxon "pluralist" practice of ad hoc and perhaps ephemeral interest groups.

4. Jean-Dominique Durand, *L'Europe de la Démocratie Chrétienne* (Brussels: Editions Complexe, 1995), 17 passim.

5. Paul Misner, *Social Catholicism in Europe: From the Onset of Industrialization to the First World War* (New York: Crossroad, 1991), 127.

6. Durand, *L'Europe de la Démocratie Chrétienne*, 41–47; Misner, *Social Catholicism*, 198–99. Emile Poulat has been among the most insistent in making this connection; see his "Catholicism and Modernity: A Process of Mutual Exclusion," in *The Debate on Modernity*, i.e., *Concilium*, no. 6, ed. Claude Geffré and J.-P. Jossua (London: SCM, 1992), 10–16, here 15: "We should never forget that Catholic antimodernism lies at the source of the Catholic social movement of which Catholic Action has been the heart: a force for progress which has played a major role in history, but which does not fit in easily as fruit of the Enlightenment and modernity."

7. Misner, *Social Catholicism*, 138.

8. Philippe Chenaux, "Les origines de l'Union de Fribourg," in *"Rerum Novarum"*: *Ecriture, contenu et réception d'une encyclique. Actes du colloque international organisé par l'Ecole française de Rome et le Greco no 2 du CNRS (Rome, 18–20 avril 1991)* (Rome: Ecole Française de Rome, 1997), 255–66; cf. Misner, *Social Catholicism*, 202–8.

9. Guy Bedouelle, "De l'influence réelle de l'Union de Fribourg sur l'encyclique *Rerum Novarum*," in *"Rerum Novarum": Écriture*, 241–54; cf. Misner, *Social Catholicism*, 220.

10. One may consult with profit the multiauthor works edited by H.S. Scholl, O.Praem., *150 ans de mouvement ouvrier chrétien en Europe de l'Ouest 1789–1939* (Louvain: Nauwelaerts, 1966), and by Joseph N. Moody, *Church and Society: Catholic Social and Political Thought and Movements, 1789–1950* (New York: Arts, 1953).

11. See, e.g., Gerald D. Feldman, *The Great Disorder: Politics, Economics, and Society in the German Inflation, 1914–1924* (New York: Oxford University Press, 1993); and John P. Windmuller, *Labor Relations in the Netherlands* (Ithaca, N.Y.: Cornell University Press, 1969).

12. Charles S. Maier, *Recasting Bourgeois Europe: Stabilization in France, Germany, and Italy in the Decade after World War I* (Princeton, N.J.: Princeton University Press, 1975), 511.

13. Alois Baumgartner, *Sehnsucht nach Gemeinschaft: Ideen und Strömungen im Sozialkatholizismus der Weimarer Republik* (Paderborn: Schöningh, 1977).

14. Heinrich Pesch, *Lehrbuch der Nationalökonomie* (Freiburg: Herder, 1924), 2:202–12; see also Clemens Ruhnau, *Der Katholizismus in der sozialen Bewährung: Die Einheit theologischen und sozialethischen Denkens im Werk Heinrich Peschs* (Paderborn: Schöningh, 1980), 263–70.

15. Pesch, *Lehrbuch,* 1:432. Volume 1 appeared in 1905 in its first edition.

16. Matthew Lamb, "Solidarity," in *The New Dictionary of Catholic Social Thought* (Collegeville, Minn.: Liturgical Press, 1994), 908.

17. Pesch, *Lehrbuch,* 2:213–84.

18. Ibid., 219.

19. Ibid., 259.

20. *Code social: Esquisse d'une synthèse sociale catholique* (Paris: Spes, 1927).

21. Bernhard Otte, "Internationaler Bund der Christlichen Gewerkschaften (IBCG)," in *Internationales Handwörterbuch des Gewerkschaftswesens* (Berlin: Werk und Wirtschaft, 1930–32), 822.

22. Franz J. Stegmann, *Der soziale Katholizismus und die Mitbestimmung in Deutschland: Vom Beginn der Industrialisierung bis zum Jahre 1933* (Paderborn: Schöningh, 1974).

23. Goetz Briefs, "Pesch and His Contemporaries: Nationalökonomie vs. Contemporary Economic Theories," *Social Order* 1 (1951): 153–60, here 159.

24. Oswald von Nell-Breuning, "The Drafting of *Quadragesimo Anno,*" in *Official Catholic Social Teaching,* ed. Charles E. Curran and Richard A. McCormick (Mahwah, N.J.: Paulist, 1986), 62–65.

25. Nell-Breuning, "Drafting," 64.

26. *Quadragesimo Anno* 79: it is a "disturbance of right order to assign to a greater or higher association what lesser and subordinate organizations can do."

27. Martin Conway, *Catholic Politics in Europe, 1918–1945* (London and New York: Routledge), 63.

28. John F. Pollard, "Italy," in Buchanan and Conway, 84.

29. Nell-Breuning, "Drafting," 63.

30. Conway, Introduction to Buchanan and Conway, *Political Catholicism in Europe,* 14–15; cf. Anton Pelinka, *Austria: Out of the Shadow of the Past* (Boulder, Colo., and Oxford: Westview Press, 1998), 139–55.

31. James F. McMillan, "France," in Buchanan and Conway, *Political Catholicism in Europe,* 48.

32. Albert Muller, cited in Paul Droulers, *Le Père Desbuquois et l'Action Populaire, 1919–1946* (Paris: Editions Ouvrières, 1981), 168–71.

33. Bernard E. Doering, *Jacques Maritain and the French Catholic Intellectuals* (Notre Dame: University of Notre Dame Press, 1983), 61–70; Michael Kelly, *Pioneer*

*of the Catholic Revival: The Ideas and Influence of Emmanuel Mounier* (London: Sheed and Ward, 1979), 31–37.

34. Jacques Maritain, *Integral Humanism: Temporal and Spiritual Problems of a New Christendom* (Notre Dame: University of Notre Dame Press, [1936] 1996).

35. McMillan, "France," 55; cf. John Hellman, *The Knight-Monks of Vichy France: Uriage, 1940–45* (Montréal: McGill-Queen's University Press, 1997). See also Jean-Pierre Le Crom, *Syndicats nous voilà! Vichy et le corporatisme* (Paris: Editions de l'Atelier/Editions Ouvrières 1995).

36. Paul Luykx, "The Netherlands," in Buchanan and Conway, *Political Catholicism in Europe,* 233–34.

37. Ger van Roon, *Neuordnung im Widerstand: Der Kreisauer Kreis innerhalb der deutschen Widerstandsbewegung* (Munich: R. Oldenbourg, 1967). See also the works of Roman Bleistein, S.J., on Delp: *Dossier: Kreisauer Kreis. Dokumente aus dem Widerstand gegen den Nationalsozialismus. Aus dem Nachlass von Lothar König S.J.* (Frankfurt am Main: Josef Knecht, 1987) and *Alfred Delp: Geschichte eines Zeugen* (Frankfurt: Knecht 1989).

38. Michael Pope, *Alfred Delp S.J. im Kreisauer Kreis: Die rechts- und sozialphilosophischen Grundlagen in seinen Konzeptionen für eine Neuordnung Deutschlands* (Mainz: Grünewald, 1994), 85.

39. Cited in Pope, *Alfred Delp S.J.,* 169, from an essay by Hans Mommsen of 1966 in which Leuschner is quoted.

40. Patrick Pasture, "The April 1944 'Social Pact' in Belgium and Its Significance for the Post-War Welfare State," *Journal of Contemporary History* 28 (1993): 708.

41. See Martin Conway, "Belgium," in Buchanan and Conway, *Political Catholicism in Europe,* 209.

42. Pollard, "Italy," 96.

43. Michel Dumoulin, "The Socio-Economic Impact of Christian Democracy in Western Europe," in *Christian Democracy in the European Union, 1945–1995,* ed. Emiel Lamberts (Leuven: Leuven University Press, 1997), 370–71. Cf. Kees van Kersbergen, *Social Capitalism: A Study of Christian Democracy and the Welfare State* (London: Routledge, 1995).

44. Pietro Scoppola, *La "nuova cristianità" perduta* (Rome: Studium, 1986), 19.

45. Luykx, "The Netherlands," 235–36.

46. Paul VI in *Octogesima Adveniens* of 1971, pars. 4, 42; John Paul II in *Sollicitudo Rerum Socialium* of 1987, par. 41.7. An interesting exegesis of John Paul II's perspective on the "moral equivalence" of communism and capitalism is given by Jonathan Luxmoore and Jolanta Babiuch, *The Vatican and the Red Flag: The Struggle for the Soul of Eastern Europe* (London: Geoffrey Chapman, 1999), 309–15. Here is noted the paragraph 2425 of the *Catechism of the Catholic Church* (1994) that "sets the record straight":

The Church has rejected the totalitarian and atheistic ideologies associated in modern times with "communism" or "socialism." She has likewise refused to accept, in the practice of "capitalism," individualism and the absolute primacy of the law of the marketplace over human labor. Regulating the economy solely by centralized planning perverts the basis of social bonds; regulating it solely by the law of the marketplace fails social justice, for there are many human needs which cannot be satisfied by the market. Reasonable regulation of the marketplace and economic initiatives, in keeping with a just hierarchy of values and a view to the common good, is to be commended.

# 4 From Political Catholicism to Christian Democracy

## The Development of Christian Parties in Modern Germany

WINFRIED BECKER

Traditional societies are frequently characterized by their religious foundations. By comparison, modern societies like those common to the western European welfare states typically display a high degree of secularization, as is evident to anyone who looks at society through the prism of the mass media and the entertainment industry. If it were not for a massive tendency toward secularization in Germany, particularly in the East, it would be impossible to explain the most serious defeat of the Union parties since 1949 during the federal elections of September 27, 1998. Issues pertaining to cultural politics, which had been the traditional domain of the Christian Democratic Union (CDU) and the Christian Social Union (CSU) since the late 1940s, hardly played a role during the election campaign, despite the fact that the erosion of traditional values, the accompanying confusion, and a growing need for new directions deserved inclusion in the political discourse of the parties. This peculiar restraint was even fostered by the actions of the churches themselves. Instead of contributing a spiritual dimension to the debate, they emphasized private social demands in discussions about the reform of a social welfare state that was close to exceeding the government's financial capabilities.

Apparently, most voters in 1998 accepted the fact that the position previously held by the Catholic Church had vanished from the political party spectrum. Indeed, there were signs that the Church had distanced itself from Christian Democracy, maybe even out of a desire to develop a higher profile. Remarkably, the most recent publications chronicling the history of the Union parties and the political Catholicism that was their most significant antecedent reject this presumably irreversible tendency toward secularization. Whereas the rare earlier treatments of Christian party formation — apart from the memoirs of individuals who had actively participated in the work of the parties[1] — frequently were controversial, things have changed.[2] In 1980 the French historian Jean-Marie Mayeur incorporated into his history of the European Christian Democratic parties a study of their roots dating back to the Restoration and the days of the Great Revolution.[3] Margaret Lavinia Anderson purposely juxtaposed her Windthorst biography (first published in 1981) to the dominant, national-liberal tradition of German nineteenth-century historiography, especially studies dealing with the history of imperial Germany. Although political Catholicism represented almost one-third of the German people, the national-liberal tradition neglected it when dealing with the government and its only viable alternative, social democracy.[4] Catholicism was portrayed as lacking the ability to grow; in fact, it was lumped together with a feudal or at best backward middle-class ideology.[5] The American historian Noel Cary traced the development of an "alternative Germany" more precisely. He pointed out a path that wove through periods of continuity as well as interruption — from Windthorst, who opposed Bismarck during the Wilhelmine era, to Adenauer, the framer of the Federal Republic.[6] By establishing a connection between the Christian-liberal beginnings in the days of the failed empire and the democratic political structure of the successful Federal Republic, he also undermined the thesis of a German "separate path," a *Sonderweg*.

Cary's purpose was to hint at a real development in German history that came into its own only after 1945. On the other hand, the theory of the *Sonderweg* viewed the National Socialist dictatorship as the final stage in an authoritarian and illiberal development that had taken root much earlier, suggesting a contradiction between the "separate path" of German development and the normal path toward democracy followed by other Western societies. Indeed, many historians regarded the Third Reich as the disastrous final stage of an aberrant development in Germany that was preprogrammed in many ways. But history had not come to a standstill in the face of the horrors of Auschwitz. The process of overcoming this infernal heritage had to be approached using various angles and starting points. This process reached a crucial stage when the National Socialists were lying in wait, artfully weighing their tactics with surprising finesse and consistency while attacking not just a religious group but religion itself. The founding of the Christian Democratic Union and the Christian Social Union parties following the defeat of Hitler has subsequently been seen by some historians as an antithesis to the antireligious activities of the National Socialists in particular, as well as of other totalitarian movements of the twentieth century.[7] These historians demonstrated that influential members from the founding circles of the Union parties derived from their experiences under National Socialism the message and the mission to henceforth pursue a political agenda that was mindful of its commitment to prepolitical, religious, and Christian values. It comes as no surprise, then, that the dignity of the human being was foremost on their mind. Even the unwavering, unqualified rejection of Communism by the CDU and the CSU was by no means a product of the Cold War; rather, it was firmly anchored in the programmatic origins at the time the parties were founded.

However, it must be stated clearly in this introduction that the two Union parties did not grow organically out of German Catholicism. They originated twelve years after the demise of political Catholicism in 1933. They differed from it not only in their programmatic platforms but also in their organizational structures and in the social background of their members and voters. Nevertheless, both groups had something important in common: their discussions (specific to their different historical contexts) about the secular concepts present in the political, social, and cultural formation of human existence.

I

The beginnings of German Catholicism date back to the Vormärz, that is, to the years 1815–48. German history has been maligned for not having experienced a great revolution comparable to the one in France; but this criticism calls for one significant qualification: the revolution from above that abolished the old empire in 1803–6 and expropriated the small principalities, the nobility, and, above all, the Catholic Church. The property of four archbishoprics, nineteen bishoprics, approximately eighty abbeys, and an even greater number of monasteries and convents came into the hands of the strengthened secular princes. The age of absolutism had prepared the way in decisive fashion for this far-reaching secularization that was highly important for political and economic as well as cultural and denominational development. As early as the seventeenth and eighteenth centuries, the German princes had restricted the freedom not only of the Church but also of intermediary authorities, such as self-governing institutions and corporations that still derived their authority from their medieval roots.[8] When compared to the Church of England and the French state church, however, the state church system advocated by the secular governments in Germany was still counterbalanced by the bishoprics dating from the former empire. The great wave of secularization did away with their independence, resulting in the disappearance of territories owned by clergy. The Church ended up with neither power nor property and was hardly able to resist secular demands for power and authority. The state expanded its domain, interfered recklessly in spiritual affairs, and even regulated in minute ways all sorts of pastoral affairs. Furthermore, these actions were frequently initiated by Protestant sovereigns, affecting in particular those Catholics who had lost their Catholic sovereign or landowner as a result of secularization and who had become subjects of a non-Catholic authority after 1803.

This unsatisfactory situation inspired several individual representatives in some of the regional diets to speak on behalf of ecclesiastical or Catholic interests. For instance, demands made in Bavaria, Baden, Württemberg, and Hesse-Darmstadt sought to restrict governmental authority over the Church, to acquire the freedom to teach and practice religion, and to permit religious congregations and orders to govern themselves in matters regarding the Church and those ecclesiastical estates that survived the revolutionary era.[9]

These complaints, which were voiced by only a few representatives, failed initially because of the unfavorable constitutional conditions. Still, they did not fall entirely on deaf ears. In 1837 the conflict between the state and the church came to a head over the issue of mixed marriages. When the archbishop of Cologne, Clemens August von Droste-Vischering, was arrested by the Prussian authorities, without a court order, for having insisted on the pope's authority over mixed marriages, people became extremely angry.[10] Joseph Görres, a professor of history and literature at the University of Munich, defended the archbishop's almost hopeless fight against the state church system in a widely read treatise entitled *Athanasius*, published in 1838. Görres's treatise generated a substantial public response.

Also, 1838 marked the appearance of arguably the most important Catholic periodical of the nineteenth century, the *Historisch-politische Blätter für das katholische Deutschland* (Historical and Political Papers for Catholic Germany). It originated from the circle of Görres supporters in Munich; subsequently, it developed into an ambitious publication that dealt seriously with politics and history, literature and art history, geography, theology, church- and state-related matters, and international law. By 1839 its circulation had grown to 1,900,[11] but it was merely the fruit of a Catholicism that had gradually become aware of itself—a Catholicism, at first scattered and fragmented, that gained strength through various publications and in private circles. The Görres circle in Munich was most influential during the Vormärz. It united writers such as Guido Görres and faithful Catholic lawyers such as Karl Ernst Jarcke and Georg Phillips, who were joined by Church historians of the caliber of Ignaz Döllinger; it also sought to establish connections with prominent French Catholics. Other groups that emerged during the same period include the circle of the "Confederates" in Bavaria, centered around Bishop Gregor Zirkel of Würzburg, the Hofbauer circle in Vienna, the Munster circle around Princess Amalie of Gallitzin, and the Mainz circle of ultramontane theologians who had gathered around the Alsatian Leopold Bruno Liebermann. In 1821 this latter group, based in the seminary at Mainz, created a publication of its own, *Der Katholik* (The Catholic), for the purpose of defending the rights of the Church.[12]

By going beyond demands dealing strictly with matters concerning the legal status of the Church, this separately emerging Catholic politics represented a starker contrast to the liberal spirit of the times. On the basis of his Romantic and interdenominational thought, the conservative Adam Müller discovered within Christianity that very force that had been instrumental in the formation of European history. He contrasted the variously fossilized and bureaucratic, institutional, and police states to an insistence on the power of a genuine community that dismissed pure self-interest and was aware of its obligation to moral laws and rights that preceded the existence of the state.[13] Müller as well as Franz von Baader provided the foundation for a Catholicism based on social issues, a foundation that enabled Catholics to criticize the Manchester methods of a purely economically oriented liberalism when the negative consequences of industrialization became apparent. With several other authors they searched for solutions—derived from the permanent or rediscovered values of Christianity—to the cultural, social, political, and legal problems of the state and of society. At the same time, a seemingly dual strategy became recognizable. On the one hand, Catholic writers and parliamentary representatives demanded for themselves those very liberties that had accompanied the revolutionary achievements. On the other hand, mindful of the shock waves that the revolutionary age had inflicted on Europe, they recalled the transtemporal, healing values of Christianity, such as the principle of fair and equal justice and respect for moral principles in the political arena.

Initially, the March movement during the revolutionary year of 1848 also liberated Catholics from the fetters of state manipulation. Pius Associations (Pius-Vereine), named after the newly elected pope, Pius IX (Mastai-Ferreti), who inspired great hope, emerged in many places. In Bavaria the Association for Constitutional Monarchy and Religious Freedom (Verein für konstitutionelle Monarchie und religiöse Freiheit) was founded. In this preparliamentary environment, four additional important benefits of the newly obtained right to free assembly manifested themselves. First, election committees met demanding free speech, and freedom of the press, and freedom of assembly and association, as well as a free municipal constitution in addition to freedom of religion.[14] Second, many members of congregations heeded the instructions of their pastors and signed petitions addressed to the German national assembly; this movement came close to being viewed as a people's movement. Third, in Mainz in 1848, the general assembly of the Catholic associations of Germany was formed. This gave birth to a tradition that still endures, namely, the annual gathering of the national Catholic convention. Fourth, taking advantage of the new freedom of movement, the first conference of German bishops met in 1848. There they discussed, as a group, those great issues of the day that related to the Church and went public with a powerful announcement. Their leader, Cologne's archbishop Johannes von Geissel, also recognized that the jointly presented demand for freedom of the Church also benefited the state. He presumed that a relaxation of the rules against the Church's teaching of religious values would equally benefit civil education.

The Catholic representatives at the assembly at St. Paul's Church in Frankfurt addressed this complex of issues more comprehensively. Approximately forty parliamentarians from various German states joined forces when the issue of the relationship between church and state was discussed. Many authoritative histories dealing with the first German national assembly treat the Catholic caucus as marginal; they consider it insignificant when compared to other parliamentary groups. By so doing, however, they imply that the representatives' positions vis-à-vis the nature of the state (republican, monarchical, or constitutional), the size of the new territory, or the abolition of hunting privileges by the nobility should weigh more heavily than the relationship between church and state.

The Catholic caucus developed a position of its own during the parliamentary debate by opposing two tendencies in particular. A few advocates of the old state church system favored continued government control over the churches by means of administrative orders and special church legislation. The Catholic speakers opposed them by demanding independence for the churches and the right to the free practice of religion as a basic right granted by the state. Naturally, this was much more suitable to the Catholics, whose ecclesiastic constitution was essentially independent, than to the Protestants, who were intimately tied to the German principalities. Radical liberals and democrats, however, demanded that the new liberal and democratic principles be applied also to the Catholic Church. This would have amounted to dissolution of the church hierarchy and the creation of a national church within which members would have been obliged to exercise their rights and duties in the fashion ordered by the new state. Thus these national democrats and liberals of the Left proceeded on the assumption that, for example, the faithful should elect their own pastors, just as they elected their mayors, or should determine the range and the contents of their faith in accordance with national needs. They did not consider churches supranatural institutions but religious communities or associations that needed to be structured in accordance with one's subjective discretion. The radicals also wanted to deprive religious orders, monasteries, and convents of the privileges of associations because of their nondemocratic internal structure and their "superstition."[15]

These debates brought into relief two significantly different concepts of the state. Because of their enthusiasm for national unity, many liberals and democrats were opposed to the existence of any sphere that fell outside the control of the state. The members of the Catholic caucus, who also had the support of a few Protestants, drew a distinction between state and society. They wanted to situate social groupings, churches, the family, corporations, and even municipal communities in a pregovernmental sphere wherein they would be independent (and also enjoy greater possibilities for exerting political influence). In the final analysis, they did not succeed in anchoring the independence of the churches in the various articles dealing with basic rights in the Constitution of 1848. The churches were equated with religious communities; however, they were granted the privilege of independent administration of their affairs and subjected only to the general laws of the state. Furthermore, the freedom to practice one's religion both privately and publicly was guaranteed. Although the Frankfurt Constitution (Reichsverfassung) was not enacted and failed together with the revolution, the articles dealing with religion proved effective. They were essentially incorporated into the Weimar Constitution of 1919 and, later, into the Basic Law of the Federal Republic of Germany of 1949.

The revolution of 1848 remained merely an episode in German history, albeit an important one. The same applies to the history of German political Catholicism; in 1848 the first outlines were sketched out for its later organization. The Catholic movement (which was supported by a few Protestants) contributed to the development of the idea of the state and of basic rights. Even though the ideas of the Catholic movement were at odds with those held by liberals and the Catholic movement did not coalesce with the civil freedom movement, it nevertheless broadened the understanding of civil freedom by combining it with the idea of religious freedom. It thus became part of a tendency that prevailed in the history of the Roman Church throughout the nineteenth century.

Since the time of Napoleon's rule over Italy—itself an outcome of the French Revolution—the secular power of the papacy had been fragile. This, however, helped to solidify the pope's spiritual power over the faithful; the curtailment of his temporal power generated renewed loyalty among his flock. In the long run, the papacy was able to mobilize laypeople who were loyal to the Church; in doing so, it relied on movements existing among the people, and hence it participated in the democratic tendencies of the time. The papacy's renewed focus on its spiritual mission and on the universalism of the promulgation of the Christian message was echoed, in a way, by the attempts of members of the Catholic Church to gain emancipation.[16] It also counterbalanced the century's nationalism embraced by many liberals with a fervor that bordered on ersatz religion. While it is legitimate to speak of partially democratic phenomena within Catholicism, one must not overlook the fact that the Curia spoke out against the democratic movement (as, for instance, in the *Syllabus errorum* of 1864). The Church attempted to rebuff those liberal ideas that frequently were indiscriminate and anticlerical. The many liberals who accused the Church of being undemocratic, outdated, and antiliberal failed to consider that spiritual hierarchy is unrelated to the worldly, political realm.

During the transitional period between 1848 and 1871, Catholicism succeeded in becoming more defined, although its outlines remained in flux and it remained dependent on the general conditions of the time. The reactionary period that followed the revolution brought with it the tentative, hesitant beginnings of a party system. Some liberals welcomed unconditionally Bismarck's national politics from 1864 and 1866 on. The left-wing liberals formed the German Progressive Party (Deutsche Fortschrittspartei) in 1861. The conservative party that had appeared in Prussia split up as soon as it was faced with Bismarck's unification policy. The labor movement, during the 1860s, remained initially under the influence of Ferdinand Lassalle and absorbed only gradually the ideas of Karl Marx and Friedrich Engels. The Catholic parliamentary group, whose presence in the Second Chamber of the Prussian parliament dated back to 1852, went beyond defending the interests of the Catholic Church and advocated a constitutional separation of powers within the state. It shrank into oblivion as a result of the polarization between the liberals and Bismarck during the Prussian constitutional conflict of 1862–66.

The new beginnings of Catholic party politics did not stem from parliamentary groups but from movements within the population that emerged largely from cultural and political mobilization. The defensive strategy against the continuing state church system, the fight against attempts to streamline and secularize education, and thus the fight against liberalism gained support among all levels of the population not only for the casino movement and the Catholic People's Party in Baden (since 1864)[17] but also for the Patriotic Party (Patriotenpartei) in Bavaria.

In spite of the rules that restricted the right to assembly in Prussia and other states, the Catholic associations experienced a temporary rejuvenation in the 1850s and 1860s. Thus the nonpolitical Kolping societies, established in 1846, were joined by Catholic workers' associations. As early as 1848, Wilhelm Emmanuel von Ketteler (who became bishop of Mainz in 1850) had called for improvement in the conditions of the impoverished and, above all, of the rising class of industrial workers. In 1864 in his treatise "Die Arbeiterfrage und das Christentum" (The Workers' Question and Christianity), Ketteler specifically criticized the liberals for their social neglect. He took the decisive step of moving beyond the issue of Christian care for the poor to address the question of the government's social politics. His concrete demands—such as the protection of workers, adequate wages, the right to form coalitions and associations—as much as the empirical facts on which he based them were pathbreaking. The government, he insisted, had the duty to grant workers the original and prepolitical right to human existence and personal development. Ketteler's theory that the state is obligated to observe rights that preceded it contributed to the subsequent development of Catholic political and social theory in Germany (the earliest lineaments of which go as far back as the Vormärz and the debates of 1848).

The conferences at Soest (Westphalia) between 1864 and 1866 lead us directly to the preliminary preparations for the formation of the Prussian and German Center parliamentary groups in 1870–71. There, members of Hermann von Mallinckrodt's circle gathered to discuss issues dealing not only with church politics but also with domestic and foreign Prussian politics. What united them there as well as in Baden and Bavaria was their shocked response to Bismarck's anti-Austrian policy and the failure to incorporate Austria into a united Germany following the battle at Königgrätz. Despite their disappointment, prominent leaders like Ketteler urged people to be realistic. Ketteler was hoping that the generous articles on religion contained in the Prussian Constitution of 1850 would be adopted throughout Germany, but he ended up bitterly disappointed.

The program of the forty-eight representatives of the Center parliamentary group in the Prussian parliament who met in December 1870 was articulated in fairly general terms. Still, it was based on a new, independent understanding of politics that combined older demands with the experience of the most recent changes.[18] The program insisted primarily on constitutionality and particularly on the freedom and independence of the Church. The earlier orientation toward a greater Germany had transformed itself into the programmatic demand for federalism. This was also the condition under which the southern Germans were willing to join the new "constitutional party." A legacy of the conferences at Soest was the commitment to parity; it was clearly voiced time and again during the later debates of the cultural struggle, or Kulturkampf. Originally, this parity was to extend not only to religious denominations but also to German ethnic groups, individual states, and social classes. Socially, from its very beginning, the Center Party advocated a program that strove for the welfare of all classes and for social harmony within the state.

The Center Party came into existence as a party with a political agenda, even though it was supported by Catholics faithful to the Church. By no means, however, could it have been confused with the Catholic Church. The party and the large group surrounding it were constituted within the framework of social interaction, that is, of Catholics coming to grips with political and social aspirations. The party had its origins in the specific circumstances of the times and manifested a definitely national configuration. To borrow from Edgar Alexander[19] and Michael P. Fogarty,[20] these Christian parties, their associations, and their pool of voters may be referred to as "manifestations of civilization," as political and social "phenomena of civilization" that are typical of a specific country and time. The political and social Catholicism of Germany that generated a significant parliamentary group in 1870 in the form of the German Center Party can be subjected to historical, sociological, or politological analysis. It would be misleading, however, if (quoting Thomas Nipperdey) one were to explain this Catholicism primarily or exclusively in terms of a "political theology" from which are derived those controversial positions referred to as "Catholic politics," that is, positions with a conservative, democratic, liberal, or social orientation.[21] This reduction to "theological" determinants misreads not only the social foundations on which political and social Catholicism rests but also its political will and its ability to form coalitions on the basis of the constitutional intentions evinced by Christian parties; it also portrays political and social Catholicism as distant from purely political and social groups. Anyone who insists that only the latter are called to political activism fails to understand that groups that are committed solely to secular concerns may also be motivated by idealistic agendas, premises, and programs.

Admittedly, the Center Party, whose initial intention was not to oppose the new empire but to be active within it, saw no other option but to immediately resort to the defense of specifically Catholic interests (pastoral freedom, the training of priests, etc.) and also of the bishops, clergymen, and religious orders that were under attack. For Bismarck intentionally launched the Kulturkampf to fight against a Catholic party that he feared might restrict his power. Bismarck was assisted by many national liberals who were convinced that by defeating France, the new Hohenzollern empire had also defeated Roman Catholicism and was called on to complete the Reformation in Germany by establishing a national church. Cultural Protestantism attacked the Catholic Church because of the latter's belief in the afterlife and a "medieval" hierarchy that culminated in the papacy; it dismissed the Catholic Church as a power that had outlived itself, that had to be overcome in order to promote general progress for the sake of the state—that is, the growth of a national culture and education.

The Center Party resorted to political means in its defense against this kind of religious warfare. Today, the campaign waged by the national liberals in favor of a new national and secular culture strikes us as almost an ersatz religion. Ludwig Windthorst, the leader of the Center Party, although never formally elected party chairman, attempted to beat the liberals at their own game. His reasons were not just tactical; he also had programmatic intentions. He insisted on a foundation of values as expressed by Christian natural law that guaranteed people and groups within the state equal civil rights and personal dignity. He defended the principles of tolerance and the constitutional state. In doing so, he simultaneously defended pluralism against the "omnipotent" state that was also interfering with church rights. Indeed, it had also been the liberals' original agenda to fight against this type of state. Faced by unjust persecution and restriction of freedom, there remained only one alternative—to appeal to the public conscience. Parliament together with the press provided a forum for this purpose. Between 1871 and 1890 the number of Center newspapers increased from 126 to 221. Circulation almost doubled—from 322,000 to 626,000.[22] Bismarck certainly failed in his efforts to make the new party comply or to force its disappearance; rather, Windthorst, a parliamentary adversary of the highest caliber, rose up against him in the Reichstag. When the time came to dismantle the Kulturkampf legislation, the small opposition in the Reichstag could claim that by adopting a constitutional stance it had advanced democracy in Germany and contributed to an alternative political culture.

Throughout the duration of the empire, the Center Party remained committed to the Christian image of man and the values shared by people of faith.[23] It was also conservative, for its mission was animated by the conviction that it was called on to represent those groups among the population who recognized a connection between the problems facing state and society and the teachings of Christianity. Those views had been widely, indeed almost universally accepted before the revolution; now, however, the pool of potential adherents was smaller because other parties offered a secular slate of values and because of the antipathy between the denominations in Germany. Recruitment was confined to the Catholic segment of the population; and, despite some tension, ties to the Catholic Church remained strong because of the Kulturkampf and the retention of basic Christian principles.

Following the prohibition and the persecution of the Association of German Catholics (Verein deutscher Katholiken; also referred to as the Mainzer Verein, Mainz Association), led by Prince Karl zu Löwenstein from 1872 to 1876, the People's Association for a Catholic Germany (Volksverein für das katholische Deutschland) was founded in 1890. Its sociopolitical and apologetic departments made it their special task to educate and organize the Catholic voting public.

The Center's hallmark was its refusal to step into a modern age characterized by a belligerent, anticlerical secularism that proclaimed the abandonment of all religious affiliation as a mark of modernity. This did not prevent the party from becoming involved aggressively and cooperatively in many areas of political and social life. It goes without saying that the Center Party emphasized cultural politics regardless of whether it concerned itself with the preservation of denominational schools or with equal employment opportunities for Catholic applicants in the administrative and justice system or at renowned universities in the Wilhelmine empire. Moving beyond the struggle for religious tolerance, the members of the Center Party proceeded to demand the kind of parity mandatory in a constitutional state.[24] To be sure, this was also an opportunity for self-criticism. Thus, for example, in an effort to reduce the self-imposed educational deficiencies among the Catholic segments of the population, Georg von Hertling, a philosophy professor at the University of Munich, called on Catholics to demand more of themselves in terms of education.

The Center Party took on a highly significant domestic political issue when, on March 19, 1877, its longtime president in Westphalia, Ferdinand Heribert von Galen, introduced for the first time in the Reichstag a bill that demanded comprehensive protection for industrial workers. The National Liberal Party and others that were committed to the supposedly objective progress of national history, as well as other "architects of history" (*Geschichtsbaumeister*), responded to such attempts at reform either with hesitation or by simply rejecting them. The bill was derived directly from the sociopolitical program that Ketteler, himself a representative in the first Reichstag, had first laid out in his treatise on the Catholics in the German Empire (*Die Katholiken im Deutschen Reich*, published in 1873).[25] It is true that the Center Party was initially unable to realize its ideas concerning the protection of workers, but it collaborated on legislation dealing with health and accident and old-age insurance, passed in 1883, 1884, and 1889. These legislative measures are widely regarded as models for social policies in other countries. Although Bismarck's social policies are rightfully interpreted as efforts to contain the increasing strength of the Social Democratic Party, one must still beware of underestimating the constructive contributions made by the various political groups in the Reichstag. The Center Party inserted its own initiatives into social policy and subsequently also into tax, finance, and customs legislation. Whenever pragmatic political and economic issues were on the table, the Center Party engaged in so-called factual politics (*Sachpolitik*); that is, it sought the right solution by weighing all facts fairly. But it also paid attention to the interests of farmers and the middle class, who were heavily represented in the party.

Regarding the Center Party's attitude toward the German nation and its foreign policy, there is no doubt that, in conjunction with its efforts to integrate Catholics into the empire, it also advocated the projection of imperial power outside of Germany. During World War I, influential representatives of political Catholicism spoke in favor of Germany's future global role and power matching other world powers such as England. Nevertheless, this goal was far less pronounced in the Center Party as compared to the ambitious ideas of the Pan-Germans (Alldeutschen) and other, less radical nationalistic groups. By this time, however, other voices such as that of the Jesuit Victor Cathrein,[26] who cowrote the political science lexicon (*Staatslexikon*) published by the Görres Society (Görres Gesellschaft), and that of Ludwig Windthorst had already fallen silent. Influenced by papal universalism and neo-scholasticism, they had advocated a political agenda that was determined by international law and aimed at international understanding. On the other hand, Matthias Erzberger, the influential Center representative who was not entirely above opportunism, advocated the peaceful coexistence among nations and the formation of a league of nations in 1917–18.[27] His attempt to redefine German foreign politics was unsuccessful, because by then Germany's defeat had become inevitable. Germany had lost its credibility with all the relevant powers; indeed, it had missed taking a decisive turn toward a politics of peace when it was still sufficiently strong.

The Center Party retained its de facto character as a denominational party until its demise in 1933. There were plenty of individual attempts aimed at expanding the party denominationally, politically, and socially. In its early years, at the time of the cultural struggle, the Center provided faithful Christians with an opportunity to align themselves against "pagan, materialistic ideas"; at the same time, it kept its doors open to any denomination willing to join the party. The party adhered to this strategy until the publication of the famous "Tower" articles in 1906.[28] In the articles Julius Bachem urged the party to nominate Protestant candidates in those precincts where it was barely able to hold its own. Moreover, various groups in the Center Party maintained that contentious policy issues could not be resolved along denominational lines. The party claimed that as a matter of principle it aimed to steer a middle course and that it would be guided in making decisions by the goal of achieving justice for the largest segment of the population. One can safely say that the Center Party not only adhered to its policy of rejecting class discrimination but also truly practiced it. Yet its readiness and ability to become a party of the people succeeded — with some qualifications — only among Catholics. The Center Party was open to all social classes, but it was never able to transcend its denominational limitations.

Practically, it was the Christian labor unions that achieved a (pluralistic) nondenominational merger of Catholic and Protestant workers. In 1899, at Mainz, they established an association that was to be headquartered in Cologne. Its energetic and distinguished general secretary, Adam Stegerwald, expanded it into the Christian-National Worker's Union by admitting organizations such as the white-collar workers' German National Employees Association (Deutschnationaler Handlungsgehilfenverband). Supported by the Cologne chapter (Kölner Richtung) of the Center Party, Stegerwald

succeeded in positioning the Christian unions against the denominationally closed Catholic Workers' associations, and in 1906, after an extended
struggle, he was able to obtain official recognition by the German bishops
and the Roman Curia. In his eyes, this move was dictated by political and
social necessity; he presumed that only his organization was able to fend off
the anticlerical, socialist-leaning free trade unions and their tendency to
resort to radical measures.

After the Center Party's National Committee (Reichsausschuß) had
invited the hitherto independent Christian-National workers to join the
party in 1914, Stegerwald tried to use the Christian trade unions as a lever
for reform. Thus he made himself the spokesman for the emancipation of
those broad segments of the population that had been mobilized during the
war. In talks and memoranda, as well as in meetings with Martin and Peter
Spahn, Wilhelm Marx, Franz Hitze, and other leading figures, Stegerwald
demanded that the Center Party become a real party of the people by integrating the masses of workers. Faced with the impending introduction of
universal suffrage in Prussia, he wanted to provide the Center Party with the
means to compete against the strongest existing party, the Social Democratic Party. He stated that to reflect the composition of the German people,
the Center Party had to reevaluate the role of conservative and farm groups
within it; in other words, he called for an internal compromise among workers, farmers, and the middle class. Moreover, the religious, Catholic character of the Center Party had to be reclaimed and its political (*staatspolitische*)
goals had to be vigorously reaffirmed. Finally, Stegerwald wanted to provide
a popular base for the reign of William II whom he envisaged as a kind of
people's emperor. In November 1918 Stegerwald planned to replace the
Center Party with a new Christian party based on the Christian trade unions,
composed of their 540,000 members and the more broad-based, one-million-
strong German Democratic federation of trade unions that he had recently
reconstituted. The core was to be made up of the workers, while conservative
and civil-democratic forces were expected to join them. The short-lived plan
foundered because the anticlerical cultural policies of Adolf Hoffmann's
Unabhängige Sozialdemokratische Partei Deutschlands (USPD) in Prussia
remobilized the old Center Party.[29] As soon as Germany became a republic,
Stegerwald joined forces with Heinrich Brüning in the Essen program of
1920 and returned to the idea of further developing the Center Party. Now
he wanted to change the Center Party into a large, national, Christian, demo-

cratic and social people's party so as to create a force within the Weimar Republic that would be capable of carrying a majority. His ideas overlapped with those of Konrad Adenauer, who called on the German Catholics—in what was, at the time, a still more general appeal—to set aside denominational distinctions and cooperate politically with similarly minded Lutheran Christians.


## II

Stegerwald's intentions could not be realized because of the crisis conditions prevailing in the Weimar Republic and because of the entrenched practices of the existing party system. Instead of becoming an inter-denominational majority party, the Center Party was merely allotted the thankless historical role of serving, from its position at the center of the political spectrum, as the honest broker for the unloved Weimar Republic.[30] After the state church system had disappeared following the demise of the Hohenzollern empire, the social domination by Protestantism was diminished. With religious freedom constitutionally guaranteed, this should have been the time for a political mandate for and a test of the Center Party. Time and again, its leading personalities, Wilhelm Marx, Heinrich Brüning, Joseph Wirth, Heinrich Brauns, Josef Joos, Adam Stegerwald, and others, had felt obliged to assume responsibility for the government even though they were facing such thankless tasks as meeting the terms of the Treaty of Versailles and overcoming inflation. Their first achievement at the end of World War I was to participate in the political life of the republic. They directed their attention primarily to questions of social order and social goals rather than to the debates on the relative merits of a monarchic or republican form of government. At the same time, they rejected revolution because it would endanger civil order. They were prepared to compromise and to continue cooperating with the other parties—as they had done in the nonpartisan committee during World War I. In other words, they wanted to find ways, whenever possible, to form coalitions with the liberal parties and the social democrats.

These frequently attempted—and failed—coalitions by the Center cannot be adequately judged by the standards of the Anglo-American two-party system. Rather, they must be understood against the background of the special conditions of the German situation and of the German past. In 1914 the parties had agreed to a truce. During World War I, the exigencies of the war led to remarkable attempts at reconciliation between disparate institutions and political groups. This atmosphere of crisis helps to explain why between 1918 and 1933 the Center Party pursued a politics of community. The continuing crisis in the interwar period and constant international tensions left the members of the Center scant opportunities to shake off their fixation on the nation. Party alliances in the Weimar Republic resulted in exactly the opposite of what they were supposed to forestall: instability. The problem was exacerbated by the formation of political wings within the parties. Even within the Center Party, despite attempts at reform in 1906 and 1914, tensions increased until, finally, a neutral clergyman, Prelate Ludwig Kaas of Trier, was elected its last president.[31]

The tension that threatened the republic affected the members of the Center Party, prompting different, partially contradictory plans for rescuing the Weimar state and leading to internal splits. Franz von Papen, even more strenuously than Heinrich Brüning, promoted changes in the constitution that were authoritarian and betrayed dictatorial tendencies; but he did this only after he had become a "renegade" and had terminated his membership in the party. The Center Party's coalition talks with the National Socialist German Workers' Party (NSDAP) were also frequently debated among the members of the parliamentary group. The talks were given serious consideration in an effort to force the "national opposition" to live up to its political duty and serve the state. Also, in this way the NSDAP's ability to form a government could be put to the test. In any case, the negotiations proved unsuccessful. The Center Party adhered to the constitutional state.[32] In exchange for his agreement to the Enabling Act of March 24, 1933, Kaas still demanded minimal constitutional guarantees such as the continuation of a Reichstag committee. Hitler dismissed those demands without blinking an eye.

In a way the Center Party benefited from the Weimar democracy; it managed to place many more of its members in government positions than was the case during the empire. In 1933, following Hitler's rise to power, the Center Party felt compelled to be considerate of its members who were civil servants and government employees. Consequently, it did not think it was appropriate to pursue a confrontational course against the Enabling Act or to challenge the new powers. Here, political interests and events worked together to determine the position of the Center Party. The policy of accommodation was in line with that of the Roman Curia, which negotiated a covenant in 1933 designed to defend the elements essential to church politics, that is, pastoral freedom, the training of priests, and religious instruction. It is highly possible that were it not for the signing of the Concordat, the Center Party would have been banned like all the other German parties. Still, two serious problems accompanied the Concordat signed by Pope Pius XI immediately after the takeover by the National Socialists. First, Hitler's position abroad gained momentum and allowed him greater power to maneuver, pushing to and beyond the limits of the treaty. Second, the treaty did not address the concerns of the German Center that was struggling for political survival during the early stages of the dictatorship. As a result, German Catholicism, with its constitutional commitment throughout the individual regions of Germany, did not get the credit it deserved for fighting against the violent methods and the ideology of rising National Socialism.[33] Its spokespersons and its press specifically attacked the racial theories of National Socialism by insisting on the Christian commitment to the equality of all people before God and eternal salvation for all people.

Immediately after the takeover, the National Socialists started to place the families of the hated "system parties" of Weimar under surveillance and persecute them. Because of its totalitarian nature and because it wanted to gain control over the entire human being, National Socialism considered even the practice of religion—participation in worship services, religious processions, religious instruction—a relapse into "political Catholicism" that was supposedly competing with it. The National Socialists took note of such nonconformist activities, punished them, and imposed sanctions on them.[34] This behavior constitutes a form of "resistance," a term that cannot be solely reserved for the men of July 20, 1944, although they are most deserving of it. Rather, resistance must also include the less spectacular deeds by nonconformists that were nevertheless considered crimes against National Socialism. Examples of these are intellectual exchanges between similarly minded people, discussions about alternatives to Hitler's dictatorship, hidden or open protests, and, finally, (rare) participation in real attempts to get rid of the dictator. All manifestations of nonconformist thinking attest to the preparedness to resist; they found expression in nuanced forms of personal conduct.[35]

The real resistance put up by the churches that quietly endured persecution, even martyrdom, for personal and ethical reasons naturally went beyond the realm of politics.[36] What I am interested in, however, is that gray area where most people lead their lives. There, many people experienced, not always consciously, hidden or overt conflicts with a regime that classified even small transgressions against its universally enforced ideology as punishable offenses. The ways in which laypeople who were faithful to their denominations engaged in resistance depended on their previous experiences, their social habits, their family backgrounds, and their inherited political and spiritual orientations. Those who had been taught to speak out against the government's excessive pursuit of power recognized more quickly that National Socialism went far beyond secular political ideologies; they tried to escape the lethal clutches of the *Volksgemeinschaft* and its new organizations. Thus Jakob Kaiser revived his old connections with groups in the Christian trade unions; he sought contact not only with Max Habermann but also with Wilhelm Leuschner, a member of the now banned free unions suspected by the Gestapo of antigovernment activities. The milieus existing before 1933 were not immediately eliminated by National Socialist rule. They provided their members and participants with a degree of immunity against the totalitarian regime of the National Socialists.

In addition to these developments, many reasonable people began to look critically at National Socialism. These initial doubts are difficult to verify empirically because of the dangers inherent in the display of antigovernment tendencies. But ever more openly, denominational lines were bridged as individuals concentrated on the Christian foundations of politics, despised by the National Socialists, who promoted their ersatz religion based on Germanness and the Germanic traditions of the past. Both Catholics and Protestants became critical of National Socialism; some concerns stemmed from fear, but they were also deeply worried about the survival of the nation and the state. An intellectual, religious, and political distaste for the ideology and practices of the National Socialist dictatorship united opponents from various denominational and political camps (who may have been unaware of one another's existence) against the regime. There were the northern German members of the Professing Church (Bekennende Kirche) Theodor Steltzer and Robert Tillmans, Catholic Rhinelanders, Leo Schwering, Johannes Albers and Karl Zimmermann of the earlier Center Party, Robert Lehr of the former German National People's Party, Walther Schreiber and Ferdinand

Friedensburg of the German Democratic Party, Paul Bausch from Württemberg and Albert Schmidt from Westphalia, both former members of the Christian Social People's Services (Christlich Sozialer Volksdienst), which was also referred to as the "Evangelical Center," Josef Müller and other members of the Bavarian People's Party, the Protestant former ambassador Friedrich von Prittwitz und Gaffron, to only name a few.[37]

All these men drafted memoranda and wrote letters that departed from the line prescribed by the regime and dealt with ideas concerning the rebuilding of Germany after Hitler. Or they exchanged within their intimate circles of friends ideas that were critical of the regime. These people were forced to remain hidden; their quiet opposition did not have external repercussions. There is no doubt that the National Socialist regime did not suffer defeat until the military advances and successes by Allied troops. Yet without this quiet or "intellectual resistance," without the intensive reflections on the events of the time, and without a subsequent willingness to become actively engaged after the collapse, one could not explain why in so many places in Germany, whether in the East or in the West, the North or the South, founding circles of the Union parties sprang to life in May 1945. The founders of the Union parties were united in their conviction that democratic politics that benefited all levels of the population and were based on basic Christian values befitted the needs of the hour.

Uniting the civil- and Christian-minded forces in a new political endeavor, despite their deeply rooted denominational and party differences, was not possible before the cataclysmic end of the National Socialist state's attempt to introduce in Germany a materialistic, biologically based, anti-Semitic, and anticlerical dictatorship. Shortly before his death, Adam Stegerwald, who had contributed decisively to the foundation of the CSU at Würzburg, Bavaria,[38] interpreted these new party and political beginnings as a kind of restitution for the aberrations of the past. Stegerwald, however, hardly celebrated the hour of this triumph. Examining his political conscience, he placed no insignificant amount of blame for the catastrophe on the fateful split within the German nation based on religious differences. It was against the background of these reflections on the dire need to redirect the course of German history that the decision to refer to the aggregate party as a "Union" was justified. Neither a new religious community nor even the introduction of a uniformly denominational entity was ever intended. Rather, the term "Union" identified a political program designed to remove historical entrenchments, to achieve a genuine political community of German people, and to shore up democratic ideals that had been buttressed much too weakly throughout the development of the German state.[39] Moreover, the former members of the Center Party and the Christian Social People's Service wished to join hands with the former members of the conservative or the liberal camp as long as it was possible to agree on a common foundation of values and basic political ideas.

In fact, there is no such thing as an organic process of continuity that leads from political Catholicism to the nondenominational Union. Though interrelated, the two phenomena are separated by the incisive interruption of 1933–45. Both the CDU and the CSU were parties of a new beginning. They acknowledged the failures and the opportunities that had been missed by their most significant predecessors, the Center Party and the Bavarian People's Party. Mindful of the lessons of the past, they set out to form broad-based people's parties and, above all, to avoid the calamity of a democratic ideal that was represented and maintained by merely a minority of the people. They were not prepared to ever again accept too great an alienation among democrats of various camps. By contrast, the Center Party reappeared, albeit mostly as a splinter party, in areas with a strong Catholic tradition (North Rhine–Westphalia, parts of Lower Saxony, and Rhineland-Palatinate). It did not lose prominence in some areas until the mid-1950s.[40] The limited resurgence of the party of political Catholicism illustrated the obstacles that had to be overcome in the effort to unite Catholics and Protestants within the Union. This unity was the decisive step that needed to be taken to supersede the political Catholicism of the German Empire and the Weimar Republic.

A more historical view that takes into account postwar developments is called for to arrive at a calmer assessment than Stegerwald did in the catastrophic year of 1945. This view would trace the roots of the renewal back to earlier layers and see how critics were able to judge the National Socialist revolution against the background of an already existing political culture. After 1945 such an analysis resulted in the selection of new avenues of political coexistence.

An examination of the connections among religion, culture, society, and politics can be at least as rewarding to historians as the study of the history of nations or social developments. This historiographical perspective has the advantage of avoiding an approach based exclusively on secular predicaments. The history of Catholicism and of the origin of the Union parties reveals the need to pay attention to the parallel existence of religious and moral motives within a political culture that still existed in the pre-revolutionary world and hence merits the attention of the historiographer.

In 1945 many people sought solace and strength in religion. After the life-threatening challenges of the past, a cultural awareness informed by Christian values proved sufficiently powerful to radiate out into politics. Internal threats to the Christian parties arose less from continued denominational differences than from a creeping lack of voter participation among Christian, especially Protestant, voters. At the same time, the ranks of Catholics who were tied more closely to the Church provided the Union parties with the most reliable pool of voters for decades.[41] In the early 1960s, however, it was exactly in those circles that a large-scale identity crisis became apparent. Half a century after the catastrophe of 1945, cultural preferences of a hedonistic and materialistic nature coupled with religious disinterest are widespread in Germany. Large groups of people appear to have lost their receptivity to the moral foundations of material culture. This is not the place to decide whether these currents are grounded in fundamental technical, economic, and social changes to which other countries are equally susceptible or whether the basis for this development may be located in the continued secularization of the masses—the seeds of which Konrad Adenauer traced back to the final throes of the empire. There is no way of telling whether these developments will gain momentum. One thing is certain, however: a return to the proven legal and political realities and to the historical foundations of a culture that is characterized by the values of the traditional denominations will provide a better position from which to counteract this trend than the seductiveness of a largely irrational, fluctuating fundamentalism that no longer possesses any institutional ties.[42]

## NOTES

1. Josef Müller, *Bis zur letzten Konsequenz: Ein Leben für Frieden und Freiheit* (München, 1975); Ernst Lemmer, *Manches war doch anders: Erinnerungen eines deutschen Demokraten* (Frankfurt am Main, 1968); Hermann Pünder, *Von Preußen nach Europa: Lebenserinnerungen* (Stuttgart, 1968); Joseph Joos, *So sah ich sie: Menschen*

*und Geschehnisse* (Augsburg, 1958); Paul Bausch, *Lebenserinnerungen und Erkenntnisse eines schwäbischen Abgeordneten* (Korntal, 1976); Johann Baptist Gradl, *Anfang unter dem Sowjetstern: Die CDU 1945–1948 in der sowjetischen Besatzungszone Deutschlands* (Köln, 1981); Anna Hermes, *Und setzet ihr das Leben nicht ein: Andreas Hermes — Leben und Wirken. Nach Briefen, Tagebuchaufzeichnungen und Erinnerungen* (Stuttgart, 1971); partly autobiographical is Leo Schwering, *Vorgeschichte und Entstehung der CDU,* 2d ed. (Köln, 1952).

2. The exceptions are the following publications: Konrad-Adenauer-Stiftung, ed., *Christliche Demokraten der ersten Stunde* (Bonn, 1966); Günter Buchstab and Klaus Gotto, eds., *Die Gründung der Union: Traditionen, Entstehung und Repräsentanten,* 2d ed. (München, 1981); Günther Rüther, ed., *Geschichte der christlich-demokratischen und christlich-sozialen Bewegungen in Deutschland,* 2 vols. (Köln, 1986); Winfried Becker and Rudolf Morsey, eds., *Christliche Demokratie in Europa: Grundlagen und Entwicklungen seit dem 19. Jahrhundert* (Köln, 1988). A more recent discussion is found in Hans Ferdinand Groß, *Hanns Seidel 1901–1961: Eine politische Biographie* (München, 1992).

3. Jean-Marie Mayeur, *Des Partis catholiques à la Démocratie Chrétienne XIXe–XXe siècles* (Paris, 1980).

4. Margaret Lavinia Anderson, *Windthorst: A Political Biography* (Oxford, 1981), 6 f. (The German edition appeared as *Windthorst, Zentrumspolitiker und Gegenspieler Bismarcks* [Düsseldorf 1988]). See also Hans-Georg Aschoff and Heinz Jörg Heinrich, eds., *Ludwig Windthorst: Briefe 1834–1880* (Paderborn, 1995).

5. David Blackbourn, *Class, Religion and Local Politics in Wilhelmine Germany: The Centre Party in Württemberg before 1914* (Mainz, 1980); cf. Winfried Becker, ed., *Die Minderheit als Mitte: Die Deutsche Zentrumspartei in der Innenpolitik des Reiches 1871–1933* (Paderborn, 1986).

6. Noel D. Cary, *The Path to Christian Democracy: German Catholics and the Party System from Windthorst to Adenauer* (Cambridge, Mass., 1996), 1–10.

7. See also the publications listed in note 2, especially the essays in Buchstab and Gotto, *Die Gründung der Union;* Winfried Becker, "Politische Neuordnung aus der Erfahrung des Widerstands. Katholizismus und Union," in Peter Steinbach, ed., *Widerstand: Ein Problem zwischen Theorie und Geschichte* (Köln, 1987), 261–92; Hans-Otto Kleinmann, *Geschichte der CDU 1945–1982* (Stuttgart, 1993), 19–21.

8. Heribert Raab, "Der Untergang der Reichskirche in der großen Säkularisation," in Hubert Jedin, ed., *Handbuch der Kirchengeschichte, vol. 5, Die Kirche im Zeitalter des Absolutismus und der Aufklärung* (Freiburg-Basel-Wien, 1985), 533–54.

9. Ludwig Bergsträsser, *Der politische Katholizismus: Dokumente seiner Entwicklung,* 2 vols. (München, 1921–23); Bruno Lengenfelder, *Die Diözese Eichstätt zwischen Aufklärung und Restauration: Kirche und Staat 1773–1821* (Regensburg, 1990).

10. Markus Hänsel-Hohenhausen, *Clemens August Freiherr Droste zu Vischering: Erzbischof von Köln, 1773–1845* 2 vols. (Egelsbach, 1991).

11. Dieter Albrecht and Bernhard Weber, eds., *Die Mitarbeiter der Historisch-politischen Blätter für das katholische Deutschland 1838–1923: Ein Verzeichnis* (Mainz, 1990), 10; Bernhard Weber, "Die 'Historisch-politischen Blätter für das katholische Deutschland' als Forum für Kirchen- und Konfessionsfragen" (dissertation München, 1983).

12. Heinz Hürten, *Kurze Geschichte des deutschen Katholizismus 1800–1960* (Mainz, 1986), 34–46.

13. Adam's principal work was *Die Elemente der Staatskunst: Öffentliche Vorlesungen in Dresden gehalten. 1808–1809,* ed. Jakob Baxa, vol. 1/1 (Jena, 1922).

14. Cologne Election Committee of April 15, 1848. Rudolf Morsey, ed., *Katholizismus, Verfassungsstaat und Demokratie: Vom Vormärz bis 1933* (Paderborn, 1988), 36–39.

15. Winfried Becker, "1848: Bürgerliche Freiheit und Freiheit der Kirche," in *Die Politische Meinung* 44:350 (1999): 80–91.

16. Karl Buchheim, *Ultramontanismus und Demokratie: Der Weg der deutschen Katholiken im 19. Jahrhundert* (München, 1963), 12–16, 516–20.

17. Franz Dor and Jakob Lindau, *Ein badischer Politiker und Volksmann in seinem Leben und Wirken geschildert* (Freiburg, 1909); Josef Becker, *Liberaler Staat und Kirche in der Ära von Reichsgründung und Kulturkampf: Geschichte und Strukturen ihres Verhältnisses in Baden 1860–1876* (Mainz, 1973).

18. Karl Bachem, *Vorgeschichte, Geschichte und Politik der Deutschen Zentrumspartei,* vol. 3 (Köln, 1927), 128, 136 f.: "Aufruf zu den Reichstagswahlen 11.1.1871."

19. Edgar Alexander, "Church and Society in Germany," in Joseph N. Moody, ed., *Church and Society: Catholic Social and Political Thought and Movements, 1789–1950* (New York, 1953), 435–54.

20. Michael P. Fogarty, *Christliche Demokratie in Westeuropa 1820–1953* (Basel, 1959), 20–24, 172–75, 184–91; Michael P. Fogarty, *Phoenix or Cheshire Cat: Christian Democracy, Past, Present and Future?* Movement for Christian Democracy Occasional Paper No. 4. (Ware, Herts., 1995), 15.

21. "Christliche Parteien," in Thomas Nipperdey, *Nachdenken über die deutsche Geschichte: Essays* (München, 1986), 127–32; Thomas Nipperdey, *Deutsche Geschichte 1866–1918,* vol. 2, *Machtstaat vor der Demokratie* (München, [1992] 1998), 342; cf. Winfried Becker, "Christliche Parteien und Strömungen im 19. und 20. Jahrhundert. Ein Forschungsbericht 1986–1994," *Historisches Jahrbuch* 114:2 (1994): 451–78.

22. Bachem, *Vorgeschichte, Geschichte und Politik,* 155.

23. Georg von Hertling, "Politik und Weltanschauung," *Historisch-politische Blätter* 145 (1910): 12–30.

24. Like the questions dealing with social balance and equity, these ideas hardly illustrated a "vague ideology" or "vague formulas," as Nipperdey put it in

*Deutsche Geschichte*, 2:343, or Wilfried Loth put it in *Katholiken im Kaiserreich: Der politische Katholizismus in der Krise des wilhelminischen Deutschlands* (Düsseldorf, 1984), 19. Cf. Martin Sebaldt, *Katholizismus und Religionsfreiheit: Der Toleranzantrag der Zentrumspartei im Deutschen Reichstag* (Frankfurt am Main, 1994), 115–23.

25. *Entwurf zu einem politischen Programm* (Mainz, 1873); cf. Georg von Hertling, "Bischof Ketteler und die katholische Sozialpolitik in Deutschland," *Historisch-politische Blätter* 121:2 (1897): 897 f.; Christoph Stoll, *Mächtig in Wert und Werk: Bischof Wilhelm Emmanuel von Ketteler* (Mainz, 1997), 83 f.

26. Anton Rauscher, "Viktor Cathrein (1845–1931)," in Jürgen Aretz, Rudolf Morsey, and Anton Rauscher, eds., *Zeitgeschichte in Lebensbildern. Aus dem deutschen Katholizismus des 19. und 20. Jahrhunderts,* vol. 4 (Mainz, 1980), 103–13.

27. Matthias Erzberger, *Der Völkerbund: Der Weg zum Weltfrieden* (Berlin, 1918); cf. Christian Leitzbach and Matthias Erzberger, *Ein kritischer Beobachter des Wilhelminischen Reiches 1895–1914* (Frankfurt am Main, 1998).

28. Julius Bachem, "Wir müssen aus dem Turm heraus," *Historisch-politische Blätter* 137 (1906); 376–386; Julius Bachem, "Nochmals: Wir müssen aus dem Turm heraus," *Historisch-politische Blätter* 137 (1906): 503–513.

29. Cf. Bernhard Foster on Adam Stegerwald (1874–1945) (dissertation in progress, Passau); Ellen Lovell Evans, "Adam Stegerwald and the Role of the Christian Trade Unions in the Weimar Republic," *Catholic Historical Review* 59 (1974): 603ff.; John K. Zeender, "German Catholics and the Concept of an Interconfessional Party, 1900–1922," *Journal of Central European Affairs* 23 (1964): 432ff.

30. Rudolf Morsey, *Die Deutsche Zentrumspartei 1917–1923* (Düsseldorf, 1966); Ellen Lovell Evans, *The German Center Party 1870–1933. A Study in Political Catholicism* (Carbondale, 1981); Karsten Ruppert, *Im Dienst am Staat von Weimar. Das Zentrum als regierende Partei in der Weimarer Demokratie 1923–1930* (Düsseldorf, 1992); Rudolf Morsey and Karsten Ruppert, eds., *Die Protokolle der Reichstagsfraktion der Deutschen Zentrumspartei 1920–1925* (Mainz, 1981); August Hermann Leugers-Scherzberg and Wilfried Loth, eds., *Die Zentrumsfraktion in der verfassungsgebenden Preußischen Landesversammlung 1919–1921. Sitzungsprotokolle* (Düsseldorf, 1994).

31. See Georg May, *Ludwig Kaas. Der Priester, der Politiker und der Gelehrte aus der Schule von Ulrich Stutz,* 3 vols. (Amsterdam, 1981–1982).

32. August 29, 1932. Rudolf Morsey, ed., *Die Protokolle der Reichstagsfraktion und des Fraktionsvorstands der Deutschen Zentrumspartei 1926–1933* (Mainz, 1969), 583f.

33. See, for example, "Aufruf der *Kölnischen Volkszeitung,*" April 9, 1932. Herbert Lepper, ed., *Volk, Kirche und Vaterland. Wahlaufrufe, Aufrufe, Satzungen und Statuten des Zentrums 1870–1933. Eine Quellensammlung zur Geschichte insbesondere der Rheinischen und Westfälischen Zentrumspartei* (Düsseldorf, 1998),

502f.; Rudolf Morsey, ed., *Das "Ermächtigungsgesetz" vom 24. März 1933. Quellen zur Geschichte und Interpretation des "Gesetzes zur Behebung der Not von Volk und Reich"* (Düsseldorf, 1992).

34. See Helmut Witetschek et al., ed., *Die kirchliche Lage in Bayern nach den Regierungspräsidentenberichten 1933–1943*, 7 vols. (Mainz, 1966–1981); Bernhard Stasiewski and Ludwig Volk, eds., *Akten deutscher Bischöfe über die Lage der Kirche 1933–1945*, 6 vols. (Mainz, 1968–1985); Martin Broszat, Elke Fröhlich, Falk Wiesemann, eds., *Bayern in der NS-Zeit. Soziale Lage und politisches Verhalten der Bevölkerung im Spiegel vertraulicher Berichte* (München, 1977), 327–368; Hugo Stehkämper, "Protest, Opposition und Widerstand im Umkreis der (untergegangenen) Zentrumspartei—Ein Überblick," in Jürgen Schmädeke and Peter Steinbach, eds., *Der Widerstand gegen den Nationalsozialismus. Die deutsche Gesellschaft und der Widerstand gegen Hitler* (München, 1986), 113–150, 888–916.

35. On church and resistance see Klaus Gotto and Konrad Repgen, eds., *Die Katholiken und das Dritte Reich*, 3rd. ed. (Mainz, 1990), 173–190; Heinz Hürten, *Deutsche Katholiken 1918–1945* (Paderborn, 1992), 537; On the Center Party and resistance see H. Stehkämper, "Protest"; Rudolf Morsey, *Christliche Demokraten in Emigration und Widerstand 1933–1945* (Köln, 1987); Günter Buchstab, Brigitte Kaff and Hans-Otto Kleinmann, *Verfolgung und Widerstand 1933–1945. Christliche Demokraten gegen Hitler* (Düsseldorf, 1986); Winfried Becker, "Widerstand aus christlicher Wurzel, vornehmlich aus dem Umkreis des politischen Katholizismus und der christlichen Gewerkschaften," in Gerhard Ringshausen and Rüdiger von Voss, eds., *Widerstand und Verteidigung des Rechts* (Bonn, 1997), 51–96.

36. Heinz Hürten, *Verfolgung, Widerstand und Zeugnis. Kirche im Nationalsozialismus. Fragen eines Historikers* (Mainz, 1987)

37. Winfried Becker, *CDU und CSU 1945–1950. Vorläufer, Gründung und regionale Entwicklung bis zur Entstehung der CDU-Bundespartei* (Mainz, 1987), 16–30; "Catholic-led anti-Nazi groupings were based predominantly in the Rhineland," in Maria Dee Mitchell, *Christian Democracy and the Transformation of German Politics, 1945–1949* (Ann Arbor, 1994), 60, 58–67.

38. December 3, 1945 in Würzburg. Peter Herde, "Die Unionsparteien zwischen Tradition und Neubeginn. Adam Stegerwald," in Winfried Becker, ed., *Die Kapitulation von 1945 und der Neubeginn in Deutschland*, (Köln, 1987), 245–295; Barbara Fait, Alf Mintzel and Thomas Schlemmer, eds., *Die CSU 1945–1948. Protokolle und Materialien zur Frühgeschichte der Christlich-Sozialen Union*, 3 vols. (München, 1993); Winfried Becker, "Gründung und Wurzeln der Christlich-Sozialen Union," in Hanns-Seidel-Stiftung e.V., ed., *Geschichte einer Volkspartei. 50 Jahre CSU 1945–1995* (Grünwald, 1995), 69–107.

39. Adam Stegerwald, *Wohin gehen wir?* (Würzburg, 1946); Herde, "Die Unionsparteien", 287–292; see also Cary, "The Path to Christian Democracy," 758–764.

40.  Ute Schmidt, *Zentrum oder CDU. Politischer Katholizismus zwischen Tradition und Anpassung* (Opladen, 1987).

41.  See Klaus Gotto and Rudolf Morsey, in Albrecht Langner, ed., *Katholizismus im politischen System der Bundesrepublik 1949–1963,* (Paderborn, 1978), 7–32, 33–59; Karl Schmitt, *Konfession und Wahlverhalten in der Bundesrepublik Deutschland* (Berlin, 1989).

42.  The susceptibility of nineteenth-century Germany to a vague form of religiousness ("vagierende Religiosität") and its political variations are pointed out by Thomas Nipperdey, *Deutsche Geschichte 1866–1918*, vol. 1, *Arbeitswelt und Bürgergeist* (1990; reprint, München, 1998), 530.

# 5 Christian Democracy and the Constitutional State in Western Europe, 1945–1995

EMIEL LAMBERTS

## POLITICAL CONTEXT

Christian Democracy became an important political force in western Europe after 1945. Religious parties already had been founded in the second half of the nineteenth century in Germany (the Center Party), Belgium, the Netherlands, Switzerland, Austria (Christlichsozialen), and, after World War I, Italy (Partito Popolare Italiano). Generally attached to the Right in their opposition to the principles of the French Revolution, religious parties nonetheless differed in several respects from conservative parties. They were more eager to defend Church rights, for example, and they were more socially progressive and internationally oriented. The political breakthrough of Fascism, however, eclipsed these centrist parties in Germany, Austria, and Italy. After the collapse of Fascism, the Radical Right was discredited. The moderate, centrist Christian Democrats now were able to integrate the rest of the Right, especially in Germany and Italy, the two most prominent defeated countries in Europe. For a brief time, Christian Democracy in the Mouvement Républicain Populaire (MRP), even became influential in France. In the first years after World War II, Christian Democracy, influenced by the Resistance movements in Italy and France and by Catholic Action, manifested leftist tendencies. The Cold War turned Christian Democracy back to the center, strengthening its domestic position and helping to establish it as a dominant political force in western Europe in the 1950s. Starting in the 1960s but especially from the 1970s onwards, Christian Democracy declined as a consequence of growing secularization, rising individualism, and the appeal of alternative ideologies. It lost voters to regionalist and liberal parties and, to a lesser extent, to socialism.[1]

Despite this recent decline, Christian Democrats were a crucial presence on the western European scene for most of the postwar era. In Germany they were in power for 36 years out of 50, in Italy for 47 years out of 52, in Belgium for 47 years out of 53, and in the Netherlands for 49 years out of 53; even in France they were influential up to 1962. The weight of Christian Democracy in Europe makes it worthwhile to examine its impact on European society. In this contribution, I focus on their impact on the elaboration and functioning of political institutions, specifically, in the founding states of the European Union. Yet it is clear that Christian Democracy has also been influential in the field of social policy (e.g., the Rhineland model) and religious-ethical issues.[2]

Immediately after the war, Christian Democrats had the opportunity to contribute substantially to the elaboration of new constitutions in western European countries. In France, the first draft of the constitution of the Fourth Republic called for a regime dominated by a single elected assembly, the *régime d'assemblée,* based on the formula of Socialists and Communists. The MRP played an important role in the defeat of this constitution in a referendum on May 5, 1946. In the subsequent election for another constitutional assembly the MRP became the largest political party in the country, with 28.2 percent of the votes. As shaped by the Christian Democrats, the second draft of the constitution included a bicameral system and strengthened the power of the president and the prime minister. Although the new draft was a compromise, it was generally acceptable to the MRP, which was instrumental in mobilizing support for the text approved in a referendum on October 27, 1946, notwithstanding the opposition of de Gaulle.[3]

In Italy, Democrazia Cristiana (DC) received 35 percent of the vote in the first postwar elections for the Constituent Assembly on June 2, 1946.[4] As a consequence, the DC had to compromise with the other parties on the elaboration of the constitution. Nonetheless, the Party dominated the coalition government, led by Alcide De Gaspari. This was even more the case when the Socialists and Communists left the government in May 1947. The new constitution, accepted on December 22, 1947, had all the characteristics of a compromise, yet Christian Democrats and, to a lesser extent, Liberals left their mark on it.[5]

In the German Federal Republic, the Grundgesetz (Basic Law) was drafted between September 1948 and May 1949 by a parliamentary council of sixty-five members chosen by the parliaments of the *Länder*. In this council twenty-seven seats were held by Social Democrats and Christian Democrats, five by Free Democrats. The Parliamentary Council was chaired by Konrad Adenauer and elaborated an institutional framework that drew heavily on the Weimar Constitution and the constitutions of the Anglo-American democracies. Although the Christian Democrats had to reckon with the differing views of Social Democrats and Free Democrats (Liberals), especially on cultural-religious issues, they were able to introduce in the constitution their conception of the balance of power between the *Länder* and the federal government, the priority of the *vorstaatliche Rechte,* and the effectiveness of the executive.[6] Also, by virtue of their powerful position in the 1950s, especially in Italy and West Germany,[7] they were able to influence the implementation of the new constitutions. In both the new constitutional regimes and the Benelux countries, where no new constitutions were elaborated, Christian Democracy was instrumental in the shaping and operation of postwar political institutions.

Let us try to distinguish some "Christian Democratic" characteristics in western European political institutions and practices after World War II. Of course, this effort is complicated by the fact that those institutions were elaborated and implemented by Socialist-Communist and eventually Liberal parties as well. But by taking into account the political ideology of Christian Democrats and their policies when they were in power, it is possible to identify some characteristic achievements.

The political ideology of Christian Democracy may serve as an important element by which to measure its influence on political organization. In this account, I focus chiefly on those elements of political ideology that are shared by all Christian Democratic parties, even taking into account the more rightist Christian Democratic Union–Christian Social Union (CDU-CSU) in West Germany and the more leftist MRP in France. At the same time, I concentrate on the substantial mark they have been able to leave on political administration.

## IDEOLOGY

Personalism, Christian Democracy's dominant ideology in the postwar period, emphasizes the individual's personal development in a social environment.[8] The principal actors in this process are the citizens themselves. Individuals can achieve fulfillment, however, only within certain social frameworks such as the family, professional associations, local communities, and the nation. Christian Democrats thus advocate a sociological pluralism. They support individual initiative, which will often be exercised through natural communities. The role of the state in both the socioeconomic and the cultural arena is supplementary. Public authority ought to intervene to create a favorable economic climate and ought to further the common good actively, for instance, through social policy. For Christian Democrats, the state is nothing more than a tool for promoting personal development in the context of one's natural community.

How should the political structures of the state be organized? Chris tian Democrats believe the parliamentary system is the best guarantor of both personal freedom and the development of natural communities. They support civil and political liberties, representative government, and the separation of powers. They are also in favor of decentralization, in line with long-established tradition, while simultaneously advocating a form of supranational authority and international cooperation.

## INDIVIDUAL AND SOCIAL RIGHTS

Before 1940 the Catholic hierarchy and the religious parties in Europe were more open to social than to individual rights.[9] In the Church's view, modern (individual) freedoms were tainted by naturalism and indifferentism. Confrontation with totalitarian regimes (Fascism and Bolshevism) and extreme violations of human rights during World War II began, little by little, to bring about a change in attitude. Participation in Resistance movements, especially in France and Italy, strengthened Christian Democrats' sensitivity to individual human rights, which henceforth were accepted as the fundamentals of every human community. After the war Christian Democrats coalesced behind the idea of the constitutional state with a duty to protect the basic rights of its citizens, including individual rights.

Nevertheless, there was always a tendency among Christian Democrats to place a collective slant on these freedoms. After all, they wanted to promote the development of the human person within a social framework. The French MRP set out, to no avail in the immediate postwar years, to incorporate so-called communal rights—rights of the families, local communities, and professional associations—in the constitution of the Fourth Republic.[10] The Italian Christian Democrats were successful in securing the recognition and protection of the family "come società naturale fondata sul matrimonio" in the constitution of their country (art. 29).[11]

By accepting "modern liberties," Christian Democrats were at the same time guaranteeing the autonomy of the churches and their affiliated organizations in western European society. They largely defended freedom of religion, education, and association in terms of the interests of the Church. The new Italian constitution safeguarded the rights of organized religion. Even more, it established the liberty of all religions before the law but recognized at the same time the special status granted to the Roman Catholic Church by the Concordat of 1929 (art. 7 and art. 8).[12] In West Germany, the Catholic and Protestant churches successfully put pressure on the CDU-CSU to guarantee, by the Basic Law, the development of religious and sociocultural associations.[13] Christian education and the charity sector were given room to expand in most countries.[14] It can be stated, therefore, that legal conditions were created for the defense of Christian views and values in society.

There had always been a greater concern for social rights in Catholic circles. This attitude facilitated the practical endorsement by the Church of the Universal Declaration of Human Rights in 1948.[15] In Italy, social rights were integrated into the constitution of 1948 with the consent of Christian Democrats.[16] In West Germany, initially no social rights were mentioned in the Basic Law, yet a climate of intensified social commitment in the 1960s led to a more explicit protection of basic social rights—a development that enjoyed Christian Democratic support. The same happened in other countries. The social rights in question included the right to work and to fair pay, to social security and health care, to legal assistance, to adequate accommodation, and to cultural and social development.[17]

## PARLIAMENTARY DEMOCRACY

It was not until the end of World War II that the magisterium of the Catholic Church dropped its reservations regarding parliamentary democracy.[18] This had not prevented Catholics in many countries with parliamentary and democratic regimes, including Belgium, Holland, Germany, and even Italy, from taking part in political life.[19] In France, Christian Democratic participation in the Resistance movement led to an enduring reconciliation between Catholics and the lay Republic. A similar phenomenon occurred in Italy. The Christian Democrats in West Germany picked up the tradition of the Center Party and helped to build a new, more democratic regime.[20] Rather surprisingly, the religious parties in the Netherlands continued to have reservations about parliamentary democracy until the 1960s, although they had operated within such a regime for many years. It was only after the mid-1960s that they began to view democracy favorably.[21]

Christian Democrats accepted the principle of universal suffrage as a logical extension of their adoption of the democratic regime. In a few countries, such as Belgium and the Netherlands, they persisted in their attempts to introduce an additional family vote, though without concrete success. On the other hand, they favored the introduction of women's suffrage in France, Italy (1946), and Belgium (1948), which did not harm their electoral interests.[22]

Generally, Christian Democrats were not champions of direct democracy and tended to oppose referendums. In West Germany, they had bad memories of the *Volksabstimmungen* during the Nazi regime. In Italy, on the other hand, where the plebiscite was more embedded in the tradition of the liberal Risorgimento, a "referendum abrogativo" was introduced in the constitution (art. 75) but was not put into practice until 1970.[23] Christian Democrats were not in favor of citizens exercising direct influence on politics, preferring instead to channel their political participation through intermediate, socioeconomic organizations, which maintained close links with the political parties. In this way, they helped to build up a system of political representation based on interest groups.

The representation of interests, a notion borrowed from the corporatist tradition, gained a great many followers among Christian Democrats. The MRP, for instance, campaigned in 1945 to set up "a representative assembly made up of delegates from local communities, professional organizations, trade unions and family associations" alongside a political chamber.[24] No such assembly or senate was established in western Europe, yet the representation of interests was realized in an indirect way through the institutional links between the Christian Democratic parties and socioeconomic interest groups.

The advocacy of proportional representation may also be viewed as an indirect strategy for introducing a system of interest representation in attenuated form.[25] Proportional representation, moreover, offered the additional benefit of enhancing the viability of Christian Democratic parties, which, as centrist groupings, were threatened by a majority-based electoral system.[26]

In terms of shaping the parliamentary system, Christian Democrats generally showed a preference for strengthening executive power while remaining explicitly opposed to a presidential regime. This became very clear in France, where the MRP rejected the *régime d'assemblée* in 1946 and was able to introduce a bicameral system and to strengthen the power of the executive. Still, the political regime of the Fourth Republic would be very unstable. For this reason, the MRP contributed to the draft of the constitution of the Fifth Republic, but it opposed the evolution, afterward, in the direction of a presidential regime. More specifically, it opposed the direct election of the president, which led to an open rift with de Gaulle. Even the MRP, the most leftist of European Christian Democratic parties, was in favor of a "parlementarisme rationalisé," "un régime parlementaire équilibré et efficace."[27]

This tendency was even more apparent in West Germany, where Adenauer introduced a system of *Kanzlerdemokratie*, although this did not hinder the development of other constitutional institutions such as the Bundestag and the Constitutional Court. In the BRD, the chancellor, who was elected by a majority vote of the Bundestag on nomination by the president, was vested with considerable independent powers and initiated government policy. He could be deposed by only a constructive vote of no confidence in the Bundestag, which made it very unlikely that he or his government would be unseated.[28]

The Christian Democrats in Belgium tried to make the government less dependent on parliament by turning from time to time to "framework laws" and, on rare occasion, to government with extended powers. They also held the view that a change of government should be avoided between parliamentary elections.[29] The religious parties in the Netherlands shared the view that parliament ought not to place itself above the government. The latter ought to be able, in certain circumstances and in the interest of the nation, to resist parliament.[30]

Christian Democrats in Italy were unable to achieve solid executive power or to establish stable governments.[31] In fact, a parliamentarian republic was installed there. The government was plagued by internal dissent and above all by rivalry among the different currents within the DC. The political system also became increasingly discredited by corruption and clientelism. Notwithstanding all this, the DC succeeded in establishing a solid constitutional state, which consistently prevailed over terrorist attacks from both Left and Right.[32]

Christian Democrats were generally in favor of the establishment of constitutional courts, as another balancing power vis-à-vis parliament. So, in West Germany, the Federal Constitutional Court (Karlsruhe), independent of both the legislative and the executive branch, successfully introduced for the first time the American principle of judicial review of legislation. In Italy, the constitution of 1948 set up a constitutional court with analogous powers.[33] In France, the MRP was already in favor of some juridical oversight of the constitutionality of legislation in 1945. In 1958 it supported the creation of the Constitutional Council, which supervises the conduct of parliamentary and presidential elections and examines the constitutionality of organic laws (i.e., those fundamentally affecting the government), much like the U. S. Supreme Court.[34]

## THE ROLE OF INTERMEDIATE COMMUNITIES

Christian Democrats attached particular importance to intermediate communities within the political structure of all countries where they exerted real influence. These communities have served as agents linking the state and its citizens. Because of their social ideology, as set out in *Rerum Novarum* (1891) and *Quadragesimo Anno* (1931), Christian Democratic parties themselves often had institutional links with socioeconomic interest groups. In this way, the religious parties in the Benelux countries developed after World War I into *standenpartijen*.[35] All of them, except for the more conservative Protestant Christelijk Historische Unie in the Netherlands, maintained structural links with Christian organizations for workers, the lower middle classes, and farmers. Later, in the 1960s, the ties between the parties and social organizations began to weaken, but even now informal links still exist.[36]

The interweaving of religious parties and Christian social organizations in the Benelux countries formed a substantial element in the societal system characterized as pillarization. The term refers to the compartmentalization of society on a religious-philosophical basis. In order for pillarization to exist, organizations have to be based on a general philosophical or religious conception, and their activities must extend into the political sphere. Entirely separate and isolated Catholic and Protestant worlds, or pillars, were created. Within these pillars, the religious parties played an increasingly pivotal role.[37]

Links between the Christian Democratic parties and socioeconomic organizations were less strong in the other western European countries. The DC, however, was a well-structured party from the outset and cultivated at least informal links with the network of Catholic social organizations. The cohesion of the party and these organizations gradually weakened from the 1960s onward, but some preferential links were maintained. From the beginning the CDU-CSU had frequent contacts with business and agriculture and some contact with trade unions. Later the party set up its own suborganization for several professions, women, young or retired people, municipal councilors, and so on.[38] In France, close, though informal contacts between the MRP and Catholic organizations existed only briefly, which also helps to explain the vulnerability of this political party.[39]

The structural or informal links with Christian Democratic parties enabled a number of socioeconomic interest groups to gain indirect access to parliament and government. They were also represented in numerous administrative bodies and consultative structures, giving them a significant say in politics. In this way, the liberal parliamentary regime was redefined, and in several countries a neocorporatist system of interest representation was introduced.[40] Christian Democrats attached special importance to intermediate organizations in all sectors of society, particularly the economy and social and cultural life. They consistently applied the principle of subsidiarity and generally allowed the state to play only a complementary, regulatory, and coordinating role.[41] The principle of subsidiarity remains a central element in the Basic Program of the European People's Party, as drafted at the Athens Conference in November 1992. It requires the exercise of power at the level needed to achieve a maximum of solidarity, effectiveness, and participation of citizens, in other words, the level at which it is simultaneously most effective and closest to the people.[42]

In most of the countries under review, intermediate organizations were strengthened to one degree or another by state subsidies in return for carrying out certain social tasks. This system of "subsidized freedom" was applied on a very large scale in Belgium and to a lesser extent in the Netherlands.[43] It undoubtedly contributed to the reinforcement of what is referred to in the Netherlands and Flanders as the *maatschappelijk middenveld,* the social midfield.[44]

## REGIONALISM AND DECENTRALIZATION

Christian Democrats have traditionally supported a policy of decentralization, but this was not pursued with the same intensity everywhere. Their degree of commitment in this respect has been governed by the political traditions of their countries and by their own interests as participants in power at the regional and national levels.

In the Federal Republic, the CDU-CSU focused strongly on the autonomy of the *Länder,* in keeping with a long-established tradition and as a reaction against the political centralization that occurred under the Nazis. The CDU-CSU viewed the *Länder* as independent regions with the character of states, which were free to act in areas in which the Basic Law did not explicitly restrain them. Particularly education, culture, and law enforcement came within the exclusive purview of the *Länder.* Those *Länder* are represented on the federal level in the Bundesrat. Members of the Bundesrat are not elected but designated by the governments of the *Länder,* the number varying according to population in the state. The powers of the Bundesrat are limited but nevertheless substantial.[45] It is also noteworthy that the CDU was a highly decentralized party until the 1970s, its branches in the individual *Länder* enjoying considerable autonomy. A more centralizing tendency subsequently arose in both federal policy and the organization of the party.[46]

In Italy, the DC set out immediately after the war to create regions with a high degree of administrative autonomy. Autonomous regional governments were soon operating in the outlying zones, whose populations differed linguistically or ethnically from the rest of Italy.[47] This was a reaction against the political centralism pursued first by the Savoy dynasty and later by the Fascists. The evolution toward regionalism was later slowed by fears of leftist domination of certain regions. The DC remained committed to regionalism in principle while in practice increasingly encapsulating itself in the central state. Nevertheless, during the 1970s, regional assemblies and governments were set up throughout Italy. There are now fifteen ordinary regions in addition to the five regions that had already been granted special autonomy. The regions acquired extensive devolved legislative and administrative powers, especially over issues concerning agriculture, social welfare, and the environment. The effects of regionalism have been profound, especially in the north.[48]

Christian Democracts in Belgium argued in favor of recognizing the two cultural regions, Flanders and Wallonia, that were viewed as natural communities. It adopted a rather conservative stance, however, toward reforming the structures of the state and embarked only hesitantly along the path of federalism. This was particularly the case with the French-speaking Christian Democrats, who did their best to slow the reform of the state, bringing them into conflict with their Flemish fellow party members on several occasions. The latter had long maintained ties with the Flemish movement. A series of compromises helped to determine the outcome of the federalization process in Belgium. This process was linked to some degree with the issue of decentralization. The intervention of the Christian Democrats enabled the provinces to win a little more freedom of action, and the administrative scope of the municipalities was broadened.[49] Christian Democrats in France, the most centralized country in western Europe, gave little more than formal approval to regionalism.[50] The same is true for the Netherlands, where Christian Democrats did not support decentralization.[51]

## INTERNATIONAL COOPERATION

In general, the religious parties retained an undeniable international orientation, in spite of the growing influence of nationalism after the nineteenth century. World War II discredited nationalism. In its aftermath Christian Democrats proclaimed their support for international cooperation and applauded the creation of the United Nations. As the Cold War took hold, they naturally lined up on the side of the Atlantic alliance because of their pronounced anti-Communism. In about 1950 they adopted a first scheme of European political integration, and they contributed substantially to the

first steps in the integration process. After 1954 the failure of the European Defense Community (EDC) dampened their enthusiasm for the project. The
strategic objective of a federal Europe with supranational political decision-
making powers was not set out clearly until twenty years later, in 1975, in the
Tindemans Report. The European People's Party (EPP) was founded in July
1976, presenting itself at the community level as a political force with a real
political project.[52]

## CONCLUSION

Christian Democrats exerted an undeniable influence on political structures in the founding nations of the European Union. In the wake of their
confrontation with totalitarian regimes, they contributed to the establishment of constitutional states committed to the protection of individual and
social rights. Within these constitutional states they were more inclined to
emphasize authority over freedom. For Christian Democrats, the state was,
in essence, merely an instrument for promoting the development of persons in the context of their natural communities. They did, indeed, reserve
a prominent place within the organization of their parties and within the
structures of the state for intermediate organizations. They evinced less
concern for the political aspirations of individuals who were not organized.
Their preference for a plurality of social and political bodies inevitably led
them to a policy of decentralization and international cooperation. As I
have noted, however, their concrete policies in this field were conditioned
by their relative strengths in each respective country or region. This gives
rise to my final conclusion: Christian Democratic parties, most of which
participated in power for a long time, have shown some inclination to reinforce the existing political system and have generally tended to interpret
their program in a conservative way.

## NOTES

1. T. Buchanan and M. Conway, eds., *Political Catholicism in Europe, 1918–1965*
(Oxford, 1996); M. Caciagli et al., eds., *Christian Democracy in Europe* (Barcelona,

1992); J.-D. Durand, *L'Europe de la Démocratie Chrétienne* (Brussels, 1995); D. Hanley, ed., *Christian Democracy in Europe: A Comparative Perspective* (London, 1994).

2. The influence of Christian Democracy on European society especially has been studied in E. Lamberts, ed., *Christian Democracy in the European Union, 1945–1995* (Leuven, 1997). This article is a revised and completed version of my contribution, "The Influence of Christian Democracy on Political Structures in Western Europe" in that volume (282–92).

3. R. Rémond, *Histoire de France: Notre siècle, 1918–1988* (Paris, 1988), 371–93; P. Letamendia, *Le Mouvement Républicain Populaire: Histoire d'un grand parti français* (Paris, 1995), 325–30.

4. The Socialists received 20.7 percent of the votes, the Communists 19.7 percent.

5. Ghisalberti, *Storia costituzionale d'Italia (1848–1948)* (Rome, 1994), 389–433; M. de Nicolo, ed., *Constituente, Costituzione, riforme costituzionali* (Bologna, 1998); G. Gonella, *L'influenza della Democrazia Cristiana sulla Costituzione* (Rome, 1976); R. Ruffli, "La costituzione italiana," in R. Papini, ed., *L' apporto del personalismo alla costruzione dell'Europa* (Milan, 1981), 159–76.

6. W. Soergel, *Konsensus und Interessen: Eine Studie zur Entstehung des Grundgezetzes für die Bundesrepublik Deutschland* (Stuttgart, 1969); P. Bucher, ed., *Nachkriegsdeutschland, 1945–1949* (Darmstadt, 1980); H. P. Schwarz, *Adenauer: Der Aufstieg, 1876–1952* (Stuttgart, 1986; English edition: Oxford, 1996).

7. In the elections of 1948, the DC would get 48.3 percent of the votes. In the BRD, the CDU-CSU would get 45 percent in 1953 and 50.2 percent in 1957.

8. See, regarding the Christian Democratic ideology and program, Durand, *L'Europe de la Démocratie Chrétienne*, 111–17; G. Dierickx, "Christian Democracy and Its Ideological Rivals," in Hanley, *Christian Democracy in Europe*, 15–30. For the CDU, see H. O. Kleinmann, *Geshichte der CDU, 1945–1982* (Stuttgart, 1993), 79–96. For the DC in Italy, see A. Giovagnoli, *La cultura democristiana tra Chiesa Cattolica ed identità italiana (1918–1984)* (Rome, 1991). For the MRP in France, see Letamendia, *Mouvement Républicain Populaire*, 5–11. For Belgium, see J. L. Jadoulle and E. Lamberts, "L'évolution du programme du PSC/CVP," in W. Dewachter et al., eds., *Un parti dans l'histoire, 1945–1995: 50 ans d'action du Parti Social Chrétien* (Brussels, 1995), 343–76. For the Netherlands, see H. E. S. Woldring, *De Christen-democratie: Een Kritisch onderzoek naar haar politieke filosofie* (Utrecht, 1996).

9. R. Coste, *L'Eglise et les droits de l'homme* (Paris, 1983); J. Punt, *Die Idee der Menschenrechte: Ihre geschichtliche Entwicklung und ihre Rezeption durch die moderne katholische Sozialkündigung* (Paderborn, 1987); *Droits de Dieu et droits de l'homme: Actes du IXe colloque national des juristes catholiques* (Paris, 1989); G. Putz, *Christentum und Menschenrechte* (Innsbruck and Vienna, 1991); J. B. D'Onorio, ed., *La liberté religieuse dans le monde* (Paris, 1991).

10. M. Einaudi and F. Goguel, *Christian Democracy in Italy and France* (Hamnden, 1969), 136; Letamendia, *Mouvement Républicain Populaire*, 327. The MRP held that family and social rights were inscribed in the Declaration of Rights of 1946, which, with the "Déclaration des Droits de l'Homme et du Citoyen" of 1789, forms part of the preamble to the Constitution of 1958 that currently governs France.

11. Ghisalberti, *Storia costituzionale*, 410–12; G.N. Modona, ed., *Stato della Costituzione* (Milan, 1998), 150–58.

12. In 1984 the Concordat of 1929 was modified. Henceforth the Catholic Church no longer had the status of an established church. It renounced much of its tax-exempt status and much of its jurisdiction over the annulment of marriages. Religious instruction in public schools would be offered only on request. Financial support for the Church was reorganized and reduced. See Modona, *Stato della Costituzione*, 35–37.

13. Burkhard van Schewick, *Die katholische Kirche und die Entstehung der Verfassungen in Westdeutschland, 1945–1950* (Mainz, 1950), 65–130.

14. The MRP failed narrowly to include freedom of education in the French constitution of 1946. In the Italian and West German constitutions, freedom of education was granted.

15. J.Y. Calvez, *L'économie, l'homme, la société: L'enseignement social de l'Eglise* (Paris, 1989); J.A. Coleman, ed., *One Hundred Years of Catholic School Thought* (New York, 1991).

16. The Italian Constitution mentioned "the obligation of the state to abolish social and economic obstacles that limit the freedom and equality of citizens and hinder the full development of individuals" (art. 3). Moreover, it recognized the right to work of every citizen (art. 4). See Modona, *Stato della Costituzione*, 12–17, 170–74.

17. Kleinmann, *Geschichte der CDU*, 269–73; F.J. Stegmann, "Sozio-ökonomische Ordnungsvorstellungen der Unionsparteien CDU/CSU," in Lamberts, *Christian Democracy*, 295–312. For the other western European countries, see the contributions of K. Kersbergen, M. Dumoulin, B. Béhouart, and L. Avagliano in the same volume (313–74).

18. A. Acerbi, *Chiesa e democrazia: Da Leone XIII al Vaticano II* (Milan, 1991); J.M. Pontier, "Pie XII et la démocratie," in J. Chelini and J.B. D'Onorio, eds., *Pie XII et la Cité* (Paris, 1988), 267–91.

19. J.-M. Mayeur, *Des partis catholiques à la Démocratie Chrétienne* (Paris, 1980).

20. Durand, *L'Europe de la Démocratie Chrétienne*, 229–84; M. Conway, *Catholic Politics in Europe, 1918–1945* (London and New York, 1997), 90–97.

21. R.S. Zwart, "Christian Democracy and the Political Order in the Netherlands," in Lamberts, *Christian Democracy*, 245–47.

22. Lamberts, *Christian Democracy*, 251, 258, 275; Rémond, *Notre siècle*, 375.

23. W. Becker, ed., "Der Einfluss der Unionsparteien auf die politische Ordnung der Bundesrepublik Deutschland," in Lamberts, *Christian Democracy*, 230–31. Letamendia, *Mouvement Républicain Populaire*, 328, 336: the MRP in France declared itself in favor of the referendum in 1946 under specific conditions but later opposed it. H. Portelli, "Le régime politique italien," in Y. Guchet, ed., *Les systémes politiques des pays de l'Union Européenne* (Paris, 1994), 291–92; Modona, *Stato della Costituzione*, 289–97. Article 138 of the Italian constitution also provided for a constitutional referendum. Under specific circumstances, constitutional changes could be submitted for popular approval.

24. Letamendia, *Mouvement Républicain Populaire*, 328; see also, for the Netherlands, Zwart, "Christian Democracy and Political Order," 246–47.

25. A. Giovagnoli, *Il Partito Italiano* (Rome, 1996), 21–22. In Italy, Christian Democrats were promoting proportional representation in order to achieve some form of interest representation.

26. The introduction in 1958 of single-member majority voting in France in two stages hastened the long-term decline of the MRP; see Rémond, *Histoire de France*, 630. Changes to the Italian electoral system in 1993 to allow majority-based voting contributed to the collapse of the DC.

27. Letamendia, *Mouvement Républicain Populaire*, 334–38; F.G. Dreyfus, *Histoire de la Démocratie Chrétienne en France* (Paris, 1988), 221–56; J.M. Mayeur, "La démocratie d'inspiration chrétienne en France," in Lamberts, *Christian Democracy*, 81–82.

28. U. Kempf, "Le système gouvernemental de la République Fédérale d'Allemagne," in Guchet, *Les systèmes politiques*, 34–38; Becker, "Der Einfluss der Unionsparteien," 229–33.

29. C. Berckx and K. Rimanque, "L'influence des sociaux-chrétiens sur l'évolution des institutions," in Dewachter et al., *Un parti dans l'histoire*, 542–44.

30. Zwart, "Christian Democracy and Political Order," 247–48.

31. Einaudi and Goguel, *Christian Democracy in Italy and France*, 46–47; F. Malgeri, "La democrazia cristiana in Italia," in Lamberts, *Christian Democracy*, 97. In 1953 Alcide De Gasperi tried to reinforce the position of the government and to install "una democrazia protetta," but his efforts failed.

32. G. Campanini, "Il significato della Democrazia cristiana nel sistema politico italiano," in Lamberts, *Christian Democracy*, 281.

33. Kempf, "Le système gouvernemental," 45–48; Modona, *Stato della Costituzione*, 566–79. The Italian Constitutional Court was set up only in 1955.

34. Letamendia, *Mouvement Républicain Populaire*, 334–36.

35. *Standenpartijen* are parties based on socioprofessional organizations. The term refers to the "Estates" of the ancien régime.

36. E. Lamberts, "L'influence de la Démocratie Chrétienne en Belgique sur l'ordre politique," in Lamberts, *Christian Democracy*, 259–60; T. Duffhues, "Confessionele politieke partijen en maatschappelijke organisaties," in P. Luykx and H. Righart, eds., *Van der Pastorie naar het Torentje. Een eeuw confessionele politiek* (The Hague, 1991), 124–45; P. Lucardie and H. M. ten Napel, "Between Confessionalism and Liberal Conservatism: The Christian Democrat Parties of Belgium and the Netherlands," in Hanley, *Christian Democracy in Europe*, 53–57.

37. There is a great deal of literature on the phenomenon of "pillarization." See, e.g., H. Post, *Pillarisation: An Analysis of Dutch and Belgian Society* (Gower, 1989); H. Righart, *De Katholieke zuil in Europa* (Meppel and Amsterdam, 1986); J. Billiet, ed., *Tussen bescherming en verovering: Sociologen en historici over zuilvorming* (Leuven, 1988); J. E. Ellemers, "Pillarisation as a Process of Modernization," *Acta Politica* 19 (1984): 129–44; E. Lamberts, "Les sociétés pilarisées: L'exemple belge," in G. Cholvy ed., *L'Europe, ses dimensions religieuses* (Montpellier, 1998), 221–36.

38. H. O. Kleinmann, "Die gesellschaftliche Basis der CDU/CSU," in Lamberts, *Christian Democracy*, 123–36; Kleinmann, *Geschichte der CDU*, 96–110, 461–80; A Parisella, "La base sociale della Democrazia Cristiana," in Lamberts, *Christian Democracy*, 189–209.

39. P. Van Kemseke, "The Social Basis of Christian Democracy in France," in Lamberts, *Christian Democracy*, 174–88. Close links existed between the Confédération Française des Travailleurs Chrétiens (CFTC) and the MRP in the 1950s. In 1964 the CFTC became the Confédération Française Démocratique du Travail (CFDT). From that moment on, the MRP could no longer count on official backing from the Christian trade unionists.

40. R. Kleinfeld and W. Luthardt, eds., *Westliche Demokratien und Interessenvermittlung: Zur Aktuellen Entwicklung nationaler Parteien-und Verbändesysteme* (Hagen, 1989); J. Wolderdorp, "Christen-democratie en neo-corporatisme in Nederland: Het CDA en het maatschappelijke middenveld," in K. Van Kersbergen, ed., *Geloven in macht: De Christen-democratie in Nederland* (Amsterdam, 1993), 141–61; R. A. Koole, "The Societal Position of Christian Democracy in the Netherlands," in Lamberts, *Christian Democracy*, 146–49; E. Lamberts, "L'influence du catholicisme politique sur la société belge," *Chrétiens et Sociétés, XVIe–Xxe Siècles* (Lyon) 5 (1998): 20–28.

41. P. Valdrini, "A propos de la contribution de l'Eglise catholique au développement de la subsidiarité et du féderalisme en Europe," *Revue d'Ethique et Theologie Morale* (Paris), supp. 199 (1996): 147–64.

42. *Europe 2000: L'unité dans la diversité* (Melle, 1994), 21, 110.

43. In the Benelux countries, not only social and cultural organizations but also private (denominational) schools are subsidized by the government. In Italy, in contrast, Catholic schools are not supported financially by the state. See V. Marcello, "La scuola nella costituzione italiana," in de Nicolo, *Costituente, Costituzione, riforme costituzionali*, 107–16.

44. Lamberts, "L'influence de la Démocratie Chrétienne," 259–62; K. Van Kersbergen, *Social Capitalism: A Study of Christian Democracy and the Welfare System* (London and New York, 1995), 153–69. In Italy, Christian Democrats inherited from Fascism a social welfare system, characterized by a parastatal organization of social security administration and the dominant position of the Church in social assistance.

45. Constitutional changes require a two-thirds vote in both the Bundesrat and the Bundestag. The Bundesrat has an absolute veto over on all legislation affecting the rights of the Länder. For other legislation, a majority in the Bundesrat can block enactment of bills passed by the Bundestag by what is known as "suspensive veto."

46. Kempf, "Le système gouvernemental," 40–45; Becker, "Der Einfluss der Unionsparteien," 233–36.

47. These zones were Sicily, Sardinia, Valle d'Aosta, Trentino–Alto Adige (including South Tirol), and, after 1963, Friuli–Venezia Giulia.

48. M. Diani, "Regionalism, Federalism and Minority Rights: The Italian Case," *Res Publica* 37 (1996): 413–28; Campanini, "Il significato della Democrazia cristiana," 276–77.

49. J. Velaers, "Les forces vives de toute une génération: La réforme de l'Etat de 1970 à 1995," in Dewachter et al., *Un parti dans l'histoire*, 492–528.

50. Dreyfus, *Histoire de la Démocratie Chrétienne en France*, 195–96, 315. The MRP even turned down de Gaulle's proposals tending to regionalism in 1969.

51. P. Lukyx and H. Righart, eds., *Van de pastorie naar het torentje* (The Hague, 1991).

52. Ph. Chenaux, "Les Démocrates Chrétiens au niveau de l'Union européenne," in Lamberts, *Christian Democracy*, 449–58. M. Greschat and W. Loth, eds., *Die Christen und die Entstehung der Europäischen Gemeinschaft* (Stuttgart, 1994); J.-D. Durand, "Christliche Demokratie und europäische Integration" *Historisch-Politische Mitteilungen* 1 (1994): 155–82.

# 6 Strategies of an Interest Group

The Catholic Church and Christian
Democracy in Postwar Europe,
1944 – 1958

CAROLYN M. WARNER

In the post–World War II era, which in western Europe has been dominated overwhelmingly by democratic political systems, the Catholic
Church has been compelled to accept its demotion to the status of a
private organization with no political authority. When Liberal governments in the nineteenth century first began to deny the Church its ancient social privileges and perquisites, the Church regarded the process
and the result as completely illegitimate and at first refused to negotiate
with them. The Church eventually had to accept the change and thereafter attempted to renegotiate its status through political channels.[1] In
the process, it began to act like—and became—an interest group. Like
many other interest groups, it then sought monopoly representation for
the social group it claimed to represent (i.e., religious practitioners),
state subsidies for its activities, legal protection against foreign and
domestic competition, and state enforcement of its sociopolitical views.
In other words, although the Church clearly had a moral purpose and
mission, it sought to use the political arena to accomplish specific policy
goals and acted like an interest group to achieve them.

After experiencing some setbacks in the early twentieth century,
the Vatican and its national churches welcomed the relief offered—
after extensive political negotiations—by the Fascist governments in

Italy, Spain, and Germany in the interwar period.[2] With the end of World War II, however, the national churches again faced the task of maintaining or possibly restoring the privileges these systems had granted. By 1946 it appeared that the churches had found at least a partial solution—in the form of the several Christian Democratic parties that appeared in these countries.

The triumph of Christian Democratic parties in much of postwar western Europe did not, however, represent the unqualified triumph of the national Catholic churches and the Vatican. From the churches' perspectives, the Christian Democratic parties were unreliable, wily, and insufficiently dedicated to their interests. Although certainly better than the alternative presented by the secular Left, the Christian Democratic parties were at best a weak compromise of the churches' preferences. While the leaders of the Christian Democratic parties built "Europe," or the European Economic Community (EEC), and oversaw western Europe's postwar economic expansion, the Catholic Church witnessed declines in its organizational strength and in attendance, resulting in waning influence in sociopolitical matters.

Precisely at the time when the Church was grappling with the new sociopolitical environment of postwar Europe, Christian Democratic parties took the reins of the new Italian, French, and German political systems.[3] These parties, Democrazia Cristiana (DC), Mouvement Républicain Populaire (MRP), and Christlich-Demokratische Union–Christlich-Soziale Union (CDU-CSU), respectively, were not creatures of the Catholic Church. They had their own goals and programs, which extended beyond and sometimes did not even include promoting the dogma and interests of the Church. They had to operate in an environment that was foreign to the national churches: democracy involved compromises on goals in the parliamentary and societal arenas. The parties faced a dramatically changed international and domestic context, yet they had to cope with the Church as an important societal institution, which many citizens still regarded as the ultimate moral authority. The fortunes of the parties also varied. The Christian Democratic parties in Italy and Germany maintained long-term electoral domination, whereas the party in France had a short-lived electoral success but remained a regular minor coalition party. The German party's success was predicated on an alliance between nominally Protestant and Catholic politicians and voters.

Contrary to standard historical interpretations, the Christian Democratic parties were not automatic political extensions of the Catholic Church. To extract resources from the sociopolitical system, the Church had to forge connections between itself and one or more political parties. These connections were subject to continuing evaluation, even possible termination, by the two "partners." To understand the trajectory of Christian Democracy and Catholicism in postwar western Europe, one must first examine the relations between the Catholic churches and the Christian Democratic parties and, in particular, the churches' strategies vis-à-vis the parties. Why did the Italian church make a deep and long-lasting alliance with the national Christian Democratic party, and why did the French party realize only a short-lived superficial alliance while the German church achieved a long-lasting alliance with a Christian Democratic party that it "shared" with a rival religion? Essentially, the churches' actions toward the Christian Democratic parties, or any party, can be analyzed as a contracting problem, with the churches seeking suppliers (a political party) of goods (public policies and subsidies) in a market (the democratic electoral system) with the attendant concerns about availability, price, monitoring, and malfeasance.

Interest groups and political parties are in a mutually dependent relationship. The party needs group support for votes, organizational infrastructure, and activists; the group needs the party for proposing and working toward the passage of legislation. From the interest group's perspective, the supply of parties is less than perfect. Parties come into being for a variety of reasons and to meet different interests; these may not match the profile of the interest group. Faced with an imperfect supply, the interest group has several choices. It can turn itself into a party, or it can create one. In either case it expends inordinate resources and alters its own organizational purpose and activities. Another option is to entice some parties to offer the desired "product" (policy). To do the latter, the group will have to commit resources to the supplier. This leads to the problems of monitoring and malfeasance: the party can then use those resources to pursue its own interests, perhaps diversifying to other "products" (interest groups, demographic categories, ideological preferences). The party's own goal is to build its desired product, not necessarily that of the interest group.

The Church recognized that interest group alliances with parties create risks for the interest group. In a blunt statement, Italy's Cardinal Ottaviani criticized the use by political entrepreneurs of Church influence to further their own ends: "In sum, everyone runs to priests to pull strings for them among the powerful, and there results a weariness and boredom in the country regarding the men of eternity transformed into electoral agents. This is not the way in which to honor the Church. Rather, this way one dishonors it. This is not serving the Church, this is serving oneself of it."[4]

Those acquainted with the works of Anthony Gill, Rodney Stark and Laurence Iannaccone, and Stathis Kalyvas will note that my approach likewise applies economic modeling to explain religious behavior, in this case that of the Catholic Church toward political parties.[5] Yet, to account for the outcomes, we must also explain why the national churches varied in the weights they accorded to similar "economic" variables. The account given here does so by paying attention to the variation in the ideological orientation of the Church and party leadership, and the institutional distance of the churches from the previous, nondemocratic regimes.

How does an interest group choose the party to which it commits its resources? How does it reduce monitoring costs and the risk of malfeasance? Why, in the face of malfeasance, does it not always exit? Because an interest group is, by definition, in pursuit of resources both to sustain itself and to promote certain policies, it will rationally look for the party that most closely shares its own policy interests. Because policy agreement is meaningless if the party cannot influence the government, the interest group may compromise its policy concerns somewhat in favor of a more capable party. Concerns about party malfeasance lead the group to prefer a party whose politicians' records are known and which the interest group can permeate, placing its own members so as to exercise direct influence and oversight. If there is malfeasance, the interest group's response will be affected by the availability of a suitable alternative party. The Italian, French, and German cases show that the ideological orientation of the leadership and specific historical contexts strongly affect the perceived payoffs to different courses of action. Which party a Church saw as an acceptable ally was affected by the Church's priorities and its worldview, not just by the situation it faced. When tensions arose, the reaction of each national church depended on a mixture of ideology and interests.

## THE VATICAN AND DEMOCRAZIA CRISTIANA

The Italian church did not throw itself behind the DC because Christian Democracy is somehow an innate part of Catholicism. Rather, it supported the DC to obtain policy outputs from the political system that would serve its priorities. The Church saw itself threatened with the loss of its prerogatives and the status that had been granted by the Concordat, including the Lateran Pacts of 1929, and its leadership had a near-pathological fear of Communism. The DC was not the Church's automatic choice, nor was it the automatic outgrowth of the Church and its ancillary organizations. In fact, the Church wanted not only a party that would respect its privileges,[6] but one that would promote explicit guarantees regarding a Catholic social program, part of the Church's goal of obtaining "a hegemonic position of control over the life and orientations of the collectivity."[7] The hierarchy demanded that the party protect Italy and the Church from Communism. For Pius XII and the Vatican establishment, these were essential elements in the Church's survival.[8]

In 1944, when the Vatican realized that its preferred political arrangement, an authoritarian regime like that of Franco's Spain, was not in the offing, it began evaluating political parties that had started to organize for democratic competition.[9] It wanted a conservative monarchist–led government and so showed no interest in the nascent Christian Democratic party of Alcide De Gasperi.[10] But the Monarchists were very weakly organized, and the neo-Fascists, whose Catholic credentials were spotty anyway, were discredited. Even in traditionally "Catholic" regions, many lower clergy initially did not "see anything wrong with [Catholics] joining one party or another; it [was] sufficient that the party [was] not in contradiction with Christian principles."[11] Other clergy criticized the DC for compromising with the Communist Party.[12] Catholics themselves were either ignorant of political options or dispersed across a range of parties, Left and Right. As a leader of a rival party noted, "Not all the Christians are in Christian Democracy."[13] Catholic Action missionaries confirmed this.[14]

Of the parties demonstrating any Catholic tendencies, Democrazia Cristiana had the most extensive, albeit unimpressive, organizational presence in the country. The drawback was that its leaders were not willing to create the strictly clerical state that most of the Vatican hierarchy advocated. Compounding the difficulty of party choice was the view of some in the hierarchy that the Church and Catholics need not concentrate their support on one party. Indeed, some argued that doing so would artificially restrict the diversity of Catholic political opinion.[15]

A number of influential leaders were wary of the selection of the DC. In 1945 two of Pius XII's closest advisers, Monsignor Tardini and Cardinal

Ottaviani, scolded De Gasperi, leader of the interim government, for not having tried, with agrarian reform and labor policies, to quell the "Communist bacillus," which, the Church argued, stemmed from poverty. One of Azione Cattolica's key leaders, Luigi Gedda, accused the DC of three errors: "the fact of having taken a position in favor of the Republic instead of remaining neutral; having let the Left develop an unjust [anti-Fascist] purge against men of good faith; finally, the feebleness of the anti-Communist campaign."[16] With those strikes against it, one might well ask why the Church then chose the DC as its ally.

First, policy stance mattered. The Church rejected other parties as potential allies when it doubted that those parties would act "in service to the Church."[17] The DC leadership advertised the party as Catholic and as having the obligation to alter some social and economic inequities.[18] In 1944 the DC stated that political action was to be "the projection of religious life into the political field."[19] De Gasperi announced, "Our party is an organization of believers which on the political-economic terrain, wants to bring about a sincere political democracy and a profound social transformation based upon justice."[20] The Church hierarchy noted approvingly that the DC founders' conception of the party was that of a Catholic party of government that would keep Italy free of Communism.[21]

Second, political capability affected the decision. In 1946 the DC had yet to prove it could marginalize or control the Communists.[22] The archbishop of Milan's daily paper admonished the DC two months before the municipal elections to raise "the heavy curtain of distrust that many have raised around the DC, accused of a dangerous acquiescence and of an organic incapacity to defend itself in a deceptive political game fraught with unknown dangers."[23] The Church nevertheless gambled on the DC half-heartedly for the 1946 municipal and constituent assembly elections, then wholeheartedly for the 1948 legislative elections. The alternatives to an ill-organized DC were worse. The Church could certainly imagine that with its investments, the party would become strong enough to supply the Church its desired policies. Still, the Church waited until the DC gave a clear signal of its anti-Communist abilities before it swung all its support to the party.[24] That signal came in mid-1947 when the DC forced the Communists out of the government.[25]

Third, familiarity may have increased the Church's confidence in the prospective policy stances of the DC. Many of its leaders came from Azione Cattolica or other Catholic ancillary organizations. The Church was familiar with these organizations, their leaders, and their political orientations. Particularly with Azione Cattolica, whose members became an influential part of the DC, the Church had been able, courtesy of the Lateran Pacts and its nominal independence of the Fascist regime, to nurture political allies. In the eyes of the Church, the DC was authentically Catholic; other parties were not: "There may be parties which, even in saying they want to defend Catholicism and its institutions, limit themselves to an exterior defense, without occupying themselves by putting into concrete action Christian thought in the social and political sector."[26]

Fourth, the views of the Church's leadership mattered: the Church's siege mentality tipped the scales. The one-party viewpoint, soon adopted by Pius XII, was that Catholic strength would lie in having the faithful united in a single party. Moreover, and as in France and Germany, the Left, generally atheist and anticlerical, was large and well organized and *their* supporters were not dispersed across numerous parties.

The alliance with the DC was not a sui generis one. It had to be arranged; its advantages and disadvantages were evaluated from the Church's perspective as well as the DC's.[27] While historical events facilitated the alliance, they did not predetermine it.

Interest group–party relations are seldom without tension, and those between the Church and the DC were not an exception. In essence, the DC started to use the resources with which the Church had provided it (i.e., domination of the Italian government) to pursue its own interests, not those of the Church. On a number of occasions, the Church expressed displeasure at DC policy and actions.[28] While in a pure market situation one would expect the aggrieved to break relations, seek legal redress, and find an alternative supplier of the desired products, in the political context of interest group–party relations, alternative suppliers often are scarce or nonexistent and there rarely is legal redress. In the Italian case, by throwing its support exclusively to the DC in the early years of the new Republic, the Church eliminated alternative parties; hence, it was left with the choice of either trying to modify DC policy from within the context of their relations or withdrawing entirely. The Church chose the former option. In contrast to the French Church's situation (see below), the Italian Church's core policy interests were still being protected by the DC, and the DC's structure was porous, allowing the Church to place its agents in the party.

## THE FRENCH CHURCH AND THE MOUVEMENT
## RÉPUBLICAIN POPULAIRE

On August 25, 1944, the cardinal archbishop of Paris was refused entrance
to the mass at Notre Dame celebrating the liberation of Paris. Though the
Church's organizational strength had grown under Vichy and many of its
clergy were eager to engage in spiritual outreach, its prestige plunged with
the rout of the Vichy regime and the end of the German occupation. During
the years of the Fourth Republic, the French Church, like other discredited
interest groups such as industrial associations and employer unions, carefully sought policy benefits from the political system via party allies.[29]

Why did Vichy matter to the Church's postwar alliance possibilities?
Vichy was an authoritarian regime according the Church a privileged, integral place. For the hierarchy and for some prominent social Catholics,
Vichy represented an opportunity to return France to its allegedly Christian origins.[30] Vichy, a self-declared "catholic" state, promised to eliminate
Communism, Jews, Freemasons, and other rivals of Catholicism and authoritarianism and restore Christian morals to public life. Catholicism was
to be an integral part of Vichy's "national revolution." Liberal democracy
merely elicited "the animal" in man.[31] Pétain seduced the hierarchy with his
language and with specific measures: restoring crucifixes to public schools
and city halls, introducing the death penalty for the performing of abor-
tions, upgrading the status of congregations.[32] Monsignor Feltin—who
was archbishop of Bordeaux during the occupation and later succeeded
Cardinal Suhard as archbishop of Paris—said that "Christian principles"
were in harmony with the National Revolution.[33] Pétain's views on replacing
the liberal order with a corporatist one echoed the hierarchy's corporatist
doctrine. Cardinal Gerlier said of the Vichy regime, "Pétain is France and
France is Pétain."[34] Even Emmanuel Mounier, a social Catholic, saw Vichy
as the opportunity to recruit new lay Catholic leaders and cultivate a Catholic vision of society.

In the aftermath of Liberation (1944–45), the French political spectrum,
like the Italian, had well-organized parties of the Marxist Left and several other
secular parties. On the center and right, there was one large party of Christian Democratic inspiration, the Mouvement Républicain Populaire (MRP);
one poorly organized, small, pro-clerical conservative party, the Parti Républicain de la Liberté (PRL); plus a variety of insignificant political groupings.[35]

A crucial difference in the Italian and French contexts is that the French Christian Democratic party had been formed independently of the hierarchy during World War II. It defined itself in opposition to the Church's recent ally—the Vichy regime—and proclaimed itself the party of the Resistance and of "Revolution within the Law."[36] With Vichy not in vogue at Liberation, neither was the Church, but with no close links to either, the MRP was.

The ties between the MRP and the Church were carefully forged, scrutinized by both organizations. The Church resorted to party politics when it needed help in protecting prerogatives granted by Vichy, which the new political context had put in question. The Church, aware that politicians' actions had serious repercussions on family and educational issues and its own organizational survival, knew that to defend its interests, it would have to find a conduit for political influence.[37] Despite assertions of the French Communist Party (PCF), which declared that the MRP stood for "Mouvement des Révérends Pères," the party was not the clergy's.[38]

Policy considerations and party capacity influenced the Church's decision to endorse the MRP in the first postwar elections. First, a factor stemming from the nature of the previous regime and the Church's relation to it affected the Church's choice. The PRL was a party of discredited conservatives, most of them tainted with Vichy.[39] Association with them would have hindered the Church's efforts to clear itself of the opprobrium of having been a willing partner in the Vichy regime. By allying, instead, with a pro-republican party such as the MRP, the Church could hope to polish its image. Since the Church had defined organizational survival partly as damage control, limiting the retribution exacted by Resistance-inspired politicians, it sought to hide under the guise of a noted Resistance party. The MRP was doubtless more progressive than the Church liked, but the Church had little choice.[40]

As in Italy, policy issues were paramount, and the Church needed an immediate ally: the question of state subsidies for private (and mainly Catholic) schools would be debated in the Constituent Assembly (1945–46), as would other matters of consequence to the Church. As the French hierarchy stressed, "l'enseignement libre" was "the question which, at this hour, retains the attention of the clergy and faithful."[41] It could not afford to wait for the dispersed and discredited conservatives to reorganize, and the MRP appeared to share many of the Church's moral concerns. The

MRP espoused Christian social principles; moreover, most of its activists and leaders had been members of Action Catholique.[42] Though the ancillary organizations were not under the direct control of the hierarchy, the Church expected that the Catholics in the MRP would be sensitive to Church interests.[43] The Church was also fearful of the policy consequences of a government led by Socialists and Communists. The MRP leader Pierre Henri Teitgen noted that those who gave the MRP their confidence had reason to be worried: "The Bishops will be terrorized if we are no longer in the government."[44]

Party capacity mattered. The Church concluded that it would do better in the long run with the larger (and generally sympathetic) party rather than with the much smaller, discredited and thus less influential PRL and the other small conservative parties.[45] The MRP's capacity for influencing government policy was important. As the Church noted at the time, the MRP had a larger share of the seats in the National Assembly than all other groups sympathetic to its social and political goals.[46] Because supporting a political party is a decision that allows various levels of support, the Church could take a low-risk, low-profile approach to the MRP, instructing Catholics at mass and through diocesan bulletins to support it but refraining from creating new organizations to campaign for the party or providing logistical resources. This is precisely what it did.[47] Its perspective on how to accomplish one of its goals, fighting Communism, tempered its inclination to sustain partisan combat. The Church viewed Communism as a moral and spiritual problem that mere party politics could not solve.

Unlike the case in Italy, however, the French church was not easily able to monitor the party's behavior. Since Action Catholique was not tightly controlled by the hierarchy and the Church's role in Vichy was an issue, the Church was both less familiar with MRP leaders and less influential over them. The Church, operating on incomplete information, probably underestimated the MRP's determination to downplay the schools issue; it probably also underestimated the MRP's determination to pursue an alliance with the SFIO (the Socialists). This lack of information would have made it more likely that the Church would see the MRP as an acceptable ally, at least initially.

The two organizations soon disagreed over the issue of state subsidies to private (Catholic) schools. In the Constituent Assembly, the MRP had agreed to a compromise that would not restore those subsidies. The Church disapproved, as did most voters, who rejected the draft constitution in a referendum. The second draft also did not guarantee "liberty of instruction" or provide automatic funding. The MRP, believing that no other alternative would win approval, supported the second draft; on this issue, in other words, it went against the Church.[48] By a slim majority and with many abstentions, voters approved the second draft. In the ensuing 1946 parliamentary election, the Church, viewing the MRP as its least offensive alternative, endorsed the party and instructed the clergy to do so with their congregations.

If the Catholic Church were not instrumentally rational in its political strategies, it would not reevaluate its links with a political party. After seeking rents from the political system by paying a party in advance for a policy product that the party then did not deliver, the French Church withdrew its support (i.e., electoral endorsements) from the MRP. Two events occasioned the reassessment. The first was the MRP's efforts in 1948 to create a political alliance with the Socialists. Doing so required the MRP to shelve the private school subsidies issue.[49] At that point, even in some traditionally Catholic areas, such as Brittany, the Church did not consistently support the MRP.[50] Only in those few parts of France where the regional MRP diverged from the national party's tactics did the Church remain supportive.[51] Second, the MRP was opposed to amnesty for those compromised by their association with the Vichy regime and those parliamentarians who had voted to cede the government to Maréchal Pétain in 1940. The Church opposed neither proposition. In 1948 the hierarchy, through its Assembly of Cardinals and Archbishops, informed MRP leaders that the Church would be "very unhappy" with a harsh and unforgiving amnesty law. A police informant noted that the MRP feared it would find itself in opposition to the hierarchy, "which until now had given it [the MRP] all its support."[52] However, fully cognizant of the consequences, the MRP refused to relent, and the Church stopped endorsing the party. The breakup of the alliance penalized the MRP's electoral future; at the same time, it left the Church without any dedicated voice in the government.[53]

While it is clear that conservatives resurfaced as a dominant factor in French politics as early as 1951 (depending on how one classifies de Gaulle's party), there was no dominant party to which the Church could turn for support of its policy goals.[54] Charles de Gaulle, though a Catholic and an avowed anti-Communist, was hostile to the French hierarchy for its having condoned the Vichy regime and the German occupation. Hence the Church could not turn to his party for assistance. The small contractors were unreliable in terms of policy content and ability to gain seats in government (as was de Gaulle's party), their coalition behavior was unpredictable, and it was often difficult to tell who had authority to speak for the "party." Sponsoring many small parties was not a viable option: transaction and monitoring costs were high, and the parties' willingness to work jointly on behalf of their shared benefactor (the Church) was highly doubtful. Cooperation and consistency have never been the hallmark of the Right in France.

In decided contrast to the situation in Italy and Germany (see below), the French church and the Christian Democratic party were not able to forge a lasting alliance. The Church's close association with Vichy and the MRP's origins and defining ideology as a party of the Resistance greatly reduced the prospects for policy agreement. The MRP sought, unsuccessfully, to transform France with the Socialists, the Church to restore its Vichy-granted prerogatives. And while the MRP was untenable as a long-term ally, French politics did not present the Church with a suitable alternative.

## THE CHURCH AND CHRISTIAN DEMOCRACY IN GERMANY

In Germany, the Church also had to deal with the aftermath of its association (even if never so close as in France) with the previous regime; this included, as in Italy, the attempt to persuade the new democratic regime to restore its privileges and status as enumerated in the Concordat signed by the Nazis and Pius XI. One aspect of the situation in Germany, however, noticeably altered the Church's options. In contrast to the de facto monopoly over religion that the French and Italian churches enjoyed, the German church had a substantial competitor: the Evangelical Lutheran Church.

How are the Church's strategies altered when it is not the only major religion in a country? One might expect an interest group that is not dominant but faces competition from other groups representing similar interests to select and invest in a political party that it would not have to share with another interest group. The German hierarchy did single out one party, yet it singled out one in which it would have a lesser voice—a mixed

Catholic-Protestant party, the CDU. Why did it not go with the mainly Catholic party, the Zentrum?

Like the French and Italian churches, the German church came out of World War II with a damaged reputation. Although the German church had never been officially incorporated into the Nazi regime, it could not claim the moral high ground. On the one hand, the Church generally rejected National Socialism, and some of its clergy had earlier even prohibited members of the Nazi Party from taking the sacraments. It frequently criticized the party's racial ideas, social policies, and, of course, its decision to establish nondenominational schooling. On the other hand, the Church encouraged the Zentrum to vote for the infamous Enabling Act, which gave Hitler's government dictatorial powers, and it readily turned over Church baptismal records to the Nazis, facilitating the latter's efforts to identify and exterminate Jews. The other black spot on the Church's reputation, though not in the eyes of all, was its failures to protect the Jews and acknowledge and denounce the Nazis' genocidal policies and actions.[55]

Like the Italian church vis-à-vis Mussolini's Fascist regime, the German church had distanced itself ideologically and institutionally from the Nazi regime. It had been neither a pillar of Nazi domestic policy nor the basis of the government's legitimacy, as had been the case in France.[56] Vatican and German church policies were directed at maintaining the Church as an institution in the face of occasional (some assert, frequent) Nazi attacks on Church prerogatives and practices. Like the Italian church, the German church was one of the very few institutions that survived the war with its basic structural characteristics intact. The Church's main loss was that the Nazis had stripped it of all but one of its many ancillary organizations, thus dramatically reducing the organizational resources on which it could rely after the war.

Again as in Italy, the Church voiced its determination to build a Catholic society, despite the fact that about half of West Germany's population was Protestant. Cardinal Archbishop of Cologne Josef Frings stated flatly, "The work of reconstruction should be done by Catholics and Protestants in alliance but each acting separately."[57] The German church seemed ready to intervene in political affairs, especially concerning the development of new parties and the status of confessional schools. Like the Italian church, it explicitly stated that even democracy and the rule of law did not give Catholics "enough guarantees" and that, because of this, Catholics had to band together and present themselves as an organized bloc. Further, the Church had no qualms about trying to eliminate political undesirables, such as the "various Catholic splinter parties that grew up following the war," especially the Zentrum and the Bavarian party.[58]

Like its Italian counterpart, the German church was determined to have the Concordat remain valid. The Reichskonkordat had not been a complete victory either for the Nazis or for the Church. For example, although bishops had to be German and trained in Germany (with a minimum of theological training), the government could object to the appointment of a bishop on political grounds and require that bishop to take an oath of loyalty to the state.[59] The state provided for the education of the clergy by funding and running the theological faculties; it could also appoint the faculty. What the Church got in return was a guarantee of confessional schools "everywhere in Germany," and it was determined that the new Federal Republic honor that guarantee.[60]

The Catholic Church in Germany chose to support only one political party, and it chose the one that included Protestants. Given that a solely Catholic party was reorganizing, there are two questions: why did the Church choose to rely on only one party, and why did it choose the one in which it would have to compete with the Evangelical Lutheran Church for influence on policy? It would make sense to support one party if the Church feared that another party would not cooperate on key policy votes, that two separate parties competing for the Catholic vote might do worse than one, that Catholics (including clergy) would feel free to vote for any party claiming to be "Christian," or because negotiating with several parties would be costly in terms of organizational time and resources. While such a multiplicity of motivations may be unsatisfactory to the social scientist, the historical record indicates that the Church was prompted by all but the first of those concerns.

The Church knew of two possible party allies, the Zentrum and the CDU. The fact that by 1945 the Zentrum had been in existence for nearly one hundred years led some of its Weimar leaders to argue that it should be revived. There were, however, some pronounced differences among its surviving leaders: some wanted to create a "centrist" party, which was not tied to a specific religious "confession"; some argued for an expressly biconfessional party; and yet others were hesitant to start a new party for fear that it might wind up dominated by "reactionaries who had no place else to turn."[61] One result was that the efforts to create any primarily Catholic political organization lagged behind the efforts of Catholic and Protestant leaders who had decided that an alternative to the old party system and its confessional affiliations was necessary. Those former Zentrum leaders who preferred to create an interdenominational party and who discovered substantial support for the idea began to organize (in Berlin) immediately after such efforts were permitted in June 1945.[62] Emphasizing their support for the creation of a democratic political system, introducing Christian values into politics to avoid scenarios like the Nazi period, and concerned that the reaction to the Nazi era might lead to a system dominated by the Left, the new organization took the name Christian Democratic Union—the latter word recognizing that the new organization was bi-denominational.[63]

Rather like the DC in Italy, the CDU emerged as a confederation of distinct local and regional sections. It did not even formally organize itself as a national party until after the first federal (Bundestag) elections, and its national party headquarters did not open until 1952.[64] The CDU at first exhibited an unusually broad range of Christian, democratic, and even socialist and nationalist policy tendencies, but as Konrad Adenauer asserted his leadership the party downplayed its confessional side, quashed the left-wing progressives, stressed pragmatic politics, and moved toward the political center-right.[65]

If anything, it was the Zentrum that demonstrated it would be the staunchest defender of the Church's interests in core policy areas, such as confessional schools and recognition in the constitution of the Reichskonkordat. Certainly it was more sure of where its interests and priorities lay—with Catholics rather than with Protestants and Catholics. Yet at the time that the Church was looking for allies, the party was having serious internal disputes about its orientation. One faction insisted that political parties should not be the embodiment or representative of an entire socioeconomic and cultural milieu, or Weltanschauung. In its view, "[a]s long as parties persisted in reducing political discourse to posturing about philosophical first principles, neither a multiparty nor a two-party system could be stable."[66] The Zentrum should not defend Catholic interests because they were Catholic interests but because defense of those interests fell under various legitimate political rights. In contrast, another faction argued that the party should "hold unmistakably fast" to "the Catholic Weltanschauung" and that the religious affairs of Catholics were also the political affairs of the party.[67] While it is plausible that these disputes discouraged the Church from supporting it, the CDU's Catholic blocs were having similar disputes.[68] Church officials later denied that policy variations had been a key factor.

Why the CDU? One could argue, as members of the Zentrum did, that a party that crossed confessional lines could hardly be an adequate defender of Catholic interests. At most, it would defend some watered-down version of "Christian" interests.[69] By supporting the CDU, the Church seemed to compromise its ability to dictate policy. Another strike against the CDU was its newness. Some clergy feared that because the CDU would face old established parties such as the SPD and KPD, it would not be able to compete with their organizational and programmatic strengths.[70] It is also possible to argue that with the demographic change brought about by the division of Germany into East and West and the increase in the relative percentage of Catholics in the new "West Germany," there was less reason to maintain an old "tower" mentality and fear Protestant domination of public institutions.[71]

While its later steadfast support of the CDU implies an initial decisiveness, the Church hierarchy was not of one mind in its choice of party. Some bishops first broached the idea of reestablishing the Zentrum; others quickly argued that the Church's fundamental interest was protection against Communism, which could only be provided by a broad-based Christian party.[72] This "concession" to the politicians and the Protestant Church was, of course, only possible when Protestants also indicated an interest in compromise.[73] The decision of the Church and many Catholic politicians not to support the Zentrum is typically credited to the Zentrum's vote for Hitler's Enabling Act "and the absence of any significant resistance activity" by Zentrum politicians or members.[74] It is also often claimed that Catholics (though not necessarily the Church) realized that the separation of faiths was no longer politically reasonable, or possible, given the Allies' demands that democratic governance be set up quickly.[75]

Policy considerations were significant. The Church balked when one of the early leaders of the CDU proposed a nonconfessional school system with religious instruction. As soon as the party altered that program, the Church was willing to support it.[76] The dispute actually delayed the official founding of the Rhineland CDU.[77] Not helpful to the Zentrum was its support in 1947 of the Social Democratic and Communist parties' economic policy program.[78] As with the MRP, the Zentrum appeared too willing to collaborate with the Marxist parties. In the Church's eyes, it was the CDU that was positioned on the correct end of the Left/Right spectrum. Perhaps even more important was the Church's estimate that "Catholics alone would not be able to assure a Catholic or Christian or conservative influence in the new German state" and the fact that the CDU was organizing rapidly while the Zentrum was not.[79] To increase the size of the "Christian" bloc, Protestants had to be brought into a joint party with a common program opposing the Social Democrats, and many Zentrum leaders were unwilling to have Protestants in their midst.[80] The single-member district element of the hybrid electoral system made the idea of joining forces in a coalition after an election untenable: on their own, a Protestant and a Catholic party might each lose in a district to the SPD or other secular parties.

Furthermore, Catholic CDU politicians had presented the Church with a fait accompli. For various reasons, they were already soliciting and working in tandem with Protestant politicians to build the new biconfessional party. In the Catholic stronghold of North Rhine–Westphalia, the CDU had active sections in twenty-one of thirty-nine electoral districts by November 1945 (the same month that they officially launched the party there). Two months later, they were in all but three of those electoral districts, and by April 1956 the CDU had sections in every district and administrative subdivision.[81] The April 1947 elections in the *Länder* clearly indicated that the CDU was the stronger party: the CDU won 38 percent of the vote, the Center Party only 10 percent (with the SPD at 32 percent, the liberal party [FDP] at 6 percent, and the Communists [KPD] at 14 percent). The Allies tipped the scales when they declared that the Parliamentary Council would have 52 seats, 20 of those going to the CDU, 20 to the SPD, 4 to the FDP, 3 to the KPD, and only 2 to the Zentrum (2 for a northern conservative party and 1 for another non-Socialist party).

The question of which party to support thus boiled down to what the Church wanted, how quickly it needed it, and whether an already constituted party could serve as an expedient solution. The Church faced an imperfect set of suppliers: it had to choose between one that, if the Church invested heavily in it, might yield returns in a number of years—the Zentrum—and one that, while not producing exactly what the Church wanted, at least had a rough facsimile already on the market in many areas—the CDU. In terms of organizational energy devoted to protecting against a perceived Communist threat, the Church had a greater incentive to support the CDU. The influential Cardinal Frings changed his position: he highlighted the virtues of supporting a party that already had a widespread organizational network and of avoiding embarrassing and debilitating divisions. He himself joined the CDU, though he was persuaded to cancel his membership under criticism from the pope and other Catholic elements.[82]

The optimal party for the German church's policy interests, the Zentrum, was also the weakest of potential allies; the party that appeared to be large enough to gain influence in the new Federal Republic, the CDU, was less interested in catering to the Church's interests. Moreover, once that party consolidated itself in the first federal election, the Church's main asset—Catholic voters—was by and large without options. The Church could not make a credible threat that it would steer Catholics away from the CDU to the Zentrum. The Church itself was convinced that the Communist threat was too great to wait for a small party to grow, even with the Church's support. An additional wrinkle was that Catholic lay leaders probably would not have accepted a directive to support the Zentrum. The Church threw itself almost frantically behind the CDU; to admit that it had been wrong would have greatly damaged its credibility. Like the Italian church, the German church was trapped by its initial decision to purchase political protection and policy goods from just one political party.

Unlike the Italian church and more like the French, the German church found itself with few institutional resources with which to affect the actual construction of the Christian Democratic party. The Church's reconstituted ancillary organizations may have assisted the CDU at elections, but they do not appear to have been central to the CDU's development. Nor is it clear that the ancillary organizations were tightly linked to the Church hierarchy: the largest and most important Catholic organizations reconstituted themselves with their own resources, making it harder for the Church to control their political orientation.

## SUMMARY

The Italian, French, and German churches chose to ally with political parties because each had policy goals that required legislative support. The preferences of the churches and the contexts in which they operated were not identical; this accounts for the divergence in levels of support that they gave the two parties. None of the churches faced an ideal set of potential allies; each had to deal with the existing supply of parties and try to use its resources to mold the parties into more amenable organizations. Policy agreement and political capability were significant. A political party is a useless ally if it does not pursue the core policies preferred by the interest group. It is also less desirable if it does not make the group's policies a high priority. If the party is politically weak, the interest group's efforts are wasted; if the party does not agree with the interest group on key policy issues, again, its efforts ("investments," if one prefers) are wasted.

The French church, hemmed in by its past association with the Vichy regime and by potent anticlericalism, approached the political scene tentatively. The Italian church, emboldened by its separation from Fascism and its heightened reputation among Italians, came on full bore. The German church, on the other hand, had to develop strategies by which to work with another Christian denomination as a political ally in order to try to attain benefits from the political system. All the churches approached Christian Democratic parties not because they thought democracy was inherently a good thing but because the alternative conservative, even authoritarian, pro-clerical parties were small and poorly organized. They most assuredly did not choose the Christian Democratic parties out of habitual association with their prewar predecessors. In fact, the Italian church opposed a renewal of Luigi Sturzo's Partito Populare Italiano (PPI), the French church had not supported the interwar Christian Democrats (PDP), and the German church had been distant from the Zentrum. The churches chose the Christian Democratic parties because their parties' programs and capacities most closely matched Church preferences. In the Italian and German cases, the alliances had to be forged, and later actions and policies played a significant role in the nature and development of the alliances.

The Catholic churches of Italy, France, and Germany were most concerned about religious and educational policy areas, yet they helped to bring to power (or did not) parties that nationalized industries, established social welfare schema, and sought to construct a united Europe. The political choices of the national churches were thus consequential for European societies. This had an impact not just within each country but also on western Europe as a whole, as it was Christian Democratic leaders who were the staunchest advocates of the European Community.

The churches' choices about party allies had repercussions for the condition of Catholicism itself in each country. The French church's withdrawal from direct politics meant it faced the issue of adapting to modernization before Vatican II. The Church had to find other means with which to retain the authority to "speak and act" on political and social issues.[83] The German and Italian churches may have acquired a false sense of security, or were certainly sluggish, in responding to changes in the conditions in which they operated, including the decline in numbers of those who attended religious services.[84] Though constrained by the dictates of Roman Catholicism, French priests, even before Vatican II, were more apt to innovate, and French Catholic Action was more responsive to the urban and rural poor than its Italian or German counterparts.[85]

Understanding that the Catholic Church, like any interest group, has demands that it seeks to have met by the political system enables us to comprehend why the Church chooses the party allies it does, perhaps breaks an alliance, or persists with an apparently suboptimal arrangement. Christian Democracy did not seamlessly evolve from Catholicism; but its history and legacy have been profoundly affected by the strategic calculations of the Catholic Church.

## NOTES

1. Stathis N. Kalyvas, *The Rise of Christian Democracy in Europe* (Ithaca: Cornell University Press, 1996). In this chapter, "Church" refers to the formal institution of the Catholic Church. It does not include other practicing or nominal Catholics per se.

2. The national churches were not mere franchises of the Vatican. They had long histories of their own and often struggled to maintain some independence from Rome. See Austin Gough, *Paris and Rome: The Gallican Church and the Ultramontane Campaign, 1848–1953* (Oxford: Oxford University Press, 1986).

3. Compared to the literature on Socialist and Communist parties, the literature on the postwar Christian Democratic parties is thin, but see François Bazin, "Les députés MRP élus les 21 octobre 1945, 2 juin et 10 novembre 1946: Itinéraire politique d'une génération catholique," 2 vols. (Thèse du doctorat, Institut d'Etudes Politiques, Paris, 1981); Geoffrey Pridham, *Christian Democracy in Western Germany* (London: Croom Helm, 1977); R. E. M. Irving, *Christian Democracy in France*

(London: Allen and Unwin, 1973); R. E. M. Irving, *The Christian Democratic Parties of Western Europe* (London: Allen and Unwin, 1979); David Hanley, ed., *Christian Democracy in Europe: A Comparative Perspective* (London: Pinter, 1994); Noel D. Cary, *The Path to Christian Democracy: German Catholics and the Party System from Windthorst to Adenauer* (Cambridge, Mass.: Harvard University Press, 1996); Joseph Verhoeven, *Démocratique Chrétienne: Origines et perspectives* (Brussels: Labor, 1979); Pierre Letamendia, *Le Mouvement Républicain Populaire: Histoire d'un grand parti français* (Paris: Beauchesne, 1995); Maria Mitchell, "Materialism and Secularism: CDU Politicians and National Socialism, 1945–1949," *Journal of Modern History* 67 (June 1995): 278–308; Anne Sa'adah, "Le Mouvement Republicain Populaire et la reconstitution du système partisan français, 1944–1951," *Revue Française de Science Politique* 37.1 (1987): 33–58. The Italian party (Democrazia Cristiana) has received considerable analysis but usually as an atypical, unique case, e.g., Gianni Baget-Bozzo, *Il partito cristiano al potere: La DC di De Gasperi e di Dossetti, 1945–1954*, 2d ed., 2 vols. (Firenze: Vallechi, 1974); or as an example of a dominant party, e.g., Giovanni Sartori, *Parties and Party Systems* (New York: Harper and Row, 1967); Sidney Tarrow, "Maintaining Hegemony in Italy: 'The Softer They Rise, the Slower They Fall,'" in *Uncommon Democracies: The One-Party Dominant Regimes*, ed. T. J. Pempel (Ithaca: Cornell University Press, 1990); Maurice Larkin, *Religion, Politics, and Preferment in France since 1890* (Cambridge: Cambridge University Press, 1995); Seymour Martin Lipset and Stein Rokkan, "Cleavage Structures, Party Systems, and Voter Alignments: An Introduction," in *Party Systems and Voter Alignments: Cross-National Perspectives*, ed. Seymour Martin Lipset and Stein Rokkan (New York: Free Press, 1967), 15.

4. Cardinal Ottaviano, pro-secretary of the Holy See's Office, in Azione Cattolica newspaper, *Il Quotidiano*, January 21, 1958.

5. Anthony Gill, *Rendering unto Caesar: The Catholic Church and the State in Latin America* (Chicago: University of Chicago Press, 1998); Rodney Stark and Laurence Iannaccone, "A Supply-Side Reinterpretation of the 'Secularization' of Europe," *Journal for the Scientific Study of Religion* 33.3 (1994): 230–52; Kalyvas, *Rise of Christian Democracy*.

6. As elaborated in the 1929 Lateran Pacts; see Martin Clark, *Modern Italy: 1871–1982* (New York: Longman, 1984), 254–56.

7. Giovanni Miccoli, "Chiesa, partito cattolico e società civile (1945–1975)," in *L'Italia contemporanea, 1945–1975*, ed. V. Castronovo (Torino: Einaudi, 1976), 378; Carlo Falconi, *The Popes in the Twentieth Century: From Pius X to John XXIII*, trans. Muriel Grindrod (Boston: Little, Brown, 1967), 264–75.

8. Andrea Riccardi, *Il potere del Papa da Pio XII a Paolo VI* (Rome: Laterza, 1988), 82–94.

9. Andrea Riccardi, *Il "partito romano," nel secondo dopoguerra (1945–1954)* (Brescia: Morcelliana, 1983), 51–55; Sandro Magister, *La politica vaticana e l'Italia*

*1943–1978* (Rome: Riuniti, 1979), 39; Jean-Dominique Durand, *L'Eglise catholique dans la crise de l'Italie (1943–1948)* (Rome: L'Ecole Française de Rome, 1991), 581–93.

10. Pietro Scoppola, *La proposta politica di De Gasperi*, 3d ed. (Bologna: Il Mulino, 1988), 49, 53.

11. Cladio Bragaglio, "Riflessioni sul blocco politico-sociale a Brescia," in *Brescia negli anni della Ricostruzione 1945–1949*, ed. Roberto Chiarini (Brescia: Micheletti, 1981), 153.

12. Archivio Centrale dello Stato [hereafter ACS], MinIntGab, fondo Situazioni Politica ed economica della regione, Lombardia, f. 2493.42, Comando Generale dell'Arma dei Carabinieri, #200/I, February 22, 1947, p. 4.

13. Roberto Chiarini and Paolo Corsini, *Da Salò a Piazza della Loggia: Blocco d'ordine, neofascismo, radicalismo di destra à Brescia (1945–1974)* (Milan: Franco Angeli, 1983), 53n. 33.

14. Archivio d'Azione Cattolica [hereafter AAC], Presidenza Generale [hereafter PG], VI.35, 1947–1949, fondo Relazioni-Missioni Religioso Sociali, anon., "Relazione sul primo giro del Carro-Cinema in Calabria," n.d., p. 2.

15. Durand, *L'Eglise catholique*, 582–88.

16. Ibid., 613.

17. Ibid., 619–20; Franceso Malgeri, "La Chiesa di Pio XII fra guerra e dopoguerra," in *Pio XII*, ed. Andrea Riccardi (Bari: Laterza, 1985), 111–22; Francesco Michele Stabile, "Palermo, la Chiesa Baluardo del Card. Ruffini (1946–1948)," in *Le Chiese di Pio XII*, ed. Andrea Riccardi (Bari: Laterza, 1986), 370; *L'Osservatore Romano*, January 2, 1945, in Magister, *Politica vaticana*, 50.

18. De Gasperi to the Congresso delle A.C.L.I., Roma, November 3, 1950, quoted in Francesco Magri, *La Democrazia Cristiana in Italia (1897–1949)*, vol. 1 (Milan: Editrice La Fiaccola, 1954), 50.

19. "Chi siamo e che cosa vogliamo [who we are and what we want]," in the DC's newspaper, *Il Popolo*, 1/7 [published from Bari], February 27, 1944, p. 1.

20. Alcide De Gasperi, under alias Demofilo, "Tradizione e 'ideologia' della Democrazia Cristiana," February 1944, p. 18, reprinted in booklet of same title, by Società Editrice Libraria Italiana, n.d.

21. DC Congresso Nazionale, November 17, 1947, held in Napoli; quoted in Magri, *Democrazia Cristiana*, 314; Msg. Borghino, Azione Cattolica director, February 25, 1946, in Mario Casella, *18 Aprile 1948: La mobilitazione delle organizzazioni cattoliche* (Lecce: Congedo, 1992), 108.

22. Magister, *Politica vaticana*, 53.

23. Durand, *L'Eglise catholique*, 612.

24. Ibid., 613–15.

25. Baget-Bozzo, *Partito cristiano*, 153–60.

26. Durand, *L'Eglise catholique*, 628.

27. See Carolyn M. Warner, *Confessions of an Interest Group: The Catholic Church and Political Parties in Europe* (Princeton: Princeton University Press, 2000), chap. 8.

28. Magister, *Politica vaticana*, 184–88; Steven F. White, "The Roman Question Reopened: Pius XII, De Gasperi, and the Sturzo Operation," paper presented at the annual meeting of the American Historical Association, Washington D.C., 1999.

29. Richard Vinen, *Bourgeois Politics in France, 1945–1951* (Cambridge: Cambridge University Press, 1995), 60–66, 72–81.

30. James F. McMillan, "France," in *Political Catholicism in Europe, 1918–1965*, ed. Tom Buchanan and Martin Conway (Oxford: Oxford University Press, 1996), 55.

31. Jacques Duquesne, *Les catholiques français sous l'Occupation* (Paris: Bernard Grasset, 1966), 65.

32. Ibid., 85–87.

33. September 1942, quoted in W.D. Halls, *Politics, Society and Christianity in Vichy France* (Oxford: Berg, 1995), 375.

34. Gerlier, in Robert Bichet, *La Démocratie Chrétienne en France: Le Mouvement Républicain Populaire* (Besançon: Jacques et Demontrond, 1980), 228; see also the presiding priest at an anniversary ceremony celebrating Vichy's defeat of de Gaulle's forces at Dakar, "You are, Maréchal, the way, the truth, and the life of the country," quoted in Duquesne, *Catholiques française*, 59.

35. On the PRL's clerical stance, see Bibliothèque Nationale, Folio Lb59 163 (1), PRL, Direction de la propagande, Note d'orientation N°1 à l'intention des orateurs du Parti, Paris, January 15, 1946; *Bulletin d'Information des Cadres du Parti*, April 1947, no. 2.

36. Warner, *Confessions of an Interest Group*, 68–71. See MRP pamphlet titled, "Le MRP, Parti de la IVe République," 4, in Widener Library, Harvard University, Mouvement Républicain Populaire, Brochures, 1945–46.

37. Adrien Dansette, *Destin du Catholicisme français: L'Église catholique dans la mêlée politique et sociale* (Paris: Flammarion, 1957), 29–30.

38. *L'Humanité*, 1945.

39. Vinen, *Bourgeois Politics in France.*

40. Norman Ravitch, *The Catholic Church and the French Nation, 1589–1989* (London: Routledge, 1990), 147.

41. SRP, 92/4770 (June 10, 1945), 331.

42. Of the 152 MRP deputies elected to the 1946 constituent assembly, 66 percent were from Action Catholique, 75 percent of those on the MRP's executive committee. On the MRP, see Bazin, "Députés MRP," 2; on its executive committee, see Irving, *Christian Democracy in France*, 79.

43. William Bosworth, *Catholicism and Crisis in Modern France* (Princeton: Princeton University Press, 1962); Marie-Josephe Durupt, "Les Mouvements d'Action

Catholique Rurale, facteur d'évolution du milieu rural," 2 vols. (Thèse du Troisième cycle, Fondation Nationale des Sciences Politiques de Paris, 1963).

44. Archives Nationales [hereafter AN] 2MRP2Dr3, January 31, 1946.

45. Vinen, *Bourgeois Politics in France*, 149.

46. Archives de la Préfecture de Police, Paris [hereafter APP], MRP box 278.247–2, June 27, 1945.

47. Semaine Religieuse de Paris, June 10, 1945, 327; ibid., November 2, 1946; AN FI CII Morbihan, Rapport du Préfet, October 10, 1946. Pierre Pierrard, *L'Église et les ouvriers en France (1940–1990)* (Paris: Hachette, 1991); Ferdnand Boulard, "Réflexions sur le péril Marxiste," *Cahiers du Clergé Rural* 82 (November 1946): 36–38.

48. Gordon Wright, *The Reshaping of French Democracy*, (New York: Reynal and Hitchcock, 1948), 138–40, 158–59, 226.

49. APP, MRP box 278/247–1, Rapport du Préfet, January 8, 1947. One-time MRP president and French prime minister Georges Bidault later stated: "We came because we refuse to have torn away from some their faith and from others their bread." Many of his contemporaries would argue that the MRP succeeded in doing neither. APP, box MRP 278.247–3, Georges Bidault at meeting of fifteenth section of the Fédération de la Seine, June 2, 1955. Bidault was MRP president from 1949 to 1952; prime minister from June to December 1946 and October 1949 to July 1950; minister of foreign affairs from September 1944 to July 1948 and January 1953 to June 1954.

50. AN FI CII Dr. 243, Morbihan, October 2, 1948; Institut Charles de Gaulle, A-RPF, BP2–56d Dr1, Rapport de la section du Rassemblement du Peuple Français, November 8, 1948.

51. AN FI CII Dr. 150, Morbihan, Rapport du Préfet, February 4, 1950.

52. APP, MRP box 278.247–1, March 11, 1948. The Assemblée de Cardinaux et Archevêques excluded Bishops. Dansette, *Destin du Catholicisme*, 73–75. Later, after hearing a speech by Cardinal Archbishop Feltin that the MRP judged too "Pétainist," party activists complained of the Church's political "meddling." APP, MRP box 278.247–2, March 2, 1951.

53. Vinen, *Bourgeois Politics in France*, 150–51. The MRP went from 25 percent of the national vote in 1946 to 11 percent in 1951 and 10.4 percent in 1956. Carolyn M. Warner, "Priests, Patronage and Politicians" (Ph.D. dissertation, Harvard University, 1994). For the MRP's perspective, see Carolyn M. Warner, "Getting out the Vote with Patronage and Threat: Constructing the French and Italian Christian Democratic Parties, 1944–1958," *Journal of Interdisciplinary History* 28.4 (Spring 1998): 553–82.

54. Paul Marabuto, *Les partis politiques et les mouvements sociaux sous la IVe République: Histoire, organisation, doctrine, activité* (Paris: Recueil Sirey, 1948); Vinen, *Bourgeois Politics in France*, 121, 234–36; Philip M. Williams, *Crisis and Compromise: Politics in the Fourth Republic* (Hamden, Conn.: Archon Books, 1964).

55. John Cornwell, *Hitler's Pope: The Secret History of Pius XII* (London: Viking, 1999); Rolf Hochhuth, *Der Stellvertreter* (Hamburg: Rowohlt Verlag, 1963).

56. William M. Harrigan, "Pius XII's Efforts to Effect a Détente in German Vatican Relations, 1939–1940," *Catholic Historical Review* 49.2 (July 1963): 173–91.

57. In Frederic Spotts, *The Churches and Politics in Germany* (Wesleyan: Wesleyan University Press, 1973), 151. On the important role of Frings and his relationship with Adenauer at the beginning of the CDU, see Rudolf Morsey, "Adenauer und Kardinal Frings 1945–1949," in *Politik und Konfession*, ed. Dieter Albrecht et al. (Berlin: Duncker and Humblot, 1983), 483–501.

58. Spotts, *Churches and Politics*, 152. The Vatican saw actual membership by its hierarchy as a violation of article 32 of the Concordat. Hans Maier, "Zur Soziologie des deutschen Katholizismus 1803–1950," in Albrecht et al., *Politik und Konfession*, 159–72.

59. Spotts, *Churches and Politics*, 191.

60. Ibid., 209.

61. Cary, *Path to Christian Democracy*, 153–56.

62. Heino Kaack, *Geschichte und Struktur des Deutschen Parteiensystems* (Opladen: Westdeutscher Verlag, 1971), 157–59.

63. Helmut Pütz, *Die Christlich Demokratische Union* (Bonn: Boldt Verlag, 1971), 36–40.

64. Susan E. Scarrow, *Parties and Their Members: Organizing for Victory in Britain and Germany* (New York: Oxford University Press, 1996), 64. On the CDU's structure, see Angelo Panebianco, *Modelli di partito: organizzazione e potere nei partiti politici* (Bologna: Il Mulino, 1982), 216–29; Scarrow, *Parties and Their Members*, 64–70; on personalities, see Pütz, *Christlich Demokratische Union*, 171–73.

65. Arnold Heidenheimer, *Adenauer and the CDU: The Rise of the Leader and the Integration of the Party* (The Hague: Martinus Nijhoff, 1960); Pridham, *Christian Democracy in Western Germany;* Kaack, *Geschichte und Struktur;* Pütz, *Christlich Demokratische Union.*

66. Cary, *Path to Christian Democracy*, 214.

67. Ibid., 219.

68. Ibid., 194–202; Pridham, *Christian Democracy in Western Germany*, 61.

69. Cary, *Path to Christian Democracy*, 190.

70. A.R.L. Gurland, *Die CDU/CSU: Ursprünge und Entwicklung bis 1953*, ed. Dieter Emig (Frankfurt: Europäische Verlagsanstalt, 1980), 17–24.

71. Ellen Lovell Evans, *The German Center Party, 1870–1933: A Study in Political Catholicism* (Carbondale: Southern Illinois University Press, 1981), 398–99.

72. Gurland, *CDU/CSU*, 472; Spotts, *Churches and Politics*, 299.

73. In August 1945 the Protestant churches at the Treysa Conference supported efforts to erase political conflict between the two faiths. There were, how-

ever, important Protestant dissenters. For the Protestant perspective, see Spotts, *Churches and Politics*, 119–49, 298–305; *Christian Democracy in Western Germany*, Pridham, 38–39; Dennis L. Bark and David R. Gress, *From Shadow to Substance, 1945–1963*, vol. 1 (Oxford: Basil Blackwell, 1989), 150–53.

74. Karl-Egon Lönne, "Germany," in Buchanan and Conway, *Political Catholicism in Europe*, 177; Evans.

75. Lönne, "Germany," 178; Richard L. Merritt, *Democracy Imposed: U.S. Occupation Policy and the German Public, 1945–1949* (New Haven: Yale University Press, 1995).

76. Karl Forster, "Der deutsche Katholizismus in der Bundesrepublik Deutschland," in *Der Soziale und Politische Katholizismus*, ed. Anton Rauscher (München: Guenter-Olzog Verlag, 1981), 220.

77. Spotts, *Churches and Politics*, 299.

78. Cary, *Path to Christian Democracy*, 189–90.

79. Evans, *German Center Party*, 397, 406.

80. Spotts, *Churches and Politics*, 307.

81. Gurland, *CDU/CSU*, 37.

82. Morsey, "Adenauer und Kardinal Frings," 495–96.

83. Brigitte Marie-Odette Vassort, "Politics and Catholic Hierarchy in France," 2 vols. (Ph.D. dissertation, Yale University, 1984), 114.

84. Stark and Iannaccone, "Supply-Side Reinterpretation,"

85. Oscar L. Arnal, *Priests in Working Class Blue: The History of the Worker Priests (1943–1954)* (New York: Paulist Press, 1986); Mark Christopher Cleary, *Peasants, Politicians and Producers* (Cambridge: Cambridge University Press, 1989); Frère Michel-Dominique Epagneul, *Semailles en terre de France, 1943–1949* (Paris: Editions S.O.S., 1976).

# 7 "Antimaterialism" in Early German Christian Democracy

MARIA MITCHELL

As West Germany's leading party from 1949 to 1969, the Christian Democratic Union (CDU) and its policies colored the new republic so completely that for many Germans it became identified psychologically with the postwar state. By dominating the first generation of West German politics, the CDU set the tone for—among other issues—the place of the family, children, and women; the nature of cultural dissent; the role of the churches; and discussion of the Nazi past. More than any other political movement, Christian Democracy succeeded in imprinting its ideology on the early Federal Republic.

The CDU was organized primarily by former members of the Center Party and Christian trade unions who had maintained their political networks through illegal meetings and anti-Nazi resistance circles. After Germany's capitulation, members of these groups—centered in Cologne, Düsseldorf, Frankfurt, and Berlin—took the decisive step of abandoning the old Center Party for an interconfessional movement. While Catholic politicians worked consistently to encourage Protestants to join their ranks, the prominence of Center Party veterans was not lost on Germany's Protestants; indeed, the CDU's image as the inheritor of the pre–1933 Center Party's undiluted Catholicism remained pervasive.[1]

This was especially true as the CDU Zonal Committee for the British Zone, under the leadership of Konrad Adenauer, emerged as the leading Christian Democratic force in occupied Germany. Because the British Zone included the historic strongholds of political Catholicism, Westphalia and especially the Rhineland,[2] the British-controlled CDU enjoyed significant infrastructural and personnel advantages over other CDU zonal groupings.[3] At the same time, it was spared the restrictions that significantly hindered CDU organization in the French and especially Soviet zones. As a result, the CDU under British occupation not only largely shaped the party's unified policy after 1947, it also highlighted and reinforced the larger CDU's links to the pre-1933 Center Party.[4]

As confessional suspicion characterized the new party's patterns of organization, religious difference also dictated the dynamics of CDU policy. Enemies or at best uneasy allies since the founding of the German Reich, devout Protestants and Catholics before 1945 had little experience in close political cooperation. The survival of Christian Democracy rested not only on Catholic success in recruiting reluctant Protestants but also on the formulation of a political program satisfactory to both confessions. This chapter examines the earliest postwar steps in the construction of a Christian Democratic ideology.

Christian Democracy as an ideological doctrine was necessarily ambiguous in 1945; nominally, it signified nothing beyond an embrace of Christianity and (obligatory) support for democracy. While Protestants and Catholics groped for positions of accord, they found greater success in focusing on what they opposed—"materialism." A stock term in Christian critiques of nineteenth- and early-twentieth-century German society, "materialism" had long been invoked by religious Protestants and especially Catholics to discredit everything associated with modernization and secularization. In coupling political Christianity with the concept of antimaterialism, early CDU leaders outlined an important base of confessional commonality and an explicit political agenda. They also set the stage for the party's earliest interconfessional battles over meanings of "materialism."

## NATIONAL SOCIALISM AS A MANIFESTATION OF MATERIALISM

Christian Democrats in occupied Germany framed much of their discussion of postwar politics in the language and context of anti–National Socialism. Civilian and military deaths, unprecedented material devastation, and widespread popular resentment of the consequences of the lost war—as well as

Allied censorship—led to a virtually complete anti-Nazi consensus among German public figures. It was therefore neither surprising nor unusual that almost every CDU program and speech published immediately after World War II began with a harsh condemnation of National Socialism.

As demonstrated by the dissolution of antifascist movements throughout Germany at the end of World War II, however, opposition to National Socialism hardly constituted an adequate basis for sustained political cooperation.[5] For both Protestants and Catholics in the CDU, the depiction of the roots of Nazism and the conclusions they drew from its collapse underscored deeper ideological commonalities. In this way, National Socialism served as an effective rhetorical and explanatory mechanism through which Christian Democrats articulated shared political objectives.

In their programs and speeches in the early postwar era, members of the CDU consistently located Nazism in a centuries-old battle between Christianity and materialism. According to this Manichaean model of competing historical philosophies, Nazism had been not simply a dictatorship led by Adolf Hitler but a culmination of anti-Christian, materialist forces that had coursed through Germany for centuries. By leading these forces of materialism to their logical and ultimate conclusion, National Socialism had waged a concerted war against the powers of Christianity; in so doing, it had revealed the innate evil and impotence of the materialist age.[6]

In the view of both Protestants and Catholics in the CDU, materialism's evil had taken a particular toll on Christians in Germany. According to an interpretation of history shared by the overwhelming majority of Germany's Christian elites, National Socialism as a manifestation of age-old secular forces in Europe had been organized specifically to eliminate the Christian churches. Drawing on decades of traditional Christian rhetoric, Christians in the postwar years characterized themselves as Nazism's principal targets and, consequently, its primary victims.[7]

The obvious historical invalidity of this claim notwithstanding, the linkage of Nazism to materialism served rhetorically not only to associate Christianity with opposition to Nazism but also to provide the CDU with a moral rationale and historical framework. With the collapse of National Socialism, Christian Democrats declared, materialism had yielded to definitive Christian triumph. As the political expression of Christian Germany, the CDU was now to realize fully the victory of Christianity over materialism. "History proved that we were right," Josef Beyerle, cofounder of the

CDU in North Württemberg, proclaimed in February 1946. "Christianity has remained victorious against those who had intended its destruction."[8]

Grounded in this conviction, the call to "Christianize" Germany appeared in almost every program and speech published by the CDU in the aftermath of the war.[9] The ubiquity of the early CDU's references to Christianization was not matched, however, by clarity in the term's implications. Protestants and Catholics may well have agreed that Christians should oppose materialism, but their understandings of materialism rested on different philosophical and historical assumptions. While Protestants, though a minority, were hardly inaudible within the party, Catholic views—reflecting the patterns of early CDU organization—held uneasy precedence.

## CATHOLIC ANTIMATERIALISM AFTER WORLD WAR II

Although political Catholicism before 1945 demonstrated that religious affinity did not ensure political harmony, a distinct "Catholic consciousness" nevertheless sustained a Catholic party in Germany until 1933.[10] Because the large majority of the CDU's founders had been members of the Center Party and the Catholic *Teilkultur*,[11] they brought a distinctly Catholic identity and Catholic worldview to Christian Democracy: in a testament to the intactness of the German Catholic *Teilkultur* in the wake of World War II, Catholic politicians in the CDU continued to operate on the political and ideological assumptions characteristic of Catholic Germany before 1945.[12]

This was nowhere more evident than in the Catholic CDU's reliance on antimaterialism. Not only had Catholics long invoked materialism as a catchall locution to discredit everything they associated with Germany's modernization and secularization, but antimaterialism had long served as a political call to arms for the Center Party. In the last years of the Weimar Republic, Center Party publications often identified materialism as the force behind the party's political opposition.[13]

Indicative of the primacy of confessional difference in nineteenth- and early-twentieth-century German politics and society, the Catholic interpretation and use of materialism had never been neutral confessionally. Because most if not all forms of perceived modernism in Europe were considered anti-Catholic, modernism and materialism had been associated consistently in Germany with non-Catholic, especially Protestant, religions and movements.[14] Antimaterialism as an axiom of Christian Democracy, then, necessarily posed fundamental questions about the interconfessionalism of early CDU ideology.

At its most basic level, the Catholic understanding of antimaterialism in the postwar era was tied to the traditional Catholic critique of modernity. Catholic theology or (Catholic) Natural Law taught that every individual, created in God's image, retained through the creation process an element of God's essence. As they had for centuries, Catholics after World War II rejected modern society's emphasis on secular individualism by stressing each individual's ties and responsibility to God and the community *Gemeinschaft.*[15]

Moreover, Catholics had long linked the rise of secular individualism to specific, apparently anti-Catholic phenomena in European history. For centuries, Catholics in Germany had traced modernism and its by-products, secularization and rationalization, to movements that placed the individual at the center of human development—the Renaissance, the Reformation, the Enlightenment, and the French Revolution.[16] After World War II Catholic Christian Democrats continued to criticize the Reformation as an assault on the Catholic individual's relationship to society;[17] they also indicted the Enlightenment for inspiring the French Revolution and ultimately leading to National Socialism.[18]

As Theodor Scharmitzel, co-organizer of the CDU in Cologne, explained in a speech in March 1946, for example, "The world view of the Enlightenment [*Aufklärertums*], Free Thinkers [*Freidenkertums*], individualism, Marxism, communism, Bolshevism, nationalism, chauvinism, militarism, and, finally . . . National Socialism, a demonic mixture of all destructive systems, undermined step by step the Christian world of ideas." For post-Nazi Germany, Scharmitzel concluded, "The forces of recovery [*des Wiederaufstiegs*] are rooted only in the uncompromising return from this false path, which led us into the abyss, to the supremacy of the Christian body of thought in the life of individuals and the state in all of its institutions and manifestations."[19]

Scharmitzel was not alone in defining the project of Christian Democracy as the reversal of the dominant trends of modern European history. From the traditional Catholic point of view, it was especially in the nineteenth century that the dangers of the materialist spirit became most threatening. By denying the individual's religious nature and attempting to examine and explain man in a rational, "mechanical" manner, materialism released individuals from their God-given responsibilities to the *Gemeinschaft* and promoted a dangerous degree of human, self-centered arrogance. Evident in such developments as industrialism, liberalism, nationalism, and socialism, the secular agenda of materialism had worked to separate Germans from their Christian God and to deny the legitimacy of Christian teachings as guidelines for societal order; National Socialism as it overtook Germany simply represented the culmination of these nineteenth-century trends.[20]

Catholics' post–World War II critique of the nineteenth century was indeed far-reaching. The nineteenth century, according to Heinrich Krone, cofounder of the CDU in Berlin, had been the "great century" or the "high point" of the "*bürgerliche* world." Throughout its decades, as invention followed invention and "modern man" became proud of his "achievements," he began to believe he had prevailed over "space and time." After the twentieth century had demonstrated "the enormous defects of the *bürgerliche* world,"[21] the man of the nineteenth century—who believed passionately in his freedom and searched desperately for the "truth"—was forced to recognize that he had become not "more free, but less free" as a result of his endeavors.[22]

Man's false assumption that he had overcome the limits of "space and time" was rooted in the nineteenth century's rise of natural sciences as well as in modern Germans' faith in technology. According to the Catholic worldview, technological progress had been falsely embraced as an end instead of as a means to serving God; as National Socialism's technological accomplishments had made clear, technology could prosper only in a soulless world infused with materialist thinking.[23] The assumption, argued Maria Sevenich, cofounder of the CDU in Darmstadt, that man could overcome the natural limits of human existence through the "discovery of steam and electricity" and "the mechanization of life" had served merely to "catapult" humans into a "fateful nothingness": In the postwar era, she explained, this "false orientation . . . calls forth in people the desire and understanding to unite themselves again in an orderly world which corresponds entirely to what God truly wants."[24]

In the same way that Catholics after World War II continued to reject materialistic science, they also condemned nineteenth-century materialism's political manifestations. Clearly echoing Center Party rhetoric, Catholic

Christian Democrats criticized Liberalism for denying the centrality of God and the responsibility of individuals to the *Gemeinschaft*. Liberals' great optimism about human progress contradicted the Catholic belief in obligatory moral laws to control human evil stemming from original sin. The most serious flaw inherent in political Liberalism, according to Emil Dovifat, cofounder of the CDU in Berlin, was its "overestimation of human nature as essentially good, the overvaluing of reason and freedom, and the over-emphasis of human attributes." National Socialism, Dovifat asserted, had demonstrated "[w]here this autonomy leads."[25]

Following the same rationale as that which rejected the Liberal belief in individual initiative, Catholics in the CDU also condemned the philosophy of free-enterprise capitalism. Of the moral directives contained in Catholic social teachings, one of the most important was respect for Christian brotherhood; devotion to the welfare of one's Christian equal proscribed financial profit at others' expense.[26] In a speech he delivered in August 1946, Karl Zimmermann explained that "the capitalistic economy neither recognizes God and his commandments as the guiding principle for its actions, nor is man in his natural dignity and freedom the goal of its indefatigable activities."[27] Based on a similarly reasoned rejection of Liberalism and capitalism, Josef André drew a widely held conclusion for postwar Christian politics: "No one can found a new state on the obsolete and economically outmoded Liberal democratic body of thought. . . . [T]he era of Manchester Liberalism is over."[28]

While Catholics in the CDU rejected consistently the philosophical underpinnings of Liberalism and capitalism as bases for postwar German reconstruction, they also condemned Liberalism's leading nineteenth-century challenger, Marxism. In a testament to the sweeping nature of the Catholic critique of modernity, Catholics depicted Marxism as a full-fledged manifestation of materialism: Marxism's origins in "the spirit of the nineteenth century"—"the natural scientific, positivistic spirit"—were in fact a logical outgrowth of Liberal "unbridled capitalism."[29] "Liberalism and Marxism," according to Konrad Adenauer, "are two sprouts from the same root, from the root which knows only this life [*Diesseits*] . . . and in whose outlook the hereafter [*Jenseits*] no longer plays a role."[30] As a manifestation of "materialism in modern times," explained the CDU in Schwäbisch-Gmünd, Marxism necessarily helped to pave "the way for National Socialism, in that it created the most important prerequisite for its reprehensible methods, namely, [it] denied the existence of God."[31]

This comprehensive indictment of all that Catholics deemed materialistic had clear implications for the Christian Democratic program. In rejecting both capitalism and Marxism, Catholics argued after 1945 for a distinctly Catholic form of societal organization. As the foundation for an antimaterialist, Christian state, the principle of the Christian individual— or *Persönlichkeit* (personalism)—beholden to God and the *Gemeinschaft* found a central place in almost every CDU publication and speech.[32]

The sanctity of *Persönlichkeit* and the related concept of human dignity (*Würde des Menschen*) undergird every Catholic stance on the German future, including perhaps the most basic, support for democracy. In contrast to the Center Party of the Weimar era, the CDU committed itself unequivocally to the principles of democratic governance. By condemning as flawed all of modern European history since at least the French Revolution, however, Catholics rejected the political and philosophical foundations for democracy as it had existed in Germany.

Instead, Catholic members of the CDU adhered to a distinctly Catholic representation of democracy's nature and origins. In a self-affirming formula that designated the conditions for democracy as uniquely Christian before concluding that only Christianity could fulfill them, Catholic CDU members rejected decades of democratic politics in Europe as materialistic: "The Christian worldview alone guarantees justice, order and moderation, value and freedom of the person and with that a true and genuine democracy. . . . We consider the high regard Christianity has for human dignity—for the value of every single person—the foundation and guiding principle of our work in the political, economic, and cultural life of our *Volk.*"[33]

In this and many other descriptions of democracy from Catholics in the CDU, the undertones of traditional, Catholic thinking, with its emphasis on organic unity, were unmistakable.[34] Employing language similar to that they had used following World War I, Catholics after 1945 portrayed democracy as the "dominion of the *Volk,* as it has grown organically in *all of its groupings,* with no preference for a *class,* a *Stand,* [or] a party."[35] In his speech at the founding assembly of the CDU in Düsseldorf in late November 1945, Karl Arnold, cofounder of the CDU in the Rhineland, proclaimed, "Democracy cannot be decreed for the *Volk* as a state gift. . . . Democracy cannot grow from top to bottom; it must come from the *Volk* and grow into governing state authority. . . . Democracy is, finally, a political atmosphere that enables forces from the moral and spiritual substance of all the strata of the

*Volk* to grow. . . . Democracy is therefore no mechanical affair but an organic and creative political manifestation of life."[36]

As the nature of democracy was rendered distinctly Catholic, so were the origins of democracy considered Catholic as well. After World War II Catholics consistently located the roots of Catholic democracy in a romanticized vision of a religiously homogeneous, premodern western Europe, the *Abendland* (Occident).[37] This construct of an organic, corporative society traced back to the pre-Enlightenment Middle Ages connoted a harmonious order integrating the family with other institutions, most important the church and state.[38] Because the state was part of a "natural" hierarchy, Catholics did not have to defend their anterior rights against it; governing authorities had no independent authority over their subjects because the entire society derived its legitimacy solely from God.[39]

At least since Oswald Spengler's *Untergang des Abendlandes,* the term *Abendland* had enjoyed great currency as the designation for a culturally unified Europe removed from the forces of secularization unleashed by the French Revolution. Although its authoritarian character for the most part disappeared after 1945, the *Abendland* had been linked during the nineteenth and early twentieth century—including the Nazi years—to a monarchical and Fascist Reich.[40] Despite its widespread use after 1945 by Protestants as well as Catholics, the *Abendland* retained a distinctly Catholic image into the postwar era.[41]

For Catholics after World War II, the *Abendland* represented more than the locus of a uniquely Catholic vision of democracy. In its sanctification of the *Persönlichkeit,* the *Abendland* offered the only basis from which Germany could recover from National Socialism.[42] In the words of the Württemberg CDU, materialism's destruction of "the united *Abendland*" had brought Germany "to the brink of destruction";[43] only a return to the *Abendland* could guide Germany in the future.[44]

The confessionalism of the Catholic CDU's vision of Christian Democracy was reinforced by Catholics' cartographic siting of materialism. While locating the roots of democratic Germany in the Catholic, western areas of Germany, CDU members simultaneously depicted Protestant Prussia as the physical embodiment of materialism. In this way, the *Abendland* and Prussia lent a geography to the otherwise spiritual confrontation between (Catholic) Christianity and materialism.

In the Catholic rendering of a Europe under siege by materialism, the *Abendland* had long been understood as explicitly anti-Prussian.[45] In the nineteenth century, many Catholics construed the unification of Germany as a deliberate violation of the *abendländische* integrity of the Reich; during the Weimar years, *Abendland* theorists attacked Prussia as a bastion of materialistic chauvinism and militarism.[46] It was in the wake of National Socialism, however, that Prussia became associated most explicitly with materialism.

Although prejudices against Prussia were by no means limited to Catholic Germans after World War II,[47] Catholics in postwar Germany burnished their own, long-standing tradition of anti-Prussianness. Consistent with the Catholic rejection of secular individualism, Catholics had traditionally linked the potency of the Prussian state to its disregard for human dignity.[48] Now, in the wake of World War II, Catholics in the CDU invoked the trope of the all-powerful Prussian state to tie Prussia directly to Nazism and materialism.[49] Materialism had found its true expression in the eastern, Protestant areas of Germany, Catholics argued; in contrast, the western, *abendländisch* areas represented the "real" and democratic Germany.[50]

In grounding their program in the Catholic worldview so clearly, Catholics in the CDU testified to the strength of Catholic consciousness in Germany after World War II. They also demonstrated the level of anti-Protestant suspicion inherent in their vision for postwar Germany, even as they worked to create Germany's first avowedly democratic interconfessional party.[51] Though dominated by Catholics, the construction of an interconfessional ideology nevertheless depended fundamentally on Protestant acquiescence. While Catholics called on Catholic traditions and social teachings, Protestants articulated their own understanding of Germany's past and future.

## PROTESTANT ANTIMATERIALISM AFTER WORLD WAR II

Before 1945 Protestants had belonged to a large number of political parties, ranging from the Christian Social People's Service (CSVD) to the German Democratic Party (DDP), the German People's Party (DVP), the German National People's Party (DNVP), and even the National Socialist German Workers' Party (NSDAP); they consequently shared neither a unifying organizational tradition nor a common political philosophy. For many anti-Marxist Protestants whose pre-1933 parties had been discredited by collaboration with the Nazis, however, a realistic assessment of postwar options left little alternative to the CDU. Particularly for devout Protestants who advocated their own Christian political agenda, members of the former Center Party were far more likely allies than Socialists or Liberals.

Of the utmost importance for the construction of a Christian Democratic ideology was the fact that conservative Protestants had long shared elements of the Catholic critique of materialism and modernism. Throughout the history of modern Germany, religious Protestants—especially the Pietists and their successors in the *Erweckungsbewegung*—had opposed secularization and modernism as passionately as had members of the Catholic *Teilkultur*.[52] Well into the twentieth century, many of these religiously devout conservatives rejected capitalism, technology, and internationalism while endorsing an organic, family-centered, *ständisch* societal order.[53]

Historically a minority in Protestant Germany, such Protestants in the nineteenth and twentieth centuries had, on occasion, regarded Catholics as natural allies in the ongoing battle against secularism and revolution.[54] During the Kulturkampf, for example, Protestant conservatives registered their disapproval of the liberal attacks on Catholic religious rights by refusing to support several anti-Catholic measures.[55] Futhermore, certain socially conservative policies, in particular, confessional schools,[56] consistently found support among conservative Protestants and Catholics.[57]

It was these common beliefs that made possible the forging of a Christian Democratic ideology after World War II. Protestants in the CDU not only rejected materialism and secularization,[58] they also linked directly the ascent of materialism to the rise of National Socialism. In answer to the question, "How could it have happened?" Otto Boelitz, a former member of the DVP and cofounder of the CDU in Soest, accused "materialism before 1933": "We had become a *Volk* that no longer searched for God with all its heart, a *Volk* unfamiliar with God that went astray."[59]

By subscribing to the Manichaean model of competing Christian and materialist forces, Protestants joined Catholics in portraying the task of postwar politics as the transformation of secular society.[60] Inherent in political activity, explained Paul Bausch, a former member of the CSVD, was the responsibility to subordinate every aspect of political life to the demands of Christian laws: "The Ten Commandments of God delineate the iron foundation for state life. . . . The task for us today is to replace a Godless government with a government that respects God's commandments and makes them the principles of the life of the *Volk* and of the state."[61] This program of Christianizing Germany, agreed Ulrich Steiner, cofounder of the CDU in Laupheim and Württemberg-Hohenzollern, implied "nothing less than the Christian revolution in all branches of human life." "We have been called to action," he continued, "and when we are not ready to organize our lives afresh and fruitfully as revolutionaries of Christian conviction, then the revolutionaries of the devil, that is to say, the revolutionaries of the materialistic idea of utilitarianism, will do it for us."[62]

Despite their agreement that only a Christian Germany could prevent the return of the evil of materialism, Catholics and Protestants grounded their critiques in two fundamentally differing worldviews. The dissimilarities, although conceptual and seemingly abstract, would nevertheless govern the dynamics of early Christian Democratic policy making. Even on such a fundamental level as the Protestant and Catholic understandings of the Christian individual, theologically based differences within the CDU shaped profoundly interconfessional cooperation.

While both confessions embraced the Christian notion of man created in God's image, Protestants differed significantly on the cultural origins of individual liberty. In contrast to Catholics in the CDU, who located the notion of human dignity in the *Abendland,* Wilhelm Simpfendörfer, former member of the CSVD and cofounder of the CDU in North Württemberg, stressed the importance of the Reformation to the development of respect for the rights of the individual. Such basic rights, according to Simpfendörfer, had been advanced for the first time by religious sects in the age of the Reformation; as these sects asserted their members' God-given dignity against the hostile powers of the state, they provided an inspirational example for people all over the world.[63]

Otto Heinrich von der Gablentz, a member of the CDU in Berlin, echoed Simpfendörfer's praise for the Reformation as the crucial historical fount of Europe's respect for "freedom of the individual." For all of human history, he maintained, man had sought to achieve a balance between the competing forces of the *Gemeinschaft* and the rights of the individual. At various times in history, the "compulsion" exerted by the *Gemeinschaft* had induced moral restraint or religious intolerance; in Germany, this had led spiritually to the medieval hierarchy of clerical rulers (*Priesterherrschaft*). In a revolt of the *Volk* determined to assert the rights of the individual, the *Gemeinschaft*-obsessed Church in Germany consequently underwent a "Reformation."[64]

In a similar rejection of the Catholic, *abendländische* interpretation of German history and the origins of democracy, numerous Protestants in the party contested the Catholic association of Prussianism with materialism. After the war, von der Gablentz proudly identified himself as Prussian and defended publicly values he considered uniquely "Prussian": "It is difficult for me to issue a harsh verdict regarding the Prussianism from which I come, today, where [*sic*] every one reviles it and it is [considered] fair to wreak one's cowardly revenge."[65] In a speech he delivered numerous times in the western zones and Berlin, "The Tragedy of Prussia," von der Gablentz declared, "Prussia belongs to Germany and has, for Germany and from the home base of Germany, an unfulfilled mission in Europe."[66]

These tensions between Catholics and conservative, religious Protestants were indicative of the profound variances that lay below the surface of early interconfessionalism. Philosophical at base, these differences on the nature of materialism quickly translated into concrete disputes over the new party's direction. Even before ideological differences prompted policy disputes, they bedeviled the early organization of the party.

Of the numerous controversies plaguing the party's formation, one open conflict concerned the inclusion of certain Protestants. In addition to conservative Protestants, who influenced most profoundly the organization of the CDU in northern Germany, the CDU attracted Protestants from the former Liberal parties, the DDP and DVP. Especially prominent in the Rhineland and Berlin, these inheritors of Germany's nineteenth-century Liberal movement represented a significant challenge to the anti-Liberalism of the CDU's antimaterialist platform.

Indeed, the Catholic reaction to Liberal elements in the party struck a considerably different chord than did the open door shown to conservative Protestants. Some Catholics in western Germany, for example, actively resisted the idea of making common political cause with former Liberals.[67] In other cases, however, Catholic CDU party propaganda listed Protestant Liberals as founding members of the post-1945 Christian Democratic alliance.[68] Especially in Berlin, where Protestant Liberal participation in the CDU was more pronounced than in most western party centers, Catholics—while continuing to denounce Liberalism as a political philosophy—accepted conditionally Liberal participation in the CDU.

In a speech delivered in January 1946, for example, Emil Dovifat condemned the ideology of Liberalism for promoting "snobby arrogance in the spiritual sphere [*im Geistigen*] just as in the purely private aim for profit in business." At the same time, however, he expanded the political definition of "Christian" to include those who did not necessarily belong to one of Germany's large churches: the CDU, based on Dovifat's broadened interpretation of "Christian," could "welcome *the* Liberal in our ranks who translates his heightened individual freedom into attainment for the people at large."[69]

Liberals themselves were unmistakably conscious of their lack of conformity to the CDU's platform of Christian antimaterialism. In July 1946, former DDP member Ernst Lemmer explained that the Nazi years had transformed significantly both Liberals and Christians in Germany so that a political union was now possible. Germany's Christians, according to Lemmer, had become "more democratic" since the end of the Weimar Republic while Democrats in turn had become "more Christian."[70] The CDU welcomed those who might not identify themselves in the first line as "Christians" but who "out of moral, humanitarian inclinations demand the return of politics to the order of moral laws." Thus "the Liberal belongs to [the CDU], too, when he accommodates his personal freedom to higher moral responsibility and utterly devotes his dogmatic individualism to brotherly help for his fellow man."[71]

That Catholic discomfort with former Liberals was not echoed by Protestant members of the CDU highlighted Protestants' and Catholics' divergent approaches to the future. Such membership questions were but one example of the practical ramifications of ideological difference. Not surprisingly, these philosophical discrepancies would become especially charged as the construction of Christian Democracy moved from a theoretical to a policy-making plane. On issues of great ideological and political conflict—above all, economic policy—Protestant and Catholic tensions influenced decisively the formation and content of the CDU program, challenging at a fundamental level the meaning of Christian Democracy.

## ANTIMATERIALISM AS POLICY: ANTISOCIALIST ECONOMICS

Antimaterialism as the ideological foundation for German Christian Democracy underwent significant testing and redefinition in the immediate postwar years. Above all, the concept of materialism was shaped by the CDU's debate about economics, particularly concerning Christian Social-ism. As the forge in which the party's ideology was shaped, CDU discourse on economic policy largely established the parameters of antimaterialism; in so doing, it helped to set the contours of interconfessional politics in postwar Germany.

The resolution of the party's confessional conflict over economic policy was influenced powerfully by outside events, particularly Allied occupation and the Cold War. The dynamics of the party's debate demonstrated clearly, however, the prominence of confessional difference. The reconfiguration of antimaterialism as an ideological and political position took place through a series of factors; religious tension was among the most important.

Reflecting the party's confessional imbalance, the CDU's discussion of economic policy was dominated by leading Catholic members of the party. Catholic Christian Democrats, consistent with their expression of antimaterialism, supported a Catholic "middle way" between communism and capitalism, between—in their words—Marxism and Manchester Lib-eralism.[72] Although in broad agreement on the need for controlled state intervention in the economy,[73] Catholics in the CDU differed on how to describe that involvement. The dispute among Catholics in the party re-volved less around the specific measures of the economic program than its terminology; the word "socialism" lay at the heart of the discord.

Just as economic programs had divided Catholics in the Center Party before 1933, the CDU debate after 1945 revealed deep fissures within the Catholic *Teilkultur*. The dividing line between low-ranking clergy and former Christian trade unionists, on one side, and middle-class Catholics, on the other, testified to the endurance of class tensions within Germany's Catho-lic population. Those tensions reappeared as activist clergy and trade union-ists promoted Christian Socialism as the economic platform of the CDU. Sharply distinguished from Marxist socialism, Christian Socialism drew on Weimar Catholic economic thought embedded in antimaterialism.[74]

Reflecting the influence of priests and trade unionists on the party's earliest organization, the term "Christian Socialism"—or the correlative expression, "Socialism Based on Christian Responsibility" (*Sozialismus aus christlicher Verantwortung*)—ran as a leitmotiv throughout early CDU publi-cations. In the party's earliest program, the "Cologne Guiding Principles," for example, the CDU demanded "social justice and social love" in order to reconcile the God-given freedom of the individual with the needs of the *Gemeinschaft*.[75] In the same spirit, the Bad Godesberg program of December 1945 embraced "Socialism Based on Christian Responsibility" as "a system of planned government control inspired by the old, *abendländische* idea of the free and responsible *Persönlichkeit*."[76]

Although widespread, such strong statements in the early CDU in favor of Christian Socialism did not meet with unanimous acclaim. Even at the earliest gatherings of Christian Democratic politicians, isolated Catholics argued against inscribing Christian Socialism into the new party's platform.[77] Nascent opposition to the term "socialism"—especially on the part of middle-class Catholics—burgeoned quickly; particularly after the first interzonal meeting of Christian Democrats in December 1945, divisions among Catholic Christian Democrats became conspicuous.

In the confessionally mixed party, however, internal Catholic conflict by no means held center stage. By virtue of their indispensability to the project of interconfessionalism, Protestants enjoyed far greater influence in the CDU than their membership numbers suggested. The Protestant reaction to Christian Socialism not only provoked the young party's most threatening internal dispute; in a larger sense, it forced a redefinition of the party's ideological foundations.

Reflecting the widely varying political backgrounds of Protestants in the CDU, there was no unified Protestant vision of Christian Democratic economics. Of crucial importance to the discussion of Christian Socialism, however, Protestants in the party were overwhelmingly middle class: no matter which party had claimed their loyalties before 1933, CDU Protestants were inveterate enemies of Social Democracy. It is not surprising, then, that Protestant Christian Democrats—with the exception of a few isolated voices in Berlin[78]—opposed unequivocally the idea of Christian Socialism. Strikingly, although class was determinate in shaping this position, Protestant stances were never characterized in class terms. Highlighting the significance of religious difference in early German Christian Democracy, the standpoint of Protestants within the party was linked consistently to their religion.

Of the Protestants in the early CDU, the most outspoken belonged to the Westphalian and especially the Rhenish party branches. Reflecting the influence of the British Zone in the larger CDU as well as of the Rhineland in the British Zone, Protestants in the Rhineland to a large degree came to represent the "Protestant" position in early Christian Democracy.[79] Better organized and more ideologically unified than their coreligionists in northern Germany, Rhenish Protestants waged a concerted campaign to increase Protestant influence on party deliberations; they would play a central role in the CDU's debate on Christian Socialism.[80]

Elected in early 1946 to represent Protestants in the party's Rhineland branch, Otto Schmidt, a founding member of the Confessing Church, enjoyed access to Konrad Adenauer as well as to other leading Catholics in the British Zone CDU.[81] Chair of the Wuppertal CDU, Schmidt used his entrée to argue for increased Protestant leverage in the party; in particular, he worked to express Protestant opposition to Christian Socialism. In an article titled "Christian Realism—An Attempt at a Socioeconomic New Order," Schmidt made clear his rejection of the economic vision common to "Romantic Catholics" and Christian Socialists: "Christian knowledge protects us from idealizing the world. It does not address the economy as an organism in the manner of Romanticism. . . . Christian knowledge does not aggrandize [*überhebt*] the individual, but [it] also does not degrade him to a mere part of the *Gemeinschaft*, to a thing or even to an animal."[82] At the same time, Schmidt asserted, "Liberal, early capitalism" may not provide for all those in need, but "it should not and cannot be disputed that, in the given circumstances, the Liberal economic principle achieved significant things. The living standard of the wide sections [of the population] was, under the influence of Liberal capitalism, far higher than in the age of the guild economy."[83]

Schmidt's position, in particular, his concern with the primacy of the individual, was typical of Rhenish and Westphalian Protestants in the CDU. In a party flyer published in August 1945, for example, Wuppertal Protestants argued that only an economic order that granted the "widest scope for private initiative" guaranteed "healthy economics," that is, the best product at the most reasonable price.[84] In September 1946 Friedrich Holzapfel, deputy chairman of the CDU Westphalian *Landesverband*, struck a similar chord when he noted that "the word 'social' is not used in our party program."[85]

Although Protestants played a key role in the party debate over economic policy, the figureheads of the conflict—not surprising in a party dominated numerically by Catholics—were the party's two leading Catholics, Konrad Adenauer and Jakob Kaiser. In large part the result of Adenauer's personal assumption of power, two fronts within the party—one associated with Adenauer, the other with Kaiser—crystallized in early 1946. While Adenauer found strong allies among western, bourgeois Catholics suspicious of all things associated with Berlin, Kaiser, a former Christian trade unionist and cofounder of the Berlin CDU, drew his support from Berliners and Catholic trade unionists. From the earliest postwar days, Kaiser strongly supported Christian Socialism.

Even more than among middle-class Catholics or from Adenauer, however, Kaiser found his most unified opponents among the CDU's Rhenish and Westphalian Protestants. Already in February 1946, for example, Otto Schmidt wrote Adenauer that the program published by the party branch in Berlin had led "to the gravest misgivings against the CDU" on the part of Protestants;[86] the CDU of the British Zone, continued Schmidt, should never place itself under the "authority of Jakob Kaiser" because Kaiser had not offered "an intellectual clarification of what is meant by Christian Socialism."[87] In March 1946 Schmidt's colleague Emil Marx expressed similar concern that the language of Kaiser and other Christian Socialists might threaten the "private initiative . . . so indispensable for construction [Aufbau]."[88]

Another influential Protestant in the North Rhine–Westphalian CDU, Klaus Brauda, was especially vocal on this matter. Kaiser's influence over social and economic policy within the party was threatening, Brauda maintained, because it represented an "attempt to transplant the radicalization of the East Zone into the West Zones." "The CDU of the West Zone," Brauda asserted, "apparently wants to accept this radicalization as an avoidable fact and necessary evil. I am sorry that what Mr. Kaiser has referred to as Christian Socialism must be described as Christian radicalism." The Rhenish Social Democrats' contention that one "could no longer recognize a difference in our mutual [beiderseitigen] views" was, in Brauda's opinion, regrettably "true."[89]

In a clear reference to the Protestants he represented within the party, furthermore, Brauda maintained that Kaiser's rhetoric would "have very unpleasant electoral [wahltaktisch] and opinion poll [stimmungsmässig] consequences." Kaiser's program had created "the greatest commotion" in the entire "middle class," Brauda contended; voters now feared "far-reaching encroachments on private property and the sphere of the small and intermediate people." "We will not make a stand against the socialist parties by outdoing them in radicalism," Brauda concluded. "Instead, we will combat them by seeking and finding in Christian realism . . . the synthesis and not the antithesis of the *Stände*."[90]

As is clear from these protests against Jakob Kaiser and Christian Socialism, Protestants resented Kaiser's influence and especially his popularization of Christian Socialism. That they reacted with such unity and passion highlights the prominence and confessional character of the early party's most important debate. Protestants may well have employed code words such as "capitalists" and "businessmen," but they could not conceal the extent to which they spoke as Protestants. Emil Marx's protest, for example, that his complaints—in contradiction to the spirit and tone of his letter— were "in no way specifically evangelical or Protestant" simply confirmed that which he sought to deny: Protestants understood their rejection of Christian Socialism as a Protestant stance within the party, not that of an interconfessional middle class.[91]

That Catholics shared this perception was evident in the shift among western Catholics against Christian Socialism in early 1946. As former Christian trade unionists began that year to reconsider their support for "socialist" economics, they made direct reference to the party's fragile interreligious alliance. In July 1946, for example, former Christian trade unionist Anton Storch wrote Johannes Albers, former secretary of the Christian trade unions and cofounder of the CDU in Cologne, that he now rejected use of the terms "Christian Socialism" or "Socialism Based on Christian Responsibility" because they weakened the party's interconfessional stance against Communism. In a clear allusion to Protestant-Catholic unity, Storch explained, "In the CDU, forces have come together which are truly in the position to give Germany a new character. We must only prevent our being maneuvered against one another" and divided into right and left wings. Making the implicit but unmistakable association of Protestants with the party's "right wing," Storch noted in reference to several Protestants he had recently met that he had "come to the conviction that they are very valuable people." In light of the long-standing confessional differences between Protestants and Catholics, Storch concluded, "[i]t is small wonder many things in a new party have to get polished."[92]

While Catholic trade unionists reconsidered Christian Socialism throughout 1946, Protestants remained concerned about its effect on attracting and retaining Protestant votes. Commenting on the September 1946 elections in the British and French Zones, for example, Wilhelm Lindner, an influential Protestant in the North Rhine–Westphalian CDU, noted that the CDU in Westphalia had done well because it had avoided the exceptionally bitter "ideological antagonism" (*weltanschaulicher Gegensatz*) plaguing the Rhenish CDU; "Christianity and socialism," Lindner opined in reference to the Rhenish CDU's debate, "go together like fire and water."[93] That same month, a party leader in overwhelmingly Protestant Thuringia complained to Jakob Kaiser that the CDU's use of the word "socialism" had "driven a considerable portion of the party's potential supporters to the Liberal Democrats." "Christian Socialism," the author explained, "did not attract the votes of SPD people, on whom we had really been counting"; instead, the Protestants who voted showed more confidence in "capitalistic Liberalism" and its proponent, the Liberal Party. To win back these Protestant voters, the Thuringian concluded, the CDU would have to drop "the propaganda for Christian Socialism."[94]

Following such exchanges in 1946, the gap between Catholic support for Christian Socialism and Protestants' stalwart antisocialism began to close. Although the debate among Catholic members of the CDU continued throughout 1947, the beginnings of a semantic and ideological compromise were manifest. That 1947 marked the unmistakable emergence of Cold War tensions was, not surprisingly, of direct consequence to the CDU's debate over Christian Socialism. Not only in the three western zones of Germany but throughout western Europe, the increased influence of the United States and the perceived belligerence of the Soviet Union discouraged support for communist and socialist domestic political forces.[95]

The discrediting of socialism neither completely ended the CDU debate nor transformed its confessional character, however. Even after the party's famous February 1947 Ahlen program marked an apparent internal consensus by avoiding the word "socialism,"[96] the specter of confessional warfare continued to haunt the CDU. As the relationship of Christian Democracy to Christian Socialism remained contested, so too did the boundaries of antimaterialism; as party developments in 1947 would make clear, an unshakable interconfessional compact for Christian Democratic politics had yet to take hold.

The palpable tensions between CDU Protestants and Catholics were evident in a number of confessionalized exchanges in 1947. Perhaps the most dramatic followed Ministerpräsident Karl Arnold's June 1947 policy statement to the Landtag of North Rhine–Westphalia. After Arnold, a prominent Catholic in the CDU, hinted at continued support for Christian Socialism by suggesting the exclusion of "private big business" from basic industries,[97] CDU Protestants reacted strongly and in force. At an official gathering in July 1947 of Rhenish and Westphalian Protestants, those present complained that Arnold had intentionally "blurred the boundaries of our conception of the economy," alienating "wide circles of the middle class" with his attempt to attract workers from the SPD.[98]

While the Protestant meeting demonstrated the unanimity of Protestants in the British Zone, Arnold's reaction to their statement was equally revealing. Defending in impassioned language his long-standing commitment to the "true and genuine values of Christianity,"[99] Arnold expressed dismay at what he considered the open confessionalization of CDU economic policy. Acknowledging what had been inherent in Christian Democratic politics from its inception, Arnold criticized Protestants for portraying the party's internal disputes as confessional: "To confuse general political questions with the thought of the confessional union and to handle them, in a way, as a Protestant problem, at a Protestant meeting, appears to me an objectively unnecessary encumbrance on the political cooperation between the confessions—[one] that I, based on the spirit of the Union [*Unionsgedanken*], deeply regret."[100]

Clearly, the interconfessional consensus undergirding the CDU remained tenuous in 1947. Christian Socialism continued to divide the confessions; at the same time, it challenged the party's antimaterialist consensus by "blur[ring] the boundaries" of Protestants' "conception of the economy." Because antimaterialism mandated a rejection of Marxist socialism, it also, according to Protestants in the CDU, dictated a full-scale rejection of Christian Socialism. Catholic support for "socialism" betrayed Protestants' understanding of antimaterialism; for the sake of interconfessionalism, Christian Socialism would have to be sacrificed.

Although Christian Socialism was ultimately defeated within the CDU, its demise was not codified by the party until the adoption of Ludwig Erhard's "social market economy."[101] The CDU's embrace of the social market economy was the product of a multilayered and complicated process, one as highly confessionalized as the debate about Christian Socialism.[102] While the CDU's interconfessional alliance owed something to the artful rhetoric of Erhard, who stressed the "Soziale" when speaking to Catholics and the "Marktwirtschaft" when addressing Protestants,[103] the groundwork for the compromise had been laid much earlier—in the disputes over Christian Socialism. By demonstrating the importance of antisocialism to Protestant Christian Democrats, the CDU's early deliberations made clear that interconfessional economics would have to be indelibly antisocialist; in this way, the formulation of CDU economic policy served to delineate the boundaries of the party's broader ideology.

The construction of a Christian Democratic ideology was among the most important developments in early West German history. Fundamental to interconfessionalism's underlying pact of antimaterialism, anti-Marxism came increasingly to define Christian Democratic politics writ large. After the founding of the German Democratic Republic and the emergence of the Social Democrats as the CDU's major rival, antisocialism superseded all other variants of antimaterialism in CDU rhetoric, coming almost to supplant antimaterialism itself. Reflecting the dominance of the CDU in the early Federal Republic, this process extended well beyond the boundaries of the party to the politics and culture of the new state. Indeed, by the 1950s antisocialism operated as the hegemonic ideology of the "constitutional and consolidational" era of the Federal Republic.[104]

The ascendancy of antisocialism could not obscure, however, the confessional tensions inherent in the CDU's origins. Despite the compelling political advantages Christian Democracy offered both Protestants and Catholics, the party's interconfessional alliance remained conflict-ridden. In 1952, for example, in response to their concern that their distinctive voice was being ignored, CDU Protestants led by organizers from Wuppertal established the inner-party Protestant Working Group (Evangelischer Arbeitskreis). Chaired by the Bundestag president, Hermann Ehlers, the Protestant Working Group almost immediately antagonized Adenauer by calling for intensified contacts with (Protestant) East Germany.[105]

As the leadership of the party remained divided by confession, so too did its membership.[106] At what point the CDU truly became a *Volkspartei*, or "catchall" party,[107] rested directly on the continued existence in the CDU and the Federal Republic of the Catholic *Teilkultur*. The impact of war-related population dislocation on the "closed village" German countryside (leading to a sudden and forced integration of Protestants and Catholics),[108] the SPD's own adjustment of its relationship to religion and the churches,[109] the abandonment of the Catholic working class for the SPD,[110] and the widespread secularization of West German society in the 1950s and 1960s all signaled the breakdown of traditional social and cultural milieus in Germany, including that of the *Teilkultur* of German Catholicism.[111]

Evident in so many ways, this profound cultural change was mirrored concretely in the shifting usage of the term "materialism." As the Cold War and economic recovery took hold and Nazism faded quickly from public concern, materialism's complexion changed dramatically, altering with it the ideological character of Christian Democracy. Rhetorically separate from the United States during the Occupation years,[112] materialism became associated in the 1950s with American-style consumerism. With the advent of Americanization in West Germany in the 1950s, Protestant and Catholic clergy members and social conservatives suspicious of American cultural influence increasingly directed antimaterialist invective against the so-called American way of life:[113] antimaterialism became the political watch-word for anti-Americanism and anticonsumerism.

The path of materialism from the immediate postwar era into the 1950s reveals much about the history of the early CDU. Initially a source of both unity and dissension, antimaterialism was necessarily refashioned to serve as an ideological foundation for interconfessional politics. By the 1950s, when antisocialism and anticommunism largely sufficed to secure interconfessional cohesion, materialism, no longer central to party politics, lay open to redefinition. That the Protestant-Catholic compact of the immediate postwar era flourished in the long run should not obscure the union's early weaknesses; indeed, the survival of Christian Democracy in occupied Germany was hardly self-evident. The challenges facing Protestants and Catholics intent on political reconciliation therefore shed important light on the crucial birthing hour of German Christian Democracy.

## NOTES

*Abbreviations for archives cited in the notes are as follows:*

ACDPStA   Archiv für Christlich-demokratische Politik, St. Augustin
BAK       Bundesarchiv Koblenz
HAStK     Historisches Archiv der Stadt Köln
HStAD     Hauptstaatsarchiv Düsseldorf
StBKAH    Archiv der Stiftung Bundeskanzler-Adenauer-Haus, Rhöndorf

1. BAK, NL 278 (Holzapfel), vol. 312, Hans Schlange-Schöningen, circular letter (October 31, 1945). Schlange-Schöningen spoke for many Protestants after World War II when he explained that "a significant percentage of the Protestant electorate sees in the Christian Democratic Union—despite its loosening of an ultramontane tie—the old Zentrum and for this reason rejects it."

2. For the importance of Rhenish and Westphalian Catholics to the Center Party in both the nineteenth and twentieth centuries, see Jonathan Sperber, *Popular Catholicism in Nineteenth-Century Germany* (Princeton, 1984), 259, 290; Ronald J. Ross, *Beleaguered Tower: The Dilemma of Political Catholicism in Wilhelmine Germany* (Notre Dame, 1976), 120; and Rudolf Morsey, *Die Deutsche Zentrumspartei, 1917–1923* (Düsseldorf, 1966), 164, 578. For a brief but helpful discussion of the two primary varieties of political Catholicism in Germany, the Rhenish-Westphalian and the Bavarian, see Jürgen Kohns, *Konrad Adenauer und der Föderalismus* (Würzburg, 1987). Because Bavarians organized separately after 1945 into their own "Christian democratic" party, the Christlich-Soziale Union (CSU), I focus exclusively on the CDU and therefore on the "Prussian" strain of political Catholicism. As a result, the majority of my citations stem from Rhenish and Westphalian Catholics.

3. While the British Zone had the lowest percentage of Catholics of the three western zones, the future *Land* of North Rhine–Westphalia was almost two-thirds Catholic. In 1946 CDU membership was proportionally higher in North Rhine–Westphalia than in any other CDU *Landesverband*. This was still true as late as 1991, when the *Land* party of North Rhine–Westphalia claimed nearly 30 percent of the total CDU membership. Joachim Beckmann, ed., *Kirchliches Jahrbuch für die Evangelische Kirche in Deutschland, 1949* (Gütersloh, 1950), 541, 561–62; Winfried Becker, *CDU und CSU, 1945–1950: Vorläufer, Gründung und regionale Entwicklung bis zum Entstehen der CDU-Bundespartei* (Mainz, 1987), 113; David Broughton, "The CDU-CSU in Germany: Is There Any Alternative?" in David Hanley, ed., *Christian Democracy in Europe: A Comparative Perspective* (London and New York: Pinter, 1994), 106.

4. The organizational and ideological dominance of the early CDU by the British Zonal Committee has been emphasized in many places. See Becker, *CDU und CSU*, 113; Horstwalter Heitzer, *Die CDU in der britischen Besatzungszone: Gründung, Organisation, Programm und Politik, 1945–1949* (Düsseldorf, 1988), 16, 166–174; Konrad-Adenauer-Stiftung, ed., *Konrad Adenauer und die CDU der britischen Besatzungszone, 1946–1949* (Bonn, 1975), 87–92; and Ute Schmidt, "Die Christlich Demokratische Union Deutschlands," in Richard Stöss, ed., *Parteien-Handbuch: Die Parteien der Bundesrepublik Deutschland, 1945–1980*, vol. 1 (Opladen, 1983), 501.

5. Daniel E. Rogers, *Politics after Hitler: The Western Allies and the German Party System* (London, 1995), 79.

6. For one of numerous examples, see BAK, NL 278 (Holzapfel), vol. 139. Christlich-Demokratische Union, Kreis Detmold, "Aufruf!" (Detmold, presumably spring 1946).

7. For the CDU's adherence to this interpretation, see Maria Mitchell, "Materialism and Secularism: CDU Politicians and National Socialism, 1945–1949," *Journal of Modern History* 67, no. 2 (June 1995): 278–308. For two of many examples of clergymen's subscription to this thesis, see Peter Löffler, ed., *Bischof Clemens August Graf von Galen: Akten, Briefe und Predigten 1933–1946*, vol. 2 (Mainz, 1988), 1233; and Albert Stohr, "Bischof von Mainz, Hirtenbrief mit richtunggebenden Worten in 'einer verworrenen Zeit,'" in Wolfgang Löhr, ed., *Hirtenbriefe und Ansprachen zu Gesellschaft und Politik, 1945–1949* (Würzburg, 1985), 37.

8. ACDPStA, I-056-019. Josef Beyerle, speech (Ulm, February 24, 1946).

9. See StBKAH, 08.54, 393–98. "Ein Ruf zur Sammlung des deutschen Volkes: Vorläufiger Entwurf zu einem Programm der Christlichen Demokraten Deutschlands, Vorgelegt von den Christlichen Demokraten Köln im Juni 1945" (Cologne, June 1945); StBKAH, 08.05, 77–78. Karl Arnold, Anton Betz, and Maximilian Freiherr von Gumppenberg, eds., Christliche Volkspartei Deutschlands vorbereitender Ausschuss, "An die Bevölkerung Düsseldorfs!" (Düsseldorf, presumably August 1945); StBKAH, 08.54, 399–403. "Leitsätze der Christlich-Demokratischen Partei in Rheinland und Westfalen" (Cologne, Bochum, Düsseldorf, September 1945).

10. Wilfried Loth, *Katholiken im Kaiserreich: Der politische Katholizismus in der Krise des wilhelminischen Deutschlands* (Düsseldorf, 1984), 17.

11. I adopt the term *Teilkultur* from Detlef Lehnert and Klaus Megerle to imply a distinct social group, the voting patterns of which are directly related to its assumptions and beliefs. I prefer the term *Teil-* as opposed to *Subkultur* (subculture) for its less hierarchical and hegemonic connotations. Furthermore, even at the peak of exclusively Catholic organization, the Catholic one-third of German society was by no means completely isolated from Protestant Germany; German Catholics interacted with other German social groups and individuals in a variety of ways. For Lehnert and Megerle's exploration of the connotations of the term *Teilkultur* and its relationship to the concepts *Lager* and *sozialmoralisches Milieu*, see Detlef Lehnert and Klaus Megerle, eds., *Politische Teilkulturen zwischen Integration und Polarisierung: Zur politischen Kultur in der Weimarer Republik* (Opladen, 1990), esp. 10–11.

12. The strength of a Catholic *Selbstbewußtsein* in post–World War II Catholic politics was also the product of the maturity of the leaders of the CDU. Because the Nazi dictatorship had prevented the democratic education of an entire generation of potential politicians, almost all of the men and women prominent in politics in occupied Germany had been politically active before 1933; most of them had formed their Weltanschauungen in the late nineteenth century. Although their political experiences in the twentieth century had contradicted or moderated certain fundamental aspects of their worldviews, most Catholic politicians never-

theless returned to nineteenth-century assumptions and language in the wake of the Nazis' collapse.

13. For two of many examples, see BAK, R43I/2658, 95, *Neun Jahre Zentrums-politik: Leistung und Aufgabe* (Flugschriften der Deutschen Zentrumspartei, 1928), 15; and BAK, R45II/62, Maximilian Pfeiffer, ed., *Zentrum und politische Neuordnung: Ein Programm* (Flugschriften der Deutschen Zentrumspartei) 2/12 (December 1918), 4, 30.

14. Hermann Lübbe, *Säkularisierung: Geschichte eines ideenpolitischen Begriffs* (Freiburg, 1965), 26–34, 40–68, 74–77, 90, 106.

15. Alexander Schwan, "Humanismen und Christentum," in Franz Böckle, Franz-Xaver Kaufmann, Karl Rahner, Bernhard Welte, and Robert Scherer, eds., *Enzyklopädische Bibliothek in 30 Teilbänden: Christlicher Glaube in moderner Gesellschaft*, vol. 19 (Basel and Vienna, 1981), 52–54; Ulrich Matz, "Zum Einfluß des Christentums auf das politische Denken der Neuzeit," in Günther Rüther, ed., *Geschichte der christlich-demokratischen und christlich-sozialen Bewegungen in Deutschland: Grundlagen, Unterrichtsmodelle, Quellen und Arbeitshilfen für die politische Bildung* (Bonn, 1989), 35–36.

16. Even as late as the 1950s some Catholics associated Protestantism with secularism, the Enlightenment, rationalism, nationalism, and Prussia. Albrecht Langner, "Wirtschaftliche Ordnungsvorstellungen im deutschen Katholizismus, 1945–1963," in Albrecht Langner, ed., *Katholizismus, Wirtschaftsordnung und Sozialpolitik, 1945–1963* (Paderborn, 1980), 79.

17. See BAK, NL 391 (Bausch), vol. 13: Josef André, speech at the first Landestagung of the CDU in Württemberg (Stuttgart, January 13, 1946); ACDPStA, I-206-20; Adam Stegerwald, "Wohin gehen wir?" (Würzburg, November 1945), 52–53; Stegerwald, "Wo stehen wir?" (Würzburg, August 21, 1945), 9–10; HAStK, Best. 1193, 421, 1–2: "Bericht über die Gründungsversammlung der Christlich Demokratischen Partei des Rheinlandes am Sonntag" (Cologne, September 2, 1945), 6; BAK, Kl. Erw. 640, vol. 11, 22; Theodor Scharmitzel, "Die Christlich-Demokratische Union Deutschlands: Ihr Wesen und Wollen," in *Schriftenreihe der Christlich-Demokratischen Union Deutschlands, Landesverband Rheinland* 1 (Cologne, March 25, 1946), 4.

18. ACDPStA, I-90-015/1, Elfriede Nebgen, speech titled "Die geistigen Grundlagen der Christlich-Demokratischen Union," delivered at an educational conference for women (November 10, 1945); and ACDPStA, I-105-045, DI/I, CDU Tübingen, outline for "Principles of Our Social Program" (Tübingen, May 6, 1947).

19. Theodor Scharmitzel, "Die Christlich-Demokratische Union Deutschlands: Ihr Wesen und Wollen," *Schriftenreihe der Christlich-Demokratischen Union Deutschlands, Landesverband Rheinland* 1 (Cologne, March 25, 1946), 9.

20. ACDPStA, I-208-005, Josef André, speech (Gerabronn, Langenburg, presumably November 1946).

21. ACDPStA, I-028-001/1, Heinrich Krone, radio address on Nordwest-deutscher Rundfunk (October 3, 1946).

22. ACDPStA, I-028-001/1, Heinrich Krone, speech titled "Volk ohne Gott? Deutsches Volk ohne Gott?" delivered at the rally of the Arbeitsgemeinschaft of the Christian churches (Schöneberg, July 6, 1947).

23. ACDPStA, I-009-005/7, 5, CDU *Landesverband* Baden, "Vom Sinn und Wesen der Kultur," report on the first Landestagung of the CDU, in *Flugschriften der Union* (Heidelberg, February 9–10, 1946). See also ACDPStA, I-059-002/3 (Bausch), Grundsätzliches zum Programm der christlich-sozialen Volkspartei (Zentrale Schwäbisch-Gmünd); BAK, NL 391 (Bausch), vol. 13, Josef André, speech at the first Landestagung of the CDU in Württemberg (Stuttgart, January 13, 1946); Stegerwald, "Wo stehen wir?" (Würzburg, August 21, 1945), 8–12.

24. Maria Sevenich, "Unser Gesicht: Abhandlung über Christlichen und Marxistischen Sozialismus," in *Politik aus Christlicher Verantwortung* 1 (Bad Godes-berg, December 14–16, 1945), 6.

25. ACDPStA, I-171-001/1, Emil Dovifat, "Liberalismus" (undated). See also BAK, ZSg. 1–17/1 (8), Karl Arnold, speech titled "Der soziale und sittliche Geist in der Demokratie," delivered at the founding assembly of the CDU (Düsseldorf, November 24, 1945), 22.

26. Joseph N. Moody, Introduction to Joseph N. Moody, ed., *Church and Society: Catholic Social and Political Thought and Movements, 1789–1950* (New York, 1953), 11; Gabriele Clemens, *Martin Spahn und der Rechtskatholizismus in der Weimarer Republik* (Mainz, 1983), 120.

27. Karl Zimmermann, speech titled "Das politisch-soziale Weltbild des christlichen Arbeiters," delivered at the meeting of the Social Committee of the CDU of Rhineland-Westphalia (Krefeld, August 8, 1946), 7.

28. ACDPStA, I-208-005, Josef André, speech titled "Der gemeinsame Weg" (undated).

29. ACDPStA, I-171-001/1, Emil Dovifat, speech titled "Was heißt 'Sozialismus aus christlicher Verantwortung?'" (undated).

30. Konrad Adenauer, speech (Düsseldorf, May 12, 1946), in *Schriftenreihe der Christlich Demokratischen Union des Rheinlandes* 10: 5–6.

31. ACDPStA, I-059-002/3 (Bausch), Grundsätzliches zum Programm der christlich-sozialen Volkspartei (Zentrale Schwäbisch-Gmünd); see also BAK, NL 391 (Bausch), vol. 13 Josef André, speech at the first Landestagung of the CDU in Württemberg (Stuttgart, January 13, 1946); Maria Sevenich, revised version of speech titled "Die Christlich-Demokratische Union in der Not der Zeit" (Stuttgart, February 23, 1946), 16–17.

32. For a typical example, see StBKAH, 08.09/1, 152–53, Konrad Adenauer, speech (Bonn, April 7, 1946). See also Karin Walter, *Neubeginn-Nationalsozialismus-*

*Widerstand: Die politisch-theoretische Diskussion der Neuordnung in CDU und SPD, 1945–1948* (Bonn, 1987), 58. For a discussion of the theological bases of the concept of personalism, see Judith A. Dwyer and Elizabeth L. Montgomery, eds., *The New Dictionary of Catholic Social Thought* (Collegeville, Minn. 1994), 724–38. I am grateful to Paul Misner for this reference.

33. StBKAH, 08.54, 404, Programm der Christlich-Demokratischen Union der britischen Zone (Neheim-Hüsten, March 1, 1946). See also ACDPStA, I-90-015/1, Elfriede Nebgen, speech titled "Die geistigen Grundlagen der Christlich-Demokratischen Union," delivered at an educational conference for women (November 10, 1945).

34. Stressing the integrality of the *Gemeinschaft* to the Catholic conception of democracy, Adam Stegerwald wrote in August 1945, "Democracy is the battle against selfishness; democracy is the battle against individual egoism and group egoism. Democracy is the happy marriage of individual freedom and awareness of the *Gemeinschaft.*" Stegerwald, "Wo stehen wir?" (Würzburg, August 21, 1945), 24.

35. Artur Ketterer, ed., "Das innere Gesetz der 'Union' (CDU) und seine politischen Folgerungen," in *Politik aus christlicher Verantwortung* 2 (Spring 1946): 7–8; emphasis in original.

36. StBKAH, 08.54, 281, Karl Arnold, speech titled "Der soziale und sittliche Geist in der Demokratie," delivered at the founding assembly of the CDU (Düsseldorf, November 24, 1945).

37. StBKAH, 08.09/1, 151–52, Konrad Adenauer, speech (Bonn, April 7, 1946). See also ACDPStA, I-182-010/01, Karl Zimmermann, speech titled, "Organisation und Arbeit des Landessekretariats," delivered at the Arbeitstagung of the Landespartei of the Christian Democratic Party (Rhineland, September 9, 1945), in *Rundschreiben* 5/45 (Cologne, October 27, 1945).

38. Franz Focke, *Sozialismus aus christlicher Verantwortung: Die Idee eines christlichen Sozialismus in der katholisch-sozialen Bewegung und in der CDU* (Wuppertal, 1978), 30–31.

39. Heinz Hürten, *Kurze Geschichte des deutschen Katholizismus 1800–1960* (Mainz, 1986), 8.

40. Doris von der Brelie-Lewien, *Katholische Zeitschriften in den Westzonen, 1945–1949: Ein Beitrag zur politischen Kultur der Nachkriegszeit* (Göttingen and Zürich, 1986), 139–40; Richard Faber, *Abendland: Ein "politischer Kampfbegriff"* (Hildesheim, 1979), 12, 16–30; Paul Kluke, "Nationalsozialistische Europaideologie," in *Vierteljahreshefte für Zeitgeschichte* 1 (January 1955): 240–75.

41. Von der Brelie-Lewien, *Katholische Zeitschriften*, 152; Walter, *Neubeginn*, 114. Both Catholics and Protestants understood *Abendland* to connote a unified, Catholic Europe not yet divided by the Reformation. Langner, "Ordnungsvorstellungen," 86; Ingrid Laurien, *Politisch-kulturelle Zeitschriften in den Westzonen,*

*1945–1949: Ein Beitrag zur politischen Kultur der Nachkriegszeit* (Frankfurt am Main, 1991), 194–97; Faber, *Abendland*, 115–17; Heinz Hürten, "Der Topos vom christlichen Abendland in Literatur und Publizistik nach den beiden Weltkriegen," in Albrecht Langner, ed., *Katholizismus, nationaler Gedanke und Europa seit 1800* (Paderborn, 1985), 149.

42. HAStK, Best. 1187, 424, Maria Meyer-Sevenich, "Die Union als Gottesarbeit im Dienst am Kreuz," *Schriftenreihe der Christlich Demokratischen Union des Rheinlandes* 4 (Cologne, December 1945): 8. See also Ossip K. Flechtheim, ed., *Dokumente zur parteipolitischen Entwicklungen in Deutschland seit 1945*, vol. 3 (Berlin, 1963), 46; ACDPStA, I-206-20, Programm der Christlich-Sozialen Union für Würzburg-Stadt und -Land, in Stegerwald, "Wohin gehen wir?" (Würzburg, November 1945), 65.

43. ACDPStA, I-105-045, Programm der CDU Württemberg/Hohenzollern (April 26, 1948).

44. ACDPStA, I-182-004/01, B.I.1, Dr. Fr. Wagner, ed., program outline for a Christian Democratic People's Party (Gelsenkirchen, July 21, 1945).

45. As early as the sixteenth century, there had existed a marked hostility between Prussia as the protagonist of the Reformation and the southern German frontrunners of the Catholic Reformation; as Prussia became more powerful during the seventeenth and eighteenth centuries, tensions between it and the ecclesiastical territories increased. Edgar Alexander, "Church and Society in Germany: Social and Political Movements and Ideas in German and Austrian Catholicism (1789–1950)," in Moody, *Church and Society*, 347.

46. At least since the nineteenth century, German Catholics had associated Prussia with specific forms of materialism, including the antiquated capitalism of the East Elbian landholders, the liberalism of the Kulturkampf, and the socialism of the SPD-led Weimar coalition. Especially since the Kulturkampf, southern German and Rhineland Catholics had regarded apostasy and secularization as predominantly Prussian-inspired phenomena. Von der Brelie-Lewien, *Katholische Zeitschriften*, 136; Faber, *Abendland*, 172.

47. The Allies' de-Nazification and de-Prussification programs were based on coherent if misinformed diagnoses of what had led to Nazism; above all else, the occupiers located the bastion of German militarism and political extremism in Prussia. Indeed, the simultaneous collapse of the Nazi regime and the dismemberment of the Land Prussia symbolized for many, including many Protestant Germans, a symbiosis between Prussianism and Nazism. Karlheinz Niclauss, "Political Reconstruction at Bonn," in John H. Herz, ed., *From Dictatorship to Democracy: Coping with the Legacies of Authoritarianism and Totalitarianism* (Westport, Conn., 1982), 41.

48. James J. Sheehan, *German History, 1770–1866* (Oxford, 1989), 561, 617; Hürten, *Kurze Geschichte*, p. 68; Hajo Holborn, *A History of Modern Germany, 1648–1840* (Princeton, 1964), 505–6; Faber, *Abendland*, 178.

49. ACDPStA, I-009-004/2, Konrad Adenauer, radio address (Nordwest-deutscher Rundfunk, March 6, 1946). See also StBKAH, 08.09/1, 152–53, Konrad Adenauer, speech (Bonn, April 7, 1946); Stegerwald, "Wo stehen wir?" (Würzburg, August 21, 1945), 18–19; Maria Sevenich, speech titled "Das Werden der neuen deutschen Demokratie!" (Wiesbaden, March 11, 1946), 3; Maria Sevenich, "Unser Gesicht: Abhandlung über Christlichen und Marxistischen Sozialismus," in *Politik aus Christlicher Verantwortung* 1 (Bad Godesberg, December 14–16, 1945): 18; BAK, NL 278 (Holzapfel), vol. 139, Bernhard Pfad, speech titled "Volk in Not: Marxismus ist Militarismus in Zivil—Christen denkt um!" (Duderstadt, undated), in *Niedersächsische Rundschau: Wochenschrift der Christlich-Demokratischen Union, Landesverband Hannover* 1, no. 3 (Hanover, June 1, 1946).

50. BAK, NL 278 (Holzapfel), vol. 265, Ernst-Albert Lotz, inaugural speech at the Consultative Assembly for the Land of the Rhineland Palatinate (November 22, 1946). Cf. HAStK, Best. 1187 (Teusch), 42, 162–63. Peter Altmeier, speech (Koblenz, November 22, 1945).

51. This suspicion was heightened by Catholic CDU members' belief in wide-spread Protestant support for—and Catholic resistance to—Nazism. See Mitchell, "Materialism and Secularism."

52. Franz Schnabel, *Deutsche Geschichte im neunzehnten Jahrhundert*, vol. 4 (Freiburg i. Br., 1937), 380.

53. A pamphlet published in 1921 by the DNVP-associated Deutschnationaler Arbeiterbund, for example, rejected capitalism and Marxism as "materialistic." Dieter Fricke, Werner Fritsch, Herbert Gottwald, Siegfried Schmidt, and Manfred Weißbecker, eds., *Lexikon zur Parteiengeschichte: Die bürgerlichen und kleinbürgerlichen Parteien und Verbände in Deutschland (1789–1945)*, vol. 2 (Cologne and Leipzig, 1984), 484–85.

54. Martin Greiffenhagen, *Das Dilemma des Konservatismus in Deutschland* (Frankfurt am Main, 1986), 41, 85, 89–91, 127–31, 157, 205.

55. Erich Schmidt-Volkmar, *Der Kulturkampf in Deutschland, 1871–1890* (Göttingen, 1962), 113, 129.

56. Clemens Vollnhals, "Die Evangelische Kirche zwischen Traditionswahrung und Neuorientierung," in Martin Broszat, Klaus-Dietmar Henke, and Hans Woller, eds., *Von Stalingrad zur Währungsreform: Zur Sozialgeschichte des Umbruchs in Deutschland* (Munich, 1990), 145.

57. Johann Baptist Müller, "Der deutsche Sozialkonservatismus," in Hans-Gerd Schumann, ed., *Konservatismus*, 2d ed. (Königstein/Ts., 1984), 199–221.

58. StBKAH, 08.54, 273–74, Robert Lehr, speech titled "Der neue Geist im neuen Staat," delivered at the founding assembly of the CDU (Düsseldorf, November 24, 1945).

59. Otto Boelitz, "Erziehung und Schule im Christlich-Demokratischen Staat: Das Bildungsideal und das Schulprogramm der CDU," in *Politik aus Christlicher*

*Verantwortung* 7 (Recklinghausen, 1946), 7. Cf. BAK, NL 391 (Bausch), vol. 13, Wilhelm Simpfendörfer, speech at the first public gathering of the Christian Social People's Party (Stuttgart, November 10, 1945).

60. ACDPStA, I-206-012/1, 1250, letter from Schlange-Schöningen to Stegerwald, dated August 22, 1945.

61. BAK, NL 391 (Bausch), vol. 13, Paul Bausch, speech (Plahingen, December 15, 1945).

62. ACDPStA, I-009-005/4, 13, Ulrich Steiner, speech delivered at the *Landesversammlung* of the CDU of Südwürttemberg-Hohenzollern (Biberach, March 30, 1947).

63. ACDPStA, I-056-003, Wilhelm Simpfendörfer, "Die wichtigsten Probleme der neuen Verfassung" (no date).

64. StBKAH, 08.29, 92, Otto Heinrich von der Gablentz, "Christlicher Sozialismus" (Berlin, June 1945).

65. ACDPStA, I-155-002/3, Otto Heinrich von der Gablentz, speech (Fröhnau, August 12, 1945).

66. ACDPStA, I-155-003/2, Otto Heinrich von der Gablentz, "Die Tragödie Preußens" (June 10, 1948). For other Protestant discussions of Prussia, see HStAD, RWN 119, vol. 2, 121, letter from Otto Aschmann of Oberhausen (Rhineland) to Otto Schmidt, dated October 7, 1946; HStAD, RWN 119, vol. 2, 122, letter from Schmidt to Aschmann, dated October 16, 1946; BAK, NL 391 (Bausch), vol. 13, Wilhelm Simpfendörfer, speech at the first public gathering of the Christlich-Soziale Volkspartei (Stuttgart, November 10, 1945); HStAD, RWN 119, vol. 2, 84, letter from Hermann Lutze to Ober-Stud. Dir. Dr. Freund, dated September 3, 1946.

67. ACDPStA, I-090-015/1, Bericht über die Sitzung der CDP (Frankfurt am Main, October 31, 1945).

68. HAStK, Best. 1187, Fasz. 41, Pamphlet titled "Christlich-Demokratische Union oder Zentrumspartei?" (presumably August 1946).

69. ACDPStA, I-155-030/1, Emil Dovifat, speech titled "Warum Christlich-Demokratisch-Sozial" (January 1946). Dovifat echoed many of these points in his article, "Wo steht der Liberale?" in *Neue Zeit* 7, as cited in BAK, NL 278 (Holzapfel), vol. 239. Christlich-Demokratische Union Deutschlands, Sondermaterial (Berlin, no date), 5/I.

70. BAK, NL 5 (Pünder), vol. 476, 220–21, Ernst Lemmer, speech (July 7, 1946).

71. ACDPStA, I-208-004/1, Ernst Lemmer, speech titled "Der Weg der Union" (Berlin, June 16, 1946).

72. Clemens, *Martin Spahn und der Rechtskatholizismus*, 120.

73. Catholics' historic distrust of capitalism was reinforced in the years following World War II by a widespread consensus on capitalism's contribution to global war and political extremism. Diethelm Prowe, "Economic Democracy in

Post–World War II Germany: Corporatist Crisis Response, 1945–1948," *Journal of Modern History* 57 (September 1985): 455; Gerold Ambrosius, *Die Durchsetzung der Sozialen Marktwirtschaft in Westdeutschland, 1945–1949* (Stuttgart, 1977), 14; David W. Ellwood, *Rebuilding Europe: Western Europe, America and Postwar Reconstruction* (New York, 1992), 13–14; Focke, *Sozialismus aus christlicher Verantwortung*, 293; Bernd Uhl, *Die Idee des christlichen Sozialismus in Deutschland, 1945–1947* (Mainz, 1975), 54.

74. On Christian socialism before 1933, see Alexander, "Church and Society in Germany," 524–26; Karl Prümm, *Walter Dirks und Eugen Kogon als katholische Publizisten der Weimarer Republik* (Heidelberg, 1984); Bruno Lowitsch, *Der Kreis um die Rhein-Mainische Volkszeitung* (Wiesbaden, 1980); Focke, *Sozialismus aus christlicher Verantwortung*, 13–14, 89, 288; Alois Baumgartner, *Sehnsucht nach Gemeinschaft: Ideen und Strömungen im Sozialkatholizismus der Weimarer Republik* (Munich, 1977), 91; Uhl, *Die Idee des christlichen Sozialismus*, 22–27, 37.

75. StBKAH, 08.54, 393–98, "Ein Ruf zur Sammlung des deutschen Volkes: Vorläufiger Entwurf zu einem Programm der Christlichen Demokraten Deutschlands, Vorgelegt von den Christlichen Demokraten Köln im Juni 1945" (Cologne, June 1945).

76. Karl Zimmermann, "Erste Reichstagung der Christlich Demokratischen Union," *Schriftenreihe der Christlich Demokratischen Union des Rheinlandes* 5 (Cologne, 1945): 7. See also BAK, NL 391 (Bausch), vol. 13, Grundsätzliches zum Programm der christlich-sozialen Volkspartei (Stuttgart, n.d.).

77. Leo Schwering, *Frühgeschichte der Christlich-Demokratischen Union* (Recklinghausen, 1963), 17.

78. BAK, NL 18 (Kaiser), vol. 88, 1–4.

79. Reinhard Schmeer, "Die Evangelische Kirche im Rheinland und die CDU 1945–1949," *Monatshefte für Evangelische Kirchengeschichte des Rheinlandes* 41 (1992): 300–337; Focke, *Sozialismus aus christlicher Verantwortung*, 298–99.

80. The Wuppertal party center represented a significant exception to the pattern in the northern Rhineland of Protestant underrepresentation (in proportion to their percentage of the area's population) in the membership ranks of the CDU. Mirroring the confessional breakdown of the Wuppertal's population, approximately 80 percent of the party's members were Protestant. HStAD, RWN 119, vol. 2, 297, letter to Werner Schütz from Otto Schmidt, dated January 10, 1947. See also Schmidt, "Christlich-demokratische Union Deutschlands," 499.

81. For the voluminous correspondence between Adenauer and Schmidt, see HStAD, RWN 119, vol. 1. On Schmidt's unique position as the "integration figure" for Protestants in the Wuppertal party center, see Schmeer, "Die Evangelische Kirche im Rheinland und die CDU, 1945–1949," 322. Schmidt was recognized widely by his colleagues in the Wuppertal party as their unofficial delegate to the

party's Catholic leadership. HStAD, RWN 119, vol. 3, 219, letter from Marx to Schmidt, dated June 12, 1947.

82. Otto Schmidt, "Christlicher Realismus—ein Versuch zu sozialwirtchaftlicher Neuordnung," *Schriftenreihe der Christlich Demokratischen Union des Rheinlandes* 7 (Cologne, presumably 1946): 5–8.

83. Ibid, 4–6.

84. ACDPStA, I-172-095/1–2, CDU flyer (Wuppertal, August 27, 1945).

85. BAK, NL 278 (Holzapfel), vol. 139, Holzapfel, speech (Buer, September 1, 1946).

86. HStAD, RWN 119, vol. 1, 31, letter from Schmidt to Adenauer, dated February 26, 1946.

87. HAStD, RWN 119, vol. 1, 68–70, letter from Schmidt to Adenauer, dated April 2, 1946.

88. HAStD, RWN 119, vol. 1, 63, letter from Marx to Albers, dated March 25, 1946.

89. HStAD, RWN 119, vol. 1, 72, letter from Brauda to Adenauer, dated April 8, 1946.

90. HStAD, RWN 119, vol. 1, 72, letter from Brauda to Adenauer, dated April 8, 1946.

91. HAStD, RWN 119, vol. 1, 63, letter from Marx to Albers, dated March 25, 1946. See also HStAD, RWN 119, vol. 1, 72, letter from Brauda to Adenauer, dated April 8, 1946.

92. ACDPStA, I-182-008/02, B. III.1, letter from Storch to Albers, dated July 24, 1946.

93. BAK, NL 278 (Holzapfel), vol. 335, Wilhelm Lindner, ed., "Christlich-Demokratische Union Evangelische Verbindungsstelle," *Rundbrief* 4 (Herford, September 1946).

94. ACDPStA, I-155-030/5, letter from Müller-Jabusch to Kaiser, dated September 19, 1946.

95. Particularly after the failed Moscow conference of the Allied foreign ministers in late spring 1947, the SPD and other socialist parties in western Europe began conspicuously to lose domestic political support. Uhl, *Die Idee des christlichen Sozialismus*, 56.

96. Antonius John, *Ahlen und Ahlener Programm: Dokumente—Ereignisse— Erinnerungen* (Ahlen, 1977).

97. *Landtag Nordrhein-Westfalen*, Stenographischer Bericht über die 6. Vollsitzung des Landtages Nordrhein-Westfalen (Düsseldorf, June 17, 1947), 8–15; see also A.R.L. Gurland, *Die CDU/CSU: Ursprünge und Entwicklung bis 1953*, ed. D. Emig (Frankfurt am Main, 1980), 273–77.

98. HStAD, RWN 122, vol. 2, 152, Robert Lehr and Helmut Lauffs, eds., *Evangelische Tagung* (Düsseldorf, July 16, 1947).

99. HStAD, RWN 122, vol. 2, 153, letter from Arnold to Lehr, dated July 23, 1947.

100. HStAD, RWN 122, vol. 2, 158–60, letter from Arnold to Lehr, dated July 31, 1947. At the same time he attacked the party's Protestants for "confessionalizing" CDU policy, however, Arnold highlighted in his own display of confessional resentment the tensions and confessional differences that characterized early CDU politics. Defending "Christian workers" as "the most active and devoted core" of the party, Arnold praised particularly the "politically and ideologically [*weltanschaulich*] well-trained Christian workers" for having displayed "in the Third Reich and also now, again, a maximum of immunity vis-à-vis Marxist, nationalistic, or other erroneous slogans." In a clear implication that Germany's Protestants showed greater susceptibility to "materialist" phenomena, Arnold concluded that "not all of the circles represented in the CDU can lay claim to the same for themselves."

101. Important works on this topic include A.J. Nicholls, *Freedom with Responsibility: The Social Market Economy, 1919–1963* (Oxford, 1994); Ambrosius, *Die Durchsetzung der Sozialen Marktwirtschaft;* and Reinhard Blum, *Soziale Marktwirtschaft: Wirtschaftspolitik zwischen Neoliberalismus und Ordoliberalismus* (Tübingen, 1969).

102. For more on the confessionalized politics of the CDU's adoption of the social market economy, see Maria Mitchell, *The Origins of Christian Democracy: Politics and Confession in Modern Germany* (Ann Arbor, forthcoming).

103. At the last meeting of the British Zonal Committee in late February 1949, for example, Erhard was confronted publicly by Johannes Albers. In response to Albers's charge that Erhard's program represented "more or less the principle of Liberal economics," Erhard countered that his political allegiance lay with the CDU, not the FDP. As an adherent of the CDU's "moral theses," Erhard declared that he was no supporter of nineteenth-century Liberalism: "I am as uncapitalist as possible." Ludwig Erhard, speech titled "Market Economics of a Modern Character" (Recklinghausen, August 28–29, 1948), in Helmuth Pütz, ed., *Konrad Adenauer und die CDU der britischen Besatzungszone, 1946–1949: Dokumente zur Gründungsgeschichte der CDU Deutschlands* (Bonn, 1975), 657–78.

104. Wolf-Dieter Narr and Dietrich Thränhardt, eds., *Die Bundesrepublik Deutschland: Entstehung-Entwicklung-Struktur* (Königstein/Ts., 1984), 4; Lothar Rolke, *Protestbewegungen in der Bundesrepublik: Eine analytische Sozialgeschichte des politischen Widerspruches* (Opladen, 1987), 138.

105. Gerhard Besier, "'Christliche Parteipolitik' und Konfession: Zur Entstehung des Evangelischen Arbeitskreises der CDU/CSU," *Kirchliche Zeitgeschichte* 1 (1990): 166–87; Peter Egen, "Die Entstehung des Evangelischen Arbeitskreises der CDU/CSU" (Ph.D. dissertation, Ruhr-Universität Bochum, 1971).

106. Helmuth Pütz, *Die CDU: Entwicklung, Aufbau und Politik der Christlich Demokratischen Union Deutschlands* (Bonn, 1971), 37–43. In 1971, when the population

of the Federal Republic was approximately 51 percent Protestant, Protestants represented only 25 percent of the CDU's members.

107. For a detailed discussion of the concept of the *Volkspartei*, see Richard Stöss, "Einleitung: Struktur und Entwicklung des Parteiensystems der Bundesrepublik—Eine Theorie," in Stöss, *Parteien-Handbuch*, 121–45.

108. Beckmann, *Kirchliches Jahrbuch*, 538. See also Hans Braun, "Demographische Umschichtungen im Deutschen Katholizismus nach 1945," in Anton Rauscher, ed., *Kirche und Katholizismus, 1945–1949* (Munich and Paderborn, 1977), 9–25.

109. Kurt Klotzbach, "SPD und katholische Kirche nach 1945—Belastungen, Mißverständnisse und Neuanfänge," *Archiv für Sozialgeschichte* 29 (1989): 37–47.

110. Schmidt, "Christlich-demokratische Union Deutschlands," 581. The election of 1969 marked the first time that a significant proportion of the Catholic working class voted for the SPD.

111. Dorothee Buchhaas, *Die Volkspartei: Die programmatische Entwicklung der CDU, 1950–1973* (Düsseldorf, 1981).

112. In August 1947 Adenauer declared explicitly that the *Abendland* included the United States, united with western Europe in the war against materialist Communism. Hans-Peter Schwarz, *Konrad Adenauer: A German Politician and Statesman in a Period of War, Revolution and Reconstruction*, vol. 1, trans. Louise Willmot (Providence and Oxford: Berghahn Books, 1995), 393.

113. On antimaterialism in Christian discourse in the 1950s, see Heide Fehrenbach, *Cinema in Democratizing Germany: Reconstructing National Identity after Hitler* (Chapel Hill and London, 1995); and Maria Höhn, "GIs, Veronikas, and Lucky Strikes: German Reactions to the American Presence in the Rhineland-Palatinate during the 1950s" (Ph.D. dissertation, University of Pennsylvania, 1995).

# 8 Christian Democracy or Pacellian Populism?

Rival Forms of Postwar Italian
Political Catholicism

STEVEN F. WHITE

The past decade has witnessed a proliferation of monographs dealing with modern Italian Catholic political and social movements, narrowing a long-standing quantitative and qualitative gap vis-à-vis scholarship on Italy's Marxist subculture.[1] From the 1950s through the 1980s, the animating ideas and accomplishments of Italy's ruling Christian Democrats interested fewer intellectuals, either in Italy or abroad, than did the *rivoluzione mancata* of Italian Communism. In recent years, a former Communist, Massimo D'Alema, has been prime minister of the Republic of Italy, and political Catholicism is benefiting from enhanced scholarly sympathy and attention.[2]

The decline of Italian Christian Democracy's political fortunes, culminating in the party's breakup in January 1994, has prompted scholars to examine in new ways that party's genesis and rise under the leadership of Alcide De Gasperi.[3] At the same time, important primary sources have become available on the careers of Vittorino Veronese, the conciliatory, moderate head of Italian Catholic Action from late 1946 to early 1952, and his domineering, integralist successor, Luigi Gedda.[4] Contemporary and retrospective "cults of personality" centered on Pius XII and De Gasperi have also been investigated in recent years[5]—indeed, each of these Catholic luminaries is presently the subject of a cause for canonization.

A clearer picture is emerging of the interpersonal and ideological dynamics that shaped relations within and among the Vatican, Italian Catholic Action, and the Christian Democratic Party after World War II. Despite ritual affirmations of obedience to the Holy Father and electoral invocations of "the political unity of Catholics," postwar political Catholicism experienced deep divisions. The reticence of Catholic protagonists and historians[6] to grapple with these divisions meant that they were, for some time, construed in a too narrowly political, even conspiratorial vein. Did Pius XII and the Vatican secretly plan to outflank Democrazia Christiana (DC) with a second, right-wing Catholic political party and eventually to establish a Salazarian regime, perhaps with Gedda playing the title role?[7] Probably not, based on the evidence at our disposition.[8]

Instead, Pius XII's challenge to De Gasperi and to the consolidation of republicanism and parliamentary pluralism[9] needs to be construed more broadly. This chapter analyzes the relationship between De Gasperian Christian Democracy and "Pacellian populism" (a political style that Cardinal Eugenio Pacelli began to elaborate as Pius XI's secretary of state even before assuming the pontifical throne as Pius XII in 1939) at four developmental stages: a gestational stage between the two world wars, in which differing experiences of the short-lived Popular Party and of the Fascist regime generated diverse Catholic agendas for the future; a stage of fruitful convergence culminating in the 1948 parliamentary elections; a crisis stage centering on the Rome municipal elections of 1952; and a conflicted aftermath period, extending until the mid-1950s, which left Catholic Action politically debilitated and Christian Democracy factionalized and befuddled—in part over the lingering question of the party's relationship with the Vatican.

During Pius XII's twenty-year pontificate (1939–58), three basic currents or positions stand out in the broad stream of Italian political Catholicism. The first of these was a "liberal-pluralist" position associated with Don Luigi Sturzo, De Gasperi, and other veterans of the Popular Party, Italy's first mass-based Catholic political party. The second was a "conservative-integralist" position championed by Gedda and Jesuit Father Riccardo Lombardi, both of whom carried forward Franciscan Father Agostino Gemelli's and Pope Pius XI's interwar vision of installing a new "Christian social order." A third "leftist-integralist" position, advanced by a younger generation of Catholic intellectuals grouped around Giuseppe Dossetti, also envisioned the transformation of Italian society based on Catholic conceptions of charity and justice but looked to the anti-Fascist Resistance legacy, entrusted jointly to the Christian Democrats and to their secular-progressive and Marxist comrades in arms, to accomplish this end.

The influence of this third position within Italian political Catholicism would decline as the heady spirit of the Resistance gave way to the sober work of reconstruction and stabilization in an increasingly polarized Cold War context. However, the rivalry between the "liberal-pluralist" and "conservative-integralist" camps would intensify during the late 1940s and early 1950s. Each of these camps found support in the Vatican, with De Gasperi and Veronese turning to their mutual friend Monsignor Giovanni Battista Montini (the future Paul VI) and Gedda looking to Cardinals Giuseppe Pizzardo and Alfredo Ottaviani and to Monsignor Domenico Tardini, Montini's rival in the Vatican Secretariat of State.[10]

During the first decade of his papacy, Pius XII had avoided occupying a fixed point along this spectrum, drawing on different perspectives and engaging different interlocutors as he saw fit. Preoccupied with the preservation of Vatican neutrality during the war and with the challenges of adapting to a rapidly shifting postwar international order, he largely delegated Italian affairs to Montini. Alarmed by the prospect that the Socialist-Communist popular front might prevail in the Italian republic's inaugural parliamentary elections of 1948, however, the pope stepped in forcefully, giving Gedda the go-ahead to form the Civic Committees that did so much to deliver an unprecedented Christian Democratic vote.

The genesis of the Civic Committees can be seen as the first major expression of Pacellian populism, the pope's own version of the "conservative-integralist" tradition of Italian political Catholicism. Aside from its almost pathological anti-Communism, Pacellian populism lacked consistent political content. In form, however, it evoked the mass-based authoritarianism of the interwar era as well as the solidarity of medieval Christendom and the zeal of the Counter-Reformation.

The pontiff launched his own series of mass religious-ideological crusades. The first of these was the 1949 Crusade for the Great Return, organized by Gedda and focusing on the "reconversion of souls seduced by Godless communism." This effort was but a prelude to subsequent mobilizations of the faithful centering on the Holy Year of 1950, the Better World Movement of 1952, led by Father Lombardi, and the Marian Year of 1954. A striking feature of these crusades, indeed of Pacellian populism itself, was their deliberate mingling of political and religious organizational forms and rhetorical tropes. In a triumphalist assertion of the magisterium of the Church, the Pope reserved the right to use any avenues available to him to foster the construction of Christian civilization.[11] Pius XII spoke and wrote of politics as constituting a dependent—and in some ways inferior—realm within which the Church reserved the right to act. He shared his predecessor's view that "when politics touch the altar, the Church has the right and the duty to intervene."[12]

Father Riccardo Lombardi of Vatican radio represented an important public mouthpiece for the Holy Father, who was fascinated with modern mass media and its unparalleled capacities for visual and verbal persuasion. Because of his organizational gifts and the quality of his deference (to Pius's own person and to the papal office), however, it was Gedda, more than any lay figure, who enjoyed the pope's confidence in these years.

## A DIVIDED INHERITANCE

Both Alcide De Gasperi and his political mentor, Don Luigi Sturzo, hailed the revival of parliamentary government after World War II as a long-awaited chance to reenter the political arena following their bittersweet experience together at the helm of the Popular Party. After the inauguration of the Fascist dictatorship, De Gasperi spent nearly a year in prison, followed by a decade and a half of humble work at the Vatican library, while Sturzo passed equally frustrating years as a political exile first in Great Britain and then in the United States.

Despite comprehensible resentments arising from the fact that from the outset De Gasperi dominated the Christian Democratic party while Sturzo was kept at arm's length, the two men shared the same basic political commitments. Hailing from opposite ends of the peninsula, the two Catholic statesmen shared a profound sense of Italian patriotism. Both regarded the Risorgimento as a positive but tragically flawed historical development: the Liberal state had been stunted by its disregard for too much of the Italian population, including devout Catholics and, more generally, the humbler classes. Each man had drunk deep at the well of Catholic social teaching, and each was eager to apply its interclassist idealism to the lacerations of a country experiencing wrenching socioeconomic change.

The two statesmen relished the give-and-take of political dialogue within a liberal, multiparty framework. Of the two, Sturzo placed more emphasis on the formulation and elaboration of political ideology; De Gasperi was more concerned with sustaining and enhancing the ethos of parliamentarism, even if this sometimes meant sacrificing or deferring programmatic points. De Gasperi particularly valued parliament's distinctive role as a mediator between state and society, while he mistrusted the politics of the piazza.[13]

Though Christian in inspiration, the Popular Party was not an officially confessional one—a stance that suited a Vatican reluctant to tie itself to an untested political venture. Sturzo and De Gasperi each treated the Roman Question gingerly, not wishing to condition or compromise papal initiatives on this matter. When the Lateran Accords and the Concordat were announced, Sturzo voiced strong reservations from his exile abroad, while De Gasperi fretted more discreetly in Italy. In truth, both men believed that Catholic values could most effectively inform and enrich the public life of their countrymen when elaborated organically from below rather than imposed diplomatically or legalistically from above.

Very different from the liberal parliamentary path favored by such *popolari* was the conservative integralism of Pius XI, Agostino Gemelli, and Gemelli's disciple, Luigi Gedda. Pius XI also wished to reconcile Italian nationalism and Catholicism—via the Lateran Accords and Concordat between the Vatican and the Fascist state signed on February 11, 1929. Two days after the signing of this historic agreement, the pope delivered a revealing speech to a visiting delegation from Father Gemelli's Sacred Heart University of Milan. Pius XI described the crossing of his path with Mussolini's ("a man free of liberal prejudices") as "providential," as the resulting accord had "returned God to Italy and Italy to God."[14]

As described in his memoirs, the Concordat greatly impressed Gedda, then a young Novara physician and rising activist within Italian Catholic Youth (generally referred to by its Italian acronym GIAC). Drawn to Father Gemelli's ideas and example through a confraternity founded by the Sacred Heart rector, Gedda credited the latter's patronage for his elevation to the presidency of GIAC in 1934. During his eleven years in this post, Gedda concentrated on amassing an ever larger number of members and subscribers for its youth magazine, *Il Vittorioso,* launched amid Italy's celebration of the 1936 conquest of Abyssinia.[15]

While Gemelli and Gedda envisioned the Catholic conquest of Italian society from above—if need be, with the help of Caesar's sword—Giovanni Battista Montini set about planting the seeds for the gradual construction of Catholic hegemony after Mussolini had had his day.[16] The son of a leading Brescian politician and Popular Party deputy, Montini served as national chaplain for the Catholic University Graduates' Association (FUCI) in the late 1920s and early 1930s. In his person and through his ideas and influence, Montini bridged the generational and experiential gap separating Popular Party veterans like his father and De Gasperi from up-and-coming FUCI activists such as Vittorino Veronese, Guido Gonella, Giulio Andreotti, and Aldo Moro. Naturally a smaller and more select group than GIAC, FUCI differed from Catholic Youth in self-consciously opposing Fascist ideology—an opposition that cost Montini his national chaplaincy in 1933. But by then the seeds had taken root. A decade later, shortly after Mussolini's dismissal and arrest, Veronese would invite his fellow Catholics to become a "creative presence within the social fabric of the Nation" and to offer an indispensable, capillary contribution to Italy's civil progress rather than, as in the past, "formally intervening as an *instrumentum regni.*"[17]

As papal secretary of state, Eugenio Pacelli viewed the Fascist regime in a manner that largely paralleled Pius XI, moving from substantial sympathy at the beginning of the 1930s to a deepening rivalry and even disapproval. He figured prominently in a sustained Catholic campaign that presented the Church, rather than Mussolini's regime, as the true inheritor and embodiment of *romanità* (Roman values as they have been transmitted and elaborated over the centuries).[18]

With regard to contemporary politics, the interwar Vatican had inclined toward a kind of constitutional agnosticism—a presumption that the structures of state power were morally neutral, so long as "the right man," possessing "the right values," was in power.[19] Nevertheless, the excesses of Fascism, and the resilience and martial performance of the Western democracies during World War II, led Pius XII to reconsider and begin to associate Catholicism and democracy in a new way. The suggestive doctrine of the "dignity of the human person" enunciated in the pope's 1942 Christmas Message was followed two years later by the pope's widely heralded reflections on "true democracy" in his message of Christmas 1944.

"The State is not a distinct entity which mechanically gathers together a shapeless mass of individuals and confines them within a specified territory," the pope proclaimed. The state may, however, realize its modern vocation if, tutored by the Church, it becomes "the organic and organizing unity of a real people." Each individual in such an authentic modern state "is the subject of inviolable duties and rights" and "is the source and end of his own social life." The Church could look forward to playing an exemplary role in the transnational renewal of the social contract that would occur once the world had returned to peace.[20]

This preliminary affirmation of Pacellian populism did not necessarily translate into a belief in parliamentary republicanism. In his celebrated 1944 Christmas Message Pius XII disclaimed any particular concern "about the external structure and organization of a democracy—matters which depend on the particular aspirations of each people."[21]

During the Allied campaign to liberate Italy, the pope and his advisers maintained a prudent reserve toward all the anti-Fascist parties, including the Christian Democrats. Pius XII was initially inclined to look to the monarchy as an institutional bulwark of postwar law and order. Still, when the popular referendum of June 1946 endorsed a republic, Pius XII went along. He now accepted parliamentary democracy—so long as those sitting in parliament were led by a Catholic elite, "a select body of men of firm Christian convictions."[22]

De Gasperi, elevated to the prime ministership in December 1945, believed that he epitomized such virtue. The Trentine leader's writings and speeches are replete with references to the Gospels, the teachings of the Church fathers, and the encyclicals of the popes as the spiritual food sustaining his political vocation.[23] De Gasperi echoed the pope's conviction that the post-Fascist state must reflect the peninsula's historically rooted Christian values to be truly democratic. To this end, the Christian Democrats saw to it that article 7 of the new republican constitution (which took effect in January 1948) retained for the Church all of the privileges it had obtained in the 1929 Lateran Accords.

## POPE AND PRIME MINISTER: A STUDY IN CONTRASTS

Before turning to the drama of the April 1948 parliamentary elections, several general observations are in order about the personalities and leadership styles of this chapter's two protagonists. Eugenio Pacelli and Alcide De Gasperi shared a number of personal traits and interests. Both men were physically similar (imposing and slender to the point of gauntness), and both were known for their personal aloofness. Each man pushed himself relentlessly in his work, and each, in his own way, was a loner. Pius XII and De Gasperi privileged foreign affairs and diplomacy in their statesmanship; for extended periods, each chose to serve as his own foreign minister.[24] The central European, German-speaking world represented a key point of reference for both men.[25]

On balance, however, dissimilarities outweighed similarities in the two figures' character and outlook. De Gasperi possessed a sense of inner certainty that sustained him even in turbulent surroundings. He distinguished himself among the leaders of the anti-Fascist liberation movement through his remarkable self-confidence and uncanny sense of political feasibility and timing.[26] Intellectually, however, his horizons remained conventionally Catholic.

De Gasperi's straightforward, unadorned manner of speaking and writing exposed him to the condescending reproof of several contemporaries, including Italian Communist Party chief Palmiro Togliatti[27] and interparty rival Giovanni Gronchi.[28] By and large, however, his plainspoken solidity and predictability were seen as assets by fellow politicians. In Catholic company, the Trentine statesman interlaced commonplaces drawn from Church doctrine with assessments of contemporary Italian problems. Yet as the Italian historian Silvio Lanaro has observed, of all the Christian Democratic leaders, De Gasperi could most credibly treat with non-Catholics in the secular, "neutral" language of liberal parliamentarism: "to their eyes— or better, noses—De Gasperi was uniquely free of the odor of incense and the sacristy."[29]

Pacelli's aristocratic eloquence stood in marked contrast. True to his Roman heritage and education, Pius XII cultivated a "grand manner" rhetorical style.[30] The Holy Father invested tremendous effort in the preparation, composition, editing, and rehearsal of his many addresses. Accomplished in seven different languages, Pius XII was not above poking fun at those whose linguistic gifts were inferior. On one occasion recorded by Cardinal Tardini, Pius XII noticed that "De Gasperi had said to the foreign press correspondents 'Nous esperons superer les difficultes.' The pope then remarked that the word which should have been used was 'surmonter.' "[31]

Whereas De Gasperi's political calling subsumed his many talents, Pius XII pushed himself to become acquainted with an encyclopedic range of disciplines so as to bring the Church's magisterium to bear on the gamut of modern society. He granted an unusually large number of audiences to persons from all walks of life and points of the globe. However, he conducted these audiences in a paternalistic and didactic rather than dialogic manner. With regard to his clerical colleagues, Pius XII wanted "'executors,' not 'collaborators.'"[32]

Much the same applied to the pope's lay Catholic interlocutors—and this fact could only redound to Gedda's advantage in comparison to De Gasperi's. Twenty-six years younger than the Holy Father, Gedda found it easier to play the dutiful son than did his Trentine rival, who was only five years Pius's junior. Even in middle age, Gedda exuded youthful dynamism. In comparison, the elderly De Gasperi came across as colorless, unflamboyant, and detached (*umbratile*).[33] During his twenty-year pontificate, Pius granted Gedda some sixty-five audiences; De Gasperi was given two.[34]

In fact, it suited both De Gasperi and Pius XII to maintain their personal distance from one another. Privately, the Christian Democratic leader counted on the pope's ongoing albeit tacit endorsement of his party as the embodiment of the political unity of Italian Catholics. However, De Gasperi resisted even the appearance of confessional subordination that frequent contact or public appearances with the Holy Father would imply. As De Gasperi remarked to Emilio Bonomelli, "We have had to comport ourselves as though thousands of kilometers, not such a small distance, separated the Vatican from the Viminal."[35] For both men, institutional loyalties and pride took precedence over personal dialogue.

De Gasperi's first postwar visit to the Vatican occurred on July 31, 1946 (more than three years after the initial liberation of Rome), when he accompanied acting president Enrico De Nicola on a state visit. On a few subsequent occasions De Gasperi took part in ceremonies at the Vatican, including the opening of the Holy Year of 1950, jubilee visits by parliamentarians, and the canonization of Maria Goretti. On one of these occasions, the prime minister found himself seated slightly lower than "certain dignitaries" affiliated with Italy's prerepublican past. "When, in the Vatican," De Gasperi wondered aloud, "will they finally give due weight to universal suffrage?"[36]

## THE PARLIAMENTARY ELECTIONS OF 1948

During the republic's inaugural parliamentary elections of April 1948, pope and prime minister formed a complementary tag team, De Gasperi traversing the peninsula with his partisan speeches while Pius XII offered "pastoral" advice from his balcony on Saint Peter's Square. De Gasperi's promises to use "whatever means necessary to prevail" provided a rhetorical foil for Pius XII's measured, flowing cadences, punctuated with Latin phrases, comparing Christ's persecution and Passion with the calumnies suffered by the contemporary Church abroad—and potentially at home—at the hands of her atheist enemies.[37] Both men presented the election as a choice between preservation of "Italic civilization" or capitulation to an alien "Marxist civilization."[38]

In the campaign Gedda's Civic Committees (nominally independent but effectively offshoots of Catholic Action) played a key grassroots role in getting the faithful to the polls. Gedda selected the modifier "civic" for his committees to finesse the 1929 Concordat's ban (now ensconced in the new republican constitution) on Catholic Action engaging in direct political activity. The work of the Civic Committees was divided into four offices, one each for propaganda, psychology, press relations, and "field expeditions" (campaigning).[39]

The decision to entrust this four-pronged structure to Gedda derived from several factors. Gedda's promotion from the helm of GIAC to the presidency of Catholic Men (a post he would continue to hold while simultaneously heading up the Civic Committees) in late 1946 demonstrated the pope's growing confidence in him. He had endeared himself to the Holy Father both because of the quality of his deference and because of his resourcefulness: several years earlier he had resolved some pressing financial problem (presumably internal to GIAC) "without ever asking for any money from the Holy See."[40]

The creation of the Civic Committees also signaled Pius XII's dissatisfaction with Veronese's stewardship of Catholic Action. In a papal audience held on February 4, 1948, he chided Veronese for slowness in passing the organization's budget, for the organizational inefficiency of some of its branches, and for its slowness in preparing for the parliamentary elections.[41]

For his part, Veronese doubted the efficacy of propaganda built "exclusively around anti-Communist themes and on the search for psychological effects." The Civic Committees might be justified as an emergency, and temporary, expedient for the parliamentary elections. But Veronese questioned their long-term compatibility with Catholic Action itself. One needed to decide between a "problematic (for Veronese a positive adjective), spiritual and fundamentally formative approach or one which sought to mold public opinion by focusing on generic 'action,' mass activities and considerations of prestige."[42]

For all of his eloquence, Veronese could not dispute the Civic Committees' effectiveness. When the ballots were tallied, the Christian Democrats and their allies scored a sweeping victory over the Socialist-Communist opposition. The Christian Democrats alone garnered a slim majority of seats in the Chamber of Deputies. But what did this electoral triumph mean?

To Pius XII, the victory heralded a broad crusade on behalf of integral Catholic values, radiating out from Rome, *la citta sacra,* encompassing Italy, and aiming, ultimately, at the re-Christianization of a Europe spiritually as well as materially bankrupted by war and totalitarianism. To this end, the pope expected the Christian Democrats to form a single-party government and to vigorously promote confessional interests in areas ranging from schooling and church construction to social welfare and the media.

De Gasperi saw the election differently. While his successive coalition governments promoted elements of this confessional agenda, particularly in the field of education,[43] the Christian Democratic leader rejected the logic of integralism. A longtime admirer of German, Austrian, French, and Belgian as well as Italian strands of nineteenth- and early-twentieth-century liberal Catholicism, the Trentine-born De Gasperi was determined to transcend the peninsula's chronic polarization between its Catholic and secular subcultures. He interpreted the spring 1948 parliamentary results in liberal pluralist terms—as a victory for the whole centrist governing coalition and therefore a mandate to renew multiparty rule in tandem with the smaller Liberal, Republican, and Social Democratic parties.

In February 1949 Prime Minister De Gasperi wrote the pope a candid letter in which he defended his politics of inclusion. As if lecturing the Holy Father on modern civics, he explained the need for patience, compromise, and even the occasional "sacrifice" of Catholic preferences. The work of postwar reconstruction—including the establishment of still-fragile republican institutions—called "for the art of the clinician rather than that of the surgeon."[44]

In a speech delivered in fall 1948 in Belgium entitled "The Moral Bases of Democracy" De Gasperi extolled patience as "the virtue most necessary to the democratic method." He urged his fellow European politicians to draw on "the merciful, forgiving patience of Christianity" in accepting humanity's hesitation and uncertainty in the face of change, even if political rivals (on the Right—even the clerical Right—as well as the Left) should accuse such politicians of a lack of political will. Working within the framework of liberal constitutionalism, the modern politician should painstakingly seek to strengthen the "conscience of the ordinary citizen" — for De Gasperi, the surest foundation of democracy.[45]

Here Christianity comes to "inhabit" modern democracy as a spiritual leaven operating between individual politicians and between parties of diverse orientations. A shared Christian context can also foster goodwill between individual voters and their elected representatives. De Gasperi elaborated on this individualized, internal reading of the nexus of Christianity and democracy on several other occasions.[46]

Meanwhile, Pius XII's thinking was moving in very different directions. The pope envisioned the "crusades" of the 1949–54 period as optimal affirmations of *cristianità*, modern manifestations of "Christendom" in the double sense of Christian civilization and Christian order. Here the pope was invoking something much more tangible than mere *cristianesimo* (Christianity)— a term with which De Gasperi was more comfortable. Pius XII's conception of Christian civilization "focused on this life, and on the collectivity, seeing religion in terms of order rather than of individual spiritual development and redemption."[47] Furthermore, *cristianità* focused on the Roman Church as a institution far more solid and enduring than any temporal power.

The Eternal City itself represented the "sacred" center and fulcrum of the Church across both time and space. Rome was to become a laboratory of Christian renewal for the rest of the world to observe and emulate. A native of the city, Pope Pius XII established an unusually intimate relationship with the Roman populace. The pope's solicitude for the city's residents during the Allied bombing attacks of 1943 and 1944 greatly enhanced his postwar stature there.[48]

## AN ILL-FATED AFFAIR

In early 1952 Rome again appeared endangered. In the pope's eyes, the barbarians this time were Marxist Italians all too ensconced inside the city's gates. The preceding spring, the Christian Democratic party had suffered a major reversal in the first round of Italy's 1951–52 administrative elections. In municipalities across the center and the north of the peninsula, the party lost 1,600,000 votes in comparison to the 1948 parliamentary elections. With the exception of the Liberals, the small centrist lay parties allied with the Christian Democrats had also done poorly.

How well would the weakened centrist coalition do in round two of the administrative elections, scheduled for Rome and for the Mezzogiorno in May 1952? If the political Center and the Right, occupied by the monarchists and neo-Fascists, continued to work at cross purposes, the Socialists and Communists might win control of the Eternal City.

Luigi Gedda now attempted to seize the political initiative. His antipathy for the Trentine leader was becoming common knowledge: in August 1951 Gedda publicly belittled the parliamentary gymnastics of "the De Gasperi virtuosos."[49] Echoing a growing sentiment in conservative Vatican and Catholic lay circles, Gedda insisted that the time had come for Italian Christian Democracy to pursue a new course: from Rome southward, the party should forge a "sacred union" with the monarchists and neo-Fascists— both of which promoted themselves as confessional parties.[50]

Set against this highly charged backdrop, Gedda's sudden elevation to the general presidency of Catholic Action in mid-January 1952 was a political bombshell. Gedda displaced Veronese without warning and despite the fact that the latter still had ten months left in his statutory term. No matter; the pope was convinced that Gedda's organizational and persuasive talents needed freer play at the apex of Catholic Action "to prepare for the Italian administrative elections."[51]

On February 10, 1952, three days after the formal kick-off of the municipal election campaign (and on the eve of the twenty-third anniversary of the Concordat and the Lateran Accords), the pope broadcast his "Exhortation to the Faithful of Rome," proclaiming, "The time has come to set aside baneful lethargy: it is time for all good souls, all those who care about the destiny of the world, to acknowledge one another and close ranks."[52] This was a thinly veiled admonition to the Christian Democrats to fall in beside Gedda's Catholic Action under the banner of Pacellian populism.

The pope called on Italy's Catholic leaders to demonstrate exceptional fortitude and imagination. The Socialist-Communist opposition had done no less, heading its list of candidates with the elderly Neapolitan radical and former prime minister (from June 1919 to June 1920) Francesco Saverio Nitti.

Over the next two weeks, Pius XII, Gedda, and Father Lombardi brought extraordinary public and private pressure to bear on De Gasperi to enroll himself and his party in their integralist crusade. In strictly political terms, the party was compelled to entertain an "opening to the Right," reaching out to the monarchists and perhaps the neo-Fascists even at the cost of alienating its centrist governing partners (the Republicans, Social Democrats, and Liberals). The person selected to mediate this delicate electoral operation was Don Luigi Sturzo, now a respected nongovernmental senior statesman. To blunt the appeal of Nitti's popular bloc list, Sturzo was charged with assembling a unified anti-Marxist list incorporating a broad spectrum of prominent centrist and right-wing individuals, who, however, were not to be veteran politicians. The *listone* (Big List) strategy appealed to Pius XII because it represented a way of depoliticizing the upcoming elections: public support could be courted not by focusing on party labels but by emphasizing the administrative capability and honesty of individuals included on the electoral list.[53] Though this so-called Sturzo Operation was not implemented in the end, its tormented history brought to a head contradictions that had been long building within Italian political Catholicism.

The major turning points in this intricate affair may be briefly summarized. Queried in early April as to whether a danger existed of the Socialist-Communist bloc winning the Rome municipal elections, Christian Democratic secretary Guido Gonella demurred, saying that "in elections, there is always risk." The DC had already begun secret negotiations with the monarchists about case-by-case cooperation in some municipalities of the Mezzogiorno. But the neo-Fascists were another matter. An April 14 meeting between Lombardi and Gonella turned into a shouting match between the two men, with the latter insisting that his party would never "dirty itself" by allying with the neo-Fascists.[54]

Two days later the pope upped the ante, directing Lombardi to visit De Gasperi at the latter's Roman apartment. Instructed by papal housekeeper Sister Pasqualina, on behalf of Pius XII, to "speak forcefully, even reprovingly," Lombardi found the prime minister obdurate. "There is no danger of Rome becoming officially Communist," De Gasperi asserted. He would enter a coalition including neo-Fascists only "if the pope were to command it," and even then against his own political judgment.[55]

Lombardi came away from the meeting flush with the belief that he had "succeeded" with De Gasperi. But Pius XII was disappointed at the outcome. "The Holy Father felt it would not do to issue commands in cases such as these to a prime minister," Lombardi recorded in his memoirs. Pius XII, he added, "suffered" greatly over his failure to wean De Gasperi from what Pius saw as an overly rigid ideological stance.[56]

As a last resort, Sister Pasqualina informed Lombardi that he should intervene with De Gasperi's wife that Saturday, April 19, at the residence of Emilio Bonomelli, manager of the papal villa at Castelgondolfo. As a former member of the Popular Party and longtime friend of the family, Bonomelli often hosted both the De Gasperis and Montini at his residence on weekends.

In an interview lasting an hour and a half, Lombardi announced that he had "come in obedience to a clear mandate from the Holy Father." "If Rome elected a Communist mayor democratically," he continued, "that would be a shame and a scandal [*vergogna*] for the Church, for the Pope, for the whole anti-Communist world and also for Christian Democracy and for the government."[57] In Maria Romana De Gasperi's celebrated account of this same encounter, Lombardi "went from flattery to threats," saying that the pope "would rather see Stalin and his Cossacks in St. Peter's Square than the Communists victorious in the elections to the Campidoglio." "Take care," he warned her, "for if the elections go badly we shall make him [De Gasperi] resign."[58] Mrs. De Gasperi agreed only "to pass on the pope's opinion" to her husband.

The next evening, while dining at Bonomelli's house, Papal Prosecretary of State Montini underscored the extent of the Holy Father's dissatisfaction with the Christian Democrats. Bonomelli asked Montini if the pope really meant to repudiate the Christian Democratic leadership in this way. "It is just that that they [the conservatives in the Vatican] want," Montini replied. "They have done nothing but repeat for a long time that the party is carrying us to ruin, and they think that Gedda and his Catholic Action is the only efficient force capable of replacing the party and standing up to Communism." When Bonomelli passed this news on to De Gasperi, the latter replied, "Only now do I realize you were right when you painted such a black picture of the state of mind nourished towards us in the Vatican."[59]

The tide began to turn in De Gasperi's favor on Monday, April 21, and Tuesday, April 22, as several intermediaries took action on his behalf. Bonomelli convinced Count Enrico Galeazzi, the architect in charge of Vatican business affairs, of the dangers of the proposed operation. Galeazzi, an influential man for whom "the pope's door was always open," then went to see Pius, accompanied by Pius's brother Prince Francesco Pacelli.[60] Half an hour later Galeazzi offered Bonomelli general reassurances that the pope was coming around and that, in extremis, he would not forsake the Christian Democrats. Bonomelli telephoned the good news to De Gasperi, who was anxiously awaiting developments back at Castelgondolfo; however, De Gasperi was afraid to put much stock in what he heard.

Several scholars have concluded that the decisive intervention was that of Giulio Andreotti, whose forceful memo reached the pope's desk, with the help of a sympathetic monsignor, Quirino Paganuzzi, and of Sister Pasqualina, on Monday afternoon. The memo, entitled "On the Roman Elections," outlined eight likely repercussions of the proposed operation. These consequences ranged from the collapse, locally and nationally, of alliances with the other centrist political parties to adverse responses "in America and in the Atlantic world." Uniformly, the Socialists-Communists stood to gain from these foreseeable complications. Having already campaigned victoriously against Communism in Italy, De Gasperi deserved to be given credit in the present difficult situation. "No less than others," Andreotti concluded, De Gasperi "feels the need for a jealous defense of the city of Rome, episcopal seat of the pope himself."[61] Tired of being pulled in different directions and anxious to extricate himself from his deepening entanglement, Pius XII seems to have been won over by Andreotti's argument.

However, none of the other principals in the affair yet realized this. The embattled De Gasperi missed the Monday, April 21, session of the Italian council of ministers. Instead, he and Gonella attended a secret summit with Gedda and several "exponents of the Vatican Secretariat of State" at Grottaferrata, not far from Castelgondolfo in the Alban Hills. The Catholic Action leader threatened to run a separate list of Catholic Action candidates in the Rome elections if the Christian Democrats did not reach an agreement with the rightist parties. In response, a weary De Gasperi agreed to renew his party's efforts to find a solution within the framework of the Sturzo Operation.[62]

On Tuesday and Wednesday morning, frenetic negotiations continued between Sturzo and top centrist and right-wing party leaders, with Gedda advising and encouraging the latter. Running short on patience, Sturzo set a deadline of midday Wednesday for the conclusion of a definitive agreement. Last-minute hairsplitting prevented the monarchists and neo-Fascists from meeting this deadline, and at 2:00 P.M., April 23, Italian state radio announced that Sturzo was withdrawing from the campaign. The Sicilian priest took this step in consultation with the DC leadership but without obtaining clearance from the Vatican. One would like to think that Sturzo's decision here reflected not only a willful disposition but also the reassertion of his anti-Fascist conscience.[63]

Pius XII was irritated with the "brusque manner" in which negotiations had been cut short. Already put out with the Christian Democratic leadership for its delaying tactics, the pope was further annoyed with them for abetting Sturzo's intemperance. Now, however, there was nothing to be done but to rally the faithful once again around the DC and its candidates. Gedda and Lombardi were both ordered to follow suit. Crestfallen, the latter felt as though he had been set aside like a "broken lance."[64]

Gedda's hand had been weakened when unexpectedly broad resistance to the Sturzo Operation surfaced from within Catholic Action itself. At a special meeting of Catholic Action's *giunta* convened on Tuesday, April 22, predictable opposition by leaders of the Catholic University Students' Association and the Movimento Laureati (Graduates' Association), groups long associated with Montini, was reinforced from other quarters. Maria Badaloni (head of the Catholic Elementary School Teachers' Association),[65] Alda Miceli (head of the Female Catholic Youth), and Carmela Rossi (head of Catholic Women) all objected to the proposed alliance with the Right. So, to Gedda's dismay, did the heretofore obedient head of Catholic Youth, Carlo Carretto. Only Agostino Maltarello, the head of Catholic Men, supported the Sturzo Operation.[66]

Badaloni's and Carretto's "defections" disturbed Gedda and the Holy Father the most.[67] Particularly fond of the Holy Father, Badaloni honored him with elaborate flower arrangements for the altar at St. Peter's every Easter. She had supported Gedda's call for a renewal of the Civic Committees at a summit of Catholic Action leaders in November 1951. Why then did she balk at the Sturzo Operation? Like many of her contemporaries, male and female, Badaloni felt uneasy with an intensity of partisanship that so deeply contradicted their initial, "Rattian"[68] conception of Catholic Action's "apolitical" mission. Perhaps a further explanation lies in Badaloni's more recent experience as a Christian Democratic deputy at Montecitorio, which underscored for her the logic of the government's commitment to centrism. Her long-standing rapport with Guido Gonella, dating from his tenure as minister of public instruction, may have played a role as well.[69]

For his part, Carretto, though an enthusiastic disciple of Gedda's, was deeply moved by De Gasperi's appearance at a convention of Catholic Youth ecclesiastical assistants held a few days after the pope's address of February 10. Speaking with deep respect and unusual candor, Carretto acknowledged that young Catholic Action activists like himself were "impatient at times and liable to get ahead of themselves" but assured the prime minister, "We are for democracy and for you: here there are no clerico-Fascists."[70] Neither Carretto's frank words nor his stand in late April were forgotten: when his term as head of GIAC expired later in the year, he was not reappointed.[71]

On April 27 the pope granted an audience to a group of young Catholics gathered in Rome for a national St. Vincent de Paul conference. Among this group were Wladimiro Dorigo, then GIAC's head of propaganda and Giorgio La Pira, the idealistic, left-wing Christian Democrat who was later to become mayor of Florence. Immediately after kissing the pope's hand, La Pira rose to offer his own high hopes that "the enemy would not prevail" in the upcoming municipal elections and that "Rome would be preserved." Surprised by these remarks, Pius XII responded with stony reserve. "Let it be, professor," the pope said, turning his shoulders, "certain refusals and certain forms of ostentation should never have occurred!" There was little question in La Pira's or Dorigo's mind that the Holy Father's remark was directed toward De Gasperi.[72]

On election day the specter of an "atheist administration" on the Campidoglio, which had so alarmed the Vatican and Roman conservative circles, was dispelled. When the ballots were tallied after the May 25 municipal elections, the centrist list (embracing candidates from the governing coalition of Christian Democratic, Liberal, Republican, and Social Democratic parties) turned back a strong challenge mounted by the Socialist and Communist parties. Some 384,000 voters backed the centrist list, while the leftist "peoples' bloc" list tallied some 314,000 votes and a separate rightist list received some 206,000 votes.[73]

## DE GASPERI'S FALL FROM GRACE

Publicly, the Holy Father, Gedda, and De Gasperi attempted to paper over the chasm that had opened between the two forms of political Catholicism they represented: to do otherwise would further demoralize and disorient the faithful, with national parliamentary elections looming in summer 1953. Privately, however, Pius XII and Gedda concluded that Catholic Action and Christian Democracy had become antithetical: in Gedda's June 17 audience with Pius XII, the latter spoke of the "bitter discoveries" that the affair had brought, lamenting that "Catholic Action, for which we have sacrificed so much, is no longer ours." "Rather than work with the Church," the pope stated, "Catholic Action now works with Christian Democracy."[74]

During this same month, De Gasperi and his wife, Francesca, requested an audience with Pius XII on the dual occasion of their thirtieth wedding anniversary and their daughter Lucia's having taken her perpetual vows as a nun. To their shock and chagrin, they were refused. The pope's snub brought home the depth of his continuing disaffection with the Christian Democratic leader in the wake of the Sturzo Operation. De Gasperi responded bluntly to the pope. "As a Christian," he wrote, "I accept the humiliation, although I can't understand how it could be justified. But I am also Italy's President of the Council of Ministers and Minister of Foreign Affairs. I cannot divest myself of the dignity of these offices even in my personal relations. For this reason I am bound to express my stupefaction at such an exceptional refusal, and must insist on clarification from the Vatican Secretariat of State."[75]

Only after De Gasperi stepped down as prime minister in July 1953 did he more directly acknowledge and articulate some of the logical implications of his breach with the pope. Addressing, as party secretary, delegates gathering for the Christian Democratic party's fifth congress in 1954, De Gasperi rejected a Vatican-backed effort to make the party an officially confessional emanation of ecclesiastical authority. "To operate in the . . . political sphere," he asserted, "neither faith nor virtue is enough: what is required is to create and nurture an instrument suited to the times: the party, a political organization with its own program, its own method, its own autonomous responsibility and democratic method." "It is not possible," he went on, "to conduct a twentieth-century democratic regime with the paternalism of a Bossuet."[76]

It is interesting to speculate as to what else De Gasperi might have realized and written had he, like Machiavelli or Dante before him, lived on for many years after being exiled from the political activity that had been his lifeblood. Clearly he had more to say: in a letter to Amintore Fanfani, written

ten days before his death in August 1954, De Gasperi defended his own, unflagging efforts to overcome Italy's age-old "Guelph-Ghibelline divide" and alluded to "secret episodes" that he wished to pass on to his successor at the helm of the party.[77] Would that he had had the chance, for a frank, sustained Catholic discussion of the balance between political autonomy and collective religious conscience at this juncture would have been healthy for both party and republic.

But De Gasperi's heirs failed to follow up the candid self-examination they had begun at the Naples congress. As secretary of the party from 1953 to 1958, Fanfani modernized and expanded its administrative structure so as to obviate the need for external "assistance" from the likes of Gedda's Civic Committees. A staunch supporter of the operational autonomy of the party, however, the opportunistic Fanfani also sided with party integralists, especially on moral issues.[78]

His Democratic Initiative faction was only one of a number of rival currents within the party that now began to organize openly despite a party statutory ban against them. Leftist currents centered on the figures of Giovanni Gronchi and Aldo Moro pushed for enhanced economic planning and more ambitious land reforms. The rightist Vespisti and Giulio Andreotti's Primavera current resisted such sweeping socioeconomic reforms in favor of a combination of economic liberalism and social integralism. Lacking more substantial common ground on domestic policy, all of these faction leaders fell back on generic affirmations of Catholicity and endless reiterations of anti-Communism to try to preserve at least a measure of cohesion at election time.[79]

The formation of such currents was a natural and indeed predictable consequence of the DC's maturation as a broadly accepted, interclass party concerned with the distribution of patronage and the balancing of various regional and socioeconomic interests. Yet their formation mocked the ideal of "the political unity of Catholics"[80] and compromised the party's moral stature in the eyes of many Italian and Church observers. This explains why De Gasperi and others in the party, including Gonella and Badaloni, deplored the currents and sought, unsuccessfully, to stem their formation.[81] The pope's conclusion is perhaps best summed up in a remark he made to former British Field Marshal Montgomery shortly before he died. Speaking of the Italian Christian Democratic party, Pius XII said that "he liked the first part" of that party's name "but not the second."[82]

## CONCLUSION

Pius XII complicated the consolidation of Italian democracy because of his policies toward Catholic Action and because of those toward Christian Democracy. Gedda's Civic Committees, as de facto emanations of Catholic Action, were vulnerable to the charge that they violated the terms of the 1929 Concordat (incorporated into article 7 of the republican constitution) that excluded the umbrella Catholic lay organization from political activity. Misgivings on this score were widespread even within Catholic Action's ruling *giunta*, as we have seen. Veronese's abrupt deposition as president general ten months shy of the end of his statutory term was shocking as well: might this internecine coup by the pontiff not presage an even more dramatic intervention at the highest levels of the Italian state?

The unfolding of the Sturzo Operation in just three months heightened such apprehensions. Father Lombardi's peremptory visitations to De Gasperi in Rome and to his wife at Castelgondolfo subjected Italy's head of government to extraordinary personal pressure—pressure that, in extremis, the devout De Gasperi could hardly withstand. That pressure, originating as from the head of another state, infringed on Italian sovereignty. The substance of Pius's diktat, in the case of the 1952 Roman municipal elections, could also be said to be "antidemocratic" as it demanded that the DC embrace, however tactically, the monarchists and neo-Fascists—avowedly antirepublican political formations of the extreme Right. If, in the end, Pius XII wavered, this reflected less a crisis of political conscience than a cool recalculation of partisan odds.

Viewed in its entirety, Pius XII's record of engagement in postwar Italian politics is an erratic and ambivalent one. Diffident toward parliamentary democracy, he nevertheless acknowledged its centrality in the era of post-Fascist reconstruction. The idealism and eloquence of his wartime Christmas messages were invaluable in empowering Italy's Catholic faithful to look ahead to the postwar era with a sense of confidence and engagement. Yet he regarded modern political parties, including the Christian Democratic party, not as goods in themselves but as tools that the Church must, perforce, be prepared to use in advancing her own interests. Between 1942 and 1948 the pope concurred with the Montinian strategy of promoting the Christian Democratic party as the embodiment of "the political unity of Catholics." After the spring 1948 elections, his appreciation of the party waned and he turned increasingly to Catholic Action as his preferred instrument for promoting a unique form of politicoreligious populism.

Despite the inspirational value of Pius's words and figure during and just after the war, the overall impact of his patronizing, judgmental leadership style was to retard the political maturation of Italian Catholics. He demanded an almost military obedience and audacity from lay leaders, yet he held himself aloof from them, reserving maximum flexibility in his choice of tactics and of "executors" of the papal will. For all their zealous dedication, neither Gedda nor Father Lombardi were able to count wholeheartedly on the mercurial pontiff, as the events of April 1952 were to demonstrate. The history of the Roman municipal election campaign, including the Sturzo Operation, revealed both the mischievous potential and the ultimate impotence of the Pacellian brand of political Catholicism.

On the other hand, De Gasperi and the Christian Democrats may be said to have "prevailed" in these elections, in the double sense of having defeated the Socialist-Communist opposition without succumbing to the pope and of Gedda's bid to dominate the party and reorient its collocation on the political spectrum. Anti-Fascism continued to distinguish the Christian Democrats and their centrist government allies from the Right, just as anti-Communism set them off from the Left.

If the Italian republican political system is imperfect, it has also proved resilient. For these things the Christian Democratic party deserves a disproportionate share of both the credit and the blame. Yet in the end the most enduring contribution of postwar political Catholicism may not have been systemic at all but instead embodied in the example of individuals such as Sturzo, Veronese, and De Gasperi. Inspired by the social teachings of the Church and the challenge of bringing their countrymen together in civil discourse, their lives testified to the fact that, conducted in the right spirit, even democratic politics might constitute a form of Christian vocation.

## NOTES

1. See Martin J. Bull, *Contemporary Italy: A Research Guide* (Westport, Conn.: Greenwood Press, 1996), 12–21; and John Davis, "Modern Italy: Changing Historical Perspectives since 1945," in Michael Bentley, ed., *Companion to Historiography* (London: Routledge, 1997), 591–612.

2. Francesco Traniello, "Political Catholicism, Catholic Organization and Catholic Laity in the Reconstruction Years," in Frank J. Coppa and Margarita Repetto-Alaia, eds., *The Formation of the Italian Republic* (New York: Peter Lang, 1989), 27–54; John Pollard, "Italy," in Tom Buchanan and Martin Conway, eds., *Political Catholicism in Europe, 1918–1965* (Oxford: Clarendon, 1996), 69–95; Douglas Wertman and Robert Leonardi, *Italian Christian Democracy: The Politics of Dominance* (London: Macmillan, 1989).

3. De Gasperi's personal papers remain in family hands; however, other significant archival collections dealing with Christian Democratic founding fathers are now being processed and opened to researchers. See Concetta Argiolas, "L'archivio storico dell'Istituto Luigi Sturzo," in *Gli archivi dei partiti politici* (Rome: Archivio centrale dello stato, 1996), 196–208.

4. Veronese's personal papers pertaining to his years with Italian Catholic Action (cited hereafter as Fondo VV-ACI) are among those held at the Istituto Luigi Sturzo (ILS). The proceedings of an international symposium focusing on Veronese's many-faceted career and hosted at the ILS have been published under the title *Vittorino Veronese un laico nella chiesa e nel mondo* (Rome: AVE, 1994). In 1998 Gedda published a political and personal memoir, centered on his numerous audiences with Pius XI and Pius XII, entitled *18 aprile 1948: Memorie inedite dell'artefice della sconfitta del Fronte Popolare* (Milan: Mondadori, 1998).

5. Steven White, "The Retrospective Cult of De Gasperi," paper delivered at the annual meeting of the Association for the Study of Modern Italy, November 23, 1996, London; Oliver Logan, "Pius XII: Romanità, Prophesy and Charisma," *Modern Italy* 3:2 (1998): 237–47; Marzia Marsili, "De Gasperi and Togliatti: Political Leadership and Personality Cults in Post-War Italy," *Modern Italy* 3:2 (1998): 249–61.

6. Pietro Scoppola critiques his fellow Catholics on these grounds in his *La repubblica dei partiti* (Bologna: Il Mulino, 1991), 209–15.

7. Carlo Falconi, *Luigi Gedda e l'Azione Cattolica* (Florence: Parenti, 1958), chap. 6 ("Quasi Salazar").

8. Andrea Riccardi, "La nazione cattolica," in Agostino Giovagnoli, ed., *Interpretazioni della repubblica* (Bologna: Il Mulino, 1998), 52; Mario Casella, "Per una storia dei rapporti tra Azione Cattolica e Democrazia Cristiana nell'eta del centrismo," in Giuseppe Rossini, ed., *Alcide De Gasperi e l'età del centrismo* (Rome: Cinque Lune, 1984).

9. Arguing that in early postwar Italy Christian Democracy's legitimacy "could only be a shadow of the legitimacy accorded to Pius XII," Patrick McCarthy dramatizes but also distorts Pius XII's problematic impact on the early republic. See his *Crisis of the Italian State: From the Origins of the Cold War to the Fall of Berlusconi and Beyond* (New York: St. Martin's, 1997), 25–26, 34.

10. Jean-Guy Vaillancourt, *Papal Power: A Study of Vatican Control over Lay Catholic Elites* (Berkeley: University of California Press, 1980), 200–201; Gedda,

*18 aprile 1948*, 156; Peter Hebblethwaite, *Paul VI: The First Modern Pope* (New York: Paulist Press, 1993), 242–53.

11. Francesco Malgeri, "Le Chiese di Pio XII fra guerra e dopoguerra," in Andrea Riccardi, ed., *Pio XII* (Bari: Laterza, 1984), 113–15.

12. Domenico Tardini, *Memories of Pius XII* (Westminster, Md.: Newman Press, 1961), 95.

13. Gabriele De Rosa, *Il Partito Popolare Italiano* (Bari: Laterza, 1988), 179–80.

14. Gedda, *18 aprile 1948*, 22–23. On Gemelli's ideas and career, see Frank Coppa, ed., *Encyclopedia of the Vatican and Papacy* (Westport, Conn.: Greenwood Press, 1999), 173.

15. Hence the magazine's title. Gedda, *18 aprile 1948*, 32–45.

16. Agostino Giovagnoli, *La cultura democristiana* (Bari: Laterza, 1991), 97–98.

17. This robust assertion comes from an article entitled "Unita e carita" (Unity and Charity), published in August 1943 both in *Studium* and in *L'Osservatore Romano*. See Carlo Felice Casula, "L'impegno 'sociale' di Vittorino Veronese," in *Vittorino Veronese un laico*, 66.

18. Emilio Gentile, "Fascism as Political Religion," *Journal of Contemporary History* 25 (1990): 229–51; Oliver Logan, "Italian Identity: Catholic Responses to Secularist Definitions, c. 1910–48," *Modern Italy* 2 (Autumn 1997): 58. On the loaded relationship, at once competitive and symbiotic, between Fascist and Catholic versions of *romanità*, see Romke Visser, "Fascist Doctrine and the Cult of the Romanità," *Journal of Contemporary History* 27 (1992): 5–22.

19. Ruggero Orfei, *Fede e politica* (Milan: Longonesi, 1977), 143–45; Frank J. Coppa, ed., *Controversial Concordats: The Vatican's Relations with Napoleon, Mussolini and Hitler* (Washington, D.C.: Catholic University of America Press, 1999), 81–82.

20. See the official English translation, 1944 Christmas Message, *The Catholic Mind* 43:986, (February 1945): 68–69.

21. Ibid., 66–67. There was little recognition here that democracy might have its own architecture—that constitutional engineering or the constructive interaction of political parties is necessary to actualize democratic governance. Alluding to the pope's temperament and upbringing, the Italian church historian Sandro Magister has in this conjunction written of Pius XII's "aristocratic indifference" to the concrete forms of the state and partisan maneuver. Sandro Magister, *La politica vaticana e l'Italia, 1943–1978* (Rome: Riuniti, 1978), 52.

22. Wilton Wynn, *Keepers of the Keys* (New York: Random House, 1988), 219; Hebblethwaite, *Paul VI*, 207–8.

23. Jean-Dominique Durand, "Alcide De Gasperi ovvero la politica ispirata," *Storia Contemporanea* 16:4 (August 1984): 552–58.

24. Pius XII left the office of Vatican Secretary of State vacant after Cardinal Maglione's death in 1944. De Gasperi served as his own foreign minister from December 1945 to October 1946 and again from July 1951 to July 1953.

25. Pacelli developed a great admiration for German culture during his sojourn as papal nuncio in Munich and Berlin during the late 1910s and 1920s. Born in Trento, De Gasperi was practically bilingual in German and Italian. He served his political apprenticeship before World War I as a Catholic deputy in the Austrian parliament; after World War II his political opponents would dub him, derisively, "the Chancellor."

26. Leonardi and Wertman, *Italian Christian Democracy*, 25.

27. Palmiro Togliatti, *Momenti di stori d'Italia* (1963), cited in Giovanni Di Capua, ed., *Processo a De Gasperi* (Rome: Ed. EBE, 1976), 918–20.

28. Stung by Gronchi's needling on this score shortly after the war, De Gasperi justified his expressive style in this manner: "I remember quite clearly how at a certain point in my political youth[,] . . . horrified by the disastrous effects of excessive rhetoric, I resolved to speak and write simply and concretely, aiming to convince rather than entrance, to persuade rather than receive applause." De Gasperi acknowledged that his words could be "fragmentary and nervous" and indeed "asyntactic at times." But this was a language that an "attentive public accepted and understood." Undated manuscript, Personal Papers of Francesco Bartelotta.

29. Silvio Lanaro, *Storia dell'Italia repubblicana* (Venice: Marsilio, 1992), 94.

30. Logan, "Pius XII: Romanità, Prophesy and Charisma," 243.

31. Tardini, *Memories of Pius XII*, 119. It is worth pointing out that De Gasperi is the only named perpetrator in the series of four linguistic or social gaffes that Tardini relates at this point in his memoir.

32. Carlo Falconi, *Popes of the Twentieth Century* (Boston: Little, Brown, 1967), 297–98; Tardini, *Memories of Pius XII*, 51–66.

33. This contrast emerges forcefully from the article "Voci e timori per la nomina di Gedda," *24 Ore*, no. 31 (February 9, 1952), Fondo VV-ACI, B.7, f. 61, ILS.

34. Gedda, *18 aprile 1948*, 233; Giulio Andreotti, *De Gasperi visto da vicino* (Milan: Rizzoli, 1986), 157, 169.

35. Extract from Bonomelli's diary published in *Concretezza* (August 16, 1964), 18.

36. Giulio Andreotti, "Riaccese la fiducia negli italiani," in Di Capua, *Processo a De Gasperi*, 110–115 originally in *Il Tempo*, August 18, 1974.

37. The Easter Sunday (March 28, 1948) edition of the Christian Democratic party newspaper *Il Popolo*, featured flanking front-page stories, one covering De Gasperi's campaign addresses at Frosinone, Cassino, and Caserta and the other depicting the pope's Easter address.

38. Oliver Logan, "Italian Identity: Catholic Responses to Secularist Definitions, c. 1910–48," *Modern Italy* 2:1–2 (Autumn 1997): 61–63.

39. "Cattolici di battaglia," interview with Luigi Gedda; and Turi Vasile (head of the Psychology Office), "Altro che spot e sondaggi," *30 Giorni* no. 3 (March 1998): 24–25, 42–45; Gedda, *18 aprile 1948*, 117–18.

40. Memo summarizing a recent meeting of Cingolani's with G. B. Montini, Mario Cingolani to Alcide De Gasperi, September 10, 1945, Spataro Papers, B. 7, f. 70, ILS.

41. Francesco Malgeri, "La presenza di Vittorino Veronese nel ACI e la rinascita democratica del dopoguerra," in *Vittorino Veronese un laico*, 35.

42. Memo, Veronese to Piazza, February 22, 1948, cited in Malgeri, "La presenza di Vittorino Veronese," 36–37.

43. See chapter 7, "Counter Reformation," in Steven F. White, *Progressive Renaissance: America and the Reconstruction of Italian Education, 1943–1962* (New York: Garland, 1991), 156–77.

44. Maria Romana De Gasperi, ed., *De Gasperi scrive: Correspondenza con capi di stato cardinali uomini politici giornalisti diplomatici*, vol. 1 (Brescia: Morcelliana, 1974), 107–13.

45. "Le basi morali della democrazia," November 20, 1948, reproduced in Maria Catti-De Gasperi, ed., *De Gasperi e L'Europa* (Brescia: Morcelliana, 1979), 55–71.

46. De Gasperi's Christian reading of democracy in terms of patience, tolerance, compassion, and "daily praxis" are explored at greater length in Steven F. White, "Alcide De Gasperi and the 'Calvary of Democracy,'" paper delivered at the annual meeting of the American Catholic Historical Association, Seattle, Wash., January 11, 1998. Angelo Braschi depicts De Gasperi's career as echoing "the trial-strewn curriculum of the Apostle of Peoples (Jesus Christ)." See his *Mussolini e De Gasperi: Vite divergenti* (Bologna: Cappelli, 1983).

47. Oliver Logan, "Christian Civilization and Italic Civilization: Italian Catholic Theses from Gioberti to Pius XII," in R. N. Swanson, ed., *The Church Retrospective* (Woodbridge: Boydell, 1997), 475, 485.

48. Logan, "Pius XII: Romanità, Prophesy and Charisma," 240–41. These same Allied bombing attacks gave rise to a bizarre campaign to discredit De Gasperi. In January 1954 Giovannino Guareschi's right-wing journal *Candido* revived a story, which had circulated late in the war, asserting that De Gasperi had *requested* that the Allies bomb Rome, or its aqueducts, to deepen Roman opposition to continued Italian participation on the side of the Axis powers. The former prime minister had no choice but to defend himself—which he did successfully—from such libelous attacks in a Milanese court. See Andreotti, *De Gasperi visto da vicino*, 276–88; and Maria Romana Catti-De Gasperi, *De Gasperi l'uomo solo* (Milan: Mondadori, 1964), 397–403.

49. This phrase appeared in a column of Gedda's in the Catholic Action daily *Il Quotidiano*, August 7, 1951. Cited in Jean-Guy Vaillancourt, *Papal Power*, 200.

50. Andrea Riccardi, *Il "partito romano" nel secondo dopoguerra (1945–1954)* (Brescia: Morcelliana, 1983), 143–76. On the confessional claims of the monarchists, see Ruggero Orfei, *L'occupazione del potere: I democristiani '45/'75* (Milan: Longanesi, 1976), 128.

51. In September 1949 Pius XII had installed Gedda in a newly created general vice presidency under Veronese, with a broad mandate to review and enhance Catholic Action's administrative efficiency. Chagrined, the diplomatic Veronese had nevertheless worked hard to smooth relations with his ambitious and unpredictable colleague. Veronese to Pignedoli, September 1, 1949, and Veronese to Gedda, s.d (but clearly September 1949), both in B. 4, f. 37, Fondo VV-ACI, ILS; Malgeri, "La presenza di Vittorino Veronese," 45.

52. Magister, *Politica vaticana e l'Italia,* 165.

53. Ibid., 195n.22.

54. Giulio Andreotti, "Montini e la politica italiana," *30 Giorni,* no. 6 (June 1999): 58; Magister, *La politica vaticana e l'Itala,* 164; Giancarlo Zizola, *Il microfono di Dio* (Milan: Mondadori, 1990), 298–99.

55. During this period, De Gasperi received letters and visits from many supporters, including "the presidents of several branches of Catholic Action," entreating him not to abandon his centrist politics. The prime minister's daughter Maria Romana recites how the bearer of one of these appeals "allowed himself in his enthusiasm to accuse the Head of the Church of interference in Italian politics." Her father "stopped him with a gesture, saying 'If it is imposed on me I will break my life and my political work, but I can do no other than bow the head.' The man saw that the eyes of De Gasperi were heavy with tears." Catti-De Gasperi, *De Gasperi uomo solo,* 328.

56. Zizola, *Il microfono di Dio,* 301.

57. Ibid., 302.

58. Catti-De Gasperi, *De Gasperi l'uomo solo,* 327–28.

59. Vaillancourt, *Papal Power,* 201–2.

60. Commemorative article by Bonomelli, cited in Di Capua, *Processo a De Gasperi,* 198; Vaillancourt, *Papal Power,* 202.

61. Orfei, *L'occupazione del potere,* 122–35; Giorgio Galli, *Storia della Democrazia Cristiana* (Bari: Laterza, 1978), 144–47; Aurelio Lepre, *Storia della prima repubblica: L'Italia dal 1942 al 1992* (Bologna: Il Mulino, 1994), 152. Andreotti's Cassandra-like memo is reproduced in Magister, *Politica vaticana,* 170–72.

62. Zizola, *Il microfono di Dio,* 305; Catti-De Gasperi, *De Gasperi l'uomo solo,* p. 330.

63. See Domenico Settembrini's thorough summary of the Sturzo operation, incorporating the sometimes inconsistent recollections of Sturzo himself, DC interior minister Mario Scelba, and GIAC veteran Wladimiro Dorigo, in *La Chiesa nella politica italiana* (Milan: Rizzoli, 1977), 253–69.

64. Zizola, *Il microfono di Dio,* 307.

65. See Badaloni's subdued letter of condolence to Veronese following his removal as head of Catholic Action. Badaloni to Veronese, January 23, 1952, Fondo VV-ACI, B. 7, f. 60.

66. Gedda, *18 aprile 1948,* 153.

67. Ibid., 153–54.

68. Referring to Achille Ratti, the future Pope Pius XI.

69. Interview with Maria Badaloni, March 16, 1982; "Verbali della Riunione della Giunta Centrale ACI," November 6–7, 1951, Fondo VV-ACI, B. 8, f. 70, ILS; White, *Progressive Renaissance*, 160–63.

70. Quoted in Magister, *La politica vaticana e l'Italia*, 166.

71. Ibid., 179–81.

72. Wladimiro Dorigo's recollections of this group audience, published originally in *Questitalia* (January–February 1959), are reproduced in his *Polemiche sull'integrismo* (Vicenza: La Locusta, 1962), 35. See also Galli, *Storia della Democrazia Cristiana*, 457 n. 10; and Settembrini, *La Chiesa nella politica italiana*, 268–69.

73. The Christian Democrats' and their centrist allies' success in Rome was a bright spot in a generally forbidding political landscape: nationwide, the party's aggregate share of the vote had fallen from 48.5 percent in the 1948 parliamentary elections to 35.1 percent in the 1951–52 administrative elections. Gianni Baget-Bozzo, *Il Partito Cristiano al potere: La DC di De Gasperi e Dossetti* (Florence: Vallecchi, 1974), 398; Norman Kogan, *A Political History of Postwar Italy* (New York: Praeger, 1966), 74.

74. Gedda, *18 aprile 1948*, 153.

75. Catti-De Gasperi, *De Gasperi l'uomo solo*, 335. See also Durand, "Alcide De Gasperi ovvero la politica ispirata," 590. According to Maria Romana, after May 1952 her father never again referred to these "deeply hurtful" events—yet "the sorrow of not having been fully appreciated and supported [by the pope] remained etched in the furrows of his brow" (336). Within a year of the appearance of Maria Romana's biography, other principal actors in the Sturzo operation sought to downplay the significance of Pius XII's refused audience. Emilio Bonomelli, who as manager of the papal summer villa at Castelgondolfo and a longtime friend of the De Gasperi family had opened his private diaries to Maria Romana, asserted that Pius XII's refusal was only consistent with his having resolved "for years not to receive Italian political figures." See his commemorative article from *Concretezza* 10, no. 16 (August 16, 1964), cited in Di Capua, *Processo a De Gasperi*, 197. Giulio Andreotti, De Gasperi's devoted but very clerical junior colleague, has construed the prime minister's note of protest as being essentially pro forma. See Andreotti's *Intervista su De Gasperi*, ed. Antonio Gambino (Bari: Laterza, 1977), 116.

76. Speech at Naples's Teatro San Carlo, June 27, 1954, in P. G. Zunino, ed., *Scritti politici di Alcide De Gasperi* (Milan: Feltrinelli, 1979), 444.

77. Romana De Gasperi, *De Gasperi scrive*, 1:334.

78. R. E. M. Irving, *The Christian Democratic Parties of Western Europe* (London: Allyn & Unwin, 1979), 78–80.

79. Giovanni Mantovani, *Gli eredi di De Gasperi: Iniziativa democratica e giovani al potere* (Florence: Le Mounier, 1976), 168–69.

80. A recent study of the persisting appeal and functionality of this ideological formula is Enzo Pace's *L'unita dei cattolici in Italia: Origini e decadenza di un mito colletitivo* (Milan: Guerini, 1995).

81. Di Capua, *Processo a De Gasperi*, 70–72.

82. John Zeender, introduction to Coppa, *Controversial Concordats*, 32.

# 9  "The Moral Question"

Relations between Christian Democrats
and Communists in Italy

ANTONIO A. SANTUCCI

Thomas Hobbes, with his famous political realism, believed that prophecies are often self-fulfilling. It is apt to begin this chapter with a newspaper headline: "Le 'profezie' di Berlinguer" (Berlinguer's Prophecies); an
interview given by the former secretary of the Italian Communist Party
to *La Repubblica* on July 28, 1981, was recently republished under this
heading.[1] Should the term "prophecy" seem hyperbolic, one might replace it with the more ordinary "prediction," but the result would be the
same. The important thing to bear in mind is that Berlinguer's analysis,
as Patrick McCarthy has pointed out in *The Crisis of the Italian State*,[2]
reappeared as a shout of protest in 1992. That year signaled the beginning of the judicial inquiry known as *mani pulite* (literally, "clean
hands"), which in just over a year would place some 2,600 people under
investigation. Of these, 325 were members of parliament, many of them
Christian Democrats. After half a century at the reins of the Italian government, the Christian Democratic party was crumbling; and in the
midst of internal divisions and electoral collapses, its odyssey rapidly
and definitively came to a close in January 1994. The phenomenon seemed
to mirror, on a smaller scale, the surprising speed with which the Soviet
empire broke up at the beginning of the decade.

What was Berlinguer's thesis? Nothing other than a reiteration of
what had already been affirmed in a document approved by the leaders
of the Communist Party in November 1980: "The moral question [*la*

*questione morale*] has now become the most important national issue."
Nevertheless, the Communist Party leader's prophecy (or prediction) did
not consist in his awareness of the existence of a "moral question" in the
political life of the nation. On the theoretical level, the relation between
ethics and politics has been a basic element of political thought since
Machiavelli. And on the historical level, the moral question has been a legitimate topic of discussion ever since the problem of political corruption first
engaged the interest of human society. In this vein, one could embark, as
John Noonan Jr. did, on a program of historiographical research stretching
back to about 3000 B.C.[3] Yet even if we do not go so far back in time and
limit ourselves to Italy, it is enough to remember the degree of violence with
which the moral question erupted on the political scene at the end of the
nineteenth century, primarily as a result of the Radical Party deputy Felice
Cavallotti's public accusations against two prime ministers, Giovanni
Giolitti and Francesco Crispi. Indeed, Cavallotti was credited with having
coined the expression "moral question." The issue was used to bring the liberal Italy of parliamentary transformism back into the framework of a
dialectic between the government and the opposition, free from the pressures of the economic interests of bankers and industrialists—not to mention a corrupt press and a bureaucracy polluted by state power. Yet in those
days Benedetto Croce still deemed the Giolitti and Crispi governments substantially sound. To be sure, scandals could still erupt, but because one
could count on an appropriate reaction in the consciences of honest people,
the proper remedies would be implemented.

In his *Storia d'Italia*, in fact, Croce does not show any leniency toward
the kind of antipolitical skepticism that viewed the Risorgimento "patriots"
as having worked for the construction of a united Italy solely out of self-
interest. Those individuals, as a common lampoon put it, "constructed Italy
only to devour it." In truth, Croce replied, "in the tales that had been told,
the evil had been exaggerated and the good omitted; . . . the deputies were
not so dependent upon the individual interests of their constituents, and . . .
the private morality of the members of the Italian Government, whether of
the Left or the Right, was with certain rare exceptions, irreproachable; they
all adhered to the simplest mode of living, and never left a large fortune to
their heirs."[4]

Ninety years later, however, according to Berlinguer, the problem had not
just become more serious and even endemic but *the most important* problem

in Italian politics, threatening, first and foremost, the natural instruments of democracy, namely, the parties. The parties, Berlinguer observes, are reduced to "vehicles of power and nepotism, with only a dim or mystified awareness of the life and problems of the populace, few or vague ideas, ideals or programs, and no feeling or civil passion—none. They manage the most diverse, the most contradictory, sometimes even obscure interests, ignoring altogether the growing human needs and demands or misinterpreting them without any consideration for the common good."[5]

Berlinguer bitterly sees the twilight of a long, even difficult season of struggle between the Communists, Christian Democrats, and Socialists, who, despite their profound ideological and political differences, had once been united in their efforts to understand and interpret the real condition of the country. Parties, trade unions, conflicting movements, moved by a "sacrosanct" anger and a shared zeal, had been unified in opposition to Fascism by liberal Democrats, Marxists, and Catholics. Even "De Gasperi showed respect to Togliatti and Nenni, and he in turn was respected by them, notwithstanding the harsh polemics." Today the parties no longer organize the populace, nor do they strive to educate society according to their ideals and strategic plans. They have turned into confederations of factions, cliques, each with its own boss. "The geopolitical map of the parties," Berlinguer affirms, "is made up of names and places. For the Christian Democrats: Bisaglia in the Veneto, Gava in Campania, Lattanzio in Puglia, Andreotti in Lazio, De Mita in Avellino, Gaspari in Abruzzo, Forlani in Marche, and so on." At the time some of the Christian Democrat representatives he mentions were already under investigation or had been indicted; in the end none of the others would emerge unscathed. Indeed, some of them would later receive severe sentences. Implicit in Berlinguer's reasoning is that Croce's interpretation has lost all meaning in postwar Italy. He states:

> The moral question is not resolved by identifying thieves, blackmailers and extortionists in high places, indicting them, and throwing them in jail. The moral question in contemporary Italy, according to us Communists, is linked to the seizure of the State by the ruling parties and their factions, to their feuds, to their conception of politics and methods of government, which must simply be abandoned and superseded. That's why I say that the moral question stands at the center of the Italian problem. That's why the other parties cannot pretend to be

serious forces of renewal unless they attack the moral question head-on and root out its political causes.[6]

This is not some incidental, intemperate attack by the leader of the largest opposition party. A comparison may help us to appreciate Berlinguer's sincerity when he moved the moral question to the center of the political debate and identified it as the decisive factor for the fate of the Italian democratic system. *Rilancio della DC?* (Renewal of the Christian Democratic Party?) is the title of the last work that Togliatti would devote expressly to the Christian Democratic party. (He wrote it in February 1964 and died in August of that year.) It is by no means a soft piece. At certain points his political criticisms of the first *centrosinistra* (center-left) government touch on some of the least edifying aspects of widespread corruption. The Christian Democratic leaders, writes Togliatti, "have been able to hold their grip on power through various strategies, political alliances, foreign support, and other means. We know it, and it is confirmed by the fact that every time we discover, in the economic or administrative sphere, a focal point of corruption, always and without exception—whether it be public agencies, bananas, or the Mafia—there is a thread or many threads leading in their direction." The accusation is firm, but Togliatti hastens to add that it is advisable "to set aside these most irritating aspects of the situation." Accordingly, he concludes: "The Christian Democratic leaders will forgive us if there is any harshness in our judgments."[7] In other words, even in a period of rampant capitalism and financial speculation, of scandals over Mexican tobacco and bananas from Somalia, of representatives of public agencies at national and regional levels working in collusion with Mafia clans to make money out of construction projects in the big cities, Togliatti still perceives a space for genuine political confrontation. In fact, in the twenty years since the struggle for liberation, some significant changes had been made, though they were not important enough to thoroughly alter the general picture. Thus, for example, even while the United States and the Soviet Union were financing the parties in a competition for hegemony over the country, certain shared rules and values were still adhered to, in particular those enshrined in the constitution of the republic.

After the seven-month-long Parri government (1945)—during which a new political stratum, born out of the Resistance, showed itself ethically rigorous and transparent—money took center stage in political rivalry.

One recalls the unforgettable picture of De Gasperi on his return from Washington in 1947: he stood on the stairway of the airplane waving the check he had received from the American government to the crowd and the photographers. Yet, compared to the future cohorts of politicians with their pockets full of checks and cash received from oilmen, shady businessmen, and publishing tycoons, De Gasperi's gesture has the appearance, perhaps, of disarming candor.

In the newly born republic, in fact, the two largest political parties — the Communists and the Christian Democrats — appeared to be working hard to revitalize their respective political cultures in preparation for free electoral contests, which had been forbidden by the dictatorship. American financial support, to some extent, went hand in hand with Rumolo Murri's old cooperative and mutual-help movement, Giuseppe Toniolo's simultaneously anti-Socialist and anticapitalist doctrine, and the anti-Fascism of Luigi Sturzo, whose vigilant eye was trained on the decline of public morality. On the other front, Russian rubles supported the organizational needs and propaganda efforts of the workers' movement; they also helped to subsidize the publication of literary and historical journals and the dissemination of Antonio Labriola's and Antonio Gramsci's writings within the framework of a cultural renewal of the nation. To be sure, that was a period of heated battles. The original Christian Democratic movement was not free from "restorationist" temptations. Catholic organizations such as the Comitati Civici (Civic Committees) adopted intimidating and discriminatory methods typical of the extreme Right. The interventions of the Vatican were often barriers on the road to pacification and dialogue. (One need only recall the decree of excommunication promulgated by the Holy Office in 1949 against the Communists and their supporters.) On the other hand, there were also Communist fringe movements that considered armed revolution the only possible means of emancipation for the exploited classes and regarded parliamentary democracy as a more or less transitional or provisional form of government. Despite everything, Togliatti's efforts to create a democratic path to socialism were no less concrete and stemmed from no lesser conviction than De Gasperi's attempts to keep the Christian Democrats from becoming a confessional party guided by a reactionary ecclesiastical hierarchy, a repository of Catholic traditionalism rather than a modern democratic party of the masses, present and vital within the whole social body.

For De Gasperi, the problem of political unity among Catholics was extremely worrisome—a problem that went back to the very formation of the party. Among other things, he was aware that even the logic of alignment produced by the Fascist/anti-Fascist dualism (which had been rendered extremely complex by the Church's connivance with the regime) would soon be superseded by other pressing issues of an economic and political nature. These political and social issues would diminish the significance of the division between Catholics and non-Catholics and heighten the importance of the differences between progressives and conservatives. Confronted with such alternatives as Communism or laissez-faire in economics and Monarchy or Republic in politics, De Gasperi wanted the Catholics to enjoy a certain autonomy and freedom of choice while adhering to certain fundamental principles. The formation of a united Catholic bloc that simultaneously embraced ex-Fascists and militant anti-Fascists, democrats and reactionaries would certainly have resulted in a conservative-leaning bloc, not much different from such movements as Catholic Action.

Confirmation of De Gasperi's views on these issues can be found in his recently published correspondence with Sturzo. For example, in a letter dated November 12, 1944, addressed to Sturzo during his New York exile, De Gasperi examined the potential danger of both a reactionary and a "Social-Communist" dictatorship in Italy. According to De Gasperi, the pursuit of a clear democratic politics, opposed to extremist unrest, would have been sufficient to forestall the right-wing temptation to restore an authoritarian regime. On the other end of the spectrum, the possibility of a Communist putsch demanded a different approach. Although the Communists had on their side "the myth and the strength of Russia," "imposing means," well-trained cadres, and "capable leaders," De Gasperi was inclined to believe that the Communists would try "to obtain a de facto dictatorship by democratic means," that is, by assuming important positions from which to exert power over government. In spite of this danger, however, the only path that seemed viable to De Gasperi was to reinforce the construction of the democratic system founded on broad popular consensus. De Gasperi concluded: "A large part of the population is anti-Communist, but we cannot assemble our forces on the basis of anti-Communism, lest we run the risk of being confused with the reactionary currents."[8]

It is true that following the extraordinary results of the elections of April 18, 1946 the Christian Democrats greatly modified the physiognomy of their open, popular party by concentrating within it the economic interests of the upper middle class, which favored a laissez-faire mode of reconstruction. At the same time, the image of the Communist Party, weighed down by its ties to Moscow and bound to its goal of superseding capitalism, provoked constant dilemmas and objections about the legitimacy of its status in the Western democratic system. It is also true that the unilateral administration of power, determined by the *conventio ad excludendum* (exclusionary pact) against the Communists, would facilitate the spread of the nodes of corruption within the majority party. Still, politics remained vital in Italy throughout the Cold War and, without exception, the parties proved themselves indispensable instruments. Togliatti's affirmation that "the parties constitute democracy in its organizational process" was never contested. In Italy, the level of public participation in politics remained among the highest in the world, even after the antiparty protests of the 1968 youth movement and the *autunno caldo* (hot autumn) period during which the trade union movement clashed with the Communist Party.

The first phase in the decline of the parties began immediately after the season of widespread terrorism that culminated in the Moro affair. Spontaneous support from ordinary citizens animated by shared idealism fell to zero. Public consensus was gained through political patronage or nepotism, which necessarily required a powerful financial base. The thick web of nepotism became inextricable and suffocated the state. In six months, between October 1980 and May 1981, the situation became critical. To begin with, Raffaele Giudice, former chief of the Guardia di Finanza (the customs and excise police), was arrested and accused of participating in a colossal $1.5 billion oil scam. Giudice was linked to Salvo Lima, an Andreotti agent in Sicily, who would be killed in spring 1992 in an ambush that had all the trappings of a Mafia-style settling of accounts. The journalist Mino Pecorelli, who at the end of the 1970s had exposed the intricacies of the oil scam, was assassinated under mysterious circumstances. In the background there were important Christian Democrats: Claudio Vitalone, deputy public prosecutor; Franco Evangelisti, undersecretary in the prime minister's office; minister Antonio Bisaglia; Giulio Andreotti himself (the Pecorelli affair would resurface in his trial for collusion with the Mafia). Judicial offices, the customs and excise agency, the secret service, the highest political strata: it was no longer just individuals who were under accusation but the entire Christian Democratic power structure.

In November an earthquake struck Irpinia, Naples, and the province of Salerno, leaving thousands of victims and incalculable damage. There was no relief; the state was absent. In their official statements and in the press, the Communists emphatically attributed the debacle to the fact that the state had been utterly debilitated by a web of corruption and intrigue. The country, they insisted, lacked an authoritative and capable political leadership, and no such leadership could be envisaged unless drastic measures were taken to guarantee honesty, fairness, and propriety in government. They called for nothing less than the renewal and revitalization of the Italian state and society. This time, an indignant president of the republic, Sandro Pertini, added his voice to that of the opposition upbraiding the inefficiency and corruption of the political class.

Berlinguer abandoned the line of "democratic solidarity" and proposed a new "democratic alternative" government. The moral question acquired a strategic role, but it did not have any effect, not even a deterrent one. On May 20, 1981, Roberto Calvi, president of the Ambrosiano Bank, was arrested in Milan. He was a major illegal fund-raiser for the Christian Democrats and the Socialists. (After various judicial proceedings, confessions, and blackmails, he would be found hung under a Thames bridge in July 1992.) That same day, the prime minister, Forlani, who had resisted until the very last moment, was compelled to make public the list of persons affiliated with Licio Gelli's "partito occulto" (covert party) of Masonic lodge P2. The Masons had been found out by the magistrates investigating the bankruptcy of Michele Sindona. All kinds of people were on the list: bankers and generals, journalists and entrepreneurs (among them, the future prime minister, Silvio Berlusconi, and the director of a national radio news program, Gustavo Selva, now parliamentary leader of Alleanza Nazionale), deputies and senators of every party except the Radicals and the PDUP (Democratic Party for Proletarian Unity). And no Communists. The Christian Democrats on the list included ministers Sarti and Foschi; former ministers Starnmati and Pedini; Forlani's cabinet chief, Semprini; Fanfani's spokesman, Cresci; Bisaglia's secretary, Del Gamba; deputies and senators, among them, Arnaud, De Carolis (now head of the city council in Milan, a member of the Forza Italia party, and currently under investigation for bribery), Danesi, Fiori, Picchioni, and Napoli.

Asked about the causes of the moral disintegration that permeated Italy in the early 1980s, Enrico Berlinguer put at the top of the list "discrimination" against the Communists, who were never represented in the government. That is the reason why the political system was blocked and the ruling political class remained unchanged and why there was an absence of alternative methods and programs. At the same time, there could be no doubt about the democratic evolution of the Communist Party, unless one were to ignore the ideas of "historic compromise" or "national solidarity" or Berlinguer's celebrated speech of 1977 in Moscow, "Democrazia come valore universale" (Democracy as a Universal Value)[9]—an evolution that led to the declaration of December 1981 that the ideas of the October Revolution had become a spent force and could not enable the renewal of eastern European society. This Communist Party in evolution (albeit a belated and slow evolution) had to deal with a Christian Democratic party that, under the leadership of Flaminio Piccoli, excluded any cooperation with the Communists and instead forged a governmental alliance with Bettino Craxi's Socialist Party. Craxi's had been a party of old, noble traditions; nonetheless, it was then in decline, and to remedy its own crisis, it appropriated modernization as a value in itself and pursued it with an insolent thirst for power and an arrogant disregard for the law. The alliance forged between the Christian Democrats and the Socialist party—known as the CAF, an acronym formed from the initials of Craxi, Andreotti, and Forlani—would prove a fatal embrace for both.

The rest is history or, rather, a judicial chronicle. Certainly, it is not *political* history in the strict sense. As Berlinguer had foreseen, politics has a boundary, something that grounds it, precedes it, and finally judges it. In the Italian situation, that boundary assumed the form of the "moral question." One cannot honestly claim that the collapse of the Christian Democratic party was simply the fulfillment or the consequence of a prophecy— Enrico Berlinguer's "prophecy." There were other important factors, the most important of which was the collapse of the Soviet system. The collapse of the Soviet Union deprived the Christian Democrats of the bogeyman they had always invoked for the purpose of presenting themselves to the electorate as the only bulwark capable of standing up to the Communist threat.

Some contemporary critics marvel at the excessive "moralism" that they believed characterized Berlinguer's party leadership in the 1980s. These criticisms have even been elaborated by his former party comrades who are now members of the new post–Communist party currently governing Italy. It is as if the insistence on the distinctiveness of the Communist Party in relation to the moral question could be reduced to an outburst of intellectual pride by its leader, a man from another era who was more sensitive to Gramsci's teachings on the moral reformation of politics than to the demands of modernity, which are as pragmatic as they are equivocal. Indeed, one might even imagine that if Berlinguer had not been so intransigent, the *conventio ad excludendum* against the Communists would have been dropped and the Communists would have been accepted earlier into the government, alongside the former Christian Democratic party in its twilight, or the Socialist Party, which was about to be demolished by a group of magistrates. Considering how events transpired, we cannot exclude the possibility that had such a coalition occurred some Communists would have ended up in jail together with former Christian Democrats and Socialists.

Some concluding considerations are needed concerning a problem that might render this discourse opaque. How can we explain to those political elements who are interested in the defense of democracy Berlinguer's "historic compromise" proposal, which, in effect, amounted to an offer of alliance with the Christian Democrats, a party that was itself "compromised" and, therefore, "compromising" as a political partner? Is it possible that, in 1970, the hope for a tactical power-sharing agreement could have induced the Communists to ignore the burden of the moral question — maybe only because it had not yet reached the unbearable level that it would attain in the following decade? Or was it because the uncompromising affirmation of the moral question in the 1980s arose as a vendetta by the Partito Communista Italiano (PCI) against the adversary that was responsible for the failure of its own political agenda? Was the "historic compromise" meant to enable the PCI to participate in the banquet of general corruption? Many hypotheses have been put forth. Some have been inspired by serious attempts at historiographical critique; others, by tendentious theses based on the view that the Communists' absence from postwar scandals was only the natural consequence of their exclusion from government (which is subjected to economic blackmail, to the pressure and the charm of bribes, etc.) rather than the fruit of their tradition of ethical rigor.

To clarify the issue, it would be useful to read again the first formulation of the "compromesso storico" and to recall the historical and political context in which it originated. Berlinguer wrote:

> We are not talking of "a left-wing alternative" but rather of a "democratic alternative" — thus of the political prospect of a collaboration and an

agreement between the popular forces of Socialist and Communist tendencies and the popular forces of Catholic tendency and also with formations of different democratic inclination. . . . The magnitude of the country's problems, the always imminent menace of reactionary adventures, and the necessity for the nation to clear a secure path of development, of social renewal, and democratic progress make it increasingly urgent and timely that we arrive at what we could define as a new, grand "historic compromise" among the forces who embrace and represent the majority of the Italian people.[10]

Berlinguer's reflections were inspired, as is well known, by the situation in Chile that resulted in the fall of the Allende government and the military coup d'état of September 1973. At first sight, the analogies between the Italian and Chilean cases did not seem evident. Nevertheless, there was no reason to doubt that if the Italian Communist Party were to acquire the reins of government—and here one should recall that in the 1975 local elections the PCI became the leading party in all the major cities and that it registered substantial gains in the national elections of 1976—it would have enjoyed only a minuscule parliamentary majority and would have had to face the pressures of an international offensive (which already weighed heavily on Italian democracy) as well as a violent subversive reaction from within. Signs of reactionary subversion had already manifested themselves. The strategy of "historic compromise"—which was also linked to a deepening of the "Catholic question" on which both Gramsci and Togliatti had reflected in the past—was put forward, therefore, in a context that made its intent unmistakably *defensive*. It was not an expansive thrust meant to garner national consensus. This antinomy is, probably, the necessary starting point for an examination of the complex reasons behind the failure of the historic compromise.

A dilemma that is destined to remain forever unresolved (like all the other missed rendezvous of history) concerns, more than anything else, the Christian Democratic party and its subsequent fate: what if the strategy of collaboration and democratic alliance with the other massive political popular force had been successfully implemented and, thus, changed the political, social, and institutional scenarios at their very roots in the Italy of the last quarter of the millennium?

## NOTES

1. Enrico Berlinguer, "Le 'profezie' di Berlinguer," *La Rinascita della Sinistra*, February 12, 1999.

2. Patrick McCarthy, *The Crisis of the Italian State: From the Origins of the Cold War to the Fall of Berlusconi* (New York: St. Martin's Press, 1995).

3. John T. Noonan Jr., *Bribes* (New York: Macmillan, 1984).

4. Benedetto Croce, *A History of Italy: 1871–1915*, trans. Cecilia M. Ady (New York: Russell & Russell, 1963), 101–2.

5. Enrico Berlinguer, interviewed by Eugenio Scalfaro, *La Repubblica*, July 28, 1981.

6. Ibid.

7. Palmiro Togliatti, *Opere*, vol. 6 (Rome: Editori Riuniti, 1984), 759–61.

8. Luigi Sturzo and Alcide De Gasperi, *Carteggio: 1920–1953* (Brescia: Morcelliana, 1999), 135.

9. Enrico Berlinguer, *Attualità e futuro* (Rome: Edizione L'Unità, 1989), 28–30.

10. Enrico Berlinguer, "Riflessioni sull'Italia dopo i fatti del Cile," *Rinascita*, September 28, 1973.

# 10 Toward a "Core Europe" in a Christian Western Bloc

Transnational Cooperation in European
Christian Democracy, 1925 – 1965

MICHAEL GEHLER AND
WOLFRAM KAISER

Transnationalism is a striking phenomenon in the European Union at the turn of the twenty-first century. The growing state structures in Europe are encouraging the formation of organized cooperation across borders, not only between the governments of the member states, but also among economic, environmental, and other interest groups, regions, and cities. Although a European political public is emerging only slowly, not least because of remaining language barriers, political parties, too, have forged closer links. Since 1976 the Christian Democrats have been united in the European People's Party, which has been extended to several conservative parties from new member states without a specifically Christian Democratic, Catholic-inspired party tradition.

Transnational cooperation among European Catholic and Christian Democratic parties evolved significantly during the twentieth century. This chapter traces its modest origins in the interwar period and in exile in Britain and the United States. It then goes on to analyze transnationalism in western European Christian Democracy during the first twenty years after 1945 in the Nouvelles Equipes Internationales (NEI), which were transformed into the European Union of Christian Democrats (EUCD) in 1965, and the Geneva Circle. Until the mid-1960s the Christian Democratic parties were particularly strong electorally and influenced European reconstruction. It seems crucial, therefore, to assess and illustrate how their more extensive transnational cooperation contributed to the formation of key policy preferences and to the evolution of European "projects," especially with regard to the reintegration of Germany into what the Christian Democrats saw as the "Christian West," and—closely related— European integration.

## TRANSNATIONALISM IN INTERWAR EUROPE AND IN EXILE

Before World War I contacts among Catholics in Europe had been organized almost exclusively by the Church. Against the background of the first European civil war, however, Catholic politicians began to establish contacts at the party level too, especially after the foundation of the Partito Popolare Italiano (PPI) in 1919 and of the French Parti Démocrate Populaire (PDP) in 1924.[1] On the initiative of Luigi Sturzo, founder of the PPI who was in exile in Britain from 1924 onward, and of PDP politicians, the first meeting took place in Paris on December 12–13, 1925.[2] The thirty-four participants were from five countries and included four representatives of the German Zentrum (Center) Party. To coordinate their contacts, they set up in Paris the Secrétariat International des Partis Démocratiques d'Inspiration Chrétienne (SIPDIC), which was run by the PDP and existed until 1939. It was only a very loose organization. The meetings of the SIPDIC executive committee—normally twice a year—were secret, and its bulletin, published three times annually between 1928 and 1931, was confidential. Only the annual congresses, which had from thirteen to forty-five delegates, were public, but after 1933, when Adolf Hitler seized power in Germany and the Center Party dissolved itself on May 5, the congresses were merely extended meetings of the executive committee.[3]

Sturzo had initially envisaged an organization of Catholic parties to forge and represent in public a common Catholic democratic front in Europe against both Bolshevism and Fascism.[4] Instead, transnational cooperation of Catholic politicians remained a marginal phenomenon. One crucial reason for the SIPDIC's weakness was the continued strength of nationalism. Nationalist claims—for a revision of the peace treaties—dominated European politics and left little room for transnationalism even for Catholic parties. In particular, Franco-German contacts were difficult to establish.[5] The participating politicians, most of whom were not leading national figures, were keen to avoid compromising their positions inside their parties and their party's position in domestic politics by too close contacts or by appearing to surrender fundamental "national interests." Their minimal consensus was procedural—to solve continuing conflicts by peaceful means. The dominance of nationalist considerations is illustrated well by the confrontation over the continued participation of the Austrian Christian Social Party in SIPDIC activities after the establishment of the authoritarian *Ständestaat* in 1933–34. Sturzo advocated the exclusion of the supporters of the Dollfuss-Schuschnigg regime on the grounds that it was undemocratic. In contrast, PDP politicians such as Ernest Pezet regarded an independent Austria allied with a friendly Italy as a necessary bulwark against Germany, irrespective of its political system, and so they insisted on their participation.[6]

The second main reason for the ineffectiveness of transnationalism in the interwar years lay in the fundamental disagreements over policy. By far the most divisive issue—not only within some parties but also between them—was their attitude to Italian Fascism and authoritarian regimes such as Austria and Portugal. When Sturzo raised the issue in 1925, the French were not prepared, on foreign policy grounds, to pass a resolution against Fascism and some German representatives because of the Vatican's enthusiastic support for Mussolini.[7] In 1926 the SIPDIC passed a resolution for democracy and against organized state violence. Just as in the case of their strong emphasis on economic corporatism at the 1930 congress[8] and their peace resolution of January 1931,[9] however, even a limited compromise was possible only because of the gross overrepresentation of progressive Catholic democrats. They were pro-democratic, for social reform, and often had links with the peace movement. Even the minimum consensus therefore did not encompass the frequently dominant conservative and nationalist wings of the Catholic parties, which had philo-Fascist views and sympathies for authoritarian government.

After the start of World War II and the occupation of the Netherlands, Belgium, Luxembourg, and France in 1940, transnational contacts could exist only in exile, primarily in Britain and the United States.[10] In the 1930s Catholic refugees like Sturzo were disturbed by the extent of philo-Fascism among the Catholic communities in both countries, which were also generally the most ardent supporters of the policies of appeasement and isolationism.[11] However, small groups of highly articulate liberal Catholics tried to provide an alternative intellectual and political focus and to create a friendlier environment for Catholic refugees. In November 1936 a group of mostly middle-class Labour and Liberal supporters, many of them converts, founded the People and Freedom Group in London. They organized speeches, many of them by Catholic refugees, and passed political resolutions that where printed in the newsletter *People & Freedom* and elsewhere. The British example inspired American Catholics to found similar groups, also named People and Freedom: in New York, where George N. Shuster acted as chairman, and in Boston, Philadelphia, Notre Dame, and Los Angeles. We have little information on the American groups, but it seems clear that, compared to the British group, they were even more marginal within their Catholic community.[12]

The People and Freedom Group facilitated transnational contacts among Catholic politicians in exile. But Sturzo, Antonio de Onaindia, a Basque emigrant, and several other refugees felt this was not sufficient and founded the International Christian Democratic Union (ICDU) in early 1941 as a platform for common thinking on postwar Europe.[13] The ICDU had the backing of leading Catholic politicians such as the Czechoslovak prime minister Jan Šrámek and General Józef Haller, chairman of the Supreme Council of the Polish Labour Party and minister of education, who, together with Sturzo, formed the ICDU's Committee of Honour. The ICDU's chairman was the Dutch professor J. A. Veraart.[14] He organized regular meetings with guest speakers who lectured on the various national party traditions and on themes of common interest.[15] The ICDU was effectively concerned with fostering contacts and debate among individual politicians in exile, not with formal party cooperation. The majority of the ICDU members, including Veraart, did not play leading roles in their own parties, and this is especially true of the western Europeans. August de Schryver, who became the first leader of the postwar Belgian Parti Social Chrétien (PSC) and was NEI president during the 1950s, sometimes participated. Maurice Schumann, who was later president (1944–49) of the Mouvement Républicain Populaire (MRP) and foreign minister (1969–73), was the official French representative during 1942–43, but he only took part once.[16] It is not surprising, therefore, that Onaindia concluded at the annual meeting in 1944 that the organization "[has] served a valuable purpose in enabling Christian Democrats of various nationalities to get to know one another . . . , but it must be admitted that it [has] not attained the influence or development that might have been hoped."[17]

Their transnational contacts probably had a certain influence on the political thinking of individual ICDU members. However, it had little if any effect on postwar planning in exile for national and European reconstruction. Moreover, there is no direct continuity, either institutionally or politically, from the rudimentary transnationalism in exile to Christian Democratic party cooperation in the NEI and the Geneva Circle after 1947. Roberto Papini claims that Sturzo founded the International Information Service in Geneva in November 1945,[18] but it seems to have existed in name only. It may well be the case that their ICDU experience made de Schryver, Schumann, and a few other Catholic refugees, who had a high political profile in western Europe after 1945, value transnational party cooperation more highly. However, these politicians were to play only a relatively marginal role in most national parties as well as in the NEI. This is especially true in the case of France, Germany, Italy, and Austria, where the new party leadership was clearly dominated by Christian Democrats—like Robert Schuman and Georges Bidault, Konrad Adenauer and Jakob Kaiser, Alcide De Gasperi and Leopold Figl—who had preferred the Resistance or internal emigration to exile.

Moreover, it is clear from analysis of the speeches and debates at the meetings of both the People and Freedom Group and the ICDU that there is no political continuity from the thinking of Catholic politicians in exile to postwar European reconstruction. The Catholic refugees were united in their much clearer rejection of *political* (i.e., state) corporatism compared to the interwar period, but so were those Catholic politicians who had stayed on the Continent during the war. They gave absolute preference to the creation of a new world organization of democratic states. They quickly became disillusioned with Allied policy long before the creation of the United Nations in 1945 but failed to advance alternative concepts. Finally, the experience of exile led the Catholic refugees to develop a strongly Atlanticist vision of postwar Europe that excluded the possibility of any continental European solution to the German question. With the notable exception of the German Catholics in exile, who almost universally regarded the "European vocation," as Carl Spiecker called it,[19] as their salvation from National Socialism, the debates in exile clearly did not anticipate the later fundamental solution of the German question through integration. On the whole, therefore, transnational cooperation in exile marked no significant advance on the interwar period and had only a marginal effect on the development of both the new Christian Democratic parties and their transnational cooperation and of western Europe after the war.[20]

## TRANSNATIONALISM AFTER 1945

### Organization and Reform

In 1945 it seemed the natural conclusion from the experience of National Socialism and World War II to treat Europe as a common political space. There was general consensus among European Christian Democrats that transnational cooperation and the coordination of their policies would be crucial for European reconstruction. Four main incentives for better organized and more intensive transnational cooperation can be identified. First, as Joseph Escher, president of the Swiss Conservative People's Party, emphasized at the first multilateral meeting of Christian politicians in Lucerne in early 1947, it was necessary to reactivate the personal and institutional links interrupted by the war.[21] Second, the evolution of the Cold War strengthened the common perception of the danger of Communism and of the need to counteract international Communist activity and propaganda at a European rather than national level. After all, as the Italian DC politician Paolo Emilio Taviani put it in June 1950, the Christian Democrats would all fight "on the same side of the barricade" in the event of a European civil war.[22] Third, the Socialist and Liberal parties in Europe also wanted to reorganize their transnational cooperation, and both political tendencies, because of their international ideologies, seemed better prepared for the expected Europeanization of national politics. Fourth, Christian Democrats wanted a unified Europe but a Europe that was Christian and *abendländisch*. Transnational cooperation also seemed crucial for defining the intellectual foundation and programmatic content of the new Europe they wished to create.

Transnationalism in European Christian Democracy after 1945 took two forms: formal, institutionalized collaboration, which took place in the NEI and then in the EUCD; and informal, secret talks between Christian Democrats from 1947 to 1955.[23] These secret meetings were attended by Bidault, Adenauer, and other leading European politicians during 1948–49. Thereafter they continued to provide a focal point of free political debate, especially concerning the Franco-German relationship and western European integration.

The NEI was named after the Nouvelles Equipes Françaises founded by Francisque Gay and Bidault in 1938 as a new democratic force of the political center in France.[24] However, the NEI was not constituted of parties but of national *équipes*. These were de facto identical to the national parties, with the notable exception of those in France and Belgium, where they were formed by individual politicians of the MRP and the PSC-CVP. The main decision-making body was the executive committee, headed by the president: the French MRP politician Robert Bichet (1947–49) and the Belgian PSC-CVP politicians de Schryver (1949–59) and Théo Lefèvre (1960–65). The secretary-general directed the small secretariat in Paris. The other members of the executive committee were the deputy presidents who came from four and then, after 1957, all six other western European national *équipes*. The NEI organized annual congresses on specific themes and passed and published resolutions on current political issues. The secretaries-general of the national parties met from 1954 onward to coordinate their electoral strategies, their political propaganda, and, increasingly, the allocation of political posts in European institutions.

The NEI's relatively weak institutional structure and its very general, French name are explained by the main fault line of postwar western European Christian Democracy between the MRP and the PSC-CVP on one side and most other parties on the other. The MRP in particular did not want to compromise its new nonconfessional image in French politics. As a result, the MRP representative, Robert Wirth, had argued at the first meeting in Lucerne that the new organization should under no circumstances look like a "black international." The papal encyclicals, Wirth insisted, "can inspire a doctrine, but one should not forget that they do not apply to politics."[25] As Barbara Barclay Carter, the British representative in Lucerne, concluded after this first international meeting, the MRP politicians feared the use of the term "Christian Democrat," which "would lay them open to a charge of clericalism and took no account of the number of nonbelievers and even, in North Africa, of Moslems among their adherents."[26] The PSC-CVP, too, did not want to be associated too closely with the Church. On the contrary, transnational cooperation in Europe, Jules Soyeur, the first NEI secretary-general, argued in a note on its creation, should assist Christian Democratic "emancipation from certain outdated political and social concepts of the Church"[27]—thus the ideologically meaningless name of the new organization that some other representatives, especially those from Italy and Austria, had wanted to turn straight away into a union of parties with a common program.

The issue of party membership in the PSC and the MRP was only resolved when they joined the NEI in 1959 and 1964 respectively. However, this was not the only difficulty the Christian Democrats encountered in their attempt to extend their collaboration after 1945. The relationship between the western European parties and the exile groups from eastern Europe was also not easy, especially when the division of Europe seemed increasingly more permanent and the NEI began to concentrate more exclusively on western European integration. Another difficult relationship was that between the Austrian and Swiss parties, which were initially active in the NEI, and the parties of the European Economic Community (EEC), which intensified their cooperation in the Christian Democratic parliamentary caucus in the common assembly of the European Coal and Steel Community (ECSC) after 1952 and especially in the European parliament of the EEC after 1958. Finally, the NEI parties also held conflicting views on the possible membership of the British and Scandinavian Conservative parties that became acute in 1961 when the issue of EEC enlargement came up for the first time. While the German Christian Democrats, who had a strong Conservative wing, were keen on such a realignment, the Italians and Belgians considered them not progressive enough in terms of their economic and social policies and vetoed their membership throughout the 1960s and beyond.

These fault lines prevented a greater deepening of the institutionalized, formal party contacts after 1945. The reform of 1965 led to a change of name and the election of an Italian EUCD president, Mariano Rumor, and of the Belgian Leo Tindemans as the new secretary-general, but only the first direct election of the European parliament in June 1979 provided sufficient incentive for the formation of the European People's Party and the formulation of a common framework for the member parties. It was precisely the difficulties the Christian Democratic parties experienced after the war, despite their general consensus on enlarging their cooperation, in agreeing on the degree of institutionalization and formal programmatic commitment that their *informal* contacts in the Geneva Circle temporarily became very important—especially before the creation of the Federal Republic of Germany and the Council of Europe in 1949.

The idea of periodic secret meetings of leading Christian Democratic politicians was the result of a German-French initiative of Johann-Jakob Kindt-Kiefer and Victor Koutzine.[28] Kindt-Kiefer was "a convinced European"[29] and a good friend of Adenauer in the late 1940s.[30] As a result of his marriage with Ilse Kiefer, daughter of a Swiss industrialist, he had the financial means to help organize the German Catholic exiles. He was a member of the board of directors of the Union of Christian Democratic Germans, a cofounder of the interparty association Democratic Germany in Switzerland, and a member of the board of directors of Christliche Nothilfe (Christian Emergency Aid). He acted as chairman of the Geneva Circle until 1951.[31] Koutzine was the interpreter of the Circle and directed its secretariat, established in 1950. He studied in Paris, qualified as an attorney in 1932, and received a degree in literature in 1937.[32] He was drafted into the French army in 1939 and was temporarily interned as a prisoner of war in East Prussia and Silesia. From late 1942 Koutzine was a political refugee in Switzerland. Beginning in October 1945 he worked from Geneva as a foreign correspondent for newspapers and also for the French foreign ministry. According to an Austrian participant in the Geneva Circle, Koutzine enjoyed the "full trust" of western European Christian Democrats.[33]

The meetings took place from November 1947 to 1955. Switzerland, a neutral state, was the preferred site for the confidential meetings. Moreover, the Allied occupation forces in Germany did not initially allow the authorized political parties to engage in activities outside Germany, and Switzerland appeared the ideal place to evade the control of the military governors. Geneva was conveniently located and, as the site of the League of Nations, also had international flair. In contrast to the NEI, the exiles from east central Europe were deliberately excluded from the Geneva meetings, which were to focus exclusively on concrete Franco-German and western

European issues. In October 1948 it was unanimously decided that the function of the meetings was "to form a contact committee of prominent European party representatives which was not public and which would make an effort to discuss concrete political questions and to implement measures which have been agreed upon."[34] The eight western European NEI parties sent from two to four representatives to the meetings. Overall, the number of participants varied from twelve to eighteen.

It is possible to identify several key motives for why the German and French Christian Democrats in particular sought to engage in secret talks. The Germans, especially Adenauer, were keen to put the bilateral relationship on a completely new basis after three wars in three generations. Moreover, for them the meetings were one step on the road toward the reintegration of Germany into the community of democratic European nations on an equal basis. They could also help to ensure effective collaboration on the reconstruction of West Germany and western Europe.[35] At the same time, the French desire to avoid close official contacts with the Germans played a role when French public opinion was still largely hostile to reconciliation.[36] The Geneva meetings provided an opportunity for MRP politicians to strengthen the Western orientation of the German Christian Democrats. Closer cooperation with (the western part of) the former archenemy was also increasingly seen as a *conditio sine qua non* for successful defense against the Soviet threat. The creation of the Geneva Circle reflected the onset of the Cold War, which made the inclusion of West Germans imperative.[37]

After 1949 the European Christian Democrats frequently discussed the future of the Geneva Circle and its relationship with the NEI. Their different priorities largely reflected the fault lines in the reform debate in the NEI. As a general rule, the Germans, Italians, and Austrians favored stronger institutionalization of the Circle and its integration, in some form or another, into the NEI. On the other hand, Bidault feared that the creation of a permanent office would spoil the secret character of the meetings that he valued most. After a lengthy debate in June 1949, the French agreed that "the Geneva Circle should be used as a kind of consultative committee within the NEI,"[38] but no formal changes were made. Thereafter, French opposition continued. When the Germans pushed for stronger party cooperation at a meeting in November 1952, for example, MRP politicians opposed "an altogether too strong link" that would lay them open in French politics to the accusation of "being a 'Vaticaninform' inspired only from there [Rome]."[39]

After summer 1949 Adenauer and Bidault no longer attended the meetings. On Adenauer's election as German chancellor, Koutzine and Kindt-Kiefer frequently came to Bonn, and Koutzine delivered confidential messages from Adenauer in Paris.[40] The Geneva meetings now took place at a lower level, but the regular briefing of Adenauer, Bidault, and others was guaranteed. In the German case, for example, Herbert Blankenhorn, Adenauer's foreign affairs adviser, and Otto Lenz, state secretary in the federal chancellory during 1951–53, took part and strictly advocated Adenauer's line.[41] The Circle now served mainly to demonstrate and reinforce the loyalty between the German and French representatives and parties. In spite of Koutzine's efforts to sustain it, however, the decline of the MRP in France and the differences in the MRP between Bidault and Schuman, who had never taken part in the Geneva Circle, contributed to its diminishing political relevance. Moreover, the Benelux parties began to have doubts about the value of the meetings, which were turning into a bilateral, Franco-German forum and were no longer directly relevant to their interests.[42] One meeting took place in Baarn in the Netherlands in 1953, but the change of location could not arrest the declining significance of the Geneva Circle. It was disbanded in 1955.

## Christian Democracy and "Europe"

Despite its institutional limitations, transnational cooperation after 1945 contributed to the Europeanization of ideological preferences and to the evolution of specific policies that were pursued by the Christian Democrats, for example, the concept of a mixed economic order as a "third way" between laissez-faire capitalism and communism that allowed for a substantial degree of state intervention in the emerging European welfare state. However, transnational cooperation was probably most important with respect to the idea of a new, institutionalized Europe that would provide a solution to the German question through Western integration. More concretely, Christian Democratic contacts contributed significantly to early Franco-German reconciliation and to the creation of the Council of Europe in 1949 and the ECSC in 1951–52.

### Europe in Christian Democratic Discourse
One of the NEI's crucial functions was to serve as a forum for the ideological rationalization of Christian Democratic policies. In particular, its transna-

tional cooperation allowed the Christian Democrats to develop their own peculiar notion of "Europe," both internally and in public discourse at the NEI congresses. Christian Democrats' contacts facilitated a common understanding of the guiding principles of their postwar European policies and helped them, despite their continuing differences, to achieve a basic ideological consensus. This consensus encompassed the strongly anti-Communist foundation of their European ideology and policies. To a large extent it continued the Catholic antibolshevism of the interwar period under the new and ideologically favorable circumstances of the Cold War, but the Christian Democrats now opposed Communism with an unambiguously democratic, non-Socialist alternative to laissez-faire capitalism that required a European framework for economic and social reform. They also agreed on a typically Catholic interpretation of the roots of nationalism and the genesis of the two European "civil wars" of the twentieth century that essentially blamed liberalism but was no longer accompanied to the same extent by antimodern rhetoric. Finally, the NEI also provided a forum for the public affirmation of a common Christian Democratic approach to the reintegration of Germany into the *Abendland,* or civilized Christian West. The Christian Democratic discourses on the genesis of the European civil wars and on the German question were closely intertwined, of course, and they were crucial for postwar reconstruction.

The German question was already the theme of the second NEI congress in January 1948, which was the first international political congress in which Germans participated. As representatives of the Christlich-Demokratische Union (CDU) and of the Bavarian Christlich-Soziale Union (CSU), Adenauer, Kaiser, and Josef Müller were in Luxembourg only as observers, but Adenauer was asked to speak. This congress not only paved the way for the early participation of the German Christian Democrats in transnational party cooperation; it also created a political climate in which the rehabilitation of the West Germans and their integration in the community of democratic states became imaginable and realistic, even for the French MRP.

The introductory speech by the Swiss national councillor Karl Wick[43] and the reports by the Luxembourger Pierre Frieden on the "spiritual and cultural aspect" of the German question[44] and the Dutchman P. J. S. Serrarens, who headed the international Christian trade union movement, on the "political aspect"[45] indicate the extent to which the Christian Democrats were prepared to reject the idea of the collective guilt of all Germans for

National Socialism, the war, and the Holocaust and to instead differentiate between "good" and "bad" Germans. Their idea of two Germanys was based on a specifically Catholic interpretation of German history. According to this interpretation, Germany west of the ancient Limes and the river Elbe was first Roman, then Carolingian, and later democratically influenced. In any case, it was "non-Prussian." In contrast, Lutheran Germany east of the Elbe had long been alienated from (Catholic) Christian western Europe and had been responsible, as Serrarens put it, for destroying "the unity of Europe" in the Reformation. According to Serrarens, there was "a direct line from Frederick the Great to Bismarck and Hitler."[46] Thus West Germany, which also was the area occupied by the Allies, seemed suited for rehabilitation and capable of integration, whereas Lutheran East Germany was under the control of Communist atheists and, for the time being, lost to the *Abendland*.[47] Despite their strong sympathies for the Catholic part of central Europe, especially Poland, this interpretation clearly facilitated the acceptance of a temporary division not only of Germany but also of Europe. It thus helps to explain Christian Democratic support for the formation of a Western bloc under American leadership and their extreme caution with respect to Soviet détente initiatives in the 1950s.

Adenauer essentially shared this interpretation, allowing him quickly to emerge as the preferred partner in European politics among the West German Christian Democrats. Others appeared less reliable, especially the leader of the East German CDU, Kaiser, who wanted to give priority to German unification, although only under democratic auspices. In his improvised speech at the second NEI congress,[48] Adenauer, referring to the Christian resistance in Germany, rejected the idea of the collective guilt of all Germans. Following on Churchill's proposal in his speech in Zurich in 1946, he also made a far-reaching offer of close Franco-German collaboration. In conjunction with the CDU-CSU's impressive showing in the 1946 regional elections, Adenauer's Francophilia led him to exclude the Center Party, which had been reestablished after the war and, like the MRP, was more leftist, from all transnational contacts in western Europe.

Another key condition for the rehabilitation of the Germans, for the quick inclusion of the German Christian Democrats in the NEI, and for integrating the newly created Federal Republic into the European community was to rid the West Germans of their moral debt through the Europeanization of the historical responsibility for National Socialism and for the crimes committed in its name. In his report, Frieden admitted that there was a specifically German contribution to the rise of Fascism and National Socialism in Europe, which he saw in the romantic and unrealistic disposition of German elites dating back to the nineteenth century that had led them to be more open to the quasi-religious ideological messages of National Socialism. On the other hand, Frieden argued, Fascism was a phenomenon that "had developed not only in Germany, but in Europe as a whole,"[49] and it is here that the Christian Democratic discourses on Germany and Europe were linked.

According to Wick, National Socialism was more "the reflection of an international *Zeitgeist* than of a national *Volksgeist*." It was really only "the teutonic expression of a more general crisis," just as "Bolshevism is the Russian-Asiatic expression of this crisis." In the end, both ideologies, Fascism and Bolshevism, could succeed only in an unfair and morally corrupt world. It was laissez-faire capitalism and free trade and thus, in the last resort, liberalism that the Christian Democrats held responsible for the decline of Christian civilization. Wick spoke dramatically of "European collective guilt," as National Socialism and Bolshevism were "really just a recapitulation of European history of the last one hundred fifty years."[50] As a Swiss, Wick was perhaps more inclined to share a portion of this European collective guilt than some others, because of his country's close cooperation with Nazi Germany during the war.[51] However, his exposition reflected the more widespread longing of Christian Democrats for a *moral* reorientation to past, apparently better times to accompany the process of economic and social modernization. The key, clearly, was for Germany to "reenter the Christian mainstream," as Frieden put it, and to "detach itself from the purely biological and positivist view of life";[52] in other words, the Germans needed to be "re-Christianized." How better to prove their moral recovery, one might add, than by being as aggressively anti-Communist as possible, which shows the link with the third main theme of the Christian Democratic discourse on the new Europe. With his warning against the "fifth column" of Communists in Western countries who were trying to undermine (Christian) democracy, Adenauer clearly fulfilled implicit expectations.

Crucially, the idea of two Germanys and the Europeanization of the guilt question also allowed the Christian Democrats to look more pragmatically at the negative consequences for Europe as a whole of the dire economic situation in the Western zones of Germany and to realize the dangers of a permanently enforced control of Germany. In his report on the economic aspects of West German integration, the Belgian Désiré Lamalle recommended a substantial increase in German coal production and exports in the short term and German economic reconstruction within a new European framework in the longer term. Germany simply could not be left in its current distress, which would leave a "source of infection in the heart of Europe from which our civilization might well die."[53] As a solution to the German question and to avoid such an infection, the Christian Democrats foresaw the formation of a European Germany after the ruthless attempt by the National Socialists to create a German Europe by force.[54] In principle, the exchanges in Luxembourg already foreshadowed the solution of the German question through the (self-)control of (West) Germany through integration into a new, institutionalized European order. Their ideological position after 1945, as it was developed and reaffirmed in their transnational party cooperation, naturally made the Christian Democrats the strongest proponents of this idea. Their support for the reintegration of West Germany was of course greatly facilitated by the fact that they had partners there in the CDU-CSU and Adenauer who stood for their vision of a morally renewed, "European" Germany and who, moreover, were prepared to give Franco-German reconciliation and Western integration absolute political preference.

## CHRISTIAN DEMOCRATIC COOPERATION AND EUROPEAN INTEGRATION

In the Geneva Circle, the closely linked issues of security and European integration were especially important. Both issues were of course closely linked to the German question, particularly in the context of the Schuman Plan of May 1950 for a European Coal and Steel Community and the Pleven Plan of October 1950 for what became the European Defense Community (EDC). In the Geneva meetings as well as in Western Europe more generally, what was seen as the desired or at least inevitable inclusion of West Germany in the evolving Western defense system led to early rejection of "Europe as a third power," that is, as a "bridge between East and West."[55] For Adenauer, the Geneva meetings provided an ideal opportunity to launch the idea of West German rearmament in secret talks with the French Christian Democrats long before the creation of the Federal Republic and before he, like Churchill, began to air this possibility in public in November and December 1949.[56] In the Geneva meetings Adenauer advocated West German contribution to European defense as early as December 1948[57] and again in March 1949 — almost two years before the Pleven Plan. He insisted that an understanding with the Soviet Union over the future of Germany and Europe was impossible. He then raised the question of whether Europe was able to withstand a possible Russian attack from the east. Half of Germany was already occupied by Russia, Adenauer argued, and the other half lay "defenseless before the Russians." If Britain did not recognize the danger, France had the enormous task to be the "protector of Europe."[58]

The theme of French political leadership in the reconstruction of western Europe ran through all of Adenauer's contributions to the Geneva meetings. In addition to reflecting his deeply held conviction that Britain was and would remain semidetached from the European continent and that his crucial task was to work for Franco-German reconciliation, it was also a crude tactical move to allay French fears of Germany, to strengthen French self-confidence, and to induce the French government, led at that time by the MRP, to take bold initiatives with regard to Europe. Indeed, the open attitude of the MRP representatives toward Germany in the Geneva meetings is quite remarkable. The MRP not only contributed much to the renewal of the French political elite at the end of the war;[59] it also paved the way for a new attitude toward Germany, and the Geneva meetings were very important in this context. Without the MRP's positive attitude, the early and constructive discussion of extremely sensitive Franco-German and European issues, such as West German rearmament, would not have been possible. In particular, Bidault's role in initiating the Franco-German rapprochement within the evolving framework of a more organized Europe should not be underestimated.

The Geneva meetings also helped to pave the way diplomatically for the Federal Republic's entry into the Council of Europe,[60] and they were used during 1950 to coordinate the Christian Democrats' public support throughout western Europe for the Schuman Plan. The Geneva talks and the close Franco-German contacts resulting from them also played an important role in the formative stages of the Schuman Plan in early 1950. At a time when the French government was already working on a plan to Europeanize coal and steel production based largely on the ideas of Jean Monnet, a Socialist technocrat and later the first president of the ECSC High Authority, Adenauer proposed in a meeting with Koutzine in March 1950 the unification of the German and French coal, steel, and even chemical sectors.[61] Koutzine forwarded Adenauer's written note to Bidault, and the strong, explicit West German support for the idea can only have strengthened the French government's resolve to submit its plan, which it duly did—after consulting Adenauer again—less than two months later, in May.

From late 1950 onward, the Geneva meetings were dominated by security policy and the negotiation and ratification of the EDC, which eventually failed in the French parliament in August 1954. Adenauer and the German Christian Democrats largely used the Geneva Circle to increase French confidence in their commitment to the economic and military integration of the Federal Republic into the West. Third way and bridge concepts were out of the question for the German chancellor in foreign policy, and there should be no doubt about that in the minds of his French partners. In one of his reports to Bidault, which was largely based on his frequent talks with Adenauer and Blankenhorn, Koutzine described Adenauer's foreign policy concept: "Adenauer has set everything on the card of European federation. Essentially, his entire foreign policy is constructed around that objective because he believes that the Franco-German entente, the key idea behind his plans, can only be realized in a wider western European context. Thus Adenauer is deliberately sacrificing German unification."[62]

The German representatives held to their clear preference for Western integration over German unification also in the context of the Stalin notes of 1952 that envisaged the unification of a neutral Germany with its own national army. In the Geneva talks, Lenz referred to the Stalin notes as "a new problem." He declared that "Adenauer is determined, as before, to integrate to the utmost. Russia ought first to prove its honest intentions by receiving the United Nations and by holding free elections [in East Germany]."[63] The German Christian Democrats in the Geneva Circle did everything to make clear that the West should not get involved with Stalin's offer. In June 1952 Lenz rejected the question put forth in Geneva as to whether the West should negotiate with the Soviet Union before the ratification of the Western treaties. He argued that the Soviets would agree to German unity only "if they have the upper hand." Stalin's notes "thus are only aimed against the West forming a bloc." Soviet policy was merely a stalling tactic. The West German government intended to "ratify the treaties swiftly."[64]

During 1953–54, the German representatives became increasingly dissatisfied with the hesitant French policy toward European integration, especially with the dragging out of the domestic debate about the ratification of the EDC Treaty. They doubted more and more the usefulness of the Geneva Circle, as one MRP assessment of the prospects of ratification after another proved overly optimistic, generating doubts about the reliability and political influence of Bidault and his advisers in the MRP and in French politics.[65] Of course, the Geneva discussions of the security issue were successful insofar as the MRP members of the French parliament voted eighty to two with four abstentions in favor of the EDC in the crucial vote on August 30, 1954. However, the French-inspired treaty failed, and the Western Allies had to fall back on the alternative, initially favored by Adenauer in 1950, of German NATO membership, now combined with the creation of the intergovernmental Western European Union (WEU) with Britain, which came into force in May 1955.

Koutzine, who had foreseen the failure of the EDC in the French parliament, became an ardent supporter of a renewed emphasis on economics in European integration. However, the Geneva Circle did not recover from the failure of the EDC and made no significant contribution to the creation of the EEC and EURATOM in 1957–58. Instead, the NEI became the focal point in transnational party cooperation not only for the formation and development of the integration ideology but also for European policy making. In a speech in Hanover in October 1954 Schuman said of the EDC failure, "We have lost a battle, but we can still win the war."[66] Only two weeks after the negative EDC vote in the French National Assembly the NEI used their annual congress in Bruges as a demonstration of the vitality of the European idea. The Christian Democrats of the six ECSC countries retained their concept of a more closely integrated "core Europe" without British participation. They also made clear that they intended to proceed with economic integration, which was seen as slightly less sensitive than defense. The NEI passed the *Manifesto of Bruges* in which they demanded the creation of a common market in western Europe with the free movement of goods, people, services and capital, which foreshadowed the EEC.[67] The resolution was formulated on the basis of a questionnaire on economic integration developed by the Belgian PSC politician Robert Houben and the detailed responses of the national NEI groups, especially the CDU-CSU and the MRP. For the first time, continuing differences in the conception of a common market, for example, regarding the harmonization of fiscal and social legislation, were made explicit, and they now no longer seemed insurmountable. The NEI also devoted their 1955 and 1956 congresses to the same theme of economic integration, and their close contacts clearly facilitated the search for compromises in the intergovernmental negotiations that finally led to the signing of the Treaties of Rome in March 1957.[68]

## CONCLUSION

In the interwar period and in exile, the early attempts at organized party cooperation among European Catholics and Christian Democrats were hampered by the dominant nationalist conflicts and severe organizational limits. In contrast, significant incentives existed after 1945 to establish closer transnational contacts and cooperation. Still, if one wanted to judge Christian Democrat party cooperation during the first two decades after 1945 against the far-reaching ambitions of politicians such the Austrian Felix Hurdes in the postwar euphoria of the 1947 Luzerne meeting, the balance sheet would be negative. The NEI did not develop into a European political party with a cohesive common program for the construction of a United States of Europe. Although the Christian Democrats increasingly operated in a common political space and had to arrive at decisions on common policies, national, cultural, and linguistic barriers prevented the evolution of a European political public that would have provided a sufficient incentive for the creation of a European party. Their transnational cooperation also temporarily became much less important for European politics with the electoral decline of the French MRP and especially after the return of Charles de Gaulle to power in 1958. Even by 2000 the European People's Party had not become a party in the narrow sense of the word but was still largely an association of national parties.[69] Nonetheless, the NEI was not merely a "debating club for idealists."[70] On the contrary, the NEI and the Geneva Circle contributed significantly to European integration, especially in its early stages.

The high level of mutual trust and strong conviction in the democratic development of western Europe achieved in the Geneva Circle was considerable.[71] The meetings always included a series of reports on the national politics of the countries involved. These and the ensuing discussions contributed to a better mutual understanding and tended to reinforce common ideological and political concepts. The Geneva Circle was probably most successful in raising the specter of a Communist peril and a Soviet threat to western Europe. The image of a common enemy contributed in no small part to its cohesion. Occasionally, the Geneva meetings also included preliminary discussions of new plans, for example, of ideas resulting in the creation of the Council of Europe. The decline of the Geneva Circle from the early 1950s was due mainly to the decline of the European movement after 1949 and of the Soviet threat, as perceived in western Europe, after the mid-1950s and to the creation of the Federal Republic and its inclusion in the Council of Europe.[72] Once direct Franco-German contacts were established at the governmental level and the bilateral process of rapprochement was initiated, the main purpose of the Geneva Circle had been achieved.

In contrast, the NEI continued, and the creation of the EEC and later the first direct election of the European parliament in 1979 reinforced the importance of the slowly growing transnational Christian Democrat networks. As in the case of the Geneva Circle, the contacts across national borders facilitated a better understanding of political concepts that gave political action at the governmental level the necessary long-term orientation and stability. Party cooperation in the NEI and the Geneva Circle amounted to a collective learning process that—against the background of the European experience of nationalist and ideological radicalization in the interwar period—the political profile of a democratic party of the center should only and, in an integrated western Europe, *could* only be shaped and strengthened in cooperation with partners in other member states. Generally, the transnational contacts also strengthened the recognition of the growing economic and political interdependence of western Europe. They taught the Christian Democrats to think about different national traditions, party programs, and party political fault lines in their own political action.

However, Christian Democratic transnationalism in postwar western Europe did not only create new forms of ideological, political, and economic cohesion. Their cooperation and the (western) European integration process also had disintegrative effects. The concept of a "core Europe" of mostly Catholic and Christian Democrat–dominated countries led to friction with Britain and the neutral countries such as Switzerland and Austria. Their anti-Bolshevism combined with the concept of a (Christian) Western bloc also made it easier for the Christian Democrats to accept the division of Europe and, despite policy differences, made the NEI parties generally reluctant to try to overcome this division. Indeed, in retrospect it is possible to argue that through strengthening their ideological profile and emphasizing their role in the defense of the free (Christian) "West," the division of Europe was actually in their narrow party interest. In some countries, especially the Federal Republic and Italy, Cold War images were consistently instrumentalized against competing parties—not only the Communists, but also the Socialists and Social Democrats, who seemed unreliable in the culture clash between the Christian West and Soviet Bolshevism and materialism.

These disintegrative effects were largely confined to the early postwar period of the hot Cold War. The Christian Democrat–dominated EEC "core Europe" quickly developed into a center of gravity that began to attract most peripheral countries into its orbit within the current European Union and its fifteen member states. Thus, it is possible to argue that ultimately the most important long-term effect of Christian Democratic transnationalism after 1945 is its contribution to a stable European culture of cooperation, which guarantees peaceful mediation of interest and common action in the European Union at the turn of the twenty-first century.

## NOTES

1. On transnational contacts after World War I, see Guido Müller, "Das 'Secrétariat International des Partis Démocratiques d'Inspiration Chrétienne'—Ein vorweggenommenes Exil katholischer Demokraten in der Zwischenkriegszeit," in Michael Gehler, Wolfram Kaiser, and Helmut Wohnout, eds., *Christdemokratie in Europa im 20. Jahrhundert* (Vienna, Cologne, and Weimar, 2000); Alwin Hanschmidt, "Eine christlich-demokratische 'Internationale' zwischen den Weltkriegen: Das 'Secrétariat International des Partis Démocratiques d'Inspiration Chrétienne' in Paris," in Winfried Becker and Rudolf Morsey, eds., *Christliche Demokratie in Europa: Grundlagen und Entwicklungen seit dem 19. Jahrhundert* (Cologne and Vienna, 1988), 153–88, 154–63.

2. Heinrich Vockel [secretary-general, Center Party], Bericht über eine Zusammenkunft christlicher Parteien Europas am 12. und 13. Dezember 1925 in Paris, Historisches Archiv der Stadt Köln, Archive of Wilhelm Marx, no. 225.

3. Ernest Pezet, *Chrétiens au service de la Cité: De Léon XIII au Sillon et au M.R.P., 1891–1965* (Paris, 1965), 115.

4. See Giuseppe Rossini, *Il movimento cattolico nel periodo fascista* (Rome, 1966), 212–14. On Sturzo's vision of Catholic transnationalism, see also Roberto Papini, *Il coraggio della Democrazia: Sturzo e l'internazionale popolare tra le due guerre* (Rome, 1995).

5. See also Jean-Claude Delbreil, *Les catholiques français et les tentatives de rapprochement franco-allemand, 1920–1933* (Metz, 1972).

6. Gabriele De Rosa, *Luigi Sturzo* (Turin, 1977), 329–34.

7. Vockel, Berichte über eine Zusammenkunft christlicher Parteien Europas.

8. Francesco Luigi Ferrari, "Etat 'corporatif' et Etat 'populaire,'" *Politique* 3 (1929): 865–88.

9. Secrétariat International des Partis Démocratiques d'Inspiration Chrétienne, *Bulletin Trimestriel*, 226, Bundesarchiv Bern (BAR), JII.181 1987/52, 2656.

10. See in greater detail, Wolfram Kaiser, "Cooperation of European Catholic Politicians in Exile in Britain and the United States during World War II," *Journal of Contemporary History* 35:2 (2000): 439–65.

11. For introductions to British Catholicism in the interwar years, see Tom Buchanan, "Great Britain," in Tom Buchanan and Martin Conway, eds., *Political Catholicism in Europe, 1918–1965* (Oxford, 1996), 248–74; Joan Keating, "The British Experience: Christian Democrats without a Party," in David Hanley, ed., *Christian Democracy in Europe: A Comparative Perspective* (London, 1994), 161–81. The influence of the Catholic constituency in the Democratic Party on American foreign policy toward Spain and in the early years of World War II is analyzed in Leo V. Kanawada, *Franklin D. Roosevelt's Diplomacy and American Catholics, Italians and Jews* (Epping, 1982), 49–70.

12. When, for example, Michael J. Ready of the National Catholic Welfare Conference in Washington attempted in April 1942 to get information on the People and Freedom branch in Los Angeles, Bishop Joseph T. McGucken made "investigations through the Intelligence Association and various other sources" but could not locate the group. In his letter, Ready had previously advised the bishop that his was "one of our lower forms of request." See Joseph T. McGucken to Michael J. Ready, May 4, 1942; Michael J. Ready to Joseph T. McGucken, April 13, 1942, Archives of the Catholic University of America, National Catholic Welfare Conference, Executive Department, 18–A Church: Hierarchy: Mitty, John J., ABP.1942.

13. "International Christian Democratic Union," *People & Freedom* 20 (1941): 4, speaks of an "initiative" of Onaindia. Onaindia emphasizes his own role and that of the ICDU's first chairman, J. A. Veraart, in his memoirs, *Capítulos de mi vida II: Experiencias del exilio* (Buenos Aires, 1974), 216–18.

14. On Veraart, see Sjef Schmiermann, "Prof. Dr. J. A. Veraart (1886–1955): Een recalcitrant katholiek democraat," in *Jaarboek van het Katholiek Documentatie Centrum* 20 (Nijmegen, 1990), 122–42, 130. On Veraart's isolation among the Dutch

politicians in exile in London, see also Louis De Jong, *Het Koninkrijk der Nederlanden in de Tweede Wereldoorlog*, vol. 9/2 ('s-Gravenhage, 1979), 1445–46.

15. On the ICDU activities during 1941–42, see also ICDU First Annual Report, Algemeen Rijksarchief, Collectie Veraart.

16. Carter to Sturzo, June 30, 1945, ALS, f.201A, c.331, quoted in Papini, *Il coraggio*, 246. According to Onaindia, Schumann participated twice. Onaindia, *Capítulos de mi vida*, 217.

17. "International Christian Democratic Union, Annual General Meeting," *People & Freedom* 61 (1944): 4.

18. Papini, *Il corragio*, 260.

19. Karl [*sic*] Spiecker, *Germany—From Defeat to Defeat, with a Preface by Professor R.W. Seton-Watson* (London, 1945), 153. Spiecker refounded the Center Party after the war.

20. Martin Conway, *Catholic Politics in Europe, 1918–1945* (London, 1997), 89, makes a similar point with regard to the Christian Democratic resistance.

21. Procès-verbal de la conférence politique internationale de Lucerne 27 février–2 mars 1947, BAR, JII.181 1987/52, 2372.

22. Geneva Circle, June 12, 1950, protocol Koutzine, Katholieke Documentatie Centrum Leuven (KADOC), Archief CEPESS, 3.1.11.

23. These talks were organized by Victor Koutzine, the son of an employee in the French diplomatic mission in Tsarist Russia, and Johan-Jakob Kindt-Kierfer, a former German emigrant in Switzerland who worked closely with the former Reich chancellor Joseph Wirth. Concerning Koutzine, see Pierre Turrettini au Direction Générale des Camps de Travail, August 21, 1943, Curriculum Vitae Koutzine and "Signalementsblatt," September 23, 1943, BAR E.4264 1985/196. Concerning Kindt-Kiefer, see Nachrichtendienst Zürich/Polizeikorps Kanton Zürich, November 12, 1943, BAR E.4320 (13) 1973/17.

24. See the reference by Robert Wirth in Lucerne to previous Franco-Belgian contacts in 1946: Procès-verbal de la conférence politique internationale de Lucerne 27 février–2 mars 1947, BAR, JII.181 1987/52, 2372. On the informal contacts of European Christian Democrats before Lucerne, especially in the context of the MRP party congress of December 1945, see Philippe Chenaux, *Une Europe Vaticane? Entre le Plan Marshall et les Traités de Rome* (Brussels, 1990), 120. On the question of whether the NEI had de facto been founded by the French and Belgians before the Lucerne conference, see Jürgen Hollstein, "Zur Geschichte christlich-demokratischer Zusammenarbeit in Europa: Die 'Nouvelles Equipes Internationales' (NEI)," *Libertas* 23 (1989): 82–117, 85–87.

25. Procès-verbal de la conférence politique internationale de Lucerne 27 février–2 mars 1947, BAR, JII.181 1987/52, 2372.

26. NEI, Secrétariat Général [Jules Soyeur], Notes préliminaires, no date [March 1947], KADOC, Archief A.E. de Schryver, 7.2.1.

27. "Christian Democrats and Industrial Democracy: A New International Body," *People & Freedom* 94 (1947): 1–2.

28. See also the recollections of Bruno Dörpinghaus, "Die Genfer Sitzungen— Erste Zusammenkünfte führender christlich-demokratischer Politiker im Nachkriegs-europa," in Dieter Blumenwitz, Klaus Gotto, Hans Maier, Konrad Repgen, and Hans-Peter Schwarz, eds., *Konrad Adenauer und seine Zeit: Politik und Persönlichkeit des ersten Bundeskanzlers. Beiträge von Weg- und Zeitgenossen* (Stuttgart, 1976), 538–65, 538.

29. Chenaux, *Une Europe vaticane?* 128. See also Kindt-Kiefer's wartime publication, *Europas Wiedergeburt durch genossenschaftlichen Aufbau* (Bern, 1944).

30. See, for example, Adenauer to Kindt-Kiefer, March 27, 1948, in Konrad Adenauer, *Briefe über Deutschland 1945–1955*, selected and introduced by Hans Peter Mensing (Berlin, 1999), 75–76.

31. For Kindt-Kiefer's wartime activities in Switzerland, see Nachrich-tendienst Zurich, July 31, 1942, BAR E.4320 (13) 1973/17. See also Ulrike Hörster-Philipp, *Joseph Wirth, 1879–1956: Eine politische Biographie* (Paderborn, 1998), 628–29, 650–60.

32. See the letter by Barbara Roth, Archiviste d'État adjointe, to Michael Gehler, May 22, 1998, quoting from Dossier Victor Koutzine (224'443), Département de l'intérieur, de l'environnement et des affaires régionales, Archives d'Etat, Répub-lique et Canton de Genève, Archives de la Police des Étrangers. The authors would like to thank Barbara Roth for her very informative reply.

33. See Bericht über die Sitzung des Büros der NEI am 18.9.1950 in Paris, Institut für Zeitgeschichte Wien (IfZg), Nachlaß Hurdes, NL 48, DO 367.

34. Vertrauliches Schreiben Felix Hurdes an Karl Gruber, November 2, 1948, and Durchschlag der Aktennotiz Hurdes über die Konferenz des Koordinations-Komitees [der NEI] in Genf, October 21, 1948, Karl Gruber Archiv Innsbruck (KGA), box 4.

35. Dörpinghaus, "Die Genfer Sitzungen," 539–40, 542.

36. Roberto Papini, *L'Internationale Démocrate-Chrétienne: La coopération in-ternationale entre les partis démocrates-chrétiens de 1925 à 1986* (Paris, 1988), 73.

37. Koutzine to Dörpinghaus, November 5, 1949, Archiv für christlich-demo-kratische Politik St. Augustin (ACDP), I-009-017.

38. Streng vertrauliche Niederschrift Hurdes über die Besprechungen im Genfer Coordinations-Comitee am 10.6.1949, Hurdes to Gruber and Figl, 20 June 1949, KGA, Box 6, Mappe M "V."

39. Gedächtnisprotokoll über die Besprechung des Informationszirkels der NEI in Genf am 3.11.1952, protocol Grubhofer, Archiv des Karl von Vogelsang-Instituts Vienna (AKVI), Box NEI (a), (b), (c), (e). See also Philippe Chenaux, "Le Vati-can et l'Europe (1947–1957)," *Storia delle Relazioni Internazionali* 4:1 (1998): 47–83.

40. Dörpinghaus to Adenauer, November 5, 1949; Koutzine to Adenauer, July 23, 1950, August 3, 1950. Stiftung Bundeskanzler Adenauer Haus Rhöndorf (SBKA),

Bestand 10 01–25, 10.01 CD/10.03 K; Dörpinghaus to Adenauer, January 21, 1950, ACDP I-009-13/1; Koutzine to Dörpinghaus, March 11, 1951, ACDP I-009-017. See also Henning Köhler, *Adenauer: Eine politische Biographie* (Berlin and Frankfurt am Main, 1994), 588, 590.

41. Tagung des Kontaktausschusses in Genf, February 13, 1950, AKVI, BPL, Konvolut BMfUnterricht 1946–50, Mappe NEI.

42. Protokoll über die Sitzung in Genf, March 2, 1952, ACDP I-172-31.

43. Karl Wick, Die deutsche Frage, Exposé zuhänden der Konferenz christlicher Politiker, Luxembourg, January 30–31, February 1, 1948, BAR, JII.181 1987/52, 2662.

44. Pierre Frieden, Le problème allemand, son aspect spirituel et culturel, NEI, Le problème allemand, Session de Luxembourg, January 30–31, February 1, 1948, BAR, JII.181 1987/52, 2350.

45. P.J.S. Serrarens, Le problème allemand, son aspect politique, NEI, Le problème allemand, Session de Luxembourg, January 30–31, February 1, 1948, BAR, JII.181 1987/52.

46. Ibid.

47. On the role of the term *Abendland* for the European debate in Germany after 1945, see Walter Lipgens, *Die Anfänge der europäischen Einigungspolitik, 1945–1950. Erster Teil: 1945–1947* (Stuttgart, 1977), 233–35. For a modern intellectual history of the term, albeit also only in a German and not a comparative European context, see Axel Schildt, *Zwischen Abendland und Amerika: Studien zur westdeutschen Ideenlandschaft der 50er Jahre* (Munich, 1999).

48. A summary of the key elements of Adenauer's speech is found in "Christlich-demokratische Internationale?" *Rheinischer Merkur*, February 7, 1948.

49. Frieden, Le problème allemand.

50. Wick, Die deutsche Frage.

51. For a very good synopsis of the controversial debate about Switzerland and World War II, see Georg Kreis and Bertrand Müller, eds., *Die Schweiz und der Zweite Weltkrieg / La Suisse et la Seconde Guerre mondiale* (Basel, 1997). See also Erwin Bucher, *Zwischen Bundesrat und General: Schweizer Politik und Armee im Zweiten Weltkrieg* (Zurich, 1993).

52. Frieden, Le problème allemand.

53. Désiré Lamalle, Le problème allemand, son aspect économique, NEI, Le problème allemand, Session de Luxembourg, January 30–31, February 1, 1948, BAR, JII.181 1987/52, 2350.

54. In this context, see also Resolution, adoptée par la conference de NEI tenue à Luxembourg du 29 janvier au 2er février 1948, ACDP, IX-002-011/2.

55. Dörpinghaus, "Die Genfer Sitzungen," 540. See also Wilfried Loth, "Von der 'Dritten Kraft' zur Westintegration: Deutsche Europa-Projekte in der Nach-

kriegszeit," in Franz Knipping and Klaus-Jürgen Müller, eds., *Aus der Ohnmacht zur Bündnismacht: Das Machtproblem in der Bundesrepublik Deutschland, 1945–1960* (Paderborn, 1995), 57–83.

56. Rolf Steininger, *Wiederbewaffnung. Die Entscheidung für einen westdeutschen Verteidigungsbeitrag: Adenaur und die Westmächte, 1950* (Erlangen, Bonn, and Vienna, 1989), 15–17.

57. Philippe Chenaux, "Les démocrates-chrétiens et la construction de l'Europe (1947–1957)," *Revue Politique* 1 (1991): 87–101, 96; Wolfram Kaiser, "Begegnungen christdemokratischer Politiker in der Nachkriegszeit," in Martin Greschat and Wilfried Loth, eds., *Die Christen und die Entstehung der Europäischen Gemeinschaft* (Stuttgart, 1995), 139–57, 150.

58. Bericht Hurdes von der Tagung des Koordinations-Komitees der christlich-demokratischen Parteien in Genf, March 8, 1949, Österreichisches Staatsarchiv Vienna (ÖStA), Archiv der Republik (AdR), BKA/AA II-pol 1949, Zl. 82.250-pol/49 (80.161-pol/49), Int. 14; see also the protocol in ACDP I-009-017.

59. Jean-Marie Mayeur, "Einige Betrachtungen über die Rolle der Christlichen Demokratie in Frankreich beim Aufbau der Demokratie und Europas nach 1945," in Becker and Morsey, *Christliche Demokratie in Europa*, 225–33, 228.

60. Koutzine to Dörpinghaus, March 23, 1950, ACDP I-009-017.

61. Proposition du Chancelier Adenauer, Koutzine to Bidault, March 22, 1950. Archives Nationales Paris (AN), 457 AP 59, Notes Koutzine. See also footnote 22 in Ulrich Lappenküper, "Der Schuman-Plan," *Vierteljahrshefte für Zeitgeschichte* 42:3 (1994): 403–45.

62. La Tactique du Chancelier Adenauer [Victor Koutzine to Georges Bidault 1951], AN, 457 AP 59, Notes Koutzine/Nemanoff. On this question, see also the excellent literature review by Klaus Kellmann, "Deutsche Geschichte nach 1945: Neuerscheinungen vor, während und nach der Auflösung der DDR und der Vereinigung beider deutscher Staaten," *Geschichte in Wissenschaft und Unterricht* 44:4 (1993): 243–69.

63. Geneva Circle, March 24, 1952, protocol Karl Count Spreti, ACDP, I-172-31.

64. Geneva Circle, June 16, 1953, protocol Grubhofer, AKVI, Box NEI c)e).

65. Koutzine to Lenz, September 14, 1953, ACDP, I-172-74.

66. Quoted in Raymond Poidevin, *Robert Schuman, homme d'Etat 1886–1963* (Paris, 1986), 381.

67. Manifeste de Bruges, September 10–12, 1954, KADOC, Archief R. Houben 246.2./3.

68. On the NEI, the failure of the EDC, and the formation of the EEC, see in greater detail Wolfram Kaiser, " 'Une bataille est perdue, mais la guerre reste à gagner': Das Scheitern der Europäischen Verteidigungsgemeinschaft 1954 und der Durchbruch zur horizontalen Wirtschaftsintegration," in Romain Kirt, ed., *Die EU*

*und ihre Krisen: Eine unkonventionelle Geschichte der europäischen Integration* (Baden-Baden, forthcoming).

69. On the development of the EVP, see also the book written by its former secretary-general, Thomas Jansen, *Die Entstehung einer Europäischen Partei: Vorgeschichte, Gründung und Entwicklung der EVP* (Bonn, 1996).

70. Jac Bosmans, "Das Ringen um Europa: Die Christdemokraten der Niederlande und Deutschlands in den 'Nouvelles Equipes Internationales' (1947–1965)," in Jac Bosmans, ed., *Europagedanke, Europabewegung und Europapolitik in den Niederlanden und Deutschland seit dem Ersten Weltkrieg* (Münster, 1996), 123–48.

71. Kaiser, "Begegnungen christdemokratischer Politiker," 151–52.

72. Chenaux, "Les démocrates-chrétiens," 96.

# 11 Parties, Populists, and Pressure Groups

European Christian Democracy in Comparative Perspective

CARL STRIKWERDA

The rise of religious social movements is one of the most important phenomena of the contemporary world scene. For Americans, the increasing influence of evangelicalism in the public activities of the Christian community and the visibility of the new Religious Right in politics are crucial examples.[1] Worldwide, the growth of Protestant evangelicalism and Liberation Theology in Latin America, the revival of a variety of Christian groups in Russia and eastern Europe, and the political role of Christians in South Korea, South Africa, and the Philippines are also striking. Understandably, an interesting debate is going on regarding the long-term importance and the possible future of these movements. To what extent will they succeed in changing their societies in the long term? A useful contribution historians can make to this discussion is to put contemporary religious social movements into the broadest possible comparative and chronological context.

An important comparative case that has largely been neglected in this discussion is the one that, arguably, has been the religious social movement with the greatest political success: Christian Democracy. For the past one hundred years, Christian Democracy, largely Catholic in inspiration, has been one of the largest political movements in continental Europe.

Because Catholic parties and social movements bridged Left and Right and cut across class divisions in a unique way, they have played an absolutely essential part in almost all battles over Fascism, the welfare state, the Cold War, and European integration. The Christian Democrats have formed the largest or second largest bloc in the European Parliament during most of its history.[2] They have also played a major role in what some social scientists have pointed out as a distinctive kind of political system, one in which divergent groups have learned to cooperate, a system sometimes described as "consociational democracy" or "segmented pluralism."[3] But the influence of Christian Democracy has gone far beyond politics. Through constituent movements such as the Young Christian Workers (Jeunesse Ouvrière Chrétienne), women's leagues, and student organizations, it has been a bulwark of Catholic Christianity. If we wish to arrive at a fully comparative view of the place of religion in modern societies, Christian Democracy is a crucial case study.

Despite their importance for mass politics, however, continental European Catholic political and social movements have been relatively understudied by what one might call the mainstream historians of modern politics; nor have they been studied by scholars interested in the comparative study of contemporary religious social movements.[4] One of the most impressive recent contributions to religious scholarship has been the great Fundamentalism project, which sought to place conservative American evangelicalism in a global, comparative perspective.[5] Yet, in its three volumes, Christian Democracy is hardly mentioned as a conservative religious political movement. Most American historians and political scientists assume that the differences between the United States and continental Europe are too vast for meaningful comparisons with Christian Democracy to be made. Strengthening this assumption is relative ignorance about central Europe. Christian Democracy has flourished not in Britain and France, the two countries Americans know best, but in the Low Countries, Germany, Austria, and Italy, with which Americans are less familiar.

The constitutional and religious differences between continental Europe and the United States are real enough. I would argue, however, that if we look beneath the level of political parties, European Christian Democrats have more similarities with—and more to teach—Christians in the United States than we usually realize. After all, continental western Europe, for most of its modern history, shares with the English-speaking world fundamental similarities as part of a democratic civilization with protected civil rights. Religion as private belief has been protected, and the existence of civil and political liberties has made these societies fertile ground for social movements. Christians in both Europe and North America have wrestled with the Judeo-Christian heritage of a sacral society—a city of God—inside a sovereign, majority-ruled political order that is not and cannot be truly Christian. Christianity demands moral engagement in the public sphere, but since the early modern era our political systems have prevented the state from being truly Christian. I do not believe that the institutional or constitutional differences between the United States, on the one hand, and the continental European countries where Christian Democracy has flourished, on the other, are so marked that comparisons between religious social movements cannot be made.

I argue that comparisons between Christian Democracy in Europe and evangelical Protestantism in the United States are valid and that, as a result, Christian Democracy has some lessons—both positive and negative—for contemporary evangelical Christians in the United States. To do this, I first explore some reasons why many English-speaking scholars have ignored Christian Democracy and argue for the validity of comparisons between continental Europe and the United States. Second, I argue that comparing Christian Democracy and evangelicalism reveals that pressure group politics are a crucial similarity among all Christian social movements. Third, I argue that the comparisons also reveal the emergence of pluralism as a key lesson that the story of European Christian Democracy holds for contemporary American religious movements.

The real success of Christian Democracy came not, I would argue, from the political parties that appear to be Christian Democracy's defining characteristic. Instead, pressure group politics or religious social movements have been and are ultimately more lasting and more effective than organized political parties in allowing individual Christians to have an influence on society. But these nonpolitical movements on which both Christian Democratic parties and the nonpartisan North American Christian community have depended must continually adjust to a diverse society that enforces compromises and coexistence with other movements.

## THE CASE FOR COMPARISONS WITH CONTINENTAL EUROPE

Why have comparisons between Christian Democracy in Europe and evangelical Protestantism in the United States not been made before? The striking feature of Christian Democracy in continental Europe for North American observers is the existence of organized political parties proclaiming themselves, at least at some point in their history, self-consciously "Christian." It is clear that the existence of religious political parties itself is a sign of more fundamental constitutional and political cultural differences between continental Europe and English-speaking countries such as the United States. Building on Enlightenment notions, the United States developed a hegemonic individualistic liberalism that has made the ideological, corporate identification with religious political parties unattractive. For much of American history, this liberalism grew up under the umbrella of a generally Protestant "civil religion." As civil religion declined with the rise of secularization in the twentieth century, liberalism more often defended a kind of negative freedom. Religious groups have had their greatest political success when arguing that they had the right not to be imposed on; they have had much less success in the United States when they argued for anything smacking of special privilege. Thus groups such as the Mennonites could be exempted from the draft, but, variously, Catholics, Reformed, and Lutherans cannot obtain state support for their schools even though they pay public school taxes.[6] As Richard John Neuhaus and others have argued, one of the forces motivating the upsurge of conservative religious politics in the United States is the shift from one kind of hegemonic civil religion to another. Up to the mid-twentieth century, an established Protestantism exerted a kind of hegemony excluding other religious expression and secularism. Struggles over church and state were relatively rare. Since the mid-twentieth century, a secular hegemony, or "naked public square," has taken hold, and almost all religious expressions are suspect. The upsurge of conservative religious politics has been a reaction to this secular hegemony.[7]

Christian political activism in the United States has not been channeled into separate political parties, in part because Protestantism served as a hegemonic civil religion. This made a separate party for Protestants unnecessary and doomed any attempt to create a party for the minority Catholics. At the same time, the two-party majority system and the division between a congressional and presidential seat of power militates against small parties and makes coalition governments not an option. In continental Europe—though again, not in Britain or France—the proportional representation system of voting ensured even small minority parties some influence and encouraged coalition governments. The recent identification of conservative

Protestants with the Republican Party in the United States mirrors in some ways the older, now largely dead tradition of Catholics' identification with Democrats. Such an alliance has always been informally at the level of voters and party activists, never an official identification of the parties themselves. This is as close as the United States has come to religious politics, and it is a far cry from the public identification of parties as Christian.

Another reason why scholars have not made comparisons between continental European Christian Democracy and societies such as the United States is because Catholicism supposedly has a unique role in continental Europe. European Christian Democracy is often seen as an essentially Catholic phenomenon, one that has little relevance for societies where Catholics are a minority. The conventional view is that the Church hierarchy, that is, the Vatican and the bishops, initiated Catholic political movements to ensure that the Church retained power in countries where it had long enjoyed special privileges. In these same countries, the dominant place of the Catholic Church had also meant that freedom of religion had had little place until the rise of liberal movements in the nineteenth century. Christian Democratic parties, in this view, were a kind of counterattack to win back through the democratic political system what the Church had lost with the decline of monarchical rule. By implication, democratic countries such as the United States have a completely different history, with the Catholic Church never having a privileged place and with religious freedom one of the bedrocks of the constitutional order.

The conventional contrast between a Europe plagued with a contentious history of church-state relations and a United States where the separation of church and state defined a wholly different political status for religion is overstated. Despite differing historical expression, useful comparisons can be made between Christian Democracy and American evangelical Protestantism. It is not the case that Catholicism alone could create Christian Democratic movements, whereas Protestantism in the political realm is intent on something wholly different. As Stathis N. Kalyvas has argued, Catholic parties did not arise from the initiative of the Vatican or Catholic bishops. Instead, the latter often opposed the growth of Catholic parties led by lay leaders. Although the Church hierarchy encouraged these parties initially because they opposed liberal anticlericalism, it then tried to restrain or even repress them as soon as they showed signs of becoming rivals to ecclesiastical authority. Christian Democracy historically grew up, in other words, more as a grassroots, lay

Catholic phenomenon than a product of the Catholic Church.[8] The parallels with Protestant evangelicalism in Britain and the United States are striking. Lay leaders often moving outside the denominational leadership of churches have organized movements from the grass roots.

Similarly, many Catholics in continental Europe and Latin America have failed to organize successful Christian Democratic movements. It is not Catholicism that by its very nature gives rise to Christian Democratic movements. Ecclesiastical and especially lay leaders in any given country have had to decide to organize mass movements for Christian Democracy to become an important force. Elitist or quietist religious movements do not give rise to political movements. In the late nineteenth century, French Catholic leaders made a fateful choice to align themselves with political conservatism and to impose rigid uniformity on political Catholicism.[9] French anticlericalism, it is true, succeeded in keeping Catholics on the defensive.[10] It was not the case, however, that French anticlericalism was too strong or the legacy of the Revolution too divisive for Christian Democracy to emerge. The same forces moving toward Christian Democracy were at work among Catholics in France as in other countries. The Abbé Lemire, a member of parliament from Armentières in the north of France, voiced the same Catholic populist sentiment as existed in Belgium and Germany.[11] The opposition to Catholic democracy was too strong *within* the Catholic community itself.[12] Nonetheless, when Catholic leaders chose to tone down their differences and exert some political influence, French Catholics in the Mouvement Républicain Populaire (MRP) played an important role in restoring democratic institutions after World War II.[13] Until then the key variable missing in France was leadership that could see the need to unite Christians and lead them in making strategic alliances with other groups.[14] As Kalyvas has argued, "Unique to France was the absence of Catholic mass organizations."[15] In Italy, too, Catholics waited too long to organize on their own. When they finally did on the eve of World War I, they were often reduced to simply supporting liberals and conservatives against Socialism.[16] However, just as in France, the same Catholic populism was at work in the activity of Father Romolo Murri, the Italian radical activist during World War I.[17]

Furthermore, Protestantism under certain conditions, usually when it feels itself a beleaguered minority, is capable of being as politicized and as tightly organized as many Catholic communities. From a sociological perspective, European Christian Democracy included not only Catholics but some

Protestant communities as well. Two very different examples of such sectarian Protestantism are the Protestants of Ulster and the arch-Calvinists of the Netherlands from the late nineteenth century to the mid-twentieth century.[18] As Ronald Wells has argued, even though political Unionism is a useful way to define the so-called "Protestant" side in the struggle in Northern Ireland, evangelical or fundamental Protestantism provides a dynamic element that is still essential to the conflict. Ian Paisley and his supporters are motivated by sectarian Protestantism and help to polarize a conflict that might otherwise be settled by a political compromise.[19] The conservative Calvinists in the Netherlands organized almost exactly like Catholic Christian Democrats in continental Europe, complete with their own labor unions, political parties, schools, newspapers, and interest group organizations.[20] Even more intriguing, from a comparative perspective that includes the United States, is the existence of small but influential Christian Democratic parties in overwhelmingly Protestant and secularized Scandinavia. The present prime minister of Norway, for example, comes from a Christian Democratic party.[21]

Another reason scholars have not made comparisons between continental European Christian Democracy and religious movements in societies such as the United States is because they believe that Christian Democrats were a liberal or radical movement. Religious movements in the United States usually have been seen as inherently conservative; if Christian Democracy has been a left-wing religious movement, then there appears to be little basis for comparison. This confusion on the part of North American observers is understandable. Already in the period in which Christian Democracy arose, some contemporaries unfortunately described them as "Christian socialists" because they tried to find solutions to the same social and economic problems as Socialists.[22] Originally, however, the Christian Democrats were in many ways more socially and religiously conservative than other Christians. Many of them, in fact, began as ultramontanists, that is, supporters of strengthening the pope's authority over the Church.[23] Traditional Catholics had opted for coexistence with the authorities and concentration on maintaining devotional life and the institutional strength of the Church. In many countries in the nineteenth century, Catholics coexisted with Liberal governments as long as the governments left them alone. Christian Democrats, by contrast, did not seek coexistence; they wanted, in their words, "a crusade against Liberalism"—and later, many would add, "a crusade against Socialism."[24]

Despite their use of progressive tactics, in their theology and religious practice Christian Democrats have almost always been an orthodox or conservative religious movement. Like many evangelical Protestants, Christian Democrats have displayed a longing for a confessional state in which the government publicly supported Christian beliefs and activities. Since the mid-nineteenth century, increasing secularization and the decline in government support for religious activity have presented both Catholics and Protestants with a new challenge. One typical reaction is to withdraw from public life and avoid politics in order to build up an alternative, private religious community. Another reaction is to accommodate as much as possible to secularization and drop any demand for government recognition of religion. Still another reaction, however, is to try to bring about through political action at least some aspects of a confessional state. Both Christian Democrats and many politically active Protestant evangelicals have been driven by a desire to restore an older world. What differentiates them from other more quietistic or more liberal Christians is their willingness to use new, even radical means for what is, in many ways, a traditional ideal.

In late-twentieth-century America, it was typically evangelicals and fundamentalists who first used television, marketing techniques, and electronic music — tactics that most of their more moderate coreligionists avoided.[25] So, too, in late-nineteenth-century Europe Christian Democrats were willing to challenge the Socialists by creating a daily press, consumer cooperatives, labor unions, and a Catholic Young Guard — means that scandalized traditional Catholics. The growth of Christian Democracy, like that of many activist Protestant movements, was spurred by radical conservatism more than by the traditionalist religious establishment.[26] In their opposition to contemporary trends, Christian Democrats in countries such as Belgium, France, Germany, Italy, and the Netherlands around 1900 had significant similarities to today's Protestant evangelicals in the United States and Latin America.

## BENEATH PARTIES TO PRESSURE GROUPS AND POPULISM

Even as Christians have become politically active, the true wellspring of religious movements in politics has been their roots in religious communities outside of politics. European Christian Democrats and Protestant evangelicals in the United States shared not only a conservative theology but also a base in religious subcultures. As Kees van Kersbergen has argued, "Christian Democratic parties cannot be properly analyzed outside the context of the Christian Democratic movement as a whole."[27] The most successful of these continental Catholic communities have been examples of what John Whyte has called "closed Catholicism," groups of Catholics who banded together to protect themselves from intellectual and cultural influences that might weaken the faith of individual believers.[28] In many ways the close-knit Catholic communities in the United States in the early and mid-twentieth century—what James Fisher calls the "Catholic Counterculture"—were similar to the Catholic subcultures of continental Europe.[29] Christian Democracy, however, went farther than Catholics and Protestants elsewhere in organizing believers in groups that would touch on as many parts of their lives as possible. It succeeded because Catholics organized farmers, workers, housewives, employers, and students and brought these groups into at least a loose alliance.

In this process Christian Democrats created a new set of tactics for religious people. They pioneered the formation of a host of organizations that both sheltered and nurtured individual believers and served as pressure groups on the government and society. These groups acted both for their members' material interests as students, teachers, housewives, farmers, and workers and, at times, for their members' religious beliefs. At the same time, these organizations created by Christian Democrats only succeeded because they adopted a strategy of populism—bringing marginal groups into the mainstream of politics and society. Farmers, lower-middle-class shopkeepers, and workers were mobilized by Christian Democrats. As the Belgian Christian Democratic leader Arthur Verhaegen put it, Catholics had "to borrow something from the Socialists[:] . . . the cooperation that they get from a well-disciplined army."[30]

The dynamism of German Christian Democrats' strength lay in their rich organizational life—clubs, singing societies, mothers' groups—and the tight web of newspapers, periodicals, and literature that knit these groups together. Among European Catholics, the Germans were the first to turn to the popular press, political organizations of workers, and state intervention to compete with Socialism. The German organization that carried out these tasks, Volksverein für das Katholische Deutschland, was founded in October 1890, along with a Catholic farmers' league, the Bauernverein.[31] The evolution of imperial Germany toward a genuine constitutional state depended more on the Catholic Center Party than on any other group, even though liberals and Socialists found it exceedingly difficult to overcome their anti-Catholic feelings and work with the Catholics.[32] The Christian labor unions of Germany formed by Christian Democrats were a remarkable social movement for their time. In a culture where denominational divisions were still deep, they brought Protestants and Catholics together. Even though they began well after the Socialist "Free" unions, they virtually matched their rate of growth between 1898 and 1914.[33] During the Weimar Republic in the 1920s, Christian unions managed to create their own labor union federation with secular white-collar and public employee unions.[34] In 1891 Belgian Christian Democrats created an association of social welfare and political action groups, the Belgische Volksbond/Ligue democratique belge (Belgian Democratic League).[35] Almost simultaneously, several Christian Democratic priests organized a national Catholic association of small farmers, the Boerenbond (Farmers League).[36] This creation of these organizations was reinforced by Pope Leo XIII's encyclical *Rerum Novarum*, which recognized the grievances of the lower classes.[37] In the Netherlands, the Catholics' campaign to obtain government subsidies for religious education was part of a larger movement to create credit unions, so-called *Raiffeisen* funds, farmers' leagues, newspapers, and workers' clubs.[38] In France, many of the most successful agricultural leagues have Catholic lay activists who had experience in the Jeunesse Agricole Chrétienne.[39] One of the largest, most well-known organizational efforts of European Catholics was Catholic Action, a network of social and religious clubs sponsored by the Church but sometimes directly supporting political activity as well.[40]

The tightly organized subcultures that Christian Democrats created in continental Europe should be seen as the result of factors at work in many other societies but which in this case led to a sometimes distinctively segmented type of society. The "pillars" or "segmented plural" communities that have characterized Catholic communities in continental Europe were not accidental creations or the result of premodern loyalties. They were thoroughly modern products of a certain constellation of forces at work in mass politics. Christian Democracy of the late nineteenth century was not a spasm of communal feeling in reaction to modernity. It was not a temporary detour on the way to an inevitably individualist future. These kinds of communities had their counterparts in Socialist or Laborite communities in many places in Europe and in certain respects even in the political "machines" in cities in the United States.[41]

The closed nature of many of the Christian Democratic organizations, of course, is not necessarily attractive or even possible in today's society. But the variety and breadth of the organizations is remarkable. What gave Christian Democracy its staying power and enabled it to become one of the defining frameworks for continental Europe for a century was its ability to tailor the collective life of believers in areas outside worship around religious organizations. Thus farmers who were Catholic might or might not belong to secular agricultural organizations, but they would also have a specifically Christian periodical, meeting place, or professional organization that was explicitly religious. One of the signs to look for, this may suggest, is whether more recent religious movements such as contemporary American evangelicalism can translate their fervor into continuing organizations that have deep roots—in other words, using Weber's terminology, whether they can translate charisma into bureaucracy.

Just as important a lesson of Christian Democracy, however, is that the true wellspring for the movement's political action was not political but rather spiritual or religious. Christian Democracy's success or failure often depended on the connection to revivalism, evangelical ministries, and spiritual support groups. In other words, the political fortunes of religious parties have depended often on the apolitical religious organizations that shape religious people's private lives. In nineteenth- and twentieth-century Europe, pilgrimages, Marian devotion, the revival of Franciscan spirituality, and confraternities all propelled Catholics to deeper religious intensity and eventually greater involvement with political and social issues.[42] As Margaret Lavinia Anderson points out, historians still have tremendous work to do in order to dispel the notion of the nineteenth century as simply a period of secularization. Established churches lost privileges and intellectual life became secularized, but parts of society, especially the rural population and the middle class, became more religious, not less.[43]

The parallels with, first, Catholic piety during the period of the late nineteenth to mid-twentieth century and, second, the Protestant evangelical revival in the late twentieth century in the United States are striking. In each case, spirituality led many individual believers to join political or social movements. In the European case, it is true, there are some complexities. The most dramatic public expressions of intense spirituality may indicate a failure to deal with social and political issues. The centers of Marian devotion—in French-speaking Belgium, France, Spain, and Portugal, that is, Lourdes, Fatima, and Beauraing—were precisely the areas where Catholics of the late nineteenth and twentieth century faced the most successful vehement anticlericalism and were least able to mount an effective Christian Democratic alternative to secular Socialism or liberalism.[44] Otherwise, however, the case of continental European Christian Democracy shows that increases in spiritual vitality have led to stronger religious social or political movements.

The social organizations of Catholic youth, farmers, women, and students and the spiritual revival movements of Catholics that together were the foundations of continental European Christian Democracy all have some similarities to the para-church groups in the United States that are the wellspring of the New Christian Right. The existence of political parties, or the absence thereof in Europe and the United States, may be less crucial than the similarities in mobilization outside of partisan politics. Where religious movements aiming at political influence in the United States and other English-speaking countries have grounded themselves in grassroots movements they have almost always had greater success than when they have focused on dramatic one-issue campaigns or high-profile, public pronouncements. Good examples of this in the United States are the contrast between the success of religious groups—Catholic, Jewish, and Protestant—in support of civil rights in the 1960s versus the isolation that many mainline Protestant churches have experienced in the 1980s and 1990s. The Protestant mainstream did not organize its own constituency in the later period, although there are signs that the situation is changing with the growth of groups such as the Interfaith Alliance. The U.S. Catholic Church in the 1980s and 1990s may provide an instructive counterexample. Its positions have often been either more liberal or more conservative than those of much of its own membership or of the public at large: too liberal in foreign policy and too conservative or at least more stridently conservative on homosexuality and abortion. Nonetheless, it still exerts a high degree of influence because of the existence of a network of organizations that allows for pressure to be brought on the political process. Another instructive contrast may be between the Moral Majority of the 1980s and the Christian Coalition of the 1990s. Unlike the Moral Majority, the Christian Coalition has gone to the grass roots and organized Protestant believers from the ground up, as it were, and also appealed to what its leaders claim are their economic interests.[45] It is no coincidence that individuals have now been offered a Christian Coalition credit card. Despite the vast differences in time and ideology, the Christian Democrats of the late nineteenth century would have understood.

The importance of pressure groups outside of organized political parties and outside the ecclesiastical establishment, I would argue, is a major comparative phenomenon of almost all religious social movements in the Western world.[46] The influence of both Christian Democrats in continental Europe and Christian movements in countries such as Britain, France, and the United States has often depended on applying "pressure group" politics, not just on party politics. A good deal of these movements' influence has come outside of partisan politics in parliament through lobbying, bargaining, and mobilizing political opinion. The Non-Conformist Liberals of nineteenth-century Britain, the Catholic Gaullists of late-twentieth-century France, and the host of social reform movements in the United States are all examples of this same kind of influence. Gladstone's personal role as a Christian is widely noted, of course, but mainstream British political history usually ignores how much support was provided him by Non-Conformists who lobbied behind the scenes in favor of numerous reforms.[47] Even after the French Christian Democratic party, the MRP, declined in the 1950s, French Christian Democrats organized in the Centre des Democrates Sociaux continued to work together as a lobbying and pressure group in French politics.[48] The actions of these European Catholics closely resemble those of religious groups in the United States. Most important, even some leading Protestant evangelical leaders in the United States have realized that the greatest and long-lasting influence their community can have is through emphasizing moral issues and individual believers' participation in politics, not through churches aligning as a group with a particular political party. As the conservative Christian minister Ed Dobson put it recently:

> While we work toward legislation, we must also do the more difficult task of challenging people's minds and beliefs on the matter. The most effective laws *follow* moral consensus — they do not bring about moral consensus. Our task as believers and followers of Jesus is to continue the tedious work of moral transformation in our culture. As we move toward

that goal, legislation will be the natural consequence of that moral transformation; it will never be the cause of moral transformation.[49]

In other words, the obstacles that religious social movements have faced
have varied. How they need to mobilize themselves to really influence society, however, can be quite similar.

One other aspect of Christian Democracy's strength that has wider
implications for the study of religious social movements in general is its
populist tendencies. In contrast to much social scientific theory, historians
have pointed out Christian Democratic movements' staying power in the
face of the modernization, urbanization, or secularization that supposedly
should have undermined their support.[50] These movements have succeeded,
however, by appealing to the disenfranchised—a set of groups much larger
and more diverse than blue-collar workers who supported Socialism or
other working-class movements. As Ludwig Windthorst, early leader of the
German Zentrum Party, stated when he defied the pope's order to support
Bismarck's military budget: "The Center party subsists simply and solely on
the confidence of the people; no other support stands at its command, and
it is . . . required, therefore, more than any other fraction, to heed the pulse-
beat of the people."[51] Usually this meant taking socioeconomic grievances
seriously. The Belgian Christian Democrat Arthur Verhaegen declared in
1891, "Charity is not enough to guarantee what is right. Next to it one must
have justice."[52]

It is true that Christian Democrats helped to create labor unions and
worked for government intervention in the economy much as Socialists did.
It was not the case, however, that Christian Democracy was pulled along
by the Socialists' agenda. The reverse is true. Most labor historians would
agree that the major program of Socialism was nationalization of industry
and the political dominance of the working class. In the end, this program
has had limited relevance for twentieth-century politics in most democratic
countries. Instead, what most Socialists had never sought came about in
most continental western European countries: a social welfare state in
which organized interest groups broker changes between themselves. All of
this looks much more like Christian Democratic programs of 1900 than like
the program of the Socialist Second International. As Robert Walton has
argued, "When the German Social Democratic Party accepted the Godesberg
Program in 1959 [which rejected Marxism] *nolens volens* they became Pope

Leo XIII's heirs."[53] It is no coincidence that the two western European countries that tried nationalization of industry on a large scale are Britain and France, the two that had the least Christian Democratic influence. Indeed, one of the most unexamined aspects in the enormous flood of social scientific research on the welfare state is that Catholicism has been a major force in creating the welfare state in continental Europe.[54] Furthermore, Christian Democrats have given the welfare state a particular emphasis: in the countries where they have had a large influence, welfare policies are aimed more at families and mothers than at individuals and mediated more by nongovernmental institutions.[55]

The contrast with Protestant evangelicalism in the United States in this area is, of course, striking. The deep traditions of limited government and individualism in the United States have long meant that politically active evangelicals have been opposed to increased welfare spending and often to any government policies in areas such the family, children, and health. Nonetheless, it is possible to argue that Protestant evangelicalism—along with the Catholic tradition—has gradually influenced social welfare policies in the United States. In the 1990s a tentative synthesis of government action and private, nonprofit efforts has emerged. The growth of charter schools, that is, private schools chartered by state governments, and the increasing disbursements of state and federal social welfare funds through nonprofit adoption and mental health organizations are two examples of this trend.

## PLURALISM

What other lessons might there be in the story of Christian Democracy for movements such as political evangelicalism in the United States and Latin America? Besides Christian Democracy's organizational genius, one of its most instructive developments is how it grudgingly came to accept a pluralist society in which Christian Democrats could maintain their separate identity but live together with their opponents. Pluralism, of course, is a complicated concept. I am talking here about what might be called a movement from "associational" pluralism to "directional" pluralism. Associational pluralism is simply the recognition that different groups exist in society because people have chosen to belong to them—Catholics, Socialists, liberals, freethinkers, and so on. Directional pluralism is much stronger; people have to decide that the diverse and perhaps mutually exclusive worldviews that lie behind many of the associational groups can all be allowed to flourish.[56] Even in the most diverse societies with a long tradition of associational pluralism—such as the United States—many people still are wary of tolerating worldviews they personally do not accept. Yet a degree of directional pluralism, accepting a diversity of views and protecting the right of this diversity to persist, is at the heart of modern, democratic society.

One has to remember what an enormous sea change this was for Christian Democrats, especially when it occasionally entailed working with Socialists. While Socialists in Belgium, for example, had denounced Catholic unionists as a "horrible popish gang," "stool pigeons," and "dompers" (duped ones or stupes), Catholics had called the Socialists tyrants, convicts, atheists, preachers of free love, and "redskins."[57] We should remember, too, that Christian Democrats in some ways faced as fierce an enemy as the secular humanism that is the target of many American evangelicals. The fundamental importance of anticlericalism as a constituent element, and fatal flaw, of continental Socialism has been neglected by scholars. In France, Spain, Italy, Switzerland, Austria, the Netherlands, and Belgium, the religious issue was almost as critical as economic grievances in the evolution of mass politics. Where anticlericalism was less of an issue, this had a major effect. The German Socialists, for example, decided to downplay anticlericalism in order to prevent losing workers to religious labor movements, a decision that may have had an importance greater than more-studied developments in German history. By contrast to the deep division between Catholics and Socialists elsewhere in continental Europe, lessening Socialist anticlericalism in Germany probably blunted the growth of Christian unionism and the Catholic Center Party.[58]

Gradually, however, groups such as Christian Democrats and Socialists learned to cooperate in politics, in setting up social welfare policies, and in representing interest groups such as working women or labor unions. During Weimar Germany, only cooperation between Socialists and Catholics held democracy together.[59] In the midst of massive nationwide strikes in 1936, Belgian Catholic and Socialist leaders went on radio together and raced to put themselves at the head of the strikers to shut out the Communists.[60]

Ironically, Socialism, which has been seen as the quintessentially modern movement, was less prepared for pluralism than Christian Democracy.

Socialism was and remained a more unitary ideology, with less room for divergent groups to coexist under its banner. Catholicism, while relatively unified in a theological sense, had long embraced divergent conservative and progressive political tendencies. Because Catholics had learned to fight a rear-guard action against the tidal wave of secularism and liberalism, they also had begun learning the difficult life of coexistence earlier than their opponents. The multiclass character of the Catholic community, which seemed an aberration to Socialists and many later scholars, in fact taught Christian Democrats how to negotiate, compromise, and coexist in the midst of conflicts. What happened in almost every country where Christian Democracy succeeded in creating a large movement was the writing of certain ground rules in education and social welfare that respected religious beliefs but required a degree of cooperation between Christians and non-Christians. Large numbers of Christians were not, and are still not, completely happy with the limited recognition or power of religious groups, but many secular citizens in these countries also resent the guarantees and influence that religious groups have won.

Pluralism developed in part because Christian Democrats gradually asserted a degree of independence from the Catholic Church authorities. While supporting religious education and strenuously fighting anticlericalism, on other issues they went their own way and became full participants in pluralist systems. Christian parties, despite their names, increasingly became nonconfessional. Even devout Catholic voters, as the common saying goes, vote with one hand and take communion with the other. This change was clearly suggested in the transformation of Christian Democratic parties after World War II into more broadly based "people's parties."[61]

The gradual weakening of the specifically religious character of the Christian Democratic parties suggests that religious movements in the United States may have a great deal to learn from the European experience. Political parties emerge out of ideology, but their future course is not predicted by ideology. Democracy survives and thrives because of forced compromises that often almost no one wanted. Given that a confessional political party is extremely difficult to maintain in a competitive democratic system over the long term, organizing as an interest group or pressure group outside of partisan politics may be the best way to both have influence and retain one's religious convictions. Ralph Reed and Jesse Jackson may have felt totally frustrated as leaders of minority movements that politicians played to and then frequently ignored, but the alternative of a separate party might have been worse. Yet the Christian Democratic experience suggests that religious people should not disdain politics either. For the Catholics of western Europe, politics provided the inevitable tools to get something done for good, or at least to prevent some evils. There are dangers in compromising one's moral absolutes in the process just as there are in clinging to them too tightly.

In the United States, of course, the problems faced by religious people—and not just Protestant evangelicals but many Catholics, Orthodox Jews, and other groups as well—is that there is so little public acceptance of religion at all today. The debate over the role of religion in public life in the United States has recently threatened to become a simplistic opposition between nostalgic, religious conservatives and secular, present-minded liberals.[62] If the impact of European Christian Democracy is a guide, the very success of a religious social movement may be ultimately to force a much greater acceptance of a public role for religious pluralism. Ironically, the people who may be most helped by a more tolerant and pluralist atmosphere for religious expression in the United States would be religious minorities from outside the Western tradition—Muslims, Buddhists, and Hindus—whose numbers are increasing rapidly as the sources of immigration have changed dramatically in the last decades but who lack any public recognition of their special beliefs.

There may be, in fact, room for a minimal level of convergence between political liberals and conservatives in the United States. Even Jim Castelli, a representative of the People for the American Way, has written, "Church and State, as institutions, must be kept separate; religion and politics, as processes of thought and action, cannot be kept separate."[63] As Stephen Carter puts it, "Religions are moral forces in the lives of their adherents, which means, inevitably, that they are moral forces in the political world."[64]

The story of Christian Democracy may also carry a warning of the dangers of religious social movements refusing to accept a degree of pluralism. Where Christian Democrats opposed Socialism so strongly that they co-operated with dictatorial movements and accepted or encouraged anti-Semitism, they almost invariably met disaster. French Christian Democracy was handicapped for decades by its flirtation with extreme right-wing Catholic elements. Only after the defeat of Vichy France in 1944, which had initially attracted strong Catholic support, was a Christian Democratic movement able to emerge as a genuine democratic movement. The Austrian Christian Social Party always had a strong tendency toward authoritarianism and anti-Semitism. Consequently, it did little to attract a working-class following and paved the way for a pro-Nazi dictatorship to replace the Austrian Republic in 1934.[65] In both countries the direct involvement of Catholic Christians in the political system through political parties weakened rather than promoted democracy, until Catholics were forced to recognize the dangerous consequences of authoritarianism.

Some degree of adaptation to pluralism by even the most uncompromising groups may be inevitable. Even where Christian Democrats succeeded in surmounting the chaos of the mid-twentieth century, they still faced the continuing need to adapt to new conditions and challenges. By comparison with their early success, Christian Democratic movements have displayed a loss of adaptability in recent decades. They survived two world wars and Communism and Fascism only to be defeated by the 1960s. It was what Reinhold Wagnleitner has called the "Marilyn Monroe" doctrine, the gospel of consumerism and hedonism, which has drained much of the lifeblood of Christian Democracy.[66] The associations that nourished Catholic social life and Catholic spirituality for a century have declined in recent decades in Europe. In many ways it is a new height of this same tidal wave of individualism and materialism that has provoked the rise of the New Christian Right in the United States and that is the greatest challenge to social Catholics in the United States as well.[67]

The story of European Christian Democracy may hold a wider significance beyond both the United States and Europe in regions such as Latin America, where Protestantism is expanding, and in Africa, where both Protestant and Catholic Christianity are growing. In both continents there are serious issues of religious tolerance among Catholics and secular forces or Muslims. Although the experience of European Christian Democracy has been largely ignored by North American scholars studying Latin America, it may ironically have particular relevance for the future of Protestant evangelicalism in both the United States and Latin America. In Latin America the connections between evangelicals and Christian Democracy are direct. In spite of all the enormous attention devoted to Liberation Theology, by far the most important political religious movement in Latin America is the set of Christian Democratic parties that has been one of the primary sources of democratic opposition to dictatorship.[68] In the few cases so far where Latin

American Protestant evangelicalism has had political importance in democratic elections, for example, in Guatemala, evangelical Protestants have voted for Christian Democratic parties, parties originally led by Catholics.[69] In Nigeria, to take only one example from Africa, pluralism is essential to Christianity's survival. Operating in a country where Muslims outnumber them and are powerfully attracted to theocratic models, Christians, both Catholic and Protestant, have had influence on the political system only when they could appeal to principles of religious freedom and pluralism. Explicitly or even tacitly, Christian political organizations can only inflame religious tensions. Working through nonpartisan educational, welfare, and social movement organizations, Christians have been able to achieve much more.[70]

Christian Democracy suggests, too, that the most effective kind of Christian political action over the long run is the nonpartisan variety, which works through changing people's hearts and minds, lobbying governments, and mobilizing the faithful to social action. Does this mean that explicitly Christian Democratic parties, such as evolved in western Europe, were a mistake? In the face of the strong liberal and socialist anticlericalism of the late nineteenth and twentieth century, some kind of Catholic defensive organization was probably necessary. But with the decline of anticlericalism and the enshrining of some form of pluralism, it is no coincidence that the need for explicitly Christian parties has waned and the parties themselves have declined or transformed themselves. This need not mean that Christians are less involved in politics or less effective. Instead, it may free them to be more active on specific issues without being tied to one party's faults. In a way, I would argue, the Christian communities of western Europe came full circle in the twentieth century. Originally, it was the social organizations, outside politics, that nourished political involvement. Now that the parties have declined or transformed themselves into more secular forms, the Catholics of western Europe are all the more free to do what in a sense they have been best at doing all along, influencing society and the political system without regard for partisan politics.

In conclusion, the success of Christian Democratic movements offers a model that allows us to see more clearly the different ways religion works as a fundamental force in modern society. Religious loyalties have lost their power much more slowly than one might assume. Even as the Church's own position as a source of authority weakened, the Catholic community found new ways to halt or even reverse secularization. The importance of religion for social movements is crucial on two levels, the personal search for a meaningful worldview and the ideological justification for a political program. Christianity, in the hands of activists able to speak to people's everyday concerns, could be both a personal guide to morality and faith and the justification for a political and social movement. Christian Democrats believed that they were simultaneously defending the Catholic community in opposing Socialist intolerance and providing a genuinely pragmatic solution to social and economic problems. More broadly, Christian Democracy suggests that religion may continue to provide a way for ordinary people to organize themselves in the midst of economic and political upheaval. From Poland's Solidarity to South Africa's Zion Christian movement to Islamic fundamentalism, religious loyalties continue to provide an alternative to secular ideologies. How secular movements deal with these loyalties and whether religion fosters or undermines a sense of pluralism may be two of the most crucial questions of our world. Christian Democrats created a new kind of politics. The richness and complexity of their hopes, defeats, and victories can still inform our understanding of how people in any time are shaped by and reshape their world.

## NOTES

1. William Martin, *With God on Our Side: The Rise of the Religious Right in America* (New York, 1996); Robert Booth Fowler and Allen D. Hertzke, *Religion and Politics in America: Faith, Culture, and Strategic Choices* (Boulder, 1995), 133–51.

2. The Christian Democratic–inspired parties have most recently formed the European People's Party, which has had approximately 30 percent of the seats in the European Parliament. "The European Parliament from Left to Right," *Europe* (April 1996): 12–13.

3. W. Becker and R. Morsey, eds., *Christliche Demokratie in Europa* (Cologne, 1988); Paul Misner, "Social Catholicism in Nineteenth-Century Europe: A Review of Recent Historiography," *Catholic Historical Review* (1992): 581–600; David Hanley, ed., *Christian Democracy in Europe* (London, 1994); Richard Wolff and Jörg Hoensch, eds., *Catholics, the State, and the European Radical Right, 1919–1945* (New York, 1987); Jean Beaufays, *Les partis catholiques en Belgique et aux Pays-Bas* (Brussels, 1973); Maurice Duverger, *Les partis politiques* (Paris, 1957), 211–55; Kenneth McRae, ed., *Consociational Democracy* (Toronto, 1974); Arend Lijphardt, *Democracy in Plural Societies* (New Haven, 1977).

4. Useful exceptions include Hugh McLeod, *Religion and the People of Western Europe* (Oxford, 1981); Ellen Evans, "Catholic Political Movements in Germany,

Switzerland, and the Netherlands: Notes for a Comparative Approach," *Central European History* 17:2–3 (1984): 91–119; Stathis N. Kalyvas, *The Rise of Christian Democracy in Europe* (Ithaca, 1996).

5. Martin Marty and Scott Appleby, eds., *Accounting for Fundamentalisms*, 3 vols. (Chicago, 1991).

6. Joshua Mitchell, *Not by Reason Alone: Religion, History, and Identity in Early Modern Political Thought* (Chicago, 1993); Paul Marshall, "Liberalism, Pluralism, and Christianity: A Reconceptualization," *Fides et Historia* 21:3 (October 1989): 4–17. I am grateful for comments by John Rooney on an earlier paper of mine that helped me clarify some of these issues.

7. Richard John Neuhaus, *The Naked Public Square: Religion and Democracy in America* (Grand Rapids, 1984), 161.

8. Kalyvas, *Rise of Christian Democracy*, 34–51.

9. Pierre Pierrard, *L'Église et les ouvriers en France (1840–1950)* (Paris, 1984), 173–312; Jean-Marie Mayeur, "Le catholicisme social en France: Orientations idéologiques," in *Een Kantelend Tijdperk/Une époque en mutation/Ein Zeitalter im Umbruch*, ed. Emiel Lamberts (Leuven, 1992): 43–47; Norman Ravitch, *The Catholic Church and the French Nation, 1589–1989* (London, 1990).

10. John McManners, *Church and State in France, 1870–1914* (London, 1972), 129–57.

11. Jean-Marie Mayeur, *Un prêtre démocrate, l'abbé Lemire* (Tournai, 1968).

12. Christian Ponson, *Les catholiques lyonnais et la Chronique sociale, 1892–1914* (Lyon, 1979), 227–68.

13. Roy Pierce, *French Politics and Political Institutions* (New York, 1968), 40–42, 114–18.

14. Pierrard, *L'Église et les ouvriers*, 393–411; Carl Strikwerda, "Catholic Working Class Movements in Western Europe," *International Labor and Working Class History* 34 (Fall 1988): 70–85.

15. Kalyvas, *Rise of Christian Democracy*, 148.

16. Donald Howard Bell, *San Sesto Giovanni: Workers, Culture, and Politics in an Italian Town, 1880–1922* (New Brunswick, 1986); Sandor Agócs, *The Troubled Origins of the Italian Catholic Labor Movement, 1878–1914* (Detroit, 1988), 88–121.

17. L. Bedeschi, "Romolo Murri," in *Il movimento operaio italiano: Dizionario biografico*, ed. F. Andreucci and T. Detti, 5 vols. (Rome, 1970), 3:616–26.

18. David Hempton, "For God and Ulster: Evangelical Protestantism and the Home Rule Crisis of 1886," in *Protestant Evangelicalism: Britain, Ireland, Germany and America c. 1750–c. 1950. Essays in Honour of H.R. Ward*, ed. Keith Robbins (Oxford, 1990), 225–54.

19. Ronald Wells, "Protestant Ideology and the Irish Conflict: Comparing Ulster Protestantism and American Evangelicalism," *Fides et Historia* 24 (Fall 1993): 3–17.

20. Arend Lijpardt, *The Politics of Accommodation: Pluralism and Democracy in the Netherlands* (Berkeley, 1968); Hans Daalder, "The Netherlands: Opposition in a Segmented Society," in *Political Oppositions in Western Democracies*, ed. Robert Dahl (New Haven, 1966), 188–237.

21. Lauri Karvonen, "Christian Parties in Scandinavia: Victory over the Windmills?" 124–29, and John T. S. Madeley, "The Antinomies of Lutheran Politics: The Case of Norway's Christian People's Party," 142–54, both in Hanley, *Christian Democracy in Europe*.

22. Francesco Nitti, *Catholic Socialism*, 3d ed. (London, 1911), 309.

23. This argument was first made by historians of French Catholicism: Jean-Marie Mayeur, "Catholicisme intransigeant, Catholicisme social, démocratie chrétienne," *Annales. E.S.C.* (1972): 483–99. For German parallels, see Christoph Weber, "Ultramontanismus als katholischer Fundamentalismus," and Klaus-Michael Mallmann, "Ultramontanismus und Arbeiterbewegung im Kaiserreich: Überlegungen am Beispiel des Saareviers," in *Deutscher Katholizmus im Umbruch zur Moderne*, ed. Wilfried Loth (Cologne, 1991), 76–94.

24. Emiel Lamberts, ed., *Het Kruistocht tegen het Liberalisme: Facetten van het Ultramontanisme in België in de 19e eeuw* (Leuven, 1984); Carl Strikwerda, "A Resurgent Religion: The Rise of Catholic Social Movements in Nineteenth-Century Belgian Cities," in *European Religion in the Age of Great Cities, 1830–1930*, ed. Hugh McLeod (London, 1995), 61–89.

25. Walter H. Copps, *The New Religious Right: Piety, Patriotism, and Politics* (Columbia, S. C., 1990).

26. Carl Strikwerda, *A House Divided: Catholics, Socialists, and Flemish Nationalists in Nineteenth-Century Belgium* (Lanham, Md., 1997), 213–64; Misner, "Social Catholicism," 189–212.

27. Kees van Kersbergen, "The Distinctiveness of Christian Democracy," in Hanley, *Christian Democracy in Europe*, 35.

28. John H. Whyte, *Catholics in Western Democracies: A Study in Political Behaviour* (Dublin, 1981), 48–95.

29. James Terence Fisher, *The Catholic Counterculture in America, 1933–1962* (Chapel Hill, 1989).

30. Arthur Verhaegen, *Vingt-cinq d'années d'action sociale* (Ghent, 1911), 93–94.

31. Horstwalter Heitzer, *Der Volksverein für das Katholische Deutschland im Kaiserreich 1890–1918* (Mainz, 1979), 17–23.

32. Wilfried Loth, *Katholiken im Kaiserreich: Der politische Katholizismus in der Krise des wilhelminischen Deutschlands* (Düsseldorf, 1984), 272–77; Helmut Walser Smith, *German Nationalism and Religious Conflict: Culture, Ideology, and Politics, 1870–1914* (Princeton, 1995), 141–65.

33. Eric Dorn Brose, *Christian Labor and the Politics of Frustration in Imperial Germany* (Washington, D.C., 1985), 157, 250.

34. William Patch, *Christian Trade Unions in the Weimar Republic, 1918–1933* (New Haven, 1985), 100–102.

35. Jan De Maeyer, "De Belgische Volksbond en zijn antecedenten," in *De Christelijke Arbeidersbeweging in Belgie,* vol. 2, ed. Emmanuel Gerard (Leuven, 1991), 19–51.

36. Leen van Molle, *Iedereen voor Allen: Hunderd Jaar Belgisch Boerenbond* (Leuven, 1990).

37. An English translation of the text of the encyclical is in *The Papal Encyclicals in Their Historical Context,* ed. Anne Freemantle (New York, 1956), 166–95.

38. Herman Bakvis, *Catholic Power in the Netherlands* (Kingston, Ont., 1981); Ton Dufflues, "Een wending naar boeren, middenstanders, en arbeiders? De katholieke volksbewegingen in Nederland," in Lamberts, *Een Kantelend Tjdperk,* 175–97.

39. John Ardagh, *France in the 1980s* (New York, 1982), 208–16.

40. Gianfranco Poggi, *Catholic Action in Italy: The Sociology of a Sponsored Organization* (Stanford, 1967), esp. 111–29 on comparisons among Catholic Action groups in Belgium, France, and Italy.

41. Harry Post, *Pillarization: An Analysis of Dutch and Belgian Society* (Aldershot, 1989); Strikwerda, *A House Divided,* 407–16.

42. Thomas Kselman, *Miracles and Prophecies in Nineteenth-Century France* (New Brunswick, 1983), 113–40; David Blackbourn, *Marpingen: Apparitions of the Virgin Mary in Nineteenth-Century Germany* (New York, 1994), 102–62, 202–49; Strikwerda, *A House Divided,* 30 31.

43. Margaret Lavinia Anderson, "The Limits of Secularization: On the Problem of Catholic Revival in Nineteenth-Century Germany," *Historical Journal* 38:3 (1995): 647–70.

44. Sandra Zimdars-Swartz, *Encountering Mary: From La Salette to Medjugorje* (Princeton, 1991); M. L. Nolan and S. Nolan, *Christian Pilgrimage in Modern Western Europe* (Chapel Hill, 1989).

45. Fowler and Hertzke, *Religion and Politics in America,* 138–42.

46. It may also be a commonality of all religious communities around the world—Muslim, Hindu, Buddhist, and more—but this comparative framework lies outside the scope of this chapter.

47. J. P. Parry, *Democracy and Religion: Gladstone and the Liberal Party, 1867–1875* (Cambridge, 1986); Boyd Hilton, "Gladstone's Theological Politics," in *High and Low Politics in Modern Britain,* ed. M. Bentley and J. Stevenson (Oxford, 1983), 28–57. D. W. Bebbington, *The Nonconformist Conscience: Chapel and Politics, 1870–1914* (London, 1975).

48. David Hanley, "Introduction: Christian Democracy as a Political Phenomenon," in Hanley, *Christian Democracy in Europe,* 9.

49. Cal Thomas and Ed Dobson, *Blinded by Might: Can the Religious Right Save America?* (Grand Rapids, 1999), 70.

50. Margaret Lavinia Anderson and Kenneth Barkin, "The Myth of the Puttkamer Purge and the Reality of the Kulturkampf: Some Reflections on the Historiography of Imperial Germany," *Journal of Modern History* 54 (December 1982): 647–86; Strikwerda, "Catholic Working Class Movements," 70–72.

51. Quoted in Margaret Lavinia Anderson, *Windthorst: A Political Biography* (London, 1974), 112.

52. Verhaegen, *Vingt-cinq*, 93–94.

53. Robert C. Walton, "*Rerum Novarum* and Political Catholicism in the Second Reich," in *The Church Faces the Modern World: Rerum Novarum and Its Impact*, ed. Paul Furlong and David Curtis (Hull, 1994), 109.

54. Harold Wilensky, "Leftism, Catholicism, and Democratic Corporatism: The Role of Political Parties in Recent Welfare State Development," in *The Development of Welfare States in Europe and America*, ed. Peter Flora and Arnold Heidenheimer (New Brunswick, 1981), 345–82.

55. Kees van Kersbergen, *Social Capitalism: A Study of Christian Democracy and the Welfare State* (London, 1995).

56. Richard Mouw and Sander Griffioen, *Pluralisms and Horizons* (Grand Rapids, 1993), 14–19. A third kind of pluralism can be called "contextual," the diversity of groups that are largely those of birth or nonvoluntary groupings based on gender, ethnicity, and race. Perhaps class can be included here as well.

57. Strikwerda, *A House Divided*, 258.

58. Hans Muller, *Sozialistische Monatshefte*, 26, December 22, 1910, 1665–69; Brose, *Christian Labor*, 374; Owen Chadwick, *The Secularization of the European Mind in the Nineteenth Century* (Cambridge, 1975), 79–85; Richard Hunt, *German Social Democracy, 1919–1933* (New Haven, 1964), 16.

59. Detlev Peukert, *The Weimar Republic* (New York, 189), 211–13.

60. Carl Strikwerda, "The Belgian Working Class and the Crisis of the 1930s," in *Chance und Illusion: Studien zur Krise der westeuropäischen Gesellschaft in den dreissiger Jahren/Labor in Retreat: Studies on the Social Crisis in Interwar Western Europe*, ed. Wolfgang Maderthaner and Helmut Gruber (Vienna, 1988), 279–304.

61. Martin Conway, Introduction to *Political Catholicism in Europe, 1918–1965*, ed. Tom Buchanan and Martin Conway (Oxford, 1996), 30; Noel Cary, *The Path to Christian Democracy: German Catholics and the Party System from Windthorst to Adenauer* (Cambridge, Mass., 1996), 147–209.

62. Robert Wuthnow, *The Restructuring of American Religion: Society and Faith since World War II* (Princeton, 1988).

63. Jim Castelli, *A Plea for Common Sense: Resolving the Clash between Religion and Politics*, foreword by Norman Lear (San Francisco, 1988), 3.

64. Stephen L. Carter, *The Culture of Disbelief: How American Law and Politics Trivialize Religious Devotion* (New York, 1993), 81.

65. Evans, "Catholic Political Movements," 180–95.

66. Reinhold Wagnleitner, "The Marilyn Monroe Doctrine, or the Promise of the Democracy of Plenty," unpublished paper, 1994.

67. Jean Bethke Elshtain, "Catholic Social Thought, the City, and Liberal America," in *Catholicism, Liberalism, and Communitarianism: The Catholic Intellectual Tradition and the Moral Foundations of Democracy*, ed. Kenneth Grasso, Gerard Bradley, and Robert Hunt (Lanham, Md., 1995), 91–114.

68. Paul Sigmund, "The Transformation of Catholic Social Thought in Latin America: Christian Democracy, Liberation Theology, and the New Catholic Right," 41–64, and Michael Fleet, "The Chilean Church and the Transition to Democracy," both in *Organized Religion in the Political Transformation of Latin America*, ed. Satya R. Pattnayak (Lanham, Md., 1995), 65–95.

69. David Stoll, "'Jesus Is Lord of Guatemala': Evangelical Reform in a Death-Squad State," in *The Dynamic Character of Movements*, ed. Martin Marty and Scott R. Appleby, Accounting for Fundamentalisms, vol. 4 (Chicago, 1991), 116. In Paraguay in the late 1990s, a largely Protestant Christian party inspired by the Christian Coalition in the United States forged an alliance with the existing Christian Democratic party.

70. Iheanyi M. Enwerem, *A Dangerous Awakening: The Politicization of Religion in Nigeria* (Ibadan, 1995); Jacob K. Olupona, ed., *Religion and Peace in Multi-Faith Nigeria* (Ile-Ife, 1992); Simeon O. Ilesanmi, *Religious Pluralism and the Nigerian State* (Athens, Ohio, 1997). For an interesting comparative case, see Meinrad P. Hebga, "The Evolution of Catholicism in Western Africa: The Case of Cameroon," in *World Catholicism in Transition*, ed. Thomas M. Gannon (New York, 1988), 320–32.

# 12 Unsecular Politics and Religious Mobilization

## Beyond Christian Democracy

STATHIS N. KALYVAS

In March 1998 the leaders of the European Popular Party (the European federation of Christian Democratic parties) decided to oppose Turkey's application for membership in the European Union (EU). The Belgian chairman of the Christian Democratic group in the European parliament, Wilfried Martens, pointed out, "In our view Turkey cannot be a candidate for EU membership. We are in favour of extensive cooperation with Turkey, but the European project is a civilisational project. Turkey's candidature for full membership is unacceptable."[1] The Islamic factor (including the presence and rise of political Islam) was presented as key in the Christian Democratic decision.

This statement says more about Christian Democracy than about Turkey. Although Islam was only one among several factors that influenced the Christian Democratic position (other factors included Turkey's political situation, human rights record, economy, and immigration potential), the reference to Islam by the European Christian Democrats is interesting insofar as it does not reflect a sectarian rejection of Islam but rather an acknowledgment of the dangers posed by the kind of politics that are informed by a religious cleavage—what I call "unsecular politics." Unsecular politics refer to a political context in which religious ideas, symbols, and rituals are used as the primary (though not exclusive) instrument of mobilization by at least one major political party (i.e., a credible contender for power). The outright condemnation by the heirs of European unsecular politics of its contemporary manifestation in other parts of the world is then indicative of two related facts—their profound political amnesia and their extremely successful integration into a liberal-secular political framework, in other words, their successful secularization.

Is it possible to lump together two seemingly different phenomena such as nineteenth-century European political Catholicism and contemporary Islamic fundamentalism in the Middle East? Here, I argue the merits of such a comparison by focusing on the main manifestation of unsecular politics: *religious mobilization.* In the first section I discuss the causes of the political and scholarly amnesia of European Christian Democracy's origins. I argue that this amnesia and the tendency to reject outright religious mobilization across the world share common causes. In the second section I focus on religious mobilization. I argue that despite widely differing religious doctrines and political and social environments, it is possible to identify a core phenomenon, religious mobilization—much as it is possible to study labor or ethnic mobilization across cultures, space, and time. I then identify the key features of religious mobilization: (a) an "antisystem" critique of liberal institutions relying on religious rhetoric; (b) the reconstruction of existing religious identities rather than just their mobilization; (c) a mass mobilization relying on the wide use of selective incentives and a concomitant focus on economic and social issues; (d) a cross-class appeal; and (e) links to pre-existing religious institutions. Although individual religious parties differ from each other in many respects, these five components tend to be constant across time and space. Identifying these commonalities enables one to address the issue of the incorporation of these parties into liberal-democratic institutional frameworks from a novel and more fruitful perspective, which I sketch in the third section. Specifically, I focus on the institutional features that facilitate or discourage the gradual transformation of unsecular into secular politics through the moderation of religious mobilization drawing on cases as diverse as nineteenth-century Belgium, Algeria, and India, among others. Overall, I integrate Christian Democracy into an analysis of contemporary religious developments in non-European politics. In so doing, I aim to show that the legacy of European Christian Democracy transcends its temporal and spatial boundaries and carries a broader significance.

## RETROSPECTIVE EXTRAPOLATION AND
## THE IDEATIONAL PERSPECTIVE

Amnesia about the (mostly) Catholic religious mobilization in Europe is not limited to European Christian Democrats. It also features prominently in many studies of contemporary Christian Democracy, where it takes the form of retrospective extrapolation: because contemporary Christian Democratic parties are liberal and secular it is assumed that they could never have been aliberal and unsecular in the past—or that if aliberal elements were present, they were somehow prevented by Christian theology from "contaminating" (liberal) political regimes. Retrospective extrapolation is methodologically fallacious; this particular one is also empirically flawed.[2]

A central cause and symptom of retrospective extrapolation is the overwhelming power bestowed on ideology: according to a widely held perception, democratization and democratic consolidation are directly linked to the (stated or interpreted) "disposition" of particular world religions (and their "political arms") with regard to liberal democracy. Thus it is often argued that Catholicism and Islam, however defined, are by nature compatible or inimical to liberal democracy. Countless debates then emerge, almost always structured around this dichotomous premise.

Yet such arguments are problematic in two ways. First, they give axiomatic value to the assumption that policy is the exclusive, automatic, and natural derivative of ideas; second, they essentialize ideas by putting forth a single and unified version of, say, Catholicism or Islam. However, religious doctrine, like all kinds of doctrines, is a contested field of meaning, amenable to a multiplicity of cultural expressions, interpretations, and political arrangements, and lending itself to multiple and continuous modifications, manipulations, and reinventions. Both Catholicism and Islam have been used to support a variety of regimes—democracy, dictatorship, republicanism, monarchy, and empire. Furthermore, ideology, especially in its theological dimension, can be a particularly flawed predictor of political action. Not only is it elastic and shifting, but it is only one among many factors that motivate social and political action. Its inadequacy as a predictor of action is revealed by an example from Iran. Shi'ite traditions recommend avoidance of direct participation by religious leaders in governments as demeaning to spiritual authority. However, Khomeini revised Shi'ite political thinking: he condemned traditional Shi'ite quietism and the practice of *taqiya* (dissimulation), arguing that the *ulamas* could rule directly. The Iranian revolution led to government by religious leaders and the creation of a clerical organization with the functional equivalent of a hierarchy of archbishops, bishops, and priests—a true revolution within Islam.[3] Ideological discourse can be an even worse indicator of future intentions. Statements of Islamist leaders in favor of democracy can be rejected as strategic posturing that obscures true intentions while open condemnations of democracy can be interpreted as reflecting true intent, thus acquiring the status of proof—and vice versa.[4]

An additional problem of retrospective extrapolation is that it tends to view religious movements as mere political arms of organized religions and to conflate the statements and ideology of the two. Retrospective extrapolation carries an important consequence: it shifts our attention away from political and religious actors and institutions and toward endless and confusing argumentation about the content of theologies. According to Abdon Filali-Ansary, "Many controversies surrounding Islamic thought focus so heavily on semantics, on names for ideas and persons, that the real issues often disappear from sight."[5] In fact, the "real issue" is precisely the interpretation of sacred texts, and this interpretation is the very object of political contention.

Retrospective extrapolation is not exclusive to religion. It is part of a view that holds the explicit commitment to democracy by the main political and social actors as a fundamental condition for the emergence and consolidation of democratic regimes: democratization requires the adoption by nondemocrats of democratic values.[6] For example, the presence of "antisystem" parties has traditionally been considered a key indicator of the stability of a democratic regime.[7]

In the case of religious movements, this view requires a transformation of their ideology through reinterpretation of sacred texts—nothing short of "an Islamic Reformation."[8] The main research implication of this view is a shift of focus to the determination of the sincerity of the espousal of democracy by religious actors. However, this can prove a futile exercise: ideological statements and political declarations are open to any interpretation, and future political action is not necessarily or always a faithful reflection of present ideological positions. Political history is replete with radical parties that became reformist.[9] While it is true that the adoption of democratic values by all major political actors is a correlate of long-term democratic consolidation, it would be incorrect to argue that democratization requires such a commitment. Moreover, the initial compliance of political actors to democratic rules does not necessarily flow from their ideological preferences; it can be the result of the largely contingent strategic pursuit of their interests under constraints.[10] Democracy can be a spontaneous and self-enforced equilibrium, possible in the initial absence of convinced democrats or mass democratic culture. The uncertainty about the outcome of political competition that is inherent to democracy, as well as the iteration that is built into the democratic process, can then transform initial commitments into long-term values. Hence democratic consolidation can be a largely endogenous process.[11]

It is my contention, therefore, that the study of religious mobilization requires that we take religious doctrines for what they are, that is, flexible and malleable statements of often ambiguous political intent, as opposed to rigidly predictive policy platforms. Hence we need to move beyond political theologies, semantics, ideology, and the search for the "essence" or the "correct interpretation" of religious doctrines and focus on actors and institutions. This requires neither a reference "to an 'absolute of divine origin'" nor "the mobilization of all resources of religious history and thought."[12]

## RELIGIOUS MOBILIZATION AND UNSECULAR POLITICS

I call "religious mobilization" a political mobilization based on the use and appropriation of religious symbols and rituals. I use the terms "religious parties" and "religious movements" generically to refer to the political actors that rely on religious mobilization. Whether or not the use of religious symbols is sincere is irrelevant—for two reasons. First, religion is never found in a "clean" state, unpolluted by other kinds of concerns. Second, no matter how "sincere" the intentions behind the use of religion (i.e., untainted by political and strategic considerations), its infusion into politics is typically accompanied by its dilution—very much like the injection of class into politics.[13]

Religious mobilization can be best analyzed and understood in comparative perspective. Often, the case study format leads to flawed comparisons between the case at hand and the author's vague or flawed perception of other cases. For example, Eric Kolodner argues that the Indian Bharatiya Janata Party (BJP) is not a religious movement "akin to the Islamist movement in the Middle East,"[14] in spite of its use of religious symbols and rituals, because its members are motivated to join by economic grievances; however, he ignores that similar grievances have been motivating the members of Islamist parties, such as the Algerian Islamic Salvation Front (FIS).[15]

Religious mobilization can be disaggregated into four essential components.

1. *An "antisystem" critique of liberal institutions relying on religious rhetoric.* Religious mobilization is centrally informed by a critique (going as far as uncompromising rejection) of secular and liberal political institutions and more generally of the liberal creed that holds that whereas politics belongs to the public sphere, religion should be assigned to the private sphere. This is true of religious movements and parties, both radical and reformist, operating in nonauthoritarian, semiauthoritarian, or authoritarian political contexts. Although religious parties that emerge in authoritarian or semiauthoritarian contexts criticize existing authoritarian institutions as arbitrary, they do not advocate the introduction of liberal democracy. Insofar as they compromise on democratization, they do it with an eye toward using liberal institutions as a stepping-stone to their preferred (religiously inspired) regime.

While the association between Catholicism and democracy may appear natural to contemporary Christian Democrats, this was not the case in the past. The ideology of the emerging Catholic movements in the 1860s and 1870s was informed by the Catholic Church's clear and unabashed opposition to liberal democracy—as expressed in the *Syllabus errorum* pronounced by the pope in 1864 that denounced freedom of speech, freedom of the press, freedom of conscience and religion, legal equality of cults, sovereignty of the people, the doctrine of progress, separation of state and church, liberalism, and the modern conception of civilization. The Church condemned as a grave error the belief that a regime that did not repress the violators of Catholic religion could be good. The German historian C. Weber has termed this project "ultramontane fundamentalism."[16]

An illustration of this trend is provided by the Belgian case.[17] The Belgian Catholic movement adopted a strongly antiliberal posture during the 1870s. It aspired to revive Catholicism and "Christianize" modernity in response to the rise of liberalism and the secularization of European states. Clerical and lay Catholic thinkers adopted the ultramontane project and unequivocally rejected political liberalism, democratic government, and the separation of church and state; they also advocated the aliberal revision of the 1830 (liberal) Belgian constitution. The revival and radicalization of Belgian Catholicism was not a matter of mere ideological declarations. The Catholic Church became the agent of sustained mass mobilization, in its own words, "a crusade against Liberalism," that began in the religious realm but quickly acquired a social and political character.[18] The objective was to use liberal institutions to destroy them. As the prominent radical Belgian Catholic thinker Camile de Hemptinne put it:

> What should subjects do if the law is indifferent and places error and truth on the same level, as it does in Belgium? . . . They must lament having to live under a regime so opposed to the rule of God and do everything they can to change it. To this effect, and since the law allows them to, they will use freedom to do good: to redress the ideas, expose the true principles, and spread the understanding of how much God abhors these general freedoms [of speech, press, conscience and religion, etc.].[19]

More generally, cross-national research suggests that there is an association between Catholicism, absence of democracy, and limited or late democratic development.[20] One can also look at interwar Austria and Portugal and postwar Portugal and Spain to discover authoritarian governments using Catholic discourse and relying strongly on the support of the Catholic Church. To use the fact that nineteenth-century European confessional parties did not overthrow existing liberal regimes in order to claim that they never posed a danger is to ignore a central fact: with one exception, these parties did not subvert liberalism because they could not. With the exception of Belgium, no confessional party won a parliamentary majority; they were either confined to the opposition or accepted as junior partners in coalition governments where their impact was necessarily limited.

One of the most commonplace arguments in the post–Cold War world is that Islamism has emerged as the most implacable enemy of liberal democracy. An extreme but hardly exceptional version of this view was expressed by the French foreign affairs minister following the electoral breakthrough of the Islamist party FIS in Algeria: "Unfortunately, the Muslim nature of Algerian society won over civilization."[21] Indeed, Islamist movements seek power using religious appeals. They criticize liberal institutions and promote a theocratic project built around religious law (*shari'a*) and antagonistic to secular and liberal democracy.

The main arguments that posit the incompatibility of Islamism and liberal democracy run along three lines: (a) empirical, based on the practice of existing Islamist states, particularly Iran; (b) circumstantial, based on the rejection of liberal democracy by many Islamist thinkers; and (c) structural, based on the purported absence from Islamic theology and culture of the essential ingredients and fundamental values of Western liberalism.[22] The Christian Democrats' statement about Turkey was informed by the last category, which stresses the antidemocratic and antimodern essence of Islamic thought and tradition: Islam requires divinely rooted sovereignty as opposed to popular sovereignty; state legitimacy derived from the application of *shari'a* and fusion of religion and politics (*din wa-dawla*) as opposed to separation of state and church and legislation without reference to religion; overlap of the political community with the community of believers (*ummah*) and hence exclusion of nonbelievers and women; rejection of political pluralism (which places on an equal footing the true "party of God" and other parties) and of majority rule (because this is based on the false idea that issues of right and justice can be quantified and disregard religiously defined morality).

Critics of this argument point out that it is based on the flawed assumption that there is one Islam, timeless and eternal, whose character is essential, primordial, and constant; the failure to grasp the breadth and depth of contemporary Islam and Muslim politics, they argued, leads to mystification. Instead, there exist different and contradictory Islamic traditions, both across time and space. Many Islamic thinkers have offered interpretations qualifying or even rejecting the concept of the indivisibility of the political and religious realms. Finally, a careful reading of the historical record indicates that politics and religion became separable not long after the death of the Prophet and the establishment of dynastic rule.[23] Both proponents and critics of the nondemocratic essence of Islam derive their arguments from different interpretations of basically the same theological corpus of Islamic doctrine and tradition. For instance, a well-developed exercise is the search for elements of Islamic law and tradition that could assist the development of some form of democracy. Such elements, compatible to the cognate principles that belong to the intellectual heritage of liberal democracy, include a disinclination to arbitrary rule, a contractual and consensual perception of sovereignty, the qualities of dignity and humility, and values such as *shura* (consultation), *ijtihad* (independent reasoning), and *ijma* (consensus).[24] In its most extreme and absurd version, this approach seeks elements of Islamic thought that could literally mimic landmarks of the historical and philosophical evolution of the West, such as the Protestant Reformation.[25] However, this is a misreading of both Islamic tradition and the history of the West, as it posits a single universal path to democracy while assuming as well that democracy only developed in Protestant countries! Plus, as Olivier Roy points out, one should not forget that the Protestant Reformation was based on a fundamentalist mode of thought.[26] As I pointed out, this debate is pointless: whether Muslim countries can adopt liberal democratic institutions or whether Islamic movements can operate under such institutions is a question that cannot possibly be answered within the framework of the discussion on the philosophical foundations of Islam.

A similar debate, anchored in conflicting interpretations of the connection between Hindu discourse, secularism, and religious toleration, has taken place with regard to recent political developments in India.[27] This debate has emerged following the impressive rise of religious mobilization in India (often referred to as the "Saffron Surge"). The Indian BJP has been described as "the largest movement of religious nationalism in the world."[28] The use of religious appeals and rituals has been central to its rise: images of Hinduism's Mother Goddess and religious festivals such as Dashehra (an autumn festival celebrating the victory of Rama, the Hindu embodiment of virtue over its archenemy) have been infused with politics, with mass Hindu organizations playing a central role—or even substituting traditional religious authorities. For example, the most solemn religious day of the year, the day of guru worship, has been turned into a heavily political festival in which the leaders of the Hindu mass organization Rashtriya Swayamsevak Sangh (RSS; National Volunteer Corps) have substituted themselves for the traditional gurus and participants present the organization with monetary offerings; its banner is worshiped as a symbol of Hindu power and solidarity.[29] The BJP's quick rise led to serious concern: If the BJP came to power, Ashutosh Varshney argued, it would mean "the end of India as we know it civilizationally (and perhaps also territorially). As Ayodhya has shown, the right wing is bigoted, communal, and exclusionary. Hatred is the cornerstone of its politics."[30] The BJP's successful bid for power in 1996 provoked open alarm: "Never before has India been so deeply polarized along religious lines, never before has the rest of the world been so alarmed by the sudden shift to the right of the world's second-most populated country."[31] The party's rise in the wake of religion-driven agitation that culminated, in December 1992, in the destruction by thousands of Hindu marchers of the Babri Masjid mosque in the town of Ayodhya (said to lie on the site where Ram, the god-king of ancient history was born) and its 1996 electoral victory were widely seen as a threat to both secularism and the Muslim minority in India. Indeed, a key tenet of the BJP's agenda was the abolition of the special marriage, divorce, and property laws applying to Muslims.

There are, obviously, many differences of doctrine, law, institutions, and values among world religions (as well as within them). One often-cited difference pertains to the relations between state and church. Christian states, it has been pointed out, have distinguished between throne and altar, whereas Islam accepts an interpenetration of cult and power. The languages of Muslim countries have no words for "secularism" or "layman."[32] Hinduism is very elastic on this matter: it has no corpus of dogma by which all Hindus must abide, and it certainly does not advance the principle that written Hindu texts constitute "the divine word." In fact, there are so few accepted fundamentals that Hindu fundamentalism is probably an oxymoron.[33] However, the decentralized and nonclerical structure of Islam and Hinduism make them less theocratic than Catholicism. Moreover, the Judeo-Christian tradition has strong historical and theological links with Islam, and, again, differences can be matched by similarities. For instance, Lisa Anderson points to the desirability of harmonious regulation of the different orders of society in both Islamic and Catholic political teaching;[34] and Shireen T. Hunter argues that Judaism and Christianity, not only Islam, are in conflict with "absolute secularism."[35]

In sum, religious mobilization tends to be "antisystem"—at least in its discourse and during its initial stages. Although this stance is informed by particular interpretations of religious doctrine, it would be wrong to remain on the level of religious ideas and discourse. Instead of comparing religions as doctrines and discourse and making grand totalizing comparisons, it is preferable to focus on the actual practice of religious parties,[36] on existing political institutions, and on religious institutions.

2. *The reconstruction of existing religious identities rather than their simple mobilization.* Religious movements constitute a social and political phenomenon that cannot be reduced to the religions from which they sprang. While they emerge in the context of a broad societal religious revival, characterized by the enforcement of stricter standards of piety and the wide diffusion of religious symbols, they do not merely mobilize existing religious identities;[37] they reconstruct them by blending religious, social, economic, and political concerns, by synthesizing traditional and modern appeals, and by mixing utopian millenarist messages with concrete political action. In short, these parties are not just an expression of dormant identities; they redefine these identities.[38] In this sense, they are revolutionary and radical not just in the context of the political regimes within which they emerge and operate but also, and this is crucial and often overlooked, within the religious structure they claim to uphold and represent. Indeed, their practice more often than not diverges in significant ways from their religious matrices.

The Catholic movements that emerged in nineteenth-century Europe aspired to revive Catholicism and Christianize modernity in response to the rise of liberalism and the secularization of European states. Like Islam before its recent resurgence, Catholicism in nineteenth-century Europe was perceived as a declining and spent force, retreating in front of modernization. Yet it reemerged dramatically to challenge the established order. The revivalist and novel form of European Catholic movements has been stressed by many authors.[39]

Islamism, a recent and modern phenomenon, emerged as a potent force in Muslim politics during the 1970s and 1980s. Indeed, it is possible to speak of a resurgence of Islam in Muslim politics, an Islamic revival, or even an attempt to Islamize modernity.[40] Islamism diverges from traditional Islam in that it is thoroughly modern in its leadership and organization and the articulation of its message. Islamist movements developed a new and modern form of organization based on the primary role of social and political action. Islamists creatively deploy selected elements of Islamic tradition to justify their actions.[41] In contrast to traditional religious organizations, Sufi mystical brotherhoods, and *ulama* associations, modern Islamist organizations have a lay rather than clerical leadership and are urban based. The *ulamas* were often criticized for being too moderate. The Islamist thinker Ali Shariati argued that because the "return to Islam" was not a retreat to the medieval Islamic worldview of conservative *ulamas* but a revolutionary vision of early Islam that would provide the inspirational basis for its modern re-interpretation, it required Islamically oriented laymen with a knowledge and command of modern thought and methods.[42]

Likewise, no unified Hindu movement existed until recently. A fore-runner, the Vishwa Hindu Parishad (VHP), emerged in 1964.[43] It focused mostly on the provision of local social services but remained of limited importance.[44] The Hindu movement really exploded in the 1980s, following a campaign of "Hindu extremism" that called for the demolition of the Babri mosque.[45] Although there has always existed a committed core of Hindu nationalists, this movement has now broadened its base of support and has successfully converted citizens who previously remained on the periphery of the movement. The Hindu movement has transcended Hindu religion since this religion does not lend itself to organized movements. As in Islam, there is no central church or recognized clergy to lead a Hindu religious campaign. Rather there exists a wide range of religious specialists, including gurus of sects, temple priests, and wandering holy men. The BJP and its associated organizations have been extremely successful in reinterpreting Hindu religious teaching (mostly through the medium of a potent anti-Muslim message) and, through this reinterpretation, creating a powerful movement.

3. *Mass mobilization relying on wide use of selective incentives and a concomitant focus on economic and social issues.*   Religious mobilization is almost always mass mobilization: religious parties share a grassroots character, the result of a pioneering use of techniques of mass mobilization. In turn, religious parties derive their strength from the creation of extensive mass organizations. The redefinition of religion is important because it is instrumental in generating mass mobilization. Yet, however important the religious message is, these parties rely as much if not more on social and political messages. In fact, religious messages act as a catalyst that mobilize a wide variety of economic and social concerns. Religious mobilization tends to take place in times of economic and social change and the concomitant processes of social dislocation and crisis.

The social profile of religious mobilization points to some important regularities. The state provides the main focus of criticism—be it the Masonic liberal bourgeoisie in Belgium or the state-rentier ones in Algeria or India. Petty bourgeois urban and rural sectors threatened by economic modernization are mobilized against these states.[46] Without generalizing too much, it is possible to remark that the "religious" cleavage also expresses the efforts of dominated actors (peasants and workers), who in alliance with the middle classes (small businessmen, low-level bureaucrats, and educated segments of the population) contest the hegemony of the ruling elites in the cultural and political arenas.[47]

Religious parties solve the collective action problem not through abstract religious ideas but through selective incentives, centered mostly on the local provision of welfare services. They provide social services (hospitals, clinics, legal aid societies), sponsor economic projects (banks, credit and investment houses, insurance companies), education (schools, childcare centers, youth camps), and wide networks of religious publishing and broadcasting. In more than one way they substitute for the state. Contrary to what one might imagine, their leaders are often the very products of modernization — graduates of major universities in medicine, science, and engineering.[48] The success they achieve in building mass organizations is reflected in the veritable countersocieties ("subcultures" or "milieus") that emerge as a result of the their efforts.

Nineteenth-century European Catholic movements combined their message with the most sophisticated political weapons of the day, such as mass organization and partisan press. Hundred of associations were created, ranging from charitable neighborhood groups and moral leagues to Catholic worker clubs and credit associations. They were built outside liberal political institutions as a distinct Catholic countersociety that would eventually grow to submerge the liberal state. This dimension of the Catholic movement was reflected in the prominent role played by laymen and the lower clergy and their critique of the Catholic hierarchy for being too moderate and unwilling to engage in open political action. It was also embodied in a revolutionary form of organization, built outside the church's clerical structure, the mass organization of laymen.[49] On the economic front, Catholic parties, such as the Belgian one, pitted a coalition of petty bourgeois urban and rural sectors threatened by economic modernization against a liberal bourgeoisie with close ties to the state.[50] The Belgian Catholic movement was particularly successful in attracting working-class support.[51]

Islamist movements share many of these elements. For example, the Algerian FIS, using both mosques and modern communications technology to propagate its message, evolved into a mass movement thoroughly integrated into the fabric of Algerian society.[52] It combined an electoralist and a grassroots strategy, weaving the fabric of a veritable countersociety.[53] Groups such as charitable neighborhood associations were gradually transformed into FIS local cells.[54] The party blended a critique of the existing regime with a utopian project: the Islamic solution and the Islamic state, concepts as vague as they are malleable. As Roy points out, the FIS mobilized the masses "around the myth of a return to an Islamic authenticity that never existed."[55] Although the FIS represented the urban poor, it would be wrong to view it only as a movement of the disenfranchised. The party enjoyed the support of peasants and workers who along with the middle strata, including small businessmen, low-level state functionaries, shop owners, lawyers, and teachers, overwhelmingly rejected the corrupt record of the governing party and the state-rentier elites.[56]

Likewise, the BJP has built a mass following in close collaboration with Hindu movements such as the RSS, a martial organization promoting an exclusively Hindu definition of the Indian nation, and the VHP, which has been campaigning to liberate Hindu sites allegedly occupied by Muslim shrines. The RSS had 1.8 million members in 1989 in about twenty thousand base units (*shakhas*); the VHP boasted three thousand local branches and more than one million volunteer workers. The Vidyarthi Parishad is India's largest student organization, and the Mazdoor Sangh has one of the largest memberships among competitive labor unions. The grassroots character of Hindu nationalism is impressive.[57]

The BJP's mobilizational muscle is largely due to its collaboration with these grassroots organizations.[58] A study of the branch of the Hindu militant organization Shiv Sena in the state of Madhya Pradesh suggests that unemployment was the driving force behind BJP's growth in membership.[59] Generally, unemployed youth are among the biggest supporters of the party along with graduate Hindu upper-caste males of urban centers.[60] According to Eric Kolodner, the BJP has proved successful because it addressed "material deprivation, psychological uncertainty, and ideological anomie," it exploited the weaknesses of the Congress Party, and it promised to clean up politics and stabilize the country.[61] According to Thomas Blom Hansen, Hindu nationalism emerged and took shape primarily in civil society.[62]

Ironically, religious movements have come to embody a condition deemed necessary for democratization, namely, the rise in civil society of a counterelite.[63] Yet the alternative culture that inspires many if not most religious movements is one opposed to liberal democracy—as is clear from even a cursory reading of their programs and declarations.

4. *Cross-class appeal.* The strength of social and economic factors underlying religious mobilization should not lead to the (Marxist) mistake of claiming that religion is just a cover for what is really a class cleavage. True, the features of religious mobilization I have discussed parallel those of class mobilization. Socialist parties rejected liberal democracy and built mass parties combining selective incentives and a utopian message of class equality. What sets religious mobilization apart from class mobilization, however, is its cross-class appeal. The social heterogeneity of religious parties, their cross-class basis, and their ability to weave together disparate or even competing social groups have been underlined by many authors.[64] Initially this task appears impossible to some observers. For example, Paul Brass has argued that "the BJP cannot integrate upper castes and backward castes in a consolidated Hindu party."[65] Yet this party managed to build such a coalition, as evidenced by survey data.[66]

Although it would be a mistake to reject religion as a mere cover for class mobilization, it would likewise be wrong to assume that cross-class appeal implies that class ceases to be a salient cleavage. Although class is deemphasized and redefined by religious parties, it does not lose its saliency. In fact, class becomes salient *within* the party. In seeking to manage their party organization and accommodate their diverse clientele, religious parties have developed remarkable skills of class mediation (often wrongly attributed exclusively to doctrines such as "social Catholicism"). The redefinition of class identities takes place *within* the party and is often reflected in the federative nature of the party organization. Many European Catholic parties adopted such an organization: in Belgium, for instance, the party was a federation of various organizations defined in class terms (workers, peasants, middle classes), called *standen.*[67] Likewise, the BJP relies on a quasi-federative structure as well, in which grassroots organizations, such as the VHP and the RSS, retain their organizational autonomy.[68] Such a structure favors a segmented set of appeals with organizations specializing in particular class target groups. For example, the Shiva Sena in Bombay and the Hindu Ekata Andolan in other parts of the Maharashtran state have targeted the needs of the lower castes and classes, whereas the BJP proper addresses the economic needs of the middle and upper classes, whose interests often conflict with the lower-caste Indians.[69]

## PATHS OUT OF UNSECULAR POLITICS

Religious mobilization is often initiated by preexisting religious institutions—churches and various religious authorities. Although these institutions often lose their ability to determine the course of religious movements and parties, the relations between the two are both a crucial feature that sets religious mobilization apart from other kinds of mobilization and an essential element in understanding how unsecular politics become secularized.

Identifying the common elements of religious mobilization is a way to address the issue of the incorporation of religious parties into liberal-democratic institutional frameworks. Indeed, the primary reason that the recent seemingly global wave of religious mobilization has attracted attention is the perception that it poses a threat and that this threat cannot be analyzed in a social science context. According to Stanley J. Tambiah:

> In the late twentieth century, a surprising number of militant and seemingly "irrational" eruptions have occurred. They challenge the confident post-Enlightenment prophecies that the decline of religion was inevitable, or that at best, it could only survive in a demythologized form; that primordial loyalties and sentiments would fade into oblivion as national integration took effect, or be carried away as flotsam by the currents of world historical process. These violent and ubiquitous explosions also challenge and strain our conventional social science explanations of order, disorder, and conflict.[70]

There is little doubt that the antiliberal and antisecular message of religious mobilization is a potential threat for emerging democracies. As Kolodner puts it, "India raises the issue of the responsibility a democratic state possesses to accommodate avowedly anti-democratic forces, that is, whether there should exist a limit to democratic tolerance, and whether the threshold should be lower in recently democratized countries, whose systems might be more susceptible to manipulative and ultimately destructive forces."[71] However, to acknowledge the existence of a potential threat is hardly sufficient. We need to specify the conditions under which religious parties will be willing and able (or not) to moderate and incorporate successfully in emerging democracies. Parties relying on religious mobilization face two major decisions: (a) *whether* to moderate, that is, decrease, the saliency of their religious goals and accept operating within competitive and secular institutional frames and (b) if yes, *how* to moderate successfully. Specifying the conditions of moderation qualifies the alarmist discourse about the rise of religious mobilization. This is precisely where a reconsideration of the legacy of Christian Democracy can be most instructive and fruitful.

Here I sketch a framework that addresses these issues. I argue that religious parties are generally *willing* to moderate because of a number of electoral and nonelectoral constraints. However, their *ability* to moderate is far more variable. Moreover, I argue that decisions about the paths that lead out of unsecular politics are typically incremental and independent of the party's ideology; they are, instead, far more dependent on the form of political and religious institutions (and institutional constraints) faced by the party in question.

## Willingness to Moderate

Like most parties, religious parties are seldom monolithic. They are typically divided into moderate and radical factions. Typically, moderates control the party's leadership, whereas radicals are strong at the grass roots.[72] The first question is, when will the moderates push for a moderate revision of their program? The main incentive for moderation is the possibility of access to power. Although the rise of new parties (of any kind) tends to be fueled by antisystem positions, the realization that power is within reach creates the incentive to moderate so as to appeal to broader sections of the electorate. There are two categories of constraints likely to induce processes of moderation, electoral and nonelectoral ones.

### Electoral constraints
The electoral performance of religious parties tends to follow the general rule according to which parliamentary one-party majorities are hard to attain. Thus they typically have to ally with nonreligious parties to form a government. These allies typically demand from the religious party and are

in a position to obtain moderation. Moderation induced by electoral constraints can be stable (by emerging as a new equilibrium) as was the case in nineteenth-century Belgium[73] even when the initial incentives for moderation are conjunctural; of course, an absence of structural incentives may prove unstable.[74]

Moderation as a result of electoral constraints was the path followed by most Catholic parties in nineteenth-century Europe.[75] I illustrate this path by using evidence from India. In 1996, for the first time in India's history, a militant Hindu party found itself in a position to govern the country. Its first opportunity lasted only thirteen days. Nevertheless, the party performed very well in the 1998 elections and led a seventeen-party coalition government. This government lasted for thirteen months, until April 1998, when it lost a vote of confidence because of a defection. New elections were called, and the BJP led a twenty-four-party coalition to a decisive victory.[76]

The rise of the BJP took place in the context of widespread religious polarization and violence, triggered by grassroots Hindu organizations. Indeed, the prospect of a BJP-led government in 1996 caused great alarm, both in India and abroad.[77] High uncertainty prevailed: "As the BJP's countdown to taking power commence[d], India [was] bracing itself for the most significant and uncertain fortnight in its political history."[78] This prospect aroused fears among both members of the one hundred-million strong Muslim minority and secular Hindus. The Indian historian Romilla Thapar argued, "It is in the nature of their kind of ideology to intimidate their enemies. . . . It will be extremely difficult for liberal elements if the BJP forms a government."[79]

Opinions about the exact course of action that the BJP would follow were divided. Many believed that the moderates in the party (like its veteran politician and candidate for prime minister, Atal Behari Vajpayee) would follow the vociferous extremist wing of the Hindu grassroots organizations. The statements of Bal Thackeray, a radical leader who had threatened "anarchy" if the BJP was not chosen to form India's government, seemed to support such expectations.[80]

However, others came to the conclusion that the BJP's accession to power would, in fact, bring moderation: "It's better that they're in power," argued a Muslim. "Now they won't resort to the kind of fanaticism they used to. They'll be saner and won't tear down any more mosques."[81] Many Muslim intellectuals and leaders thought that the harsh realities of power would make the BJP "behave differently in office"; they "concluded that things are not as bad as that. Any menace from a BJP government may be short-lived, they said, because the party ha[d] not rallied a parliamentary majority behind it."[82] The BJP "strove to project itself as a moderate, inclusionary force capable of forging a national consensus and furnishing stability at the center."[83] In a televised interview soon after he was named prime minister for the first time, Vajpayee declared that the first BJP government would not mean a radical shift. The country, he pointed out, would remain secular, and Muslims, 11 percent of the population, should not fear discrimination. "Hinduism will not be the state religion," he added. Moreover, BJP president Lal Krishna Advani made a stark declaration: "We are committed to secularism."[84]

The trend toward moderation was confirmed in the following years, culminating in the electoral victory of the BJP-led alliance in October 1999.[85] The party formed a coalition with secular partners; in exchange for their support, the party "promised that it [would] not pursue the agenda that ha[d] raised the hackles of Muslims and secularists alike."[86] Indeed, the electoral campaigns it ran were largely free of ideology,[87] and the BJP resorted to strategies of moderation at the state level.[88] Following the party's decisive victory, the *New York Times* ran the following editorial comment: "[Mr. Vajpayee has] managed to rid his party of some of its Hindu chauvinist reputation by agreeing not to institute the party's most virulent anti-Muslim measures."[89] Likewise, the international media recognized the party's move toward moderation. According to *The Economist:*

> The BJP rose to national prominence in the early 1990s on a programme of Hindutva—Hinduness—and attracted zealots who wanted to tear down Muslim mosques and erect Hindu temples in their place, notably in Ayodhya in Uttar Pradesh. But, recognising that it could not form a government alone, the BJP fought this election as the leader of the 24–party National Democratic Alliance, whose manifesto promised a moratorium on "contentious" issues such as the building of the temple at Ayodhya.[90]

Those who had previously brushed aside any prospect of moderation for the BJP now recognized that "[t]he logic of Indian politics has made it clear to the BJP that if they want to be in power they must find enough coalition partners in the South and East, which is impossible without ideological moderation."[91] The BJP's platform attempted a tightrope walk between hard-line and moderate factions, but the direction of the tilt was clearly toward greater moderation. Pratap B. Mehta summarizes this remarkable trajectory:

> The rigors of the democratic process have chastened the BJP and led it to try to smooth down some of its rougher edges. It has bent over backwards to project itself as a moderate party of the center right, capable of being inclusive and providing good governance. In the states where it holds power—Gujarat, Rajasthan, and Maharashtra—it has indeed behaved like a moderate party that recognizes good governance as the key to staying in office. It has relied less on ominous rhetoric of Hindu self-assertion, and moderates in its ranks have been in the driver's seat.[92]

It is particularly interesting to note here that Vajpayee's political career began in the grassroots Hindu movement: he joined the fundamentalist Hindu organization RSS and worked as a journalist in the RSS magazine *Rashtradharam*. Examples of Islamist parties that have appeared willing to moderate under similar constraints are those in Jordan and Pakistan.[93]

*Nonelectoral constraints*

What happens when religious parties manage to win parliamentary majorities? The "safety valve" of minority governments is obviously not available and secular minorities feel threatened. These situations are described as follows:

> Secularism is the dream of a minority which wants to shape the majority in its own image, which wants to impose its will upon history but lacks the power to do so under a democratically organized polity. In an open society the state will reflect the character of the society. Secularism therefore is a social myth which draws a cover over the failure of this minority to separate politics from religion in the society in which its members live.[94]

Similar statements can be made about nineteenth-century Belgium and other Catholic countries in Europe, with the exception of France, and many contemporary Muslim societies.

Because many religious parties operate in the semiauthoritarian environments of countries undergoing democratization, they face heavy non-electoral constraints. A central constraint is the fact that ruling elites control or are closely associated with military establishments. When this is the case victorious religious parties will have to become moderate to accede to power, otherwise the military will be likely to subvert their victory (and the process of democratization). Belgium in 1884 and Algeria in 1992 are cases in which the structure of choices facing the political actors conformed to this situation: religious majorities with no military might faced ruling minorities with military might. In Belgium democratization succeeded but not in Algeria.[95]

## Ability to Moderate

As Roberto Michels pointed out a long time ago, if the (moderate) leadership of a party is willing to push for a less radical agenda, it has the means to impose its will on radicals.[96] Ignacio Sánchez-Cuenca has developed a long-overdue formal model that explores how moderates tackle this task with respect to their radical rank and file and voters and shows how they succeed.[97] However, in situations in which victorious religious parties face hostile military establishments, it is the religious parties' ability rather than their given willingness to moderate that matters.

I have argued elsewhere that ex ante credible signaling of ex post victory behavior is of crucial importance in the successful outcome of democratization processes where religious actors win parliamentary majorities.[98] Unfortunately, the moderate leadership of young parties may have the willingness to moderate but lack the ability to silence the radicals and to send the right kind of explicit and unambiguous signals that will satisfy ruling elites. A solution to this problem can be provided by religious institutions. Centralized, authoritarian, and hierarchical religious institutions can have a positive effect by shouldering the responsibility of silencing the radicals. The empirical prediction here is that Catholic movements should be more successful than Islamist or Hindu movements to send credible signals. Hence unambiguous electoral victories that make one-party cabinets possible in Islamic countries or India will be likely to fit the alarmists' expectations. This was the case in Algeria but not in India, where the BJP did not win a parliamentary majority.

A final caveat is warranted: a religious party might be willing and able to moderate yet still be excluded from power. The Welfare Party in Turkey is such an instance. In semiauthoritarian regimes, ruling elites have the option to shut out of power religious parties that threaten their hold on power. In such situations, the outcome is independent of the religious parties' strategy—or of religious mobilization altogether.

## CONCLUSION

The European Christian Democratic experience can be integrated into a comparative approach that stresses actors and institutions. This approach has a triple advantage. First, it dodges the pitfalls of deadend dichotomous debates on ideologies and theologies. By bypassing the issue of political theology, it is possible to focus on issues that are otherwise overlooked: instead of concentrating on whether a religious ideology is structurally compatible with democracy, the analysis has to focus on the nontrivial issue of *how* and *when* religious parties moderate. Second, this approach generates empirical predictions such as the ones I have suggested; these predictions qualify the prevalent indiscriminate alarmism about the rise of religious "fundamentalist" parties. Third, by pointing to the importance of religious institutions, this approach reintroduces (and reconceptualizes) religion in social science investigation where it continues to remain absent.[99] Fourth, this approach suggests that the legacy of European Christian Democracy transcends its temporal and spatial boundaries and carries a more universal significance—both for politics and for political science research.

## NOTES

I thank Kanchan Chandra for comments and Caroleen Marji for research assistance.

1. Quoted in Andrew Mango, "Turkey and the Enlargement of the European Mind," *Middle Eastern Studies* 34:2 (1998): 171–92. The European Union eventually accepted Turkey as a candidate in 1999.

2. Stathis N. Kalyvas, "Democracy and Religious Politics: Evidence from Belgium," *Comparative Political Studies* 31:3 (1998): 291–319.

3. Ali E. Hillal Dessouki, "The Islamic Resurgence: Sources, Dynamics, and Implications," in *Islamic Resurgence in the Arab World,* ed. Ali E. Hillal Dessouki (New York: Praeger, 1982); Bernard Lewis, "Islam and Liberal Democracy: A Historical Overview," *Journal of Democracy* 7:2 (1996): 52–63; Robin Wright, "Islam and Liberal Democracy: Two Visions of Reformation," *Journal of Democracy* 7:2 (1996): 64–75.

4. For opposite interpretations of similar statements by Islamist leaders, see John Waterbury, "Democracy without Democrats? The Potential for Political Liberalization in the Middle East," in *Democracy without Democrats? The Renewal of Politics in the Muslim World,* ed. Ghassan Salamé (London and New York: I.B. Tauris, 1944), 40; and François Burgat, *L'Islamisme en face* (Paris: La Découverte, 1996), 14–15). Likewise, ideology can be a flawed predictor of foreign policy. According to Roy, the "cultural opposition [of Islamic states] to the West is unrelated to the strategic choices made by states. Anti-Christian attitudes and discourse reach their highest pitch among the Saudis, who strategically are in the western camp, but who forbid the erection of churches on their soil, whereas Iran never had an anti-Christian political position and has always accepted a certain Christian visibility (to the point of authorizing the Armenians to make wine)." Olivier Roy, *The Failure of Political Islam* (Cambridge, Mass.: Harvard University Press, 1994).

5. Abdou Filali-Ansary, "Islam and Liberal Democracy: The Challenge of Secularization," *Journal of Democracy* 7:2 (1996): 78.

6. Juan J. Linz and Alfred Stepan, "Toward Consolidated Democracies," *Journal of Democracy* 7:2 (1996): 16.

7. G. Sartori, *Parties and Party Systems: A Framework for Analysis* (Cambridge: Cambridge University Press, 1976).

8. Wright, "Islam and Liberal Democracy," 75.

9. Ignacio Sánchez-Cuenca, *The Logic of Party Moderation,* Working Paper 135, Instituto Juan March de Estudios e Investigaciones, 1999.

10. Kalyvas, "Democracy and Religious Politics," 291–319; Adam Przeworski, *Democracy and the Market: Political and Economic Reforms in Eastern Europe and Latin America* (Cambridge: Cambridge University Press, 1991); Dankwart Rustow, "Transitions to Democracy: Toward a Dynamic Model," *Comparative Politics* 2:3 (1970): 345–53.

11. Przeworski, *Democracy and the Market.*

12. Burgat, *L'Islamisme en face,* 98, 19.

13. Stathis N. Kalyvas, *The Rise of Christian Democracy in Europe* (Ithaca: Cornell University Press, 1996); Adam Przeworski and John Sprague, *Paper Stones:*

*A History of Electoral Socialism* (Chicago and London: University of Chicago Press, 1986).

14. Eric Kolodner, "The Political Economy of the Rise and Fall (?) of Hindu Nationalism." *Journal of Contemporary Asia* 25:2 (1995): 244.

15. Pradeep K. Chhibber, "State Policy, Rent Seeking, and the Electoral Success of a Religious Party in Algeria," *Journal of Politics* 58:1 (1996): 126–48. Of course, the scope of the religious agenda can vary—both within and across religions.

16. C. Weber, "Ultramontanismus als katholischer Fundamentalismus," in *Deutscher Katholizismus im Umbruch zur Moderne*, ed. W. Loth (Stuttgart: W. Kolhammer 1991).

17. For detailed evidence, see Kalyvas, "Democracy and Religious Politics," 291–319.

18. Emiel Lamberts, "Het Ultramontanisme in België, 1830–1914," in *De Kruistocht tegen het Liberalisme: Facetten van het ultramontanisme in België in de 19e eeuw*, ed. Emiel Lamberts (Leuven: Universitaire Pers, 1984).

19. Camile de Hemptinne, *Questionnaire Politique No. 2, Le libéralisme* (Gand: Siffer, 1877), 11–12.

20. Samuel P. Huntington, *The Third Wave: Democratization in the Late Twentieth Century* (Norman: University of Oklahoma Press, 1991), 75.

21. Quoted in Rhaba Attaf, "La dimension moderniste du FIS," in Reporters sans Frontières, *Le drame Algérien: Un peuple en otage* (Paris: La Découverte, 1994).

22. Burgat, *L'Islamisme en face*, 186–88.

23. Dale F. Eickelman and James Piscatori, *Muslim Politics* (Princeton: Princeton University Press, 1996); John L. Esposito, *The Islamic Threat: Myth or Reality?* Rev. ed. (New York and Oxford: Oxford University Press, 1995); Roy, *The Failure of Political Islam.*

24. Laith Kubba, "Islam and Liberal Democracy: Recognizing Pluralism," *Journal of Democracy* 7:2 (1996): 87; Lewis, "Islam and Liberal Democracy"; Jean Leca, "Democratization in the Arab World: Uncertainty, Vulnerability and Legitimacy. A Tentative Conceptualization and Some Hypotheses," in *Democracy without Democrats?* 48–83.

25. Wright, "Islam and Liberal Democracy," 64–75.

26. Roy, *Failure of Political Islam*, 21.

27. For a summary, see Robert G. Wirsing with Debolina Mukherjee, "The Saffron Surge in Indian Politics: Hindu Nationalism and the Future of Secularism," *Asian Affairs, an American Review* 22:3 (1995): 194–201.

28. Mark Juergensmeyer, *The New Cold War? Religious Nationalism Confronts the Secular State* (Berkeley: University of California Press, 1993), 83.

29. Kolodner, "Political Economy," 244–45.

30. Ashutosh Varshney, "Contested Meanings: India's National Identity, Hindu Nationalism, and the Politics of Anxiety," *Daedalus* 122:3 (1993): 255.

31. John Zubrzycki, "Hindu Nationalists Rule India—But How Long?" *Christian Science Monitor*, May 17, 1996.

32. Lewis, "Islam and Liberal Democracy," 61–62.

33. Kolodner uses these features to claim that the Hindu movement is fundamentally different from the Islamist movement—another example of a flawed noncomparative inference. "Political Economy," 236.

34. Lisa Anderson, "Obligation and Accountability: Islamic Politics in North Africa," *Daedalus* 120:3 (1991): 96.

35. Shireen T. Hunter, *The Future of Islam and the West: Clash of Civilizations or Peaceful Coexistence?* (Westport, Conn.: Praeger, 1998), 56.

36. The usefulness of a comparison of Islamism and political Catholicism is hinted at (but not pursued) by some students of Middle East politics, such as Roy, *Failure of Political Islam;* Ghassan Salamé, "Introduction: Where are the Democrats?" in Salamé *Democracy without Democrats?* 9; and Gudrun Krämer, "The Integration of the Integrists: A Comparative Study of Egypt, Jordan, and Tunisia," in Salamé, *Democracy without Democrats?* 204.

37. Dessouki, "The Islamic Resurgence"; Tom Buchanan and Martin Conway, eds., *Political Catholicism in Europe, 1918–1965* (Oxford: Oxford University Press, 1996).

38. This is consistent with Mark Tessler and Jodi Nachtwey's finding from survey data that there is a clear empirical distinction between the personal and political dimensions of religion. "Islam and Attitude toward International Conflict: Evidence from Survey Research in the Arab World," *Journal of Conflict Resolution* 42:5 (1998): 634.

39. Kalyvas, *Rise of Christian Democracy;* Margaret Lavinia Anderson, "The Limits of Secularization: On the Problem of the Catholic Revival in Nineteenth-Century Germany. Historiographical Review," *Historical Journal* 38:3 (1995): 647–70; David Blackbourn, *Marpingen: Apparitions of the Virgin Mary in Nineteenth-Century Germany* (New York: Knopf, 1994).

40. Joel Beinin and Joe Stork, "On the Modernity, Historical Specificity, and International Context of Political Islam," in *Political Islam: Essays from Middle East Report*, ed. Joel Beinin and Joe Stork (Berkeley and Los Angeles: Univeristy of California Press, 1997); Esposito, *The Islamic Threat.*

41. Beinin and Stork, "On the Modernity, Historical Specificity, and International Context of Political Islam."

42. Esposito, *The Islamic Threat*, 107–8.

43. The RSS was launched in 1925, and the VHP was initially its affiliate. However, its founder, Keshav Baliram Hedgewar, was not religious and kept the RSS away from religious activities, a tradition that only recently has been discarded. Walter Andersen, "Many Faces of Hindu Nationalism," paper presented at the South Asia Seminar, Center for International Affairs, Harvard University, 1994, 3.

44. Kolodner, "Political Economy," 235.

45. Sudipta Kaviraj, "The General Elections in India," *Government and Opposition* 32:1 (1997): 9.

46. Chhibber, "State Policy, Rent Seeking," 126–48; Rolf Falter," De Kamerverkiezingen van 10 juni 1884," in *1884: Un tournant politique en Belgique—De Machtswisseling van 1884 in België*, ed. Emiel Lamberts and Jacques Lory (Brussels: Publications des Facultés Universitaires Saint-Louis, 1986).

47. Séverine Labat, *Les islamistes Algériens: Entre les urnes et le maquis* (Paris: Éditions du Seuil, 1995), 15; Chhibber, "State Policy, Rent Seeking," 127.

48. Esposito, *The Islamic Threat;* Lamberts, "Het Ultramontanisme in België, 1830–1914."

49. Kalyvas, *Rise of Christian Democracy.*

50. Falter, "De Kamerverkiezingen van 10 juni 1884."

51. Carl Strikwerda, "The Divided Class: Catholics vs. Socialists in Belgium, 1880–1914," *Comparative Studies in Society and History* 30:2 (1988): 333–59.

52. Roy, *Failure of Political Islam,* 4.

53. Benamar Mediene, "Une société en mal d'expression," in *Demain l'Algérie,* ed. Gérard Ignasse and Emamnuel Wallon (Paris: Syros, 1995), 114–15.

54. Rabia Bekkar, "Taking Up Space in Tlemcen: The Islamist Occupation of Urban Algeria," *Middle East Report* 179 (1992): 15.

55. Roy, *Failure of Political Islam,* 195.

56. Chhibber, "State Policy, Rent Seeking," 127; Labat, *Les islamistes Algériens,* 15; Benjamin Stora, "Les origines du Front islamique du salut." In Reporters sans Frontières, *Le drame Algérien,* 175.

57. Thomas Blom Hansen, *The Saffron Wave: Democracy and Hindu Nationalism in Modern India* (Princeton: Princeton University Press, 1999).

58. Christophe Jaffrelot, *The Hindu Nationalist Movement in Indian Politics* (New York: Columbia University Press, 1996); Kanchan Chandra and Chandrika Parmar, "Party Strategies in the Uttar Pradesh Assembly Elections, 1996," *Economic and Political Weekly* 32:5 (1997): 214–22.

59. Kolodner, "Political Economy," 245–46.

60. Kaviraj, "General Elections in India," 19.

61. Kolodner, "Political Economy," 238, 242.

62. Hansen, *The Saffron Wave,* 4.

63. Guillermo O'Donnell and Philippe C. Schmitter, "Tentative Conclusions about Uncertain Democracies," in *Transitions from Authoritarian Rule,* ed. Guillermo O'Donnell, Philippe C. Schmitter, and Lawrence Whitehead (Baltimore: Johns Hopkins University Press, 1986).

64. Labat, *Les islamistes Algériens,* 184; Els Witte and Jan Craeybeckx, *La Belgique politique de 1830 à nos jours: Les tensions d'une démocratie bourgeoise* (Brussels: Editions Labor, 1987), 87; Kolodner, "Political Economy," 243.

65. Paul Brass, "The Rise of the BJP and the Future of Party Politics in Uttar Pradesh," in *India Votes: Alliance Politics and Minority Governments in the Ninth and Tenth General Elections,* ed. Harold A. Gould and Sumit Gangul (Boulder: Westview, 1992), 276.

66. Kaviraj, "General Elections in India," 9; Wirsing and Mukherjee, "Saffron Surge in Indian Politics," 189.

67. Emmanuel Gerard, "Du Parti Catholique au PSC-CVP," in *Un parti dans l'histoire: 1945–1995. 50 ans d'action du Parti Social Chrétien,* ed. Wilfried Dewachter et al (Louvain-la-Neuve: Duculot, 1996), 11–31.

68. Kolodner, "Political Economy," 236.

69. Ibid., 243.

70. Stanley J. Tambiah, *Ethno-Nationalist Conflicts and Collective Violence in South Asia* (Berkeley: University of California Press, 1997), 342.

71. Kolodner, "Political Economy," 223–53.

72. See Stathis N. Kalyvas, "Commitment Problems in Emerging Democracies: The Case of Religious Parties," *Comparative Politics* 32:4 (July 2000): 379–99. for a detailed description of Belgium and Algeria; Kaviraj, "The General Elections in India," 11, 14–15, for India.

73. Kalyvas, "Democracy and Religious Politics," 291–319.

74. Chandra and Parmar, "Party Strategies," 214–22, argue that the BJP had the weakest incentives to retain its moderate strategy in Uttar Pradesh after the 1996 elections. Yet three years later it apparently followed the same moderate strategy.

75. Kalyvas, *Rise of Christian Democracy.*

76. Founded in April 1980, the BJP grew from only 2 seats in the 545–seat lower house in 1984 (7.4 percent of the popular vote) to 88 in 1989, 119 in 1991 (21 percent of the popular vote), 194 in 1996 (together with its declared allies; 160 on its own; 23.5 percent of the popular vote), 182 seats in 1998, and 294 seats in 1999 (as a 24–party coalition; 182 on its own), making it the largest single party in India. At the same time, the party achieved considerable success in state elections, at some point ruling over an area constaining as much as one-third of the Indian electorate.

77. Zubrzycki, "Hindu Nationalists Rule India."

78. Ibid.

79. Quoted in Zubrzycki, "Hindu Nationalists Rule India," 6.

80. John-Thor Dahlburg, "India's Muslims Both Anxious, Hopeful," *Los Angeles Times,* May 18, 1996, p. 8.

81. Quoted in Dahlburg, "India's Muslims Both Anxious, Hopeful," 8.

82. Dahlburg, "India's Muslims Both Anxious, Hopeful."

83. Pratap B. Mehta, "India: Fragmentation and Consensus," *Journal of Democracy* 8:1 (1997): 65–66.

84. John-Thor Dahlburg, "Hindu Nationalists Vow Fair, Secular Rule in India," *Los Angeles Times,* May 16, 1996. This does not mean that policies are totally secular. While liberal democracy is not threatened as an institution, policy outcomes should move toward the median voter and, thus, be less secular. Nineteenth-century Belgium illustrates this point. Kalyvas, "Democracy and Religious Politics," 291–319.

85. Ashutosh Varshney, "India's 12th National Elections," *Asia Society* (February 1998), 5–19.

86. Celia W. Dugger, "Hindu-first Party Wins Solid Victory in India's Election," *New York Times,* October 8, 1999, A1.

87. Chandra and Parmar, "Party Strategies," 214–22.

88. Chandra and Parmar ("Party Strategies," 217) list the steps that the BJP took toward moderation. It chose an unimpeachably secular rather than a pro-Hindu party as an alliance partner; it did not make the construction of the Ram temple a central issue, even in the constituency of Ayodhya; there was no statewide coordination with the VHP, and several VHP leaders were kept away from the party's electoral rallies. They conclude that the BJP "had now regulated the mention of its own Hindu identity to a barely perceptible whisper."

89. *New York Times,* October 8, 1999.

90. *Economist,* October 9, 1999.

91. Varshney, "India's 12th National Elections," 15.

92. Mehta, "India: Fragmentation and Consensus," 66.

93. Glenn E. Robinson, "Can Islamists Be Democrats? The Case of Jordan," *Middle East Journal* 51:3 (1997): 373–87; S. V. R. Nasr, "Democracy and Islamic Revivalism," *Political Science Quarterly* 110:2 (1995): 261–85.

94. T. N. Madan, "Secularism in Its Place," *Journal of Asian Studies* 46:4 (1987): 748–49; the statement is about India, where it is questionnable whether antisecularism is majoritarian.

95. Kalyvas, "Commitment Problems in Emerging Democracies."

96. Roberto Michels, *Political Parties: A Sociological Study of the Oligarchical Tendencies of Modern Democracy* (New York: Free Press, 1966).

97. Sánchez-Cuenca, *Logic of Party Moderation.*

98. Kalyvas, "Commitment Problems in Emerging Democracies."

99. A recent survey of 727 articles published in leading journals of comparative politics between 1982 and 1996 found that religion is among the most underdeveloped issues of "prime importance." Adrian Prentice Hull, "Comparative Political Science: An Inventory and Assessment since the 1980s," *PS: Political Science and Politics* 23:1 (1999): 123.

# Contributors

**Winfried Becker** is Professor of Modern and Contemporary History at the University of Passau. He holds advanced degrees from Bonn University and Regensburg University. He has edited and contributed to a number of works dealing with politics and religion in modern Germany, including *Die Minderheit als Mitte: Die Deutsche Zentrumspartei in der Innenpolitik des Reiches, 1871–1933* (1986) and *Die Kirchen in der deutschen Geschichte: Von der Christianisierung der Germanen bis zur Gegenwart* (1996).

**Joseph A. Buttigieg** is the William R. Kenan Jr. Professor of English and a Fellow of the Nanovic Institute for European Studies at the University of Notre Dame. He has written extensively on modernism and the relationship between culture and politics. He is also the editor and translator of the complete critical edition in English of Antonio Gramsci's *Prison Notebooks.*

**Martin Conway** is Fellow and Tutor in Modern History at Balliol College, the University of Oxford. He received his Ph.D. from the University of Oxford. He is the author of *Collaboration in Belgium: Léon Degrelle and the Rexist Movement, 1940–1944* (1993) and *Catholic Politics in Europe, 1918–1945* (1997), and coeditor of *Political Catholicism in Europe, 1918–1965* (1996).

**Michael Gehler** is Adjunct Assistant Professor at the University of Innsbruck, Austria. Dr. Gehler received his Ph.D. from the University of Innsbruck. He is coauthor (with Wolfram Kaiser) of *Christdemokratie in Europa im 20. Jahrhundert* (1999) and author of *Studenten und Politik: Der Kampf um die Vorherrschaft an der Universität Innsbruck, 1918–1938* (1990).

**Raymond Grew** is Professor in the History Department at the University of Michigan and has also taught at Princeton University and the Ecole des Hautes Etudes en Sciences Sociales. He received his Ph. D. from Harvard. He is the author of *A Sterner Plan for Italian Unity* (1963), coauthor of *School, State, and Society: The Growth of Elementary Schooling in Nineteenth-Century France* (1991), and was editor of *Comparative Studies in Society and History* from 1973 to 1997.

**Wolfram Kaiser** is Lecturer at the Institute for Contemporary History at the University of Vienna. He received his Ph.D. from the University of Hamburg. He is the author of *Using Europe, Abusing the Europeans: Britain and European Integration, 1945–1963* (1998), and coauthor (with Michael Gehler) of *Christdemokratie in Europa im 20. Jahrhundert* (1999).

**Stathis N. Kalyvas** is Associate Professor in the Department of Politics at the University of Chicago. He received his Ph. D. from the University of Chicago. He is the author of *The Rise of Christian Democracy in Europe* (1996), which was awarded the Greenstone Prize of the American Political Science Association.

**Thomas Kselman** is Professor of History at the University of Notre Dame. He received his Ph. D. from the University of Michigan. He is the author of *Death and the Afterlife in Modern France* (1993) and *Miracles and Prophecies in Nineteenth-Century France* (1983) and editor of *Belief in History: Innovative Approaches to European and American Religion* (1991).

**Emiel Lamberts** is Professor of Modern History at Louvain University, where he has also served as Dean of the Faculty of Arts. He received his Ph. D. from Louvain University. Lamberts has published several books on relations between the Catholic Church and modern society, including *Kerk en liberalisme in het besdom Gent, 1825–1857* (1972) and *Une époque en mutation: Le catholicisme social dans le Nord-Ouest de l'Europe, 1890–1910* (1992). He is also the editor of a major collection of essays based on a conference held at Louvain in 1995, *Christian Democracy in the European Union, 1945–1995* (1997).

**Paul Misner** is Professor in the Theology Department at Marquette University. He received an S. T. L. from the Gregorian University of Rome and a

Ph.D. from the University of Munich. He is the author of *Papacy and Development: Newman and the Primacy of the Pope* (1976) and *Social Catholicism in Europe: From the Onset of Industrialization to the First Cold War* (1991).

**Maria Mitchell** is Assistant Professor in the History Department at Franklin and Marshall College. She received her Ph.D. from Boston University. Her book, *The Origins of Christian Democracy: Politics and Confession in Modern Germany*, will be published by the University of Michigan Press.

**Antonio A. Santucci** earned his doctorate in Philosophy from the University of Rome. For several years he was director of the Center of Gramscian Studies at the Gramsci Institute in Rome. He has taught political philosophy and historiography at the Universities of Sassari and Cagliari and at the Istituto Universitario Orientale in Naples. He is currently Professor of Communications and Politics at the University of Salerno. He is the author of numerous essays on political philosophy and political history and has edited the works of Diderot, Marx, Engels, Labriola, and Gramsci.

**Carl Strikwerda** is Associate Dean in the College of Arts and Sciences and Professor in the History Department of the University of Kansas. He received his Ph.D. from the University of Michigan. He is the author of *A House Divided: Catholics, Socialists, and Flemish Nationalists in Nineteenth-Century Belgium* (1997) and coeditor of *The Politics of Immigrant Workers* (1993) and *Consumers against Capitalism? Consumer Cooperation in Europe, North America, and Japan* (1997).

**Carolyn M. Warner** is Assistant Professor of Political Science at Arizona State University. She received her Ph.D. from Harvard University, where she also taught as a visiting assistant professor. She is the author of *Confessions of an Interest Group: The Catholic Church and Political Parties in Europe* (2000).

**Steven F. White** is Associate Professor of History at Mount Saint Mary's College (Maryland). He received his Ph.D. from the University of Virginia. He is the author of *Progressive Renaissance: America and the Reconstruction of Italian Education, 1943–1962* (1991), and of scholarly articles in American and Italian journals. Currently he is working on a political and intellectual biography of Alcide De Gasperi.

# Index